BY CHARLES BUKOWSKI

Flower, Fist and Bestial Wail (1960)
Longshot Pomes for Broke Players (1962)
Run with the Hunted (1962)
It Catches My Heart in Its Hands (1963)
Crucifix in a Deathhand (1965)
Cold Dogs in the Courtyard (1965)
Confessions of a Man Insane Enough to Live with Beasts (1965)
All the Assholes in the World and Mine (1966)
At Terror Street and Agony Way (1968)
Poems Written Before Jumping out of an 8 Story Window (1968)
Notes of a Dirty Old Man (1969)
A Bukowski Sampler (1969)
The Days Run Away Like Wild Horses Over the Hills (1969)
Fire Station (1970)
Post Office (1971)
Mockingbird Wish Me Luck (1972)
*Erections, Ejaculations, Exhibitions and General Tales of Ordinary
    Madness* (1972)
South of No North (1973)
Burning in Water, Drowning in Flame: Selected Poems 1955–1973
    (1974)
Factotum (1975)
Love Is a Dog from Hell: Poems 1974–1977 (1977)
Women (1978)
*Play the Piano Drunk/Like a Percussion Instrument/Until the Fingers
    Begin to Bleed a Bit* (1979)
Shakespeare Never Did This (1979)
Dangling in the Tournefortia (1981)
Ham on Rye (1982)
Bring Me Your Love (1983)
Hot Water Music (1983)
There's No Business (1984)
War All the Time: Poems 1981–1984 (1984)
You Get So Alone at Times That It Just Makes Sense (1986)
The Movie: "Barfly" (1987)
The Roominghouse Madrigals: Early Selected Poems 1946-1966 (1988)
Hollywood (1989)
Septuagenarian Stew: Stories & Poems (1990)
In the Shadow of the Rose (1991)
The Last Night of the Earth Poems (1992)
Screams from the Balcony: Selected Letters 1960–1970 (1993)

CHARLES BUKOWSKI

SCREAMS

FROM THE

BALCONY

SELECTED LETTERS 1960–1970

EDITED BY
SEAMUS COONEY

BLACK SPARROW PRESS
SANTA ROSA — 1993

Black Sparrow Press books are printed on acid-free paper.

LIBRARY OF CONGRESS CATALOGING-IN-PUBLICATION DATA

Bukowski, Charles.
    Screams from the balcony : selected letters, 1960-1970 / Charles Bukowski ; edited by Seamus Cooney.
       p.   cm.
    Includes index.
    ISBN 0-87685-915-5 (cloth) : $25.00. — ISBN 0-87685-914-7 (pbk.) : $15.00. — ISBN 0-87685-916-3 (cloth signed) : $40.00
    1. Bukowski, Charles—Correspondence. 2. Poets, American—20th century—Correspondence. I. Cooney, Seamus. II. Title.
    PS3552.U4Z48   1993
    811'.54—dc20
    [B]   93-36411
                                          CIP

Editor's Note

The last thing this book needs is an academic introduction—so the few comments I have to offer will *be* the last thing, relegated to an Afterword.

All that's required here is an explanation of how the letters have been edited. Working from photocopies of letters in private and public collections available to me, I have transcribed and selected roughly 50% of their contents. My only criterion was vividness and interest of the contents, while trying to minimize repetition. Except for three or four word changes, there has been no censorship or expurgation. Letters from the seventies and later will appear in a subsequent volume, where earlier letters found too late for printing here may also be included. Headnote comments about his correspondents are quoted from notes Charles Bukowski made at my request.

A few reproductions of letters (not all of them transcribed for inclusion) will let readers glimpse what this book cannot render: the total visual effect of many Bukowski letters, often decorated with drawings, painting, or collages. Not only are such visual components regrettably sacrificed, but making a readable text has also meant imposing some regularity on Bukowski's spacing, spelling, and the like. There is no way these things could be fully preserved in setting type, in any case. And after a few instances (some of which I've preserved), typos grow distracting. But to give the flavor, I have presented a couple of representative letters verbatim and uncorrected.

Other editorial changes are regularizing of dates and the omission of most salutations and signoffs. For emphasis and for titles in his letters, Bukowski often typed in ALL CAPS. In a book these are hard on the eye. Here, when they are for emphasis, we print them as SMALL CAPS; when they name titles, we print them in regular title format: italics for books, quotes for separate poems or stories. I have indicated editorial omissions by asterisks in square brackets. A few editorial additions are similarly bracketed. A minimum of explanatory material has been included preceding some letters. References to *Hank* are to the biography of Bukowski by Neeli Cherkovski. "Dorbin" refers to Sanford Dorbin's *A Bibliography of Charles Bukowski* (Black Sparrow, 1969).

The title for this volume was supplied by Charles Bukowski.

Acknowledgments

The editor and publisher are grateful to the owners, institutional and private, of the letters here printed. These include:

The University of California, Santa Barbara, Special Collections
Boston University Libraries
State University of New York at Buffalo, Poetry/Rare Books
    Collection
Mr. Louis Delpino
Mr. Joseph Erdelac
Mr. Arthur Feldman
Mr. Carl Weissner

Some letters are reprinted from their appearance in the following books and magazines:

Magazine, 3 (1966), ed. Kirby Congdon
Down Here, 1 (1966), ed. Tom McNamara
Wormwood Review, 14 (1964), ed. Marvin Malone
All's Normal Here: A Charles Bukowski Primer, ed. Loss Pequeño
    Glazier (Fremont: Ruddy Duck Press, 1985).

A section of photographs follows page 180.

SCREAMS FROM THE BALCONY

Selected Letters 1960–1970

· 1 9 5 8 ·

In mid-1958, the time of the earliest letters available, Bukowski had recently begun working in the post office in a permanent position as a mail sorter, after an earlier spell of three years as a mail carrier. Not long before, he had resumed writing after a ten-year interval, and by now had a handful of little magazine publications. E. V. Griffith, editor of Hearse *magazine, had agreed to do a chapbook. But the delay in publication was to test Bukowski's patience to the limit. He finally received his author's copies in October, 1960.*

Until May 1, 1964, Bukowski's letters are dated from 1623 N. Mariposa Avenue, Los Angeles 27, California.

(The following letter is printed in full.)

[To E. V. Griffith]
June 6, 1958

Dear E. V. Griffith:

Here are some more. Thanks for returning others. No title ideas yet. Post office pen no damn good. Trying to say—no title ideas yet.

Fire, Fist and Bestial Wail? No. Thought about using title of one of my short stories—"Confessions of a Coward and Man Hater." No.

"The Mourning, Morning Sunrise." No.

I don't know, E. V.

I don't know.

Anyhow, I'm thinking about it.

Sincerely,
Charles Bukowski

Gil Orlovitz (1918–1973) frequently published pamphlets of verse.

[To E. V. Griffith]
July 9, 1958

I still think *Flower, Fist and Bestial Wail* just about covers the nature of my work. If you object to this title I'll send along some others.

I'm quite pleased with your selections. "The Birds," which I had just written, I like personally but I found others would not like this type of thing because of its philosophical oddity. Poem, by the way, is factual and not fictional. All of my stuff you have is, except "59 and drinks" & "[Some Notes of Dr.] Klarstein."

Thanks for sending *Arrows of Longing.*

As to Orlovitz, I find him at his best, very good. Certainly his delivery seems original.

Do you have my short stories about anywhere?

I suppose I mentioned I unloaded one at *Coastlines* and a couple at *Views* (Univ. of Louisville), but I think what you picked is pretty much my best stuff, and I have been honored to have been singled out by you and gathered up this way.

•

· 1 9 5 9 ·

Griffith published Carl Larsen's Arrows of Longing *as Hearse Chapbook no. 1 in 1958. He was also the editor of* Gallows, *in the first issue of which Bukowski had two poems printed.*

[To E. V. Griffith]
August 10, 1959

Verification of existence substantiated.

I am alive and drinking beer. As to the literary aspect, I have appeared recently in *Nomad #1*, *Coastlines* (spring '59), *Quicksilver* (summer '59) and *Epos* (summer '59). I haven't submitted further to you because I have sensed that you are overstocked.

There are 10 or 12 other magazines that have accepted my stuff but as you know there is an immense lag in some cases between acceptance and publication. Much of this type of thing makes one feel as if he were writing into a void. But that's the literary life, and we're stuck with it.

I am looking forward, of course, to the eventual chapbook, and I hope it moves better for you than the Larsen thing. Of course, I don't consider Carl Larsen a very good writer and am always surprised when anyone does. But to hell with Larsen, now where was I? Oh yes, I have never received a copy of *Gallows* and since you say I have a couple in it, I would like a copy. Could you send one down?

Well, there really isn't much more to say . . . the horses are running poorly, the women are f/ruffing me up, the rent's due, but as

11

I said, I'm still alive and drinking beer. Glad to get your card. Don't forget to send me to the *Gallows*. Thanx.

[To E. V. Griffith]
October 3, 1959

Dashing this off before going to the track with a couple of grifters. I hate these Saturdays—all the amateurs are out there with the greed glittering in their eyes, half-drunk on beer, pinching the women, stealing seats, screaming over nothing. [* * *]

Thanks for card and news of *Hearse* fame in *Nation* and *Poetry* (Ch.). Can't seem to find the correct issue of *Nation* for this but am still trying. Success is wonderful if we can achieve it without whoring our concepts. Keep publishing the good live poets as in the past.

[To E. V. Griffith]
early December, 59

Are you still alive?

Everything that's happening to me is banal or venal, and perhaps later a more flowery and poesy versification—right now drab and bare as the old-lady-in-the-shoe's panties.

I don't know, there's one hell of a lot of frustration and fakery in this poetry business, the forming of groups, soul-handshaking, I'll print you if you print me, and wouldn't you care to read before a small select group of homosexuals?

I pick up a poetry magazine, flip the pages, count the stars, moon, and frustrations, yawn, piss out my beer and pick up the want-ads.

I am sitting in a cheap Hollywood apartment pretending to be a poet but sick and dull and the clouds are coming over the fake paper mountains and I peck away at these stupid keys, it's 12 degrees in Moscow and it's snowing; a boil is forming between my eyes and somewhere between Pedro and Palo Alto I lost the will to fight: the liquor store man knows me like a cousin: he cracks the paper bag and looks like a photograph of Francis Thompson.

•

· 1 9 6 0 ·

Jory Sherman, described by Bukowski as "an early talent," was a poet then living in San Francisco and publishing alongside Bukowski in little magazines like Epos, *whose editor, Evelyn Thorne, suggested the two men should correspond (*Hank, *p. 116).*

[To Jory Sherman]
[April 1, 1960]

Tell the staunch Felicia to hang on in: you are, to my knowledge, the best young poet working in America today. And rejections are no hazard; they are better than gold. Just think what type of miserable cancer you would be today if all your works had been accepted. The beef-eaters, the half-percepted wags who give you the pages and the print have forced you deeper in to show them the sight of light and color. [* * *]

Hell, if you want to read some of my poems, go ahead. I embrace you with luck. But I am tired of them, I am tired of my stuff, and I try very hard not to write anymore. I suppose I might sound like Patchen although I have not read much of him. Jeffers, I suppose, is my god—the only man since Shakey to write the long narrative poem that does not put one to sleep. And Pound, of course. And then Conrad Aiken is so truly a *poet*, but Jeffers is stronger, darker, more exploratatively modern and mad. Of course, Eliot's gone down, Auden's gone down, and William C. Williams has completely fallen apart. Do you think it's age? And E. E. Cummings blanking out. Sherman's coming on, though, taking them in the stretch, stride by stride, clomp, clomp, clomp, Sherman's coming on toward the wire and the ugly crowd screams. Bukowski drinks a cheap beer. [* * *]

Sheri Martinelli, mentioned in this next and several subsequent letters, was an American artist for whose book Ezra Pound wrote an introduction: La Martinelli *(Milan, 1956). Bukowski notes, "She wrote heavy letters, downgrading me. Everything was, 'Ezra said . . . ,' 'Ezra did . . .' She was said to be a looker. I never met her. Lived in San Francisco."*

[To Jory Sherman]
[ca. April, 1960]

[* * *] Rather like Sheri M. altho when she sent back my poems she tried to relegate me with some rather standard formula and I had to take the kinks out of her wiring. [* * *] The Cantos make fine reading, the sweep and command of the langwidge (my spell) carries it even o'r the thin spots, although I have never been able to read the whole damn thing or remember what I've read, but it's going to last, I guess, just for that reason: a well of Pounding unrecognized.

[* * *] Thanks again for *Beat'd.* Anonymous poem not good because guy thinks he can compromise life. There is no compromise: if you are going to write tv rifleman crap, tv rifleman crap will show in your poems, and if he thinks he's an old timer at 34, he'd better towel behind the ears and elsewhere too, because Bukowski, who nobody's heard of will be 40 on August 16th., and Pound who everybody's heard of will be almost twice that old and has never compromised with anybody, nations or gods or gawkers and has signed his name to everything he has written, not for fame but for establishment of point and stance. Let the baker compromise, the cop and the mailman, some of us must hold the hallowed ground . . . [* * *]

"S & S" is Scimitar and Song, *whose March 1960 issue prints a Bukowski poem, with a typographical error.*

[To Jory Sherman]
[ca. April, 1960]

[* * *] Do you double space your poems? I know that one is supposed to double space stories, articles, etc. for clarity and easy reading but thot poem due to its construction (usually much space) read easy enough singled. And I think a double-spaced poem loses its backbone, it flops in the air. I don't know: the world is always sniping sniping so hard at the petty rules petty mistakes, I don't get it, what doesn't it mean? bitch, bitch, bitch. meanwhile the point going by: is the poem good or bad in your opinion? Rules are for old maids crossing the street.

Saw your poem in *S & S.* [* * *] She messed up my poem—eve instead of eye, but it was a rotter anyway. She's a very old woman and prints the same type of poesy. Wrote me a letter about how the birds were chirping outside her window, all was peace, men like me who liked to drink and gamble, oh talented but lost. I saw a bird when I was driving home from the track the other day. It was in the mouth of a cat crouched down in the asphalt street, the clouds overhead, the sunset, love and God overhead, and it saw my car and rose, cat-rose insane, stiff back like mad love depravity, and it walked toward the curbing, and I saw the bird, a large grey, flip broken winged, wings large and out, dipped, feathers spread, still alive, cat-fanged; nobody saying anything, signals changing, my motor running, and the wings the wings in my mind and the teeth, grey bird, a large grey. *Scimitar and Song,* yes indeed. Shit. [* * *]

The poem "Death Wants More Death" was published in Harlequin *in 1957. Sherman must have proposed reading it aloud to an audience.*

[To Jory Sherman]
[Spring 1960]

[* * *] On "D. Wants More D.," I am afraid it would disturb an audience a bit too much. My father's garage had windows in it full of webs, flies and spiders churning blood-death in my brain, and tho I'm told nature has its meaning, I'm still infested with horror, and all the charts and graphs of the chemists and biologists and anthropologists and naturalists and sound-thinking men are nothing to the buzzing of this death.

"Crews" is Judson Crews, since 1949 a prolific author of books and pamphlets from the little presses.

[To E. V. Griffith]
April 25, 1960

No, I haven't seen any of the Crews clip-out type production, and know very little of the mechanics of this sort of thing. But does this mean that a poem must have been published elsewhere in some magazine before it can be included in the chapbook? On much of my published work I only have one magazine and I would not care to tear them up for the chapbook. And you also hold much work of mine that has never been published. I don't quite know; it is all rather puzzling. And I know that if we had to go after the missing magazines to get the clips it would take long long months, and perhaps many of them could never be acquired.

I wish you could write me a bit more on how this works, for as you can see I am mixed up. What would it cost some other way? Or do they *have* to be published pieces?

The prices seem fair enough and I could go up to the 32 pages if you have enough material to fill them. Perhaps we might add the 2 poems out of *San Francisco Review* #1, and I have some stuff coming out in the *Coastlines* and *Nomad,* due off the press any day now, I'm told. I don't know if you'll like it or not. And you've probably seen some of my other crap around. I think "Regard Me" in *Nomad* #1 was pretty good, but it's hard for me to judge my own work and I'd rather leave that task up to you.

Right now I don't know how many pages you can fill or just whether or not this clip-out method restricts the filling. So I guess we'll have some more delay while you are kind enough to write me and fill in my ignorance.

Hoping to hear from you soon,

[To E. V. Griffith]
June 2, 1960

Good of you to write or even think chapbook while auto-torn. Like your lineup of poems ok, and should they run into more pages, please do let me know and I will money order you the difference. I would rather send you more than have you cut out a poem you want in there but are restricted on pages. I guess it's pretty hard to tell how many pages the thing will run at a loose glance like that and you will probably find out from your printer. Let me know how things work out this way on the pages. [* * *]

I just hope you can move a few copies so you won't get stung too badly on your end of the deal. I have visions of chapbooks stacked in a closet gathering dust and nobody knowing Bukowski and Griffith are alive and I begin to have horrible qualms. Maybe not. Maybe if this works out ok, sometime in the future we can go in on another half and half deal. It seems *very* reasonable since you do all the work and are promoting *another* person's work and not your own. The money end, from my side of it, seems less than nothing, but I realize that from your end with so many things going, different mags, chapbooks, it can get very very big, mountain-like. Well, hope all is ok, and you needn't write for a while, I realize you are in tough shape—unless you have some suggestions or et al. I feel pretty good that this thing is going thru, although it's hard to finally realize. [* * *]

Norman Winski was editor of the little magazine Breakthru.

[To Jory Sherman]
June 28, [1960]

[* * *] Winski, he's been phoning and I've been ducking. Jesus, I can't see any sense in it but I don't want to hurt his feelings. He pinned me down and I told him I'd be over to his place last night, but at last minute I phoned his wife and told her something had come up, I couldn't make it. She sounded pretty hurt and in about 10 minutes the phone started ringing, Winski I suppose and I just laid there slugging down the beer. I guess I'm insane, a mess-up. He told me to bring over some of my poems, wanted me to read something. Jesus, I can't do that sort of thing, Jory!

[* * *] Do, if you see Sheri, tell her I said hello. She wrote me a wonderful 3 page letter bout Pound and things, almost a poem, the whole thing. Deserves answer but I can't get untracked. [* * *]

[To Jory Sherman]
[July 9, 1960]

u in bed weigh & I am answering right off altho I do not know if I have anything to say but will let the keys roll and see what comes off. not me, I hope. No women around. One lugcow just left, sitting on couch all old out of shape red in face fat, jesus I told her I'm really going to heave a big one, one old big shitsigh when u drag it outa here. I'll have a brew and fall on the springs and begin to dream sweet dreams, only I did not say it in exactly this manner and she laughed. old women everywhere, lord. [* * *]

Spicer stupid to ask if you have read Lorca. Everybody has read Lorca. Everybody has read anything, everything. Why ask. I hate these meetings. Have u read. oh yeah. he's good. how about. o yeah. he's good too. [* * *]

Stan phoned yesterday. told him I was going to races. phone me, see me that night. I didn't hear. guess he pissed. well, what is there to see . . . me . . . old man on couch or edge of chair trying to think of something to say, and all the time everybody thinking, is *this* the guy who wrote those poems? No, it can't be!

WHAT PEOPLE FORGET IS THAT YOU *WRITE* THE POEM, YOU DON'T *TALK* IT.

to hell with everybody but Jory Sherman, S. Martinelli, Pound, Jeffers, T. Williams and the racing form. you are not a bastard and I do not like to hear yourself call urself one, and I am not a saint. let's go with the poem, straight down the stretch to the wire, first. sure.

Hearse Chapbook no. 4 was Mason Jordan Mason's A Legionere *(1960). Bukowski's book would be no. 5 in the series.*

[To E. V. Griffith]
August 1, 1960

Again the long silence from Eureka, although I see in *Trace* 38 you are coming on with more Mason Jordan Mason as fast as Crews can write it, also a couple of more editors. Well, that's all right. What you do is yours. I hate to bitch, but is anything happening with the *Flower and the Fist etc.* I have told a couple of more magazines, and few people and I am beginning to feel foolish because as you know, this is the second time around with the same act. Let me hear something or other. Stamped self-addressed enclosed.

Marvin Bell and a couple of others seem to think my "Death of a Roach" in *Epos*, Winter 1959, is a pretty good poem? Too late to work it in? More loot? You don't care for poem? Anyway, I'll be glad when it's all over. The thing has become more than a few pages of my poems. It has been going on so long that it has become like a disease, an obsession, purgatory, Alcatraz. . . . how long has it been? 2 years? 3? Please, E.V., be reasonable. Let's get this thing out of the way. Let Mason screw his lambs for a while. I am beginning to talk to myself in the mirror.

ps—I see where Witt crossed you up on "Lowdermilk," having appeared with it in *Decade* 1953. How they want their fame! over and over again! instead of writing something new. Frankly, E.V., I'm getting pretty sick of the literary world but I don't know where else to go. Yeah. I know. I can go to hell. I dropped a hundred and fifty on the ponies Saturday. Riding back on the train drunk, all the women looking at somebody else. Bukowski old and grey and shrunk. all the rivers dry. all the pockets empty. best anyhow, damn it, they haven't dropped the bomb yet.

The broadside referred to in the next letter was the first separate Bukowski publication, a poem called "His Wife the Painter," published by E. V. Griffith and included as an insert in the magazine Coffin, *no. 1 (1960).*

[To E. V. Griffith]
August 6, 1960

Thank you for the quick response on inquiry. Hope I have not piqued you.

Yes, this little mag game discouraging and that is why I try to keep quiet and not scratch at editors, just write the poem. When I bitch occasionally it's just the nerves reaching the throat, mine really, and I'm eating at myself rather than anybody else.

Thank you for broadsides: they are beautiful type jobs. I have at least a half dozen friends, places in mind that I'd like to see these. Tonight I am mailing out the ones you send. They are wonderfully presented, can't quite get over that. Do you have a few more sets? [* * *]

No, I don't have any particular mags in mind for review copies. I don't have any particular feuds going nor, on the other hand, any strong supporters who would swing for me. [* * *]

Nice to hear from you Griff and I promise not to cry anymore.

A little outa the way, but I rec. a note from Ann Reynolds of the *Sixties* this morn. little photo a duff and bly. I roasted Duffy and he ducked out and joined the French Foreign Legion. Who says I'm not a tough baby? [* * *]

P.S.—If this works out ok, perhaps sometime in the future—the far future—we can work out another half-and-half deal. I think right now we have both suffered too much with it . . . . [* * *]

The next letter records the first contact with Outsider *magazine and its editors and publishers, Jon and Louise Webb, a connection which was to prove so beneficial to Bukowski. It also, like the preceding letter, notes his incompatibility with the kind of poetry being furthered by Robert Bly's magazine* The Sixties

(formerly The Fifties*). Bukowski had eleven poems in* Outsider *No. 1 (Fall 1961), under the collective title "A Charles
Bukowski Album."*

[To Jory Sherman]
August 17, 1960

[* * *] Martinelli called me down something . . . called me a
"prick," said I built "ass-hole palaces," called me "bug-job," I can't
remember all. [* * *] I can't be bothered with gash trying to realign
my outlook. And Pound may have been "lonely" and "fell in love
with a great sSSPLLLANGggg" "like a rain in a dry dusty summer,"
but I am not Pound and I am not lonely. The last thing I wanna
see is more gash and more people.

No, regarding Griff, broadsides not of book, but insert style thing
to be slipped into pages of *Coffin* and *Hearse* loosely, later to be
assembled into collection of some sort. I am broadside #1, *Hearse*.
Tibbs freelance pen ink sketcher who fulfills frus[trations] by playing little mag pages with scratchy pen. Rather ordinary talent, I think,
but not too much compo[sition]. Think I could do better but I am
supposed to be a poet.

No, I'm not in *Sixties*. One reject they sent me, trying to place
me in *Evergreen Review* class, had hangover and straightened them.
Hence this bit of corres., photo etc., which I am not going to answer,
my point already have b. made, and I don't care too much to leave
the poem and jaw unless it is crit. article. Ann Reynolds sounds like
somebody to fill Duffy-gap. [* * *]

Thanks for word on *Outsider* Finally got card from them through
Coastlines. Asking me for contributions. Ah, well.

Bukowski's birthday is August 16th.

[To Jory Sherman]
August 17, 1960

it's all over, I'm 40, over the hill, down the other side . . . made the rounds Sunday nite . . . alone . . . sat in strip joint, watched them shake and wiggle like something going on . . . bored . . . $1.25 for beer, but drank em like water. water hell. I don't drink much water. Place after place . . . faces sitting there empty as jugs. shit. shit. oh, I got a lovely buncha coconuts! nothing. woke up with cracked toe, blood, couldn't walk. oh I got a lovely buncha, a lovely buncha coconuts!

old girlfriend sent over huge buncha flowers, all kinds, quite nicea her. like a funeral, like a beautiful funeral, buried at 40 . . .

sick today. [* ★ *]

Do you mind if I sign myself Charles? it is old habit. when I write or when somebody writes me I am Charles. When they talk to me in a room I am Hank. This, my solidification. A chunk of 40 stone.

[To Jory Sherman]
[August 22, 1960]

black day, they have kicked my horse-ass good. 3 rejects, *San Fran. Review, White Dove,* and *Oak Leaves.* [* ★ *]

Girlfriend said I was as drunk the other night as she'd ever seen me. I used vile lang. and yanked the mattress off her bed and then leaned back in chair and gave 2 hours lecture (while drinking) on the arts and what they meant or didn't mean, and who was what and why.

Kid, I am definitely cracking. These last 3 or 4 months have ended me. I think I'm written out. I've said it all. What the hell else? I don't care. I've still got the horses and the whores and Schlitz. Let these 19 year old editors gobble the gugga of rooster.

I'm going to try to buy a shack somewhere and give everything up. Just be dirty old man waiting to die. I'm sick of all the 8 hour faces and laughter and babble, Dodger talk and pussy-talk and zero-talk. A roof, no rent. That's my aim. Pick up enough washing dishes 3 times a week or pimping. Lord, I'm sick of it all. And poetry too.

No wonder Van Gogh blasted his head off. Crows and sunlight. Idle zero. Zero eating your guts like an animal inside, letting you shit and fuck and blink your eyes, but nothing, a nothing. I couldn't die stretched in a blizzard because I'm already dead. So let Pound have it. And Keats. and Shelley. and belly. piss. the mailman with his smirking white rejectee envelopes, and all the grass growing and the cars going by as if it all doesn't matter. Christ, I'm watching a guy water his lawn now. His mind is as empty as a department store flowerbowl. Water. water. water. make the grass grow green. GREAT. G R E A T. [* * *]

[To E. V. Griffith]
[September 19, 1960]

Got you plug in *Quagga* vol. I, no. 2, just off the press: "Charles Bukowski's new book will be off the press early next month, *Flower, Fist and Bestial Wail.* It is being published by Hearse Chapbooks in California." So you see, I'm working at it. Pretty lively poem in *Quagga* about a riot that occurred while I was in Moyamensing Prison. Might instigate the sale of a couple of chapbooks. I feel that you have been somehow reluctant to put out the Wail, perhaps feeling it would not move, since I am an isolationist socially speaking and have only enemies, but life is sometimes odd Griff, and it might be that this thing will put some dough in your pockets. I feel I am a more lively writer than Crews, Creeley, Mason, etc., Eckman, but we'll see.

[To E. V. Griffith]
Mid September, [1960]

Got your note on chapbook progress the other day. It appears to me that you are doing too much at once, getting out too many chapbooks at once, and although mine was started long ago others seem to be coming out ahead of me. I don't know what the hell to make of it all and often wonder how another writer would have taken it. From my experiences as an editor I found they wail and bitch pretty much, and can be quite damned nasty. This thing is even beginning to get me. Now the pages have come out wrong sequenced . . . what kind of a printer is that?

Well, I hope this thing does get done . . . sometime . . . somehow. The strain is getting unbearable.

[To E. V. Griffith]
October 7, 1960

My dear E. V. Griffith:

Since you have failed to contact me since about last August— "and I should have something in your hands by the end of the month"—and then the note about wrong sequenced pages—"and I should have something in your hands in just a few more days," I haven't heard and we are now sailing well into October.

It seem to me that all mistakes could have been rectified by now! My famed patience, has at last, after a 2 years wait, *had* it.

And in case you have forgotten, I finally sent you some money— between 30 and 40 bucks—to help you get this thing rolling.

You have put me out on the limb by again asking me to make announcements to the magazines that *Hearse* is to issue *Flower, Fist and Bestial Wail.* This is getting to be the joke of the literary world, but I am no longer laughing.

I am going to wait a short period longer and if no results are achieved I am going to write *Trace,* the San Francisco newspapers and the editors of other literary magazines of the whole history of this notorious and impossible chapbook nightmare. I can not see it that sloppy and amateur editorialism, a downright horror of coldness and cruelty and ineptness go unchallenged.

If you feel that I am being unfair, hasty or unreasonable, I would be most glad to get any statements from you. However, further silence or delay, would be construed to mean that you intend to continue your slipshod policies and the writer be damned.

We of the literary world, we like to feel that we are not here to wrangle or to claw, but to create. Protest is more a political and worldly thing, but even as a poet, I feel I have a right and a duty, in this case, to make public protest.

[To E. V. Griffith]
October 14, 1960

I went down to the post office this morning with card left in my box yesterday—and *yowl!*—there it was, set of *Hearse* chapbooks by one Charles Bukowski. I opened the package right in the street, sunlight coming down, and there it was: *Flower, Fist and Bestial Wail,* never a baby born in more pain, but finally brought through by the good Doctor Griffith—a beautiful baby, beautiful! The first collected poems of a man of 40, who began writing late.

Griff, this was an event! Right in the middle of the street between the post office and a new car agency.

But then the qualms came on and the fear and the shame. I remembered my last letter to you when I had finally cracked, scratching and blaming and cursing, and the sickness came.

I DON'T KNOW HOW IN THE HELL TO APOLOGIZE, E. V., BUT JESUS I ASK FORGIVENESS. That's all I can say.

It's a beautiful job, clean and pure, poem arrangement perfect. I'm mailing out copies to some people who think I am alive, but first off with this letter to you.

I hope I can live down any disgust I have caused you.

•

• 1 9 6 1 •

[To Jory Sherman]
[1961?]

[* * *] The fact that the poets of the world are drunk is a damn good indication of its shape. Cresspoolcrews says something about the essence of poetry being in the shape of a woman's body. It must be wonderful to be so beautifully simple and uninvolved. Sex is the final trap, the closing of the steel-kissed door. Lawrence was closer in seeking muliebrity from flesh to soul, and to perstringe [sic] the awkward-working and the ugly. Crews simply swallows sex in great drunken drafts because he doesn't know what else to do, which, of course, is common Americana: thinking about it, simpering about it, carrying dirty pictures in the back pocket, and yet this country, for it all, is the most puritanical you can find. Women here have put the price too high and the boys go behind the barn with the cow. Which makes it tough on boys, cows, and women.

I have just read the immortal poems of the ages and come away dull. I don't know who's at fault; maybe it's the weather, but I sense a lot of pretense and poesy footwork: I am writing a poem, they seem to say, *look* at me! Poetry must be forgotten; we must get down to raw paint, splatter. I think a man should be forced to write in a roomful of skulls, bits of raw meat hanging, nibbled by fat slothy rats, the sockets musicless staring into the wet ether-sogged, love-sogged, hate-sogged brain, and forevermore the rockets and flares and chains of history winging like bats, bat-flap and smoke and skulls ringing in the beer. Yes. [* * *]

Ben Tibbs, a printer, a poet and artist who published alongside Bukowski in many little magazines, lived in Kalamazoo, Michigan. He did the cover art for Flower, Fist and Bestial Wail.

[To Ben Tibbs]
June 8, 1961

Sorry I can only ship one copy but I am down to the end of mine. Other people have written me that Griffith does not respond either to money or written request. I have attempted to send copies to all those who asked for them but Griffith only sent me a limited number. What has gone wrong up in Eureka I really don't know.

Thank you for doing the Art work on *Flower, Fist.* I think you caught the spirit of the poems and the title quite well.

•

• 1962 •

Carl Larsen published Bukowski's third book, Longshot Poems for Broke Players, *at his 7 Poets Press in New York early in 1962.*

[To Ben Tibbs]
[early 1962]

I had meant to ask you not to send dollar; certainly this is one hell of a price to pay to see the fine cover you did for Griffith. But instead of sending the dollar back, I am going to suffer you with a copy of *Longshot Poems for Broke Players.* Am sending the buck on to Larsen for this purpose, but am having the beers anyhow. Many thanks for your graciousness and understanding.

Neeli Cherkovsky, then known as Neeli Cherry, recounts an incident of Bukowski's reacting to Cherry's writing a poem about him by throwing the MS *in the fire. Cherry retrieved it, Bukowski praised it, but added "I hope you don't devote a career to writing about me" (*Hank, *p. 293). Cherry published the poem in his magazine,* Black Cat Review, *no. 1, June 1962.*

[To Neeli Cherry]
Sunday [early 1962]

without too much reverence

Thank you for the poem. Are you going to devote a career writing about me? Better chose yr subjects more carefully.

Your poetic style is good. I mean that it is loose enough to allow truth to enter or anything you want to say enter

> without worry about preconceptions
> or the poetic line
> which thoughts
> choke up most of them
> before they begin
> I mean, before they begin
> they have ended.
> they are done.

a good style is important. style is what makes you different from the run. it lets yr voice be heard. Some good men have learned this.

to wit: Shakespeare, Hem, Sherwood Anderson, D. H. Lawrence, Gertie Stein, Faulkner, Picasso, Van Gogh, Stravinsky.

Stein had more style than genius. Her style was her genius. Faulk was next. He put very little fire into a forge of style that fooled almost everybody. Hem had style and genius that went with it, for a little while, then he tottered, rotted, but was man enough, finally, and had style enough, finally. Lawrence was a cock-freak who never had nerve enough to face the world as a man and so faced the world behind a nerve-soothing soul-soothing whirl of sex proteins, but who ever and nevertheless wrote some penetrating lines. Sherwood A. was just a good old fuck who suffered without too much pretense but who was aware of style, of cutting words into paper so you could see them, like blood or paint. This is important. It is a painting. Writing is painting and the sooner people realize this the less dull crap will dull the market and I will have to get drunk that much less. Picasso does with paint what I would like to do with words, only some day may try to do with paint, only not, fuck of course like P. but like B., and style only means opening into light simply and cleanly. Van Gogh, of course, was never insane. He simply realized the world was elsewhere. And his style, the purest of styles.

A good style comes primarily from a lack of pretentiousness, and what is pretentious changes from year to year from day to day from minute to minute. We must be ever more careful. A man does not get old because he nears death; a man gets old because he can no longer see the false from the good.

Enough of speech-making. [* * *]

Ann Bauman was and is a poet living in Sacramento, publishing in some of the same little magazines Bukowski appeared in. (On her marriage, she became Ann Menebroker.) Evidently their correspondence began with her note of appreciation for a poem of his which appears in Signet, *May 1962. Bukowski notes: "Fair poet. I believe we bucked each other up for a while, perhaps she helped me more than I helped her. There was an off-hand, rather ho hum attitude from her, more toward life than toward me."*

[To Ann Bauman]
May 10, 1962

got yr note on "Dead Stay Alive Too Long" and etc., and it filled a hole in the mailbox where a rejected poem usually sits. Am sitting here having a beer and staring out the same window, 3 floors up, miles out into the nowhere of Hollywood. If you saw something in the poem (or poems) good. Yet a little praise is a bad thing, and a lot of it is worse. We cannot be too careful. It is better for the artist to work out of a vacuum, going from creation to creation, each a new beginning, until it is all over, until he is dead in the sense that he can no longer create or he can no longer create because he is dead (physically). The latter, of course, is preferable.

Jory is another case entirely, and it would do little good to discuss him here.

Joyce Odam wrote a poem for me about the death of a lady, for which I wrote her my thanks.

I recall seeing a large group of your work somewhere (*Signet?*). Well, keep going. But we have to, don't we?

[To Ann Bauman]
[May 19, 1962]

rec. yr letter but I am a bastard and usually do not bother with these correspondii? or haven't you heard? this has nothing to do with fathead or fat in the frying pan or limping dogs.

all my elements are hung up like a shirt on a hanger and there is not much I can do with them.

Yes, everything I do is "breathlessly new"—for this same reason people continue to make love. I am not interested in history or theory—or argument. The best argument is a new poem.

It is may the 19th somebody has just told me. Fine.

what does one do at poetry festivals? surely, dear, there must be a better way.

I sent yr Friedman at SIGNET a poem but have not heard and she is pretty quick usually. I told her it was a bad poem and this might have her confused. It's called "Keats and Marlowe." I told her it was bad and then I rewrote it. It might still be prob. bad.

God, I am running out of beer! this is madness . . .

ah, hahah ahha ha ha ha ha!

[To Ann Bauman]
May 21, 1962

Getting this off while drinking a beer and listening to a little Sibelius before going to work. I am sorry you do not believe I do not like to argue. I believe you are bothered with too many concepts.

You should avoid these poetry festivals etc. as they are nothing but a melting pot of watered-down talents, high-class lonely heart club for those with typewriters. [* * *]

Study yr keeds. Kids. There are a lot of poems there. But don't write about yr kids. Write about the human, what's left of him, where he's going, what he dropped on the floor.

Don't tell me about insanity. I wrote a short story about a man who murdered a blanket that fell in love with him and appeared to look at him and follow him around. "Very believable," wrote back the first mag, "but this man appears too bizarre." Or this is the condensation of it. I do not believe in writing a short story unless it crawls out of the walls. I watch the walls daily but very little happens.

The review mentioned in the next letter was among the very earliest published recognitions of Bukowski's work. R. R. Cuscaden's "Charles Bukowski: Poet In a Ruined Landscape" appeared in Satis, *no. 5. Cuscaden, editor and publisher of* Midwest *magazine, brought out Bukowski's* Run With the Hunted *(1962).*

[To Ann Bauman]
June [20?], 1962

Yes, Sibelius later went into hiding and shaved his head; I'm told he was a handsome and vain man, and age bothered him, but for it all

> he wrote the long-striding line
> stepped around the mountains
> and died.

It is 26 minutes before 9 a.m. and I am out of beer. [* * *]

I include herein *Satis* an English magazine that has printed a couple of poems that fall into the non-uplifting category. You can get the other kind anywhere. Also, a review of my 3 books by Cuscaden. It is a good damned thing I do not wear a hat or I could not get it around my head after reading these reviews.

Darling, this is the trap: BELIEVE YOU ARE GOOD WHEN THEY TELL YOU YOU ARE GOOD AND YOU ARE THEREBY DEAD, DEAD, DEAD. dead forever. Art is a day by day game of living and dying and if you live a little more than you die you are going to continue to create some pretty fair stuff, but if you die a little more than you live, you know the answer.

Creation, the carving of the thing, the good creation is a sign that the god that runs you there inside still has his eyes open. Creation is not the end-all but it is a pretty big part. End of lecture #3784. [* * *]

Corrington, a poet then teaching at Louisiana State University, was to write the introduction to Bukowski's first Loujon Press book, It Catches My Heart in Its Hands, *which would finally appear in the fall of 1963. Bukowski notes, "An early booster of my work." He adds that their long correspondence "stopped after he wrote his novel and went to Hollywood."*

[To John William Corrington]
June 24, 1962

IN KIND OF A NUMB STATE LATELY? I mean, me. THE END OF THE SOUL. mebee. Anyhow, just crawling out of the sack and looking around, that's about where I am at. They've machine gunned me down to this nub. good. cigarettes, cigars, candy?

Jon's hard at the book, I know. How about yours? I heard that your San Francisco Review has folded or will change hands. Weren't they going to bring out a new collection of your poems? Check your tires for air.

Just off a four day drunk. Bloody ass. Glass on floor. Broke. Coffeepot now going in front of me: GLUGGLE, GLUGGLE, GLUKE GLUKE!! I think a new piece of ass would fix me fine. This old stuff gets so hard to handle. That their eyes spray me with love is not enough. It is the sagging of the tit, the worn-flesh? If I could only once have a drink of clear spring water. Everything has mud in it and sticks and discarded socks. Well, I am not so much myself. Crows don't sleep with peacocks. I've got to realize this. [* * *]

Wormwood Review *published the following letter as Bukowski's response to the editor's explanation that the payment for publication was four copies "which we will mail to anywhere, anybody or anything...." (M.S. is presumably a slightly disguised reference to Sheri Martinelli and C.W. to John William Corrington.)*

[To Marvin Malone]
[August 1962]

well, ya better mail one to M.S. or she'll prob. put her pisser in the oven, she thinks she is a goddess, and maybe she is, I sure as hell wd't know
like some of the boys tell me,
then there is C.W. who does not answer his mail but is very busy teaching young boys how to write and I know he is going places, and since he is, ya better mail 'm one . . .
then there's my old aunt in Palm Springs nothing but money and I have everything but money . . . talent, a good singing voice, a left hook deep to the gut . . . send her a copy, she hung up on me, last time I phoned her drunk, giving evidence of need, she hung up on me . . .
then there's this girl in Sacramento who writes me these little letters . . . very depressed bitch, mixed like quite some waffle flower, making gentle intellectual overtures which I ignore, but send her a magazine
in lieu of a hot poker.
that makes 4?
I hope to send you some more poems anytime because I got to figure that people who run my poems are a little mad, but that's all right. I am also that way. anyhow,—
I hope meanwhile you do not fold up before I do.

A note by the recipient identifies this as accompanied by the gift of a bobby pin. The "her" in question is presumably Jane Cooney Baker, who had died early in 1962. For Bukowski's relationship with her, see Hank, *chapters 4 and 5.*

[To Ann Bauman]
[September 1962]

Death does *not* take everything, god damn it.
I hope you can use this in your hair to keep alive a something that I should have died in front of. o my god my god yes I am drinking.

and who cares? I love her. simple swine words. use it, in your hair. Thank you, Sacramento fog, fountains, odd voice, grief of wretched breathing, phantom love, oh child, wear it in your hair, honor me, her, the mountains, the hot great tongue and flash of God.

Thank you.

[To Ann Bauman]
September 4, 1962

Disregard my last letter. Strings became undone. A little sawdust spilled out. Beer. Wine. German gloom. These things can fetch anyone. A waterglass looks like a skull. Horses run into the rail. Insomnia. Job trouble. Toothache. The body bleeds. Retching. Flat tire. Traffic ticket. Lack of love. Sleep, then nightmare. Paper everywhere. Trivial bits of paper. Nothing ever done. Flooded sink. People in the hall with cardboard faces. Sure, sure, sure.

Today I will walk in the sun. I will simply walk in the sun. [* * *]

[To Jon Webb]
September 4, 1962

Regarding the death of my woman last Jan. 22, there is not much to say except I will never be the same again. I might attempt to write it sometimes but it is still too close, may always be too close. But that time in the charity ward years ago a little Mexican girl who changed the sheets told me that she was going to shack up with me as soon as I got well, and I began feeling better right away. I had one visitor: a drunken woman, red and puffy-faced, a bedmate of the past who reeled against the bed a few times, said nothing and walked out. Six days later I was driving a truck, lifting 50-lb packages and wondering if the blood would come again. A couple of days later I had the first drink, the one they said would kill me. A week or so later I got a typewriter, and after a ten-year blank, after selling to *Story* & others, I found my fingers making the poem. Or rather the bar-talk. The non-lyrical, non-singing thing. The rejects came

36

quickly enough. But they made no indentation, for I felt in each line as if I were talking the thing out. Not for them, but for myself. Now I can read very little other poetry or very little other anything. Anyway, the drunk lady who reeled against my bed, I buried her last Jan. 22. And I never did see my little Mexican girl. I saw others, but somehow she would have been right. Today, I am alone, almost outside all of them: the buttocks, the breasts, the clean live dresses like unused and new dishtowels on the rack. But don't get me wrong—I'm still 6 feet tall with 200 lbs. of ableness, but I was able best with the one that's gone.

Bukowski's "WW 2" appeared in Mica *7 (November 1962). Previously, three poems were published in* Mica *5 (Winter 1962). The magazine was edited by Helmut Bonheim and Raymond Federman from Santa Barbara.*

[To Helmut Bonheim]
September 28, [1962]

Thanks the stamps, and good you like "ww 2" which is more factual than inventive, but what the fuck, you've got to give me credit for putting it down anyhow because it's what to know what to leave out that makes me different from the garage mechanic, if we are too much different. There is another story I have written—about a man who murders a blanket. Sent it to *Evergreen*, 6 months now, no response. Wrote stamped, self-add. thing. No response. I don't keep carbons. I suppose I'll see it in print some day under the name of Francios Marcios or Francis Francis or F. Villon. I keep getting reamed this way. But it is good for me. It reminds me that the world is pretty shitty. and this keeps me deftly abdulah and stasher of cannons. Anyhow, on "ww 2," change and shift lines at your will . . . to fit page or to help readability;—although I personally garbled it a little, voices and ideas running together—to throw nails.

I'll send you more poems since you ask for them, but haven't written any, and they don't come back. I don't mean they are accepted; I mean the swine simply do not return them; they sit on them like pillows, friend. aye.

37

This is garbage talk.

I have come through a green and red war these last 2 month. My side lost but I am still more alive than ever, in a sense. We have to pass through these things, again, again—arguing with a knife blade, a bottle, weeping like a frigging cunt in menopause, afraid to step out a door . . . afraid of birds, fleas, mice . . . encircled by a clock, a typewriter, a half-open closet door full of ghouls, killers, horrors like sea-bottoms. And then it ends. You are calm again. As calm as . . . a garage mechanic. I think of a D. H. Lawrence title: *Look We Have Come Through.*

Anyhow, I'll try you with some poems, although I don't know if they can be like the *Mica* things. They will just have to be what they are . . . If you read somewhere that I cursed editors and other critters, you prob. read correctly. I deal pretty much alone and don't care for ties. Tits, yes. Ties, no. I never wear ties. Creation and flow are the factors. Survival is not too important to me, either in any sense of immortality or in any sense of today—paying the rent, eating a sandwich, dreaming of a good fuck etc. etc. Although I get pretty scared sometimes when the world tries to kill me. Not the death-part, for as Socrates explained, this cannot be too bad. It is the getting there. The eyes. The flies. the ties. rubber tires. dead fish. fat landladies. buttons falling off shirt. dirty laundry. garage mechanics . . . .

savannah and eggplant

The Webbs were preparing the third issue of their magazine, The Outsider, *which would be devoted mainly to Bukowski, whom Webb proclaimed recipient of a special award as "Outsider of the Year." The issue would include tributes to Bukowski as well as photographs of him and poems and letters by him. It was to be followed by the publication of a "Loujon Press Award Book" collecting Bukowski's poetry.*

[To Jon Webb]
September 28, [1962]

[* * *] I have been doing some thinking. I would like to write you another letter of acceptance re the OUTSIDER OF YEAR 62 thing,

and I will anyhow, and it should be arriving in a day or 2 [* * *]

As per writing more letters, as you know, this can't be done just like that any more than a poem can; in fact, a letter is tougher because the letter mood seems to fall less upon me than the poem thing. Yet I think the letter is an important form. You can touch about everything as you run around. It lets you out of the straightjacket of pure Art, and you've *got* to get out once in a while. Of course, I don't restrict myself as much in the poem as most do, but I have made this my business, this freedom with the word and idea, because . . . to be perfectly corny . . . I know I'll only be around once and I want to make it easy on myself. [* * *]

[To Jon Webb]
[ca. October 1, 1962]

[* * *] Sherman was up yesterday to borrow 5 bucks. Said it was raining and his windshield wiper wasn't working. I hate to be a bitch but this kid is getting to be real pain in the ass. He's got a $150 a week job and he keeps borrowing from me, and then he's got guts enough to claim he's paid me back. [* * *] I'm going to have to cut off relations with Sherman. You are the editor, but if he sends in anything on me on congrat. for 1962 OUTSIDER, I wish you wouldn't run it because congrats from this person are not congrats at all. Enough of this type of bitching which is a little bit swinish . . . if it were only the borrowing it would not be so bad, but there are other facets of personality here in Sherman that you wouldn't find in a low-grade polecat. Enough. [* * *]

[To Jon Webb]
[ca. October 1, 1962]

I am enclosing another letter of acceptance which I much prefer to the other one I sent you. Of course, I do not know exactly what you want, and even if I did, I couldn't do it. This one might be a little too long for you, or the ending rather sudden. I don't know.

I am over my menopause or whatever the hell it was. It only lasted a month; maybe it was something else. I don't mind going mad so long as it is clean. I don't like the sloppy thing. Yet, you surely know that any of us who work with the word are open to anything, I mean any day we might test the cliff's edge. This is the nature of remaining as alive as possible: while other men die slowly, we are more apt to blow out the fire with one quick fucking blast—see Van Gogh, see Hemingway, see Chatterton, see the whole thing back down and through. Or if we don't kill ourselves, the State kills us: see Aristotle, see Lorca. And Villon, they ran him out of Paris just because he did a little thievery between poems. We are in for hard times, Jon, any way you look at it. Even those of us who are not giants. But it is harder for the giants. Their bones are the same as ours but they have strained and made the leap. Then there's a lot of pap and shit: people who write drivelly little poems while maintaining a time-clock, children, new-car, new-home decency. They'll make with the poem as long as nothing *else* is lost. It won't work. Man can't *divide* his impulses and expect to have power down every corridor. Now, the original Beats, as much as they were knocked, had the Idea. But they were flanked and overwhelmed by fakes, guys with nicely clipped beards, lonely-hearts looking for free ass, limelighters, rhyming poets, homosexuals, bums, sightseers—the same thing that killed the Village. Art can't operate in Crowds. Art does not belong at parties, nor does it belong at Inauguration Speeches. It belongs sitting across from Khrushchev but only if it drinks a beer with the man and talks anything but politics. . . . and there are so many good beginnings. A strong young talent makes it. Then can't stand light. This is nothing but the plain old-fashioned fathead and shows that the Artist was not *ready* in the first place. The days speak; the years tell; the centuries throw out the garbage.

God oh mighty, another lecture. Is this a sign of old age? Let me tell you that by saying these things to myself, and to you, I protect myself from rot. I've seen so much rot. And I may be rotting myself and may not know it. It's just like when someone else is sleeping with your wife: you are the last to find out, or you never find out. Such is the soul. We are tested when we lace our shoes, or in the manner in which we scratch our back. [* * *]

The following is from the letter accepting the "Outsider of the Year" Award that Bukowski sent for publication.

[To Jon Webb]
[ca. October 1, 1962]

[* * *] I have always been pretty much *outside* it all, and I don't mean just the art I try to send down through my typewriter, although there it appears I stand outside the gate also. It appears from many rejections that I do not write *poetry* at all. Or as a dear friend told me the other day: "You do not understand the true meaning of poetry. You are not lyrical. You do not *sing!* You write bar talk. The type of thing you write you can hear in any bar on any day."

I have always been one of those people who do everything wrong. This is essentially because I am not involved in the march.

Nothing is quite real to me. Streetcars. bombs. bugs. women. lightglobes. areas of grass. All unreal. I *am* outside. Death which is *true* enough, even this appears unreal. Not so long ago I was in the charity ward of a hospital in one of our greater cities. This is wording it badly: the whole god damned hospital was a charity ward, a place to crawl around in, a kind of purgatory on earth where the dying are allowed to lay in the stink of their sheets for days and the appearance of a nurse is redemption and the appearance of a doctor is like God Himself. All this is pretty much *outside*. They *do* keep the men and the women in separate wards. This is about all the individuality, all the identity we were allowed to retain: what's left of the gender. [* * *]

[To Ann Bauman]
October 8, 1962

[* * *] I have taken a 30 day leave of absence (without pay) from my post office job. The job was driving me mad (if you'll allow a platitude), but I find this time to drink and gamble—think—also leads to madness.

I was 42 on August 16th. That I have lived this long is a true miracle. I cannot hope for many more days. They will catch me.

They will get me in their bloody net and I will have done.

I wish Sacramento were around the corner. I am usually—in spite of all doubt and razors and grief—fairly strong, but tonight I would have liked to talk to you. This letter then will have to do—and perhaps tomorrow—t & t & tomorrow—I will be more the hard steel German-Polack who bats out the sounds of living from the top of a beercan.

Photographs were needed for the Outsider *feature.*

[To Jon Webb]
[?October 15, 1962]

Well, I have been shot. It's all over.

J. phoned and I told him I needed to be shot and J. is a great contact man and he came up with a brother-in-law, one John Stevens who works in a factory and shoots on the side, so over they came from Pasadena, J. and Stevens and J.'s wife and some other young man (I never did quite get where he fit), and they dragged the stuff in, and somebody said, "This guy doesn't even look like a writer," which is something I have heard before and before and before. Such as, "You wouldn't think he was the guy who wrote those poems . . ." Or, "I don't know, I expected, I expected well, more *fire* out of you." People have these ideas of what a writer *should* be, and this is set up both by the movies and by the writers themselves. We can't deny that such people as D. H. Lawrence, Hart Crane, Dylan Thomas and so forth had a scabbard of personality that cut down into people. I say or do nothing brilliant. The most brilliant thing I do is to get drunk—which any fool can do. If there is any dramatics in me, it must wait on the Art Form. If there is any ham in me it must wait on the Art Form. If there is any D. H. Lawrence in me it must wait on the A.F. I am pretty much tired and when it comes to playing writer, somebody else will have to do it.

Anyhow, they set the thing up and I got out the beer and J. and his wife talked to me, trying to make me forget the camera, but I'd be a fool to forget the camera, my mind is not that bad. If there were a snake in the room I would not forget the snake in the room. And flick, flick, you could hear the thing going. It is not essentially a happy mood and I kept thinking, this has nothing to do with the poem, this is how men die. Kennedy might phone me any day now and ask me to do a foreword to a campaign speech or something, and I will have to tell him what Frost did not. So flick, flick, more beer, another chair, another shirt, another cigarette, J.'s wife laughing, enjoying it all, like watching a bear poked with a cigarette. Then they stuck me behind the typer and asked me to type and I wrote: "It is only when I read of suicides that I feel happy at all. To know that there are other votes in that direction." Flick, flick, there was plenty of beer and plenty of cigarettes and evidently plenty of film. The thing finally ended and I went into the can to piss and then I found we had probably messed up everything. In the beginning, I had scratched the top of my head and here was this floater of hair sticking up on top of my head like a coxcomb or whatever. Everything ruined. Why didn't they tell me? I came out and told them I had a flag on my head but they intended to ignore it. The camera won't.

I got some more beer and we stopped off at J.'s, and here more trouble. I went into J.'s can and when I flushed the thing it ran over and out into the hall. He's been having trouble with the thing and his landlady can't seem to get it fixed and this set J. off. He has the true writer's temperament and he ran down the stairs to fix his teeth in the landlady. I guess he was embarrassed about the toilet (I was too), and maybe the only way sensitive people can override embarrassment is to howl. I do not. When something bad happens I say nothing. What's wrong with me there, I do not know. Anyhow, J. got his teeth in the landlady and a scene spouted up. She came up the stairs crying and had this mop and mopped the floor, and it was funny in a tragic way: here she was with the mop, weeping, poet J. standing over her saying, "Now, Mrs. M., I think you get simply too *emotional* over these things!" Anyhow, she went weeping down the steps, and J. came in and paced up and down cursing the toilet. He said he liked the view. You can see the whole horrible city of Los Angeles. J. likes to look at it. But he's new in town. I've seen the welts of L.A. too long. I never go to the window. Not to look out at the city. To look at a bird maybe, all right. Anyhow, I guess you can't blame him on the can: when a man wants to piss (or worse) you can't piss in a view. Anyhow, we had another beer and left. I drove Stevens and his friend back to Pasadena, a city I am not too familiar with. My night was not over. When I left them out they said, "You see that blue light down there?" I told them I saw that blue light down there. They said, friend, when you get there, turn right. You'll hit the freeway in about 2 or 3 miles. Well, I never did find the freeway. Maybe it was because I was too busy looking for a liquor store. It was about one thirty a.m. and they close at 2. But in Pasadena they close about 10 p.m. My old man said 30 years ago, "Pasadena is a one-horse town." It was one of the few times he was on beam. And it still goes today.

To make it worse I got lost. I drove and drove and drove. And everything was closed. Gas stations, everything. Cafes, everything. On the largest boulevards there was not a single person on the streets. Just signal lights, street corners, and no direction signs and if there were direction signs they only said Arcadia and I had no idea where Arcadia was. I kept driving almost under a sense of panic. I get into these things time and time again. I got to thinking of Kafka, how he wrote about going into these buildings, one room after another, being shuffled and buffoned [*sic*] about, nothing making any sense. I am sure if Kafka had been driving with me this night he would have had another novel. Panic, sure, all you want is a bed and a cool beer and here you are driving in a peopleless world of smooth and efficient streets that only lead you further and further away and you can't stop because this would then be real panic, you understand? I kept driving, and then it became really nightmare. I ended up in the hills! A small road going up into the hills and over one of the hills I saw a thing that looked like a Chinese temple. Jesus Christ, Jon, I was in Tibet! And sure enough, halfway through the hills here was this kind of Chinese village-inn type of thing, but no people, just these Chinese signs, and I began to feel as if I were going mad and I swung around the village driveway and shot back down out of the hills the way I came.

I must have driven an hour more, seeing no one, getting nowhere, backtracking, turning, going North, South, East, West. Then I saw a human being. He had one of these gas trucks and was running gas into a gas station. I asked him, "How do I get to L.A.?" "Whereabouts you want to get in L.A.?" he asked. "I don't care *where*," I told him, "just show me the city hall." "Well, buddy," he said, "you are going in the wrong direction. Just turn around and follow this street straight on in." That simple.

But going back, I got found, I recognized some of the streets leading to Santa Anita racetrack and I was on my own route back home. I can get you to any racetrack from California to Mexico but don't ask me where anything else is at.

I got to my sweet room, full of empty beercans and bottles and

I went to the refrigerator. Luck. There sat one chilled and lovely glass bottle of Miller's. I drank that and went to bed.

And that was the night of the photos. I hope something comes out of it because I don't think I can go through with it again. Not this year, anyhow. I mean, other people can do these things easily. Me, I'm a frog on a dissection table. I guess that's why I write. They keep cutting me open. It's nothing profound, but so odd. And all these photos with this hunk of hair standing up on my head. I can't even walk across a room with success. This morning I stepped on a can opener that was on the floor. No shoes on, of course. Another minor tragedy. Yet the spirit is not suicidal. I tend to linger just to see how many more odd turns the gods can throw on me. I suppose somebody will tell me I need the couch. Well, we all need the couch. Don't tell me that with our Berlin walls and our stockpiles that our part of the universe is healthy and makes sense. If I need the couch they had better start building a lot of couches. I won't deny that I might be somewhat off, don't get me wrong But if you are going to try to show me a leader or a way out, I am going to ask a lot of questions.

Anyhow Stevens is supposed to phone me about the pictures. He has them in Pasadena and is going to put them into the soup. And I guess I am supposed to—ha, ah ha, ha, ha!!!—drive over and pick them up!

I will airmail them if I ever get to Pasadena and back again, and if you use any of them, I do wish you would give him a line: Photo or photos by John Stevens. Something like that.

Well, Jon, that's how it went. I tried. Only wish my hair had been combed. Do you figure this ever happened to Hem or Willie the Faulk? I guess not. Going out to mail this now, get some beer and some sleep. To hell with the world's series. I couldn't sleep last night—steaming about the cockscomb.

[To Jon Webb]
Wednesday [?October 17, 1962]

[* * *] Tired today, from horses and other things, but hope to have a prof. photog up here tomorrow or Friday, and chances are he'll have a better camera and know-how. That is, if I don't go mad,

or just don't fall through the floorboards. This picture-taking has some semblance of horror in it to me. I go through the same thing whenever I get a haircut. And sometimes the bastards will spin you in the chair and show you yourself in the mirror. God. [* * *]

. . . I have all these letters Corrington has sent me, and I began to worry a while back when I was not feeling so good mentally and physically. I might have to get them off my hands and may ship them back through you and have Bill pick them up when he sees you. There is kind of an ivory-carved quality to most of these letters and they are much better than his poems. In the poem he still sometimes has this E.E. thing mixed with Auden plus a kind of hysterical abstract and fancy glibness. When the letters catch up to the poems (and I think they will)—I mean when the letters become the poems—they can't catch them, being past them, Corrington will be a poet to listen to. He's getting better now, which is much better than laying still. His politics and outlook a little too far right of center but this is the Southern Aristocrat somewhat, and doesn't mean he lacks heart. Anyhow, if some day you get a pack of Corrington letters, I know you are busy, but flip through a few and hold the pack for Willie. They make the Miller letters look like burnt apple pie. [* * *]

[To Ann Bauman]
[November 22, 1962]

[* * *] No, I am not feeling better. I need an operation for one of my maladies but don't know if I have either the guts or the time for it. I never get splendid clean diseases that you can talk about over a cup of tea, like heart attack, stroke, amnesia, etc., but instead, ulcers and hemorrhages, madness, boils, ingrown toenails, rotten teeth, and now hemorrhoids, which, my dear, is a malady of the ass. [* * *]

It is more than difficult for me to survive. My present job has me by the throat and I don't know how much more I can take. I have no special trade and am getting old. It will all end somewhere down the line: an old dirty demolished German pig, sitting on a doorstep looking in the sand for a razor.

Life is for achievement? Even Hegel's achievements are paling. See how we waste? Life is avoidance of pain until death. Life is finding that love between 2 people only goes one way. One is always the master, the other the slave. Life is Tuesday afternoon in a cage. I do not like to talk about life. It gets silly. It sounds silly. Death is the master. [* * *]

[To Jon Webb]
November 25, 1962

[* * *] Very little new out here. Just difficult to believe you are working on this Outsider of Year thing about me. I keep thinking of a certain paper shack I ended up once in in Atlanta without light, heat, food, typewriter or drink. A most cold, most dark end. Yow. I have slept on park benches in the warm parts of the country and there seemed air and light and easiness, but somehow this was so closed and finished. My ass was really in the trap, the first gilded shape of hell reaching out. I did have a pencil and I sat there in the dark daytime ice writing things on the edges, the margins of old newspapers that I found on the floor. How I got out of there I don't remember, but I did and I left the writing there. It was quite mad, most of it, I guess. Now I have 3 collections of poetry, have been photographed by imbeciles, and you are giving me the honor and light of the O. of Y. award, almost as if much of my misery had been recorded right along as it happened. So many of our writers now have teaching positions, they teach the thing they do, and it's no wonder the writing has no lumps, no rawness. But in spite of this, I am sure that right now there is some poor bastard freezing-starving somewhere, writing sonnets on toilet paper. Not all of us can go through the college degree teaching bit. We cannot jump through the hoops; no wiseness in practical sense of survival. If an English teacher can write, good enough for me. You don't have to be thrown into half a hundred drunk tanks to be shaken into or out of life. But there is something about their lives that is too safe, too pat. Their intrigues of the day are political, bitchy and petty, feminine. Very few of them come to class drunk. They know what they are doing, even when they sit down to a typewriter. Corrington seems to have escaped much of this but I keep thinking they will get him. [* * *]

[To Ann Bauman]
Late November, 1962

[* * *] Kafka, unlike your Henry James, was not ordinarily intelligent and discerning. Kafka was a god damned petty clerk who lived a good damned [*sic*] petty life and wrote about it, the dream of it, the madness of it. There is one novel where a man enters this house, this establishment, and it appears that from the viewpoint of others that he is guilty of something but he does not know what. He is shuffled from room to room, endlessly, to the rattle of papers and bureaucracy, a silent simmering horrible living dream of ordinary mad and pressing, senseless everyday life. Most of his books are on this order: the shadow, the dream, the stupidity. Then there are other things—where a man turns into a bridge and lets people walk across him. Then there is another where a man gradually turns into a giant cockroach ("The Metamorphosis") and his sister feeds him as he hides under the bed. Others, others. Kafka is everything.

Forget Henry James. James is a light mist of silk. Kafka is what we all know. [* * *]

[To Jon and Louise Webb]
November 30, 1962

[* * *] Yes, disgusting the rent they charge of a dive in the business districts of anywhere, and the landlord doesn't have to do anything but sit back and take it in while you hope to make it—somehow. Hang on, you're getting an *award* too, somewhere, somehow; this is lit. history like *Poetry* when Ez was European editor and full of beans, or even like Mencken's *Mercury*; or *Dial*; but you are essentially the new center and the part of this age, only people never realize the blood sweat weariness disgust breakdown & trial of soul that goes into it; and the puking little criticisms of milk-white jackasses. [* * *]

Federman was coeditor of Mica, *the last issue of which appeared in November 1962. Bukowski's story, "Murder," was published not in* Mica *but in* Notes from Underground, *no. 1 (1964). Dorbin records no earlier story in* Mica, *although one was published in* Canto *(Los Angeles), winter 1961.*

[To Raymond Federman]
December 6, 1962

Rec. your O.K. on "The Murder." I write very few short stories—you've taken the only 2 I have written in years. Both of them were very close to a type of personal experience and feeling that just did not seem to fit into the shorter poem-form.

You might call "The Murder" a prose-poem as I have worked with the poem so long that when I do try the story-form I still feel as if I were laying down the poem-line.

It might interest you to know that over drinks and in conversational lulls with the few odd people that get in here I have told the story of "The Murder," first telling them what made me write it, what was happening to me at the time, and how I took this and made it into a story—or whatever it is.

Their comment at the finish was usually, "Jesus Christ!," which I took more as a criticism than a vindication.

[To Ann Bauman]
[Tuesday] December 18, 1962

Terrible happenings. Got drunk Sunday night and thrown in jail. Must see judge on Wednesday. Fell and twisted ankle—swollen now, might be broken. Missed 2 days work. Judge might give me 120 days. This is not first offense. Will mean loss of job, of course.

Have been laying here in horrible fit of depression. My drinking days are over. This is too much. Jail is a horrible place. I almost go mad there.

I don't know what is going to become of me. I have no trade, no future. Sick, depressed, blackly, heavily depressed.

Write me something. Maybe a word from you will save me.

49

[To Jon Webb]
[December 19, 1962]

I lucked it. Easy judge. Nobody got a day all the time I was in court, but all fined. A good 40 or 50 appeared ahead of me. Jail might be full. Christmas. Whatever. [* * *]

Don't be angry, Jon, but there are very few editors holding my recent stuff, so I can't write them. And the other stuff, the older stuff has *disappeared* and I don't keep records and/or carbons so it's pretty much lost. I've dropped 200-to-300 poems this way since 1955, and I used to try to get some of these poems back, the larger batches of 20 or 40 that I remembered anyhow, but I have found that the elongated keepers of poems or destroyers of poems WITHOUT EXCEPTION do not respond to polite and reasonable inquiry with proper stamped self-addressed envelope enclosed. There is a mucky dismal breed out there . . . unmoral, immoral unscrupulous . . . homos, hounds, sadists; curious, blank children; blood-drinkers . . .

And then some people wonder why I write an occasional anti-editor poem. You and Gypsy are a pair of the few editors I know who operate in a professional and straight manner, and the gods have been more than good to me in that you have seen some light in some of my work and are handing me this OUTSIDER OF YEAR shining tray of honor, plus the book.

[To Jon and Louise Webb]
[December 21, 1962?]

Got to thinking about the telephone call the other night, and how you weren't going to mention this or that, and well, I think pretty slowly, but I hope now, thinking it over, that you aren't going to make a white rabbit outa me. I've got nothing to hide. Feel free. It's a person's eccentricities that give him whatever he has. Don't be too cautious with excerpts from letters, except I agree with you that mentioning a name directly (false initials will do) might be bad taste, especially if that person has very little literary standing. If he has literary standing, use the name and the hell with it. I hope this does not get to you too late. That I drink or play the ponies or have been in jail is of no shame to me.

As you can see, I have recovered from my depression [* * *]

50

[To Jon and Louise Webb]
December 27, 1962

Got your six page letter which I read through a couple of times
while drinking a Miller's, and the sun's out good, but it's cold &
I have a heater on and the stove on, and somehow there's a feeling
of peace today—I feel like a fat man who ate a lot of turkey, and since
this feeling does not arrive too often, I take it, I take of the good
of it without examining it, without feeling selfish. That's what's good
about being 42: you know when to go with what's left of the soul.
I spent Xmas in bed asleep. I hate to go out on the streets on Xmas
day. The fuckers act like they are out of their minds. They strain
at the thing; round-eyed and hacked-out they drive through red lights,
they look at each other and say things but they don't know what
they're saying: their mouths have long ago been cut out and thrown
away. Christmas, to most of them, is like owning a new car. They've
got to do it. They don't have the guts—or the sense—to pass it up.
Enough. Did I say I was feeling at peace? [* * *]

[To Jon Webb]
[December 28, 1962]

No, as to title, I don't care for *Naked in the Womb* or the *Alcatraz*
one. When I said you think up title, I was only thinking in terms
of a *summary* title such as *Selected Poems* or etc. As to the *other* type
of title, I don't think it would be fair for you to submit titles any
more than it would be fair for you to put one of your poems in there
under my name. Surely, you understand this? I have been trying to
think up a *summary* title, but if you want a straight title, I will send
you a half dozen or so in a day or two. I'm glad this came up. Please
do not use one of your titles that is *not* a summary title (such as *Collected Poems, Selected Poems*) as this would take the heart out of me.
I will be strictly dreaming titles from here on in, say like *Beer and
Frogs Legs* or *I Can't Stand the Sunshine When People Walk Around
in It* or *For Jocks, Chambermaids, Thieves and Bassoon Players*. I almost
like the last one. It carries summation plus the rest. Yes. [* * *] or
Tonic for the Mole. Meaning these type of poems for those who duck

51

out to the world, ya know. or *Minstrels Would Go Crazy Singing This.* [* * *]

Know it cost you money to have your man work on photos but glad he perked up a couple. I cannot get over the nightmare of those photos, and maybe some day I can write about it, but it's still too close. [* * *]

•

· 1 9 6 3 ·

The title settled on is a phrase taken from a poem by Robinson Jeffers. Permission to use it had to be obtained from Random House.

[To Jon and Louise Webb]
January 2, 1963

christ, I'm glad you liked the title (*It Catches My Heart in Its Hands*), and yes I'm sending book (this piece "Such Counsel You Gave to Me") to you [* * *], and no, I'm *not* going to change my mind, THAT'S IT, and so if you are going to or have set up an ad using title, fine. Also glad you and Louise have accepted dedication. I have been worried about both ends of this: title and dedication, and now all's well. [* * *]

No, I don't know how many copies of each of the 3 earlier books there were. Although I believe Cuscaden (*Run With*) mentioned 200, and I believe *Longshots* around 200 too. On Griffith (*Flower, Fist*), I don't know, and also, he doesn't answer his mail. [* * *]

Must say again, very glad you went for title and dedication. Yes, the title is in my head too. It says so god damned much. Jeffers, when he got good, he got very good. There were these long periods when he flattened out and had a tendency to preach his ideals of rock & hawk, but when he did get the word down . . . he got it down in a way, that to me, made our other contemporaries or newly deads seem not so much. [* * *]

53

p.s.—my photo on cover only another miracle on miracle that has been occurring. It does not seem too long ago that I was considering the blade. If I never write another decent poem it's your fault, Jon. I've got my alibi ready.

[To Jon and Louise Webb]
January 6, 1963

[* * *] I am glad on Corrington for intro. He knows me—and my work—better than anyone, and he possesses the style and manner to do a patrical job. (I wanted to say "pat" but it looked like "pot," so I changed it to patrical, whatever that means.) Anyhow, Corrington's the only one, and his own writing is improving. His lines seem clearer and harder—he sent me a poem called *Communion.* It has a holy edge and fervor, quite good. Quite. [* * *]

Photo of Sandburg in *This Week* holding little girl on his knee and underneath poem about death. Death is hush, says the old boy. Well, I guess so. Only I wish he'd crop or comb that sickly flange of white hair that looks like a wig. If I EVER get that old, they'll find me under the bed drunk
with the Racing Form AND
a big OLD girl. [* * *]

Roman Books, run by Jim Roman in Fort Lauderdale, Florida, published in 1963 a ground-breaking catalogue called " 'The Outsiders': a collection of first editions by avant-garde and 'beat' generation authors of prose and poetry since World War Two." Bukowski is giving his approval to Jon Webb's sale of manuscripts to the dealer.

[To Jon and Louise Webb]
January 7, 1963

[* * *] On ROMAN BOOKS, I understand. In your position, why not? Someday when you are gone they will talk about the force and

vitality of the *Outsider* in mid-20th century literature, and how you stood in front of that press feeding it your blood and your hours and your life. It will very *very* romantic *then*. But now? Shit, nobody ever cares about NOW. They are always looking *back*. They moon for the pain of Mozart or Lorca bulleted in the road. But there are always new Mozarts and Lorcas, new *Poetry* Chicagos, new *Blasts*, new *Brooms*, etc. If you can swing a buck from ROMAN for a few wilted manus in order to go on, hell, do it. YOU ARE LIVING NOW. If you have any manus you want me to sign, ship them here, I will sign and return. Ink is cheap. [* * *]

[To John William Corrington]
January 14, 1963

[* * *] my cock average size but mostly out of action lately, desire there still, but price too high, trouble too much, I do not search like a highschool boy, and some night finally it is there, or at a motel outside Del Mar track in August it is there, and then it is gone, the color of the dress I remember, some words spoken, but the act is really secondary, they have hung the cock on me, I have dipped, but really, the walls are large.

Born Andernach, Germany August 16th, 1920. German mother, father with American Army (Pasadena born but of German parentage) of Occupation. There is some evidence that I was born, or at least conceived out of wedlock, but I am not sure. American at age of 2. Some year or so in Washington, D.C., but then on to Los Angeles. The Indian suit thing true. All grotesques true. Between the imbecile savagery of my father, the disinterestedness of my mother, and the sweet hatred of my playmates: "Heinie! Heinie! Heinie!" things were pretty hot all around. They got hotter when I was in my 13th years on, I broke out not with acne, but with these HUGE boils, in my eyes, neck, back, face, and I'd ride the streetcar to the hospital, the charity ward, the old man was not working, and there they'd drill me with the electric needle, which is kind of a wood drill that they stick into people. Stayed out of school a year. Went to L.A. City College a couple of years, journalism. Tuition fee was two dollars but the old man said he couldn't afford to send me anymore. I went to work in the railroad yards, scrubbing the sides of trains with

OAKITE. I drank and gambled at night. Had a small room above a bar on Temple Street in the Filipino district, and I gambled at night with the aircraft workers and pimps and etc. My place got to be known and every night it was packed. It was hell getting my sleep. One night I hit big. Big for me. 2 or 3 hundred. I knew they'd be back. Got in a fight, broke a mirror and a couple of chairs but held onto the money and early in the morning caught a bus for New Orleans. Some young gal on there made a play for me, and I let her off at Fort Worth but got as far as Dallas and swung back. Wasted some time there and made N.O. Roomed across from THE GANGPLANK CAFE and began writing. Short stories. Drank the money up, went to work in a comic book house, and soon moved on. Miami Beach. Atlanta. New York. St. Louis. Philly. Frisco. L.A. again. New Orleans again. Then Philly again. Then Frisco again. L.A. again. Around and around. A couple of nights in East Kansas City. Chicago. I stopped writing. I concentrated on drinking. My longest stays were in Philly. I would get up early in the morning and go to a bar there and I would close that bar at night. How I made it, I don't know. Then finally back to L.A. and a wild shack job of seven years drinking. Ended up in same charity hospital. This time not with boils but with my stomach torn open finally with rot gut and agony. 8 pints of blood and 7 pints of glucose transfused in without a stop. My whore came to see me and she was drunk. My old man was with her. The old man gave me a lot of lip and the whore was nasty too, and I told the old man, "Just one more word out of you and I'm going to yank this needle outa my arm, climb off this deathbed and whip your ass!" They left. I came out of there, white and old, in love with sunlight, told never to drink again or death would be mine. I found among changes in myself, that my memory which was once pretty good was now bad. Some brain damage, no doubt, they let me lay there a couple of days in the charity ward when my papers got lost and the papers called for immediate transfusions, and I was out of blood, listening to ham-mers against my brain. Anyhow, I got on a mail truck and drove it around and delivered letters and drank lightly, experimentally, and then one night I sat down and began writing poetry. What a hell of a thing. Where to send this stuff. Well, I took a shot. There was a magazine called *Harlequin* and I was a fucking clown and it was out in some small town in Texas and maybe they wouldn't know bad stuff when they saw it, so—. There was a gal editor there, and the poor dear went wild. Special edition. Letters followed. The let-ters got warm. The letters got hot. Next thing I knew the gal editor was in Los Angeles. Next thing I knew we were in Las Vegas for marriage. Next thing I knew I was walking in a small Texas town with the local hicks glaring at me. The gal had money. I didn't know she had money. Or her folks had money. We went back to L.A. and I went back to work, somewhere.

The marriage didn't work. It took 3 years for her to find out that I was not what she had thought I was supposed to be. I was anti-social, coarse, a drunkard, didn't go to church, played horses, cursed when intoxicated, didn't like to go anywhere, shaved carelessly, didn't care for her paintings or her relatives, sometimes stayed in bed 2 or 3 days running etc. etc.

Very little more. I went back to my whore who had once been such a cruel and beautiful woman, and who was no longer beautiful (as such) but who had, magically, become a warm and real person, but she could not stop drinking, she drank more than I, and she died.

There is not much left now. I drink mostly alone and discourage company. People seem to be talking about things that don't count. They are too eager or too vicious or too obvious.

I hope this clears up some things and that I have not Ferlinghettied you. I can tell you things that happened like this and it takes nothing away because it is only a LISTING in a sense, and what happened, the living of it, it is still there. I have played some bad lutestrings and taken some knocks in the head, but it was the only way, there was only one path.

As to the other, I like the EARLY Hemingway, and like the rest of us, was affected somewhat by T.S. and Auden, but not so much in a sense of *content*, but in a clean and easy way of saying. I like Wagner and Beethoven, Klee and Stravinsky, Rachmaninoff and rabbits. This is all pretty common, I realize. So is breathing. Then too, there's Darius Milhaud, Verdi, Mussorgsky, Smetana, Shostakovich, Schumann, Bach, Massenet, Ernst von Dohnanyi, Menotti, Gluck, Mahler, Bruckner, Franck, Gounod, Handel and Zoltan Kodaly. Brahms and Tchaikovsky somehow become less and less to me. In Jeffers, I like the longer works, where the style is almost prose, but where everything is hard brick and breaking, where everything is up against the knife and very real. Jeffers almost admires his nonthinking man-brutes as opposed to etc. . . . that gives his work the touch of truth. He writes believably and the pages are in your hands like warm things, difficult to believe that type and machine also put them together. As to contemporaries, they do not do much for me. I do not mean the poets still living who have stopped writing,

I mean those living now and writing now. I cannot see much. A great alikeness. A carefulness. What a stinking age! What a set of ass-lickers.

Enough of that. [* * *]

Got a letter from Germany today from some Heinie telling me that he has translated "Candidate Middle" and "The Life of Borodin" and that they will be used in a radio feature. This calls for cold chills all around. I, who can no longer speak or understand the language of my birthplace, will be going back into my own tongue from the place I left. This is some kind of magic, like black horses turned loose and running on a hill. [* * *]

Weekend shot. Sherman haggling with Norman Mosher who studies under T. Roethke. Real bitter stuff. I have long ago said that I do not care for the poets. I would like to see one once in a while with a little self-doubt instead of this cockiness and the unsheathing of the nails. I am just about now getting over it. People climb into my mind, kick around, piss around, and it takes some time for them to leave.

. . . a part of the ankle will not go down. I will be the club-ankle poet. Lord Byron, make way!

I told Jon to let you have your head in the intro. If you want to go long, go long; if you want to go short, go short. It is a tough job at best. But you must know that I am honored to have you for my barker: "And now, ladies and gentlemen, we give you—," and Bukowski steps out from behind the tent flap with 3 red hairs on his chest, and can of beer in one hand and a German shepherd pup in the other.

Keep your bones in good motion, kid, and quietly consume and digest what is necessary. I think it is not so much important to build a literary thing as it is not to hurt things. I think it is important to be quiet and in love with park benches; solve whole areas of pain by walking across a rug.

you got it.

dip the brush in turpentine,

p.s.—I asked Webb not to send proofs of the section. I'd rather see it all at once, quietly with a cold beer audience. And maybe think of other days & bad days to come, like all this is well, but the wall will be coming down. [* * *]

[To Jon and Louise Webb]
[?February 1963]

Enclosed copy of *Literary Times*. I might suggest when book comes out you send them a review copy. Arnold Kaye over last night to interview me, I suppose a la Ben Hecht. He gave me the old bullshit about me being a legend, and he had a list of questions. I was fairly drunk and don't remember what I told him. Some of the questions rather vapid like: "What effect does Mickey Mouse have on the American public and culture?" I don't know if they are going to run the interview; I might have been fairly bitter and vulgar. The guy had just come from Zahn's where Curtis had babbled on and on, I am told. At least I kept it short and hot. Anyhow, what with the horses and interviews and the bottle and being a LEGEND . . . I have not written any poetry lately, and this is how we go down the drain: doing everything but creating. There are enough traps in this world to kill a man before he becomes five years old.

At any rate I had sense enough to turn down an invite to be on a panel thing on the radio with Zahn and Kay and some editors. J. B. May etc. I still believe in more privacy and less talk. Badly hung over today but I see no broken furniture and my knuckles are not bruised so there was no fight. Good. May told this guy, "Bukowski's kind of unfriendly." These people don't understand that the living takes time and that the talking about it is unnecessary. You do. I think that when they knock on your door you feel the same way I do. That's why we pretty much get along.

Anyhow, going now.

I think the bastard took my pen.

[To Jon and Louise Webb]
Early March, 1963

[* * *] As to dedication of book to you, Lou, it is all pretty simple. When I heard you over the phone and you did not give me a

bunch of literary doubletalk, accent, etc. etc.—your complete sense of *un*falsity, this led me to suggest the dedication to you. This, plus the fact that it being the first book in your series (you and Jon: *Loujon*), it seemed in a sense of history—and literary history is the only one that seems to have some sense—the only dedication. As to being on cover with you, great, but it does not seem real, it is a conjecture sort of thing and I will not know it, really, until the magazine is in my hand and I stand here in this room with it and something in my head says, it happened. I will have a drink on it, a good scotch and water, and I will think of myself down in the alleys again or in all the rooming houses in hell, and the jails, freezing, madness etc., and it will come through to me good. You know, for all this, I still feel pretty much outside of everything yet. It is as if, any moment, somebody is going to knock on my door and a couple of guys are going to enter some day, "All right, friend, we've come to cut off your arms." Psychologically speaking, there might be a reason or a term for this, but we do not live with reason or terms, unfortunately. [* * *]

[To Jon and Louise Webb]
March 17, 1963

starting to thunder . . . like a dark closet in here, but I've still got #3 to my right here, and I hope you people understand why I did not phone upon rec. copy, but rather wrote. The phone calls have been mostly when I was pretty high, and a sense of madness there, and yet not. Anyway, what I am trying to say is that on the phone the voice does not say as much what the mind is thinking as the typewriter does. Somewhere the thought in coming down from the mind and out into the voice, the thought becomes dispelled, distorted, petty and so forth. So, upon rec. #3, I thought it best to WRITE about it rather than TALK about it. Anyway, as I said, my section was done with a good, sure hand, a beautiful hand, and better and gentler and cleaner than I might have dreamed. . . . but this, mainly to say I've gone on reading more of #3, after getting Bukowski out of the way, and GOD!!! ya really laid the whip on Creeley!!! What you say I agree with, find true, but I'm afraid that as many teeth as you put into him I'd havta add another: CREELEY CAN'T WRITE, nor can the rest of them. They affect to write, and out of this affectation, of course, they need powers, groups, blather, underground lines, handshakes, imputations, delegations and barkers to make the thing go. However, I'm glad you took a swing at them: they need a spanking, these little pricks in their walking shorts and mountain cabins and goats and money and teaching positions. They are fondled enough by society without the rest of us having to put their spittle in cups before the shrine.

Your story an odd one, Jon, but has the taste of air and being, kind of like Sherwood would do, Sherwood Anderson, and this is not a knock . . . I do not believe that the short story has gone forward beyond Anderson. He's been dead a long time now, but the way he put down the word is not. I suppose Anderson has influenced me as much as Jeffers, but in a different way—the cleanliness he had of getting a line down, it is hard to beat.

And it was quite a thing, of course, to read that Genet liked "Old Man Dead in a Room" best of all the poems in your #1. There were a lot of poems in #1. And I always get the unholy chills when I think of the language switch. Think of this Frenchman sitting in a room reading "Old Man" in French to Genet, the walls there, the chairs, while I am asleep at the time or betting on a horse. Life is oddly wild, full of miracles as well as horrors. [* * *]

More thunder. Burroughs, of course, is important because he keeps the air-holes open. We need a Joyce or Burroughs or Gertrude S. every age to keep us loose and let us know that everything needn't be so, the way it seems or the way the herd-writers want it to seem. These people are valuable, in a way, beyond their work—icebreakers, knockers down of policemen. . . . Yes, the Millerboy finally got around to working Walter over and he did put him straight enough on politics and Art, and it still stands today. I am not saying ART is going to save us . . . it might save me, for a little while . . . but politics isn't going to either; politics got us this far, and see what we're doing now: tossing the bomb back and forth, back and forth, and the first one to drop it: o, blaAAHHHHHHH! [* * *]

Mid-March [1963]

Know I have not written, and am bastard slob this way, drink, madness et al., but I always figure that I am no good for a woman anyhow, and any way I can save her from myself is all to her good. Meanwhile, as you might have guessed, I write for selfish reasons: I have a book on the press now, Selected Poems 1955-1963, *It Catches My Heart in Its Hands* . . . Loujon Press, 618 Ursuline st., New Orleans, 16, Louisiana. 2 bucks, baby, and an autograph, even. Christ, y've got 2 bucks somewhere, haven't you? What I mean is, I don't get any money out of the book at all—as if it mattered—but I am pumping for these people because 2 bucks to them might mean such a simple thing as eating on this day or not. They eat one meal a day and forward such bastards as I, and I figure if they can do this (and sometimes they don't make the one meal), I figure I can forget immortality and carefulness and isolation and maybe even myself and go out and ask people to buy the g.d. book. If you think this is slick sales talk, it is not. I have thrown money into the fire. I have thrown my guts into the fire. I know more than this. But these people are the oddest set of living gods ya ever saw. She sells picture postcards on the sidewalks for meek coin and he stands 14 years hours a day poking paper into a cheap press he has hustled somewhere. I can't tell you more than this, only that these people are giants in a world of ants. If you can get hold of *The Outsider* #3 (same address) (as book) perhaps you will understand more of what I mean.

Meanwhile, glad your car running good. Mine lets up this cul de sac cloud of gaseous nauseous burning oil continually, until people stare as I go by . . . like a forest fire.

I lost your photo. How could I do this? Ya don't have another around, do you? Perhaps some day we will meet over a beer. It's a long way to Sacramento, but perhaps a good horse . . . a little luck? And then we'd only be bored and disgusted with each other. Keep working with the poem; if you treat it right, it is the most faithful and truest of all.

62

[To Jon and Louise Webb]
March 26, 1963

[* * *] If you think the interview with Kaye (*Lit. Times*) was rough for me in the sense of the poppyseed question, you should have heard afterwards . . . when we'd both had a bit more to drink:

K: "Look, if the world were going to end in 15 minutes what would you do, what would you the tell the people?"

B: "I wouldn't tell 'em anything."

K: "Now LOOK, man, you're not cooperating! If the world were going to end in 15 minutes, I wanna know what you would do!"

B: "I'd lay down and rest, just like I'm doing now."

K: "But what would you tell the people, man, the PEOPLE!"

B: "Don't forget your streetcar transfer."

And the odd thing is, you tell these people the truth and they think you are not cooperating. [* * *]

[To Jon and Louise Webb]
March 28, 1963

[* * *] I have already caught hell, in person, for #3, and I was going to spare you some of this, but it may prepare you for what's to come. I bought him a bottle of wine and he arrived an hour later than he said he would—which is bad form; when I tell someone I will be there at a certain minute, I arrive *on the minute*. However, it gave his wine a chance to chill, and he fingered his drink and began, mostly telling me that there was *another* type of poverty that nobody knew about and he was going to write about it. What he means is that he has a $200 a week job and he somehow can't MAKE IT! I told him that I had little sympathy with this type of poverty, that one hundred and sixty million out of 180,000,000 in this country lived that way. I think it an entirely different thing to want something to eat and not being able to eat, and a place to sleep and rest the tired body, and only having the benches, the streets, the ice, the rain. Because a man needs 2 cars, a tv set, 12 pairs of shoes for his wife, this signifies to me only an unhandsome sort of greed that is needed to fill a hole where something else should be. I did not tell him all this but let him talk. Then he got on his job, writing blurbs for the

pictures in nudie magazines, and then he said, "Oh, I know you were offered the job first and you turned it down, X. told me about it and I am tired of hearing about it, and you were offered the job again, there was another opening and you turned it down again . . . but you could not have gone up the ladder the way I have!" What he means is that he has been promoted from writing the nudie blurbs for the magazines that lay around in barbershops chairs and that he has been elevated to writing books about legitimate nudism . . . nudist camps, etc. He is right: I would not have gone up the ladder. I wouldn't have lasted one day writing blurbs. I would rather wash dishes and go at night to the glory of a small box-like room with swinging electric light and the other torn people walking up and down the halls, half out of their minds, miserable, waiting to die, wanting to get drunk. I let him talk on. I am not much of a talker. I think very slowly, very. I have some bad teeth and I lisp once in a while. But mainly, when you're talking, you're going OUT, burning away, and although I don't mind much burning, I don't care for haggle, argument, point and counter point. I am not a lawyer. I am not a movie star. I don't know what I am. But as I go on, the feeling is toward a gentle center somewhere. Anyhow, he went on and I listened, and he said, "I could have had my picture on the cover of *The Outsider* myself. . . . and then, there's Corrington . . . you and Corrington. You dedicated a book to him and then he writes this stuff about you. Look at my face. Why don't you look at my face? Are you afraid of me?"

"That is not why I do not look at your face," I told him.

"I love you," he said, "I guess I still do, but you are not the person you used to be. I mean, dedicating a book to an *editoress*. That's cheap. And, in #3, The Editor's Bit, it was too long and it cheapened everything."

"Don't you think," I asked, "that the way he tore up Creeley was a courageous thing?"

"I threw *Outsider* 3 in the toilet," he said, "I flushed it down the toilet."

(Cavelski [*Kabalevsky?—ed.*] on now. Something *Brilliant Suite*, so clean, so sharp. There have been men in the world, thank the gods, thank the tulips, thanks the dead horses, thank the Winters and the midgets and the grass growing.)

"I told my wife I would only be gone 10 minutes," he said. "I have wasted a half hour. Well, these people think you're GREAT, there's a lot of space separating you from them, they don't know you like I know you, so they'll keep thinking you are great. You are safe."

Then he got up and moved toward the door. "Just keep on living your small, little insignificant life the way you are doing."

"Slam the door when you leave," I asked him.

He got in the last punch. "I'll leave it for you to close," he said and walked out leaving the door open.

He won. I had to get up and close the door.

Now, I can't pretend that all this did not bother me. I am very full of self-doubt, self-doubt twists me in the vise forever, and I know that I often do badly and write badly and I don't live exactly like a saint, but it does appear to me that I ought to be allowed to think along my own lines and live in my own way. The trouble with this writer is that he has built an image of me, probably from my poems, that I do not seem to stand up to in the flesh. Well, maybe I lie in my poems. I try not to. But if I do not present a flaming torch while sitting in a chair drinking a beer, I can't help it. I don't believe much in extra talk. I can talk for hours on paper because there is only the click of the keys and this brown torn shade pulled down in front of my face. It is a clean white thunder. That is why I do not like opera. Somebody I know pretty good and who knows I like the classical symphonies [* * *] asked me, "How come you do not like opera?" and I answered, "Because it contains the human voice." "What's wrong with that?" she asked. "I don't know. I just don't like the human voice. I think it's fake. Almost anything that comes out in voice is fake. I don't care if it is singing or the Gettysburg Ad., I don't like it. Here you have some bitch singing ultra-soprano who beats her kids and squats over a bowl and drops turds like the rest of us, and she is through the Art-form trying to become purified and trying to purify the rest of us. I just don't like the human voice: it drags down, it wears, it will simply not let things alone."

But she was fairly sharp. "You like the violin, or some of the horns, don't you?"

"Yes, at times," I said.

"But don't you realize that these instruments are played by human beings and that the human voice is just another instrument?"

Which is a pretty damning argument, but I still say the voice is more *direct*, and that something is gained (not lost) by letting it come down through the fingers (violin or piano). Which is essentially why I am *ashamed* of the one or 2 drunken phone calls g.d. put through to you: because I had only the voice and the voice could not say, never damn can. [* * *]

And what my bottle bloody knife fireblast friend said was right: I am glad there is space between us, so that if I am a phoney or a coward or a rotten human being you will jes. christ never know it

because all you see is a sheet of ape ass paper

and you don't see me

or what I really am—

which is not much,

but which is me and which is working toward some saliva and red end of everywhere, and which is repeat the rift of the wind and I am tired, shit, and you are tired, listening . . .

Only the boy who came in and spewed his venom on me, I have, for a long time, been trying to get rid of but did not want to hurt his feelings. I hope this does it. But I sense that he will be back. It is too good this way.

But life does not always hold the Brutus within its sleeve. I was walking out toward the parking lot after the 9th race and somebody shoved 50 cents at me and said, "Can you give me a ride, my friend pulled out without me." I asked where he was going and since it was a couple of blocks away, I told him to forget the 50 cents and get in. Turns out I had driven him in earlier in the year only I was drunker and didn't remember, only that time I was a big winner and flashing broken teeth and mug. And so we talked, quietly, weary, smashed, as I tangoed in and out of traffic, slipping through with my sometime smoking car, and we talked the gambler's talk, the rough days, the good days, but essentially nothing important. I let him off at Hollywood and Western. "Goodby, Hank," he said. "So long, Nick," I said, and I took a right, circled round and came back into the liquor store where I billed an I-owe-you for $11.50.

Now, this is not bad, It adds up into living. No great words. Nothing. But somehow good. How can you explain it? [* * *]

[To Jon and Louise Webb]
April 1, 1963

[* * *] I agree with you on the Creeley, but am not too amazed that a lot of people don't. They believe you have pot-shotted him, but they seem to forget that you have published *him* and *his*, plus their theories. You are going to hear a lot of stuff about how there

were always "schools," and you are going to hear some big names of the past mentioned as proof of those who have created and created damned well in spite of (or, they would like to say, because of) schools. What these good people forget is that the past does not prove the present. The past may have called for schools, whether they were created for self-survival of IDEA, or whether created by critics. The present, I feel, does not call for schools; with our speed-up of transportation and communication, it MIGHT become apparent to some sensible & feeling people that *we touch too much*, we are now slowly becoming ground down to the same thing. The only hope of survival is to escape as much as possible from the mass-hypnosis, of which the "school," be it Black Mountain, Kenyon and/or etc., is still part of the grouping-thing and too many men in a closet (or make it *bed* for some of them). The only defense of a bad work is to create a better work, not to have some disciple of a school come to bat for you. In some places it helps them to teach English; in other places they gather as homos or smokers of pot. They need the trunk and then they feel pretty good as branches. Politics is often, it seems, involved with Art; and as Politics often stinks, their creations do too. If I want to join a Lonely Hearts Club I will go to a genuine place where I might make some old woman happy. Otherwise, all I need is a typewriter, some ribbon, paper, envelopes, stamps and soul. School—is out.

. . . anyhow, I have an idea that this Creeley-blast might be good for *The Outsider*'s circulation, you'll see. You took a swing but don't back down; if you back down, you're dead. Give them space, but don't forget there's *creative* work to be published, new people, new Buks, new Creeleys . . .

"Kaja" is Kaye Johnson, of whom Bukowski notes, "She wrote very literary letters a bit on the pretentious side."

[To Jon and Louise Webb]
April 9, 1963

[* * *] If you do write Kaja, please tell her that her "White Room" has a lot of the female race laughing because it's true and

sobbing because it's so. Women, g.d. them, tho, must learn that there are other things besides LOVE, I mean, concentrating, centering on it; the man is not actually callous but more divided—he plants his seed and moves on, not nec. toward another woman but away from the *concentration.*

[To Jon and Louise Webb]
April 22, 1963

[* * *] Heard from Kaja today and also Harold Norse—so not being much of a reader I had to open #3 and read the Norse poem, and luckily it was pretty damned good, although a little too poetic for me, I like my cake plain, but he seems filled with the fire, so, o.k. I should read more, but reading bothers me. [* * *]

oh yes, heard from Malanga today. He sent me some of his poems, which he self-praises but which do not get to me. He thinks you've got something against him because he rubs elbows with Auden and the New York Crowd. Me, I don't think you care where a man comes from as long as he lays the line down. By the way, the boys didn't like the photos you sent, said they were too "domestic." Wants a head portrait, or something. So to hell with it. I told him to write in space where my photo supposed to be: "Charles Bukowski wishes these poems to be his photo." [* * *]

[To Jon and Louise Webb]
April 26, 1963

[* * *] The book is beginning to well into my mind as a possibility. It's like, you know, you meet a beautiful woman, have some talk with her, but really think nothing of it because everything seems pretty much out of reach and you turn to leave and find that she's walking beside you, and she walks up the steps with you and stands there while you open the door to your room and then she walks in with you. The book's like that. A little too much to behold. I've had so

many knives stuck into me, when they hand me a flower I can't quite make out what it is. It takes time. [* * *]

[To Neeli Cherry]
April 29, 1963

enclosed bad photo from leftover stash I had taken for some art-ist who thinks he might do a drawing for *Cold Dogs in the Courtyard*, Cyfoeth, Chi. Lit. Times, out in May, I'm told. Anyhow, Jory over for small drunk, saw reject photo and said I should send it to you. O.k., I said, o.k. But I didn't and J. has kept hounding, so here it is, whatever it is. Which explains nothing.

Picked up a couple of Borestones the other day. One for "The House" and one for "The Singular Self." They will come out later in the year, *Best Poems of 1963*. I've never seen one of their collec-tions. Might be pure crap. Most poetry is. Almost everything is.

Tell Sam to keep working out. I think I can find room for a good 4 round man down at Santa Monica. I hear all you havta do is keep the gloves laced.

More and more black cats everywhere, but there's a *white* cat here, that means *luck,* brother. He has an angular scar down the left side of his head. Proud; a real shit-head. [* * *]

[To John William Corrington]
May 1, 1963

god damned quarter horses worse than money stealing sluts, hot enough out there to take the bark off an oak tree, and everything in kind of a yellow-sandish grit, like a cheap dream, and you peel the money off—your last poor bloodsmeared 5 or ten, and here they come, damp, fear-peeling, and the number goes by and it is the wrong number. you are fucked again but the most noticeable part is that you are getting used to it. some day in an alley I'll wish I had back g.d. once more, the green, and the milk from ma's tit, but it will be old newspapers and hacked-out minds and blue wind and young cops. What I am trying to tell you here is that I lost at Los Alamitos, and they all lose, they stand there stunned and greyfaced, the dream all gone. And I hit down the freeway in a borrowed blue 1954 Buick that drove like an ice truck. Tomorrow night she'll be over and I'll have to hear all about the horrors of the Right (as opposed to Left) and how soon we'll have a sort of Gestapo dragging people screaming down the streets. She'll have 2 tickets to a lecture by James Baldwin and I will refuse to go. As to Gestapos, Gestapos have always been—and hooeva is in powa has his own kinda Ges., only they call it something nice the The Federal Bureau of Investigation or Vets of For. Whores, or the A.M.A. or the Y.W.C.A.; when these shits gona realize the Gestap. has always been here? that Life is Blood? Control? Fences? only a guy like Gandhi did without and they got him. What I am trying to say, I lost at Lost Alamitos. [* * *]

[To Ben Tibbs]
[May 1, 1963]

Thanks for the drawing. It is the best one I have seen of yours. Don't be pissed, but I think it so good I'd almost use the dirty word "genius." I want Webb to see it. Going to write to him about it. But I want it back because you sent it to me.

I will stoke up something for you—eventually—perhaps a series of small ones, if I don't get run over or pressed out.

Meanwhile your work lights up this dump on this grey day like one thousand searchlights. Thank you, Ben.

Yes, the death of a good woman, it is a bad thing.

I heard about the death of your wife, but take hold, man, your work is getting stronger, so put down the ink the way you do, go on, maybe she's watching, and if she isn't, go on anyway—she'd tell you to.

Thanks again (a small thing to say) for the fine drawing. do continue.

[To Jon and Louise Webb]
May 1, 1963

[* * *] Ben Tibbs shipped me a drawing which he says [he] has not submitted anywhere and he wants me to have it, only it seems so quite warmly funny and good . . . I would like you to see it for possible *Outsider* use, but I would like the original back. I guess he just drew it for me, but hell hell, it's something . . . called "Idyll" and it has one of Ben's little old men with life-filled child eyes, hat on, reading a book in a rocking chair, and it's out on the grass, and there's a bed and the woman is putting a sheet on this bed and you can see part of the body through the sheet and just where the THING is, there is a patch on the sheet—oh, it is not vile ugly dirty but warm laugh clean and love—and then on the sidelights: there is some kind of bird sitting on the head of the bed, and he's looking at the patch, and there's a tree back there. Ben wants me to send him something in ink, but hell hell I can't match, it's trying to draw to an inside straight with a short deck.

And yet I know that Ben is not trying me in contest. He has liked some of my drawings. Well, this is good, but drawing hardly interests me now—little does—and I draw like Thurber
which is o.k. only if
you are
Thurber
and T.'s dead so he's ahead of me on 2 counts, only o you should see the Tibbs, this is the best I've seen of his. Did you know he's an old man? Not that this should prejudice judgement of a work. I see whatever I can see that is there. But when you get an old man who still has velvet in his dreams you get something coo, dad, and mama. [* * *]

[To Ann Bauman]
[May 2, 1963]

I am writing this right after you have phoned, and you have so little money and you should not have, and yet this makes it better, and for it all, it was a sound out of the darkness, and I love you for it, and there's something good in you, you may not know it, but there is, and forgive all the comas and loose talk . . . it is so odd to hear a sound out of all this madness. I am not so good at talking on the phone, or talking at all and though I say small things, hesitant dull things, it is only shame and lack of heart and lack of ability and all the lacks that keep me from expressing what should be, and when the phone is put down I always feel as if I have failed—not only in ordinary failure but in a failure that affects everything: myself and you and tomorrow morning and any way the smoke blows. [* * *]

Ann, I think you should know this—I am not primarily a poet, I hate god gooey damned people poets messing the smears of their lives against the sniveling world, and poets are bad and the world is bad and we are here, ya. What I am trying to say is that poetry, what I write, is only one tenth of myself—the other 9/to hell tenths are looking over the edge of a cliff down into the sea of rock and wringing swirl and cheap damnation. I wish that I only could suffer in the classic style and carve out of great marble that would last centuries beyond this dog's bark I now hear outside of my 1963 window, but I am damned and slapped and chippied and wasted down to the nothingness of my arms and eyes and fingers and this letter tonight, May first or second, 1963, after hearing your voice upon the phone.

I deserve to die. I wait upon death like a plumed falcon with beak and song and talon for my caged blood. This may sound pretty god damned pretty but it is not. The poetry part of me, the seeming actuality, what I write, is dung and dross and saliva and old battleships sinking. I know that when the world—which is fairly cheap and stylish and what? what?—forgets a little of the poetry that I have written, it will not be entirely the fault of the world—mainly because I do not *think* of writing, and only the edge of the knife . . . where I spread the butter or cut the onion keeps practice in the verse of my mind.

You do not know how much your call meant although I was seemingly dull and drab and stupid, but I do wish you would not do it again because I know how things are going for you and yours (not so good) and I don't want the few good people of the world hurt because of buk the puke. (Someone once wrote me that Buk rhymed with puke and she was correct, not only in manner, which is bad, but also in the way the chandeliers work their still lightning in an empty room) and I say, everything is pretty good now but I of course don't know when or if or what the next o my god stroke of everything will bring, which is a coward's viewpoint, and all drowning men are cowards, hear them scream, and life is what? what? going down into the water, and it is not the cutting off of air and light and lung and eye and love that counts—it's the itch they put into us making us wonder why the hell we are here. For these few things. Like a phone call from Sacramento at 7:30 p.m. I don't know, I don't know, and it is so sad. If I could give tears to make it right we would all drown in my sick tears. I hardly know what to do. I drink too much. Or not enough. I gamble. I make love to women who only exist within their bodies and I look against the flakes of their eyes and I know that I am lying to myself and to them because I am no less than a dog, and love or the act should contain more than a couple of steaks in a frying pan or else all is lost like weeds in a garden or snails stepped upon and crushed and left in some sort of slime which contains life, smashed life forever and foreboding.

This poetry-thing is the worst sort of crutch. It weakens a man. And if a man is weak before he writes poetry he becomes, finally, through the strumming of shadows and wailing, he becomes finally what he is—just another fine pink juicy boy doing his god damned job in the frailest and most vomiting way.

You've got to understand that there are other ways of facing the horn except through the typewriter. Those who are known to us may just be a bad choice of chance. Never take the Arts as a holy mirror. Very little is just, and that includes all the centuries. The most honorable countries do not survive through courage nor do the ages survive us the best artists. Everything is chance and shit and the strumming of the winds. Please forgive the center word. If I hate anything it is a vile word said vilely or a dirty joke or the making of sex and life and woman and man into the thing they seem to want it to be.

I am probably fairly insane and you should know this (a more somber note with golden screeching undertones) and I do not mean to knock your verse plays . . . some have been done well . . . Racine, etc., only it is too much and ever so easy to mock and cajole when you do not *give* or try, and I say go ahead: verse, or phone calls or cards or death or love or vast areas of bathing in arenas of sound and stroke and midnight moments, I thank you for going on and I, too, go on a little while more.

p.s.—don't hate me for feeling more than is (perhaps) necessary. It may be best that the lost frogs and space-burnt nylon and neon air . . . it may be best that we are creatures of gesture instead of reality and marriage is reality with life and very few of us can stand either marriage or reality or life. [* * *]

[To Jon and Louise Webb]
May 7, 1963

[* * *] Gypsy, when I phoned last I remember saying "Good-bye, Baby," and it bothered me for hours afterwards. It is simply terminology, crass yes, hell yes, but you should know all the people I know who toss this term, and it can mean everything—to you it meant simply the best of everything: luck, love of the kind I know, rising spirits, grace, 7, the nose in front, holy Mary, you name it. That's what it meant. and you know it. and you stay out of this, Jon.

[To John William Corrington]
[?Mid-]May, 1963

[* * *] . . . on the blood yes, it is not too good, and I know the cancer-bit. I remember my mother. She couldn't straighten her legs. womb. gut. she kept telling me all along, "Your father is a great man." I knew what my father was. She didn't. I took her a rosary on Christmas eve or Christmas day, I can't remember. She was dead. Fry was with me. Fry was dead too.

I pretend that the blood from my mouth is bad teeth and the blood from my ass is from hemorrhoids and then I feel better and take another drink. What man wants to waste his time in hospitals? I am not so particularly concerned with writing poetry as I am concerned with standing around in the sun or just sleeping or getting drunk or looking at the poor face of some old woman I have made love to and watching her eyes eating into my face, into my body, this delight delight, until I am ashamed and turn my eyes down. I am tired as hell but the longer I live the more something begins to take shape. I thought the whiskey would finally ride my brain down, and maybe it has, and as I type this to you I am listening to some new Broadway musical, they are pretty similar, it is more Artless in its shouting than a blowjob whore, but it is a moment, a sound, not bad, and I am writing this to you and I am drunk but I am still alive, and we write on, over and over, live on, your wife, your kids, myself, Jon, Lou, WILDCAT, and tomorrow's entries. The fucking stage, yeah, the fucking stage, we are all there. [* * *]

Jory Sherman's My Face in Wax *with an introduction by Bukowski was published by Windfall Press, Chicago, in 1965.*

The end of this letter refers to Karl Shapiro's introduction to the first book of Jack Hirschman (A Correspondence of Americans [Indiana Univ. Press, 1960]), who in the 1960s was teaching at UCLA. "Was invited to dinner by Jack and his wife Ruth," Bukowski notes. "I drank a lot of wine and made an ass out of myself. Jack has the ability to get off some strong lines and poems, strange and original."

[To John William Corrington]
May 23, 1963

got yr 2 letters right one on the other, and I am hanging in (yet); sometimes I think u think I think I am sliding under the table. Drunk phone calls are my specialty. Cost me 50 bucks a month, which if the mules don't start dancing, I'm gona haveta stop doing, but don't worry, there's bloody ass but windows with screens, and how are YOU doing? They went bad again today, and my feet hurt, and no money ha, but that's not it, it's the TIME melting like vanilla, boy, and I am going ha, and that's it, a crotch, a crotch of grey waiting to stretch out and stop farting, and fucking old things, but the drinking's not bad, the drinking lifts, verily, John, fills the gap I'm not filling at the time, it's beans on the shelf, things going, radios, and all the words of silence that crawl the walls like cockroaches. Bang, bang, you're dead. [* * *]

I'm not worried about the Southern problem; that will work itself loose into another problem. And the bomb. That will, slovenly thing, solve itself. You know the ol' hack—we cure the obvious and the subtle takes over, and if it's subtle enough some grow fat and happy and others grow mad. I know this woman (pretty well), she marches on City Hall, the protest thing, either the black or the bomb, and she asks me, why don't you do something? and I don't say it, but I think I AM DOING SOMETHING, I am fucking you and you seem to like it a lot more than I do.

But I tell her, down where I work at night, I know plenty for there are 4 thousand people in this building and three thousand five hundred of them are black or mostly black, and I get along solidly with those I like, but here the problem is in being WHITE, and I have faced the problem in the factories and the slaughterhouses, I have been the WRONG color most of the time, but I can't expect sensibility when they nailed christ on the cross for pulling miracles, I don't go around pulling rabbits out of the hat. I have gotten close to their women and I have seen a black walk up to these women with a piece of white chalk in his hand and draw a line of white on his skin and ask one of these women, now will you have ME?

The fact that he was a sloppy strutting egocentric bastard, he did not take into consideration, only the fact that he was black. It's hard being black. It's even hard being white. It's hard being alive.

She listens to this and says, At the meeting today I saw the most *beautiful* thing. This girl, she took this man's shoes and stockings off and washed his feet in a pan of water, and then, after carefully and tenderly washing his feet, she kissed his feet, she was so young and beautiful and had this long hair and it fell over her face, and she kissed his feet, kissed his feet, and then she put his stockings on and then she put his shoes on.

Now this woman did not tell me the color of skins involved here, but I knew, of course. And I said, Well, I guess when we find out God is black we'll all feel better and get around to raising roses. don't get me wrong willie, but don't get me right, either, it's so easy to be RIGHT AND DO THE PROPER THING when you figure you've got the proper *cause,* and nothing to worry about, and that's what puts old men and women in churches on Sundays in their proper clothes— there's no drawback, and it seems like courage, it seems like knowing. This is a pretty good feeling. Some people go around looking for easy good feelings. Like a young girl kissing a black's feet in front of a Los Angeles crowd and feeling good because everybody knows you're going to fuck him later when nobody's around. Because your parents didn't understand Proust or Conrad Aiken. A psychologist could tell you a lot more about this than I can. But the human mob never solves a problem straight on; it generally fucks up in a mesh of shit and carries further problems to the problem, and the weak ones protest the most and do the most because there is this hungry space within them that can only see the immediate, the thing that can answer back and boy, they feel good; it's either a war or a pol. party or a magnet of some sort, and when they are long dead to the worms, somebody a couple of centuries later, when it gets cooler and clearer, decides that they have done the WRONG thing. I hate to leap into dishwater. Like you know guys used to go to doctors and the docs would put these suction cups on them and draw out their blood and they would pay for this. Then there's the history of wars. I am bullshitting a loghead tonight but the mules were bad and this too is a sort of colossal type of righteousness blah to right the torn-up tickets. But I know my madness more properly than many others. I hope, ya. I have an idea the medics are some day going to find out that cutting out cancer with a knife was the quickest way to death. Or that teeth never should have been pulled. These are guesses but I am a pretty good guesser and I know that rot should be removed but not with such force and gesture, and further bullshit. [* * *]

On the foreword to Sherman's book you will see that I am talking mostly about myself, which is savage and lets out air and sometimes a little light. Don't worry about me laying out any bolognas out on the stage. I mostly blast Shapiro in it, in opening, not mentioning name, about using his name to promote another college Eng. teacher, and giving the grand come-on, I found the pages not to be like that at all. This is just part of it. I went over drunk one time and ate with man and wife in their house, the book I speak of with Shapiro foreword, and I told them I didn't like it, that it shouldn't have been done, it was bad for Shapiro and it was bad for them. Now I do not argue and I do not take stands but sometimes an idea will come out of me drunk during a drink and I will say it.

You know what he said?

Well, the book never would have gotten printed without it. That's what he said. [* * *]

[To Jon and Louise Webb]
June 3, 1963

Well, I got the plaque, it was leaning against the door when I opened it—the bastard didn't knock, or I was asleep. Anyway, it's on the wall now, it's a fine thing and it holds the walls up . . . "the poet Charles Bukowski." Sometimes it's all in the dream-state and I don't know who Bukowski is. Sometimes I expect somebody to walk out of my bathroom and say, "Give me a smoke, man, I am Charles Bukowski." Anyhow, something like this which you needn't have done at all and did do with this beautiful gesture of warmth . . . this thing on the wall will be mine, and as the years go on—saving I hang around—this plaque will mean more and more to me. [* * *]

Our boy Sherman has a book coming out in which I write a long introduction. It was done sometime back when I was feeling pretty good. I speak more of myself . . . if I remember . . . than I do of Sherman. Neeli Cherry was orig. going to bring book out and Sherman asked me if I would do intro. I said I didn't know and then one day sat down and found myself writing it. I hope they have not cut it because then it would not make sense. [* * *]

[To Ann Bauman]
June 3, 1963

[* * *] If you should ever come down here your problem will be to keep the conversation "dull." I am an old wolf and after a few beers begin to imagine myself a young bull. I would always rather chance that they go away angry and unloved than unangry and unloved. It is better, of course, for them to leave unangry and loved, but of the other choices, at least I will know that I have tried. [* * *]

The review mentioned here is not listed in Dorbin's bibliography.

[To Jon and Louise Webb]
June 24, 1963

A little good news. Yesterday, Sunday, in the *Los Angeles Times* book review section, we, LOUJON PRESS and Buk and *It Catches* was mentioned by Jack Hirschman. Some bit about my style of writing (according to Hirschman); that the book was on the press, price of book and address of LOUJON PRESS given. Also several other books reviewed and a kind of eulogy for Creeley by Hirschman. Anyhow, we have been mentioned, and maybe a few sales because of it? It might pay to send Hirschman a review copy when the book comes out? [* * *]

The U. gave Corrington a grand ($1,000) to lay around and write so he wouldn't have to teach Summer School. Well, this is o.k. if you can work it. Also, I think, a $2,500 advance on his novel. He's now thinking about going to Europe. I guess they all do that. They start running around the world. (See Ginsberg, Corso, Kaja, Burroughs, etc., etc.) I don't know quite what it means, but I'd rather side with Faulkner who g.d. figured there was more than enough just around his doorstep. This culture hunt smacks too much of a Cadillac sort of acquisition.

All right, hang in tough.

Corrington published "Charles Bukowski and the Savage Surfaces" in Northwest Review *for fall 1963.*

[To John William Corrington]
[June 1963]

Don't worry yourself shitty on the *Northwest Review* article, I understand, and I hold to the savage side with the honor of my teeth. I know damn well I don't wax the golden poetic and I don't try to because I believe it to be essentially outside of life—like lace gloves for a coal-stoker. On the other hand, I don't believe in being tough because life is tough. I like my sunlight and beer and cigars and occasional pussy just like any matador or prelim boy, but there's still room for a good symphony written in 1700 or 1800 or the disgust-strike of sadness at seeing a cat crushed flat by wheels upon asphalt. There's room for things, and I once tried to straighten these things into REASON by reading Plato and Schope and F.N., Hegel, the whole host of boys, but I only found that they were tilting silver water, getting lost in it, and as long as I was getting lost I figured it might as well be in a cheap bar where I could listen to sounds that were not being written, and if I found love it was some other old dog's bone. Because if the answer isn't at the top, it isn't at the middle, and you'll find just as much at the bottom which was where I was at anyhow. It's not so much savage as it is discarding the whole facade of knowledge and education and looking as directly as you can into your own sun. You can get blinded this way but at least a lot of it is your own doing. Like suicide or betting the 9 horse. The next cold drink is God, and the next cigarette isn't cancer; it's the next one after, the one you haven't gotten to. And you realize all along that you are not getting very near anything, but if it's not the razor, you toddle along like a kid shitting in its pants, and the game is corncobs and dollars and buttons and an occasional Easter candle. [* * *]

I get touches and hints of the book from Jon, and this man and his wife weave things like a golden dream, touching it, tasting it, adding, subtracting, loving, o loving, they touch again and again the thing they are working with, it takes design, it takes them, they heave to it like good steak or a visitation by the angels; these people are blessed beyond blessedness, and my unholy mad luck has made this work of mine fall into their hands and I look through the curtains, and the cars on the street and the people and the sidewalks have become real and carved and yet soft like pillows because these people have touched me with the wand. All my luck came at once, and it won't last, I don't want it to. There will be a time of looking back, and I am ready. I came out of absurdity and I will go back, back, but now now all the dogs and flowers and windows laugh with me, and it is a stirring a stirring like an approaching army marching or a butterfly coming out of the cocoon. [* * *]

I await the *K. Review,* and your probable 18th century sonnet. This is all right. The *K. Review* is good fat book, stirs with a kind of dusty knowledge and unreality, but some of the critical articles hold little strokes of lightning, the taste and stir of the good long word mixed with the near-slang. This beholds one in an amusing sort of way. [* * *]

[To Ann Bauman]
[mid-June, 1963]

if you come to LA someday I hope you come to see me, part of that time anyhow. The only problem being that I work about half the weekends and the other I don't. If you come by bus, would be glad to meet you at bus stop, or drive you anywhere around town you want to go, or if you don't want to go anywhere we can have a beer at my place and make dull and polite conversation. However, I know that your idea is only half-resolved, a thought in between many other thoughts while things are going on, and that it prob. will not be followed through.

I am signing pages for the book, a huge stack of purple pages arrived in a box with instructions and this Sunday I will quietly drink beer and smoke and listen to my radio and look out the window and sign the pages.

Webb sent me a dummy copy of the book and it is a real thing of beauty—the paper, the type, the cover etc. etc. [* * *]

[To Jon and Louise Webb]
July 1, 1963

[* * *] If you are serious about a 2nd book to follow *Outsider* #4, I can say no more than that the miracles are still coming, the honor laid out like all the horses dancing in my dreams. Should you people change your minds—because of circumstances or conditions later, that will be o.k. too. I've got to go with you. YOU HAVE EXCLUSIVE RIGHTS TO PUBLISH THE NEXT BOOK AFTER *It Catches My Heart in Its Hands* [*dated and signed*].

This is real nice to say—as if I were giving *you* a break or something, after you break your backs to make me known! Don't worry about a notary: my word is good, and when my word is no longer any good then my poetry won't be either. I'm glad to go with you, much more than glad; you are my kind of people. Not a bunch of phoney literary bullshit or slick-assed business people, but people in love with their work and their lives, asking nothing but enough to continue to stay alive in order to continue to do the thing.

Your danger after putting me out in such fine style in *It Catches* would not be from the little chapbook operators but from the big boys, the bigger publishers, who might think I would go. But they can go to hell. I'm with you, and same arrangements with 2nd book, no royalties, but would like some copies. I'm afraid, tho, we will never come up with such a good title again, but meanwhile I will be thinking, gently thinking of one, as I go in and out of bars or watch them run. [* * *]

I don't write letters . . . too much . . . anymore, because it was simply it is simply a time of no letters. It may change. But I get to thinking IT IS THE ART-FORM THAT COUNTS, and all the letter-writing in the world won't excuse a bad poem or make it any better. Then I am still drinking, and the drinking often takes over and I don't know quite where I am or what I am anymore. Right now this place has newspapers in it that date 3 weeks back, onion stems, beer-cans, coffeepots on the floor. This woman comes over once in a while and straightens up but then she starts in with THE INTELLIGENT TALK, and I let her win her precious little arguments, I hate haggle, but just the same I get a little sick with how PROUD people are with the mind, how they want to ram it through you like a sword, how they want to talk talk talk. Don't they know that there is simply something nice about sitting in a room and drinking a beer and not saying much, feeling the world out there, and sitting there, sitting there, resting? [* * *]

I will send you a tape of a poetry reading of mine I made on my machine and which was broadcast over KPFK in August 1962. Of course, they deleted a lot of vulgarity, had to, so it is not quite the same thing I sent them. They asked me to come to their studios, which is like asking me to go to church with a hangover, so instead I mailed them what I had made in my room among the beercans, and, lo, they accepted it and played it over the air. Jack Hirschman's wife runs the literary and drama end of KPFK. Anyhow, when the thing finally came on over the radio . . . at 11:15 p.m. . . . I was drunk and did not hear it, but somebody retaped it off the radio and I was able to hear it afterward. [* * *]

Bukowski had three poems in El Corno Emplumado *no. 7 (July 1963), published in Mexico City. He had previously appeared in no. 3.*

[To John William Corrington]
July [22], 1963

shd. change ribbon but I am too tired—*Mutiny* editors are correct: I am a bastard: would rather kiss the king's ass than change a ribbon.

Heard from Jon. His spirits seem high, which does me good, as I would hate him to bite into the book and get this bad taste in his mouth. . . . Got copy #7 of *El Corno*. They seem to be falling off from a good start. Of course, I can't read Spanish or Mexican either, so it doesn't help my broad-minded eye. I got to figure that what I can't read isn't any good. That's how flies get fat. [* * *]

[To Jon and Louise Webb]
July [28], 1963

[* * *] In case you decide to send a copy of *the book* to Jack Hirschman for review for *L.A. Times,* his address is 10543 Bradbury Rd., Los Angeles, Calif. I know, I broke all rules and went there for dinner once, drunk. He thinks Creeley is God and Robert Frost 3/4s God but then he teaches at a University and therefore some of this is understandable. They see the underside softside of the wing. But he may have ordered the book anyway, and we may be in trouble, but I kind of like trouble sometimes—I mean, in my rather long foreword to Sherman's book (out July 21st, I believe), along with other ramblings, I take to task Karl Shapiro for writing a misleading introduction to Jack Hirschman's book. Names are not mentioned but, I guess, rather obvious. And at the dinner I told Jack that the introduction was bad but he told me that the book would have never been published without it, that there was only one good poem in there. Which might have been modesty but let's not pick at bones. This is the trouble with getting involved with literary talk; soon you are covered with slime and haggle, and creation is forgotten, So far, I have often forgotten creation because of drink or gamble or plain forget, but so far, very little shit-paddle has stopped me and I hope I remain as lucky.

When I took this woman home today she showed me a collection of the early poems of Ernie Hem. Out of the *Little Review* etc., but although most of them were not very good, they were not very bad either, and there was one poem in there . . . after the style of Ger. Stein and you can see how much this woman *did* affect him, which we all know but which we tend to forget after Hem and Stein are both gone and Hem more or less remains. However, these poems are encouraging to any young (or old) writer to show that something almost can come out of almost nothing. It is simply buttoning a button right and knowing how to open a door. It is easy as hell, really, it is so easy that almost nobody can do it. [* * *]

[To Jon and Louise Webb]
August 6, 1963

[* * *] Then there's the bush down there, the same bush with orange blossoms forever, and the old man down there poking in his wooden mailbox. He must be a writer or a madman; he keeps looking in there as if some long-limbed thing sheathed in nylon is going to take him back to the full bright dream. I'm hungry. It's good to be hungry when you can afford to eat. Right now, I can afford. I like crab. You can get a big crab down at one of the stores for around 80 cents and it takes you all day to eat him and you don't feel very sorry for the crab. That makes it nice. Although they say they boil them alive? But they boil me every time I walk out the door. Swosh. sure. I'm lucky to have a rented door to walk out of. haven't read a book in ten years or seen a movie in fifteen and don't give a damn. Airplanes and sirens now. Do you think it is going to rain this Winter? I've got to throw out the cans again. There's the mailman. Hot damn, look at the ol' man run!! [* * *]

[To Ann Bauman]
[August 14, 1963]

[* * *] I was jailed for common drunk 6 a.m. Monday morning, bailed out 8 p.m. Monday night. went to court this afternoon (Wednesday). judge gave me choice 3 days vs. $30. I figure easier to lose money than mind.

. . . I must be more careful. I am all right if I drink where I live. Good manager here, good people. But when I go out on the street, BANG.

Anyhow, I am alive yet. Maybe.

I do not even feel depressed. It is all so very odd. my god, what they'll do to a man, over and over again, for nothing.

I never understood society. I understand that it works somehow and that it functions as a reality and that its realities are necessary to keep us from worse realities. But all I sense are that there are plenty of police and jails and judges and laws and that what is meant to protect me is breaking me down. I know that I am not much good in the network and the miracle is that I have remained around this long.

Now: off to work, if my terrible job is still there.

Bukowski contributed to the symposium on "Little Magazines in America" in Mainstream, *June 1963. The editor was Walter Lowenfels.*

[To Jon and Louise Webb]
August 22, 1963

[* * *] Wrote to *Mainstream* and sent a buck, they sent money back, and then mailed 2 copies. Said had mailed twice before to WRONG ADDRESS. The whole picture there has been jumbled from the start. It always is when Lowenfels gets a finger in anywhere. First I was contacted by Larsen who said *Stream* had written me but he had misplaced the letter in a bottom drawer for a couple of months, but here it is Buk. Meanwhile, Larsen's article on the littles had already appeared. Not that it matters. But everything always works in a bugged-up fashion and I find more and more that there just aren't any people around. Everybody's clay or horseshit or posing.

As far as that goes I cannot seem to get unstrung either. I just lay in the sack or stare out the window and I say to myself, come come, old man, this is not the way to create Art. And then another voice says, well, hell, EVERYBODY's busy creating ART, and maybe that what's the matter. They're all trying to MAKE IT, trying to hustle up their little snail walls. God damn the prince and Tolstoy and Norman Mailer. [* * *]

The Webbs eventually published an issue of The Outsider *featuring a "Homage to Kenneth Patchen" section, but not a separate book by him.*

[To Jon and Louise Webb]
August 23, 1963

[* * *] Good on the Patchen; he's not believed in his fame or he knows that a man working out of fame is the same as a man working out of failure—each time the one or the other begins again, they begin even. You might call this innocence or you might call it non-innocence or you might call it anything, but whatever it is, it is good that he has it.

Does accepting the Patchen book mean that Buk book #2 is off? This will be o.k. if you cannot bear the load, and remember I told you I did not hold you to a second book—which it looks like we don't have the poems for anyhow.

It Catches is plenty for me, I can only bear about so much good. [* * *]

[To Jon and Louise Webb]
September 18, 1963

[* * *] Got rid of a mass of your rejects to *Targets* for $25 for his next issue as a Signature. Also Holland took a couple, so the luck holds. With *It Catches* coming up, I might need another 10 years off to get my senses back. There is always the danger of writing too much or pushing beyond yourself. Something kills writers and kills them pretty fast, and then we all die anyhow like the fly and the flower, the wail . . . shit, so . . . some dullard outside honking his horn; somebody else hammers. Still the insomnia thing but most of the bleeding has stopped. nasty letter from a churchboy who was handed one of my poems. . . . I'm interested in the Patchen section, of course. Do try to get some DRAWINGS from him along with photos. Do you know that I haven't read any of his books, never seen one? Just a poem here and there, mostly a reprint and mostly all good in this awesome softly real good way; but then, I have not been much of a reader for some time. I get the idea, though, that he has remained *alive* as an Artist. On the back-thing, I really don't know. I am somewhat confused on the back-thing. I think *everybody* with a bad back should be taken care of, including Patchen. I mean,

have the medical thing. But the poems are Patchen, and the drawings. And he's as OUTSIDE as any, sure. [* * *]

[To Jon and Louise Webb]
September, 1963

[* * *] It took a lot of guts to turn down the Roman offer but hell, you've been there and you know it is only finally chopchop and twist and chop and demand and then you've had it. You depend on their money and the "free editorial reign" but they've got ways of pulling their money out or getting nasty, and all these fingers running through your brain like neckties. I know that I have always felt better broke than not because when you are broke you have nothing to lose and are loose, and when you get it you worry about protecting it and you don't do *anything but* protect it. [* * *]

Gypsy, take vitamins, even I do—99¢ for a month's supply— and eat bread and potatoes, and when you can't sleep at night don't fight it, get up and read a newspaper, something dull, the financial sect., war, marches, weather reports, so forth. And be kind to yourself when you're feeling bad, try to think of something good that once happened to you or of something good that might happen to you. We are often too tough with ourselves. I know that this sounds like a corner preacher or etc. but try a little of it: OL' BUK'S EASY WONDER CURE. I wish I could give you about 20 of my pounds; I am a swine; in a morgue I would look like a stuffed turkey. [* * *]

 [P.S.] no man is an island but why are so many of them flecks of dirt?

[To Neeli Cherry]
September 20, 1963

well, kid, I got your burnt Bukowski poem bust-out booklet, and it was somewhat like finding angels female with good figures and some wing in *The Daily Racing Form*, and I thank you for the toast (burnt) and I guess you are neva gon forget I threw one a your poems

87

in the fire. but you've got to remember it was a hot night and the fingers of my mind were sweating, I was almost out of stuff to drink and your old man kept running in and out of the back door with this constant stagger of logs and I was standing in front of the fireplace and it got hotter and hotter and I thought I was a wheel from the old Lafayette Escadrille and when you handed me a poem there was nothing left to do but dump it along with the rest of me. ;;;ah, a hell of an excuse. !!!

well, the booklet had some good poems in a kind of blaring hard-stone sense that is really closer to feeling than the perfumed hanky drillwork of OUR contemporaries; but I remember your bedroom and you asleep in there like a sick frog, and pictures of Hem on your walls, pictures of Hem and maybe Faulk and so forth, well, this is better for a kid than Henry Ford and almost as good as ice hockey but look someday the pictures have to come down, the walls will have to be as bare as say the ass of your own reflections getting pinched by the light, and paeans to a minor poet c.b. must stop. It is pretty hard, as you must guess, not to die before the last Supper of your 30th. birthday in our American Society, and then you are never safe, you can go at any time like any Mailer or Jones, although I do not know their ages nor am I interested. The novel nowadays has become the guillotine. You can last longer growing inside and around the poem although it isn't any news that you won't make any money but you'll live longer even if you sell papers on the corner than you will hustling The Book of the Month Club. This is stale advice from an old man to a young man, and much of the bad breath of old age is that the old tend to tell the young where the sun comes up. I think maybe it is time for the old to listen to the young but since I am at this moment handing it out, I will continue to slough it. Don't ever write a novel unless it hurts like a hot turd coming out. You will know when this happens; it has not yet happened to me but it can happen to you. If you ever feel like pressing, get drunk or draw something on a piece of paper or a piece of ass. There are plenty of doors to go out of that breaks the place of yourself up but if there's enough left when you get back maybe you got a hustle going. [* * *]

[To Jon and Louise Webb]
October 1, 1963

I did not make work tonight, and so there it goes: the job on the edge of the cliff again, and I do not like work and have no trade but I do like to eat, so this is basic, the basic training of slaves to fear, but I wrote some poems and it does not matter whether they are good or not—yes, it does, everything should be as sharp as possible: I talk like a fool; what I mean is, it is good to hear the typewriter running again across my brain like a lawnmower or a machinegun or what is left of anything. You've got to get the idea of this breakfast nook here, it's always hot, and mostly always beer, but sometimes just the window and I look out the window and like any other damn-fool writer I begin to wonder where the soul went, and I used to think this was foolish, but no more, I know that the soul does *go*: ZIP, and then that's that. Only you don't think of it like an expensive item, like a big diamond, more like a good solid piece of ass with eyes of sea that walked out for somebody with more $$$ or more dangle or more natural decency toward his fellow being. ow. [* * *] There are good days, tho, when the whole world unfolds . . . unfolds like what? like a lie. Most of us hold onto jobs if we can, sell brooms door to door, work in post offices, slaughterhouses, collection agencies, all that hell. Hell and hell and hell, on and on. I no longer wonder about Rimbaud running the guns and hunting gold and going buggy in Africa. He only wanted time to write poetry, I think. And he wanted it so bad that he didn't write anymore. Starvation may or may not make artists; I only know that it gets very tiresome to STARVE while guys pass you on the streets with faces that look like dishpans and bellyfuls of porterhouse and fries and all those things that kill: like penthouse blondes and collections of Mozart, ow. I mean, I write better, I think, when I am not worried about the belly or the rent or scraping up a piece of ass. These things are primaries and when you get them out of the way you can begin to worry or unworry about a hell of a lot of other things you wouldn't have time to think about in the first place. I don't mean I am for Harvard educations. I'm not. If I had one I would probably say they are o.k. but since I don't have one they can't be o.k. for me because it is not happening. I paid the rent today and if I walk on the job tomorrow and they do not barber me too much we will have PEACE for 3 or 4 days, maybe. There is always this sense of futility and disgust that you have been hammered finally into something which you do not WANT TO BE, and as long as you are conscious of this and not man enough or clever enough to find a way out, you are going to be pretty generally unhappy like with hot tongs gripping your guts most of the time. This is sad but it makes me glad I've written a few poems today, bad and/or?, and this is madness too, I know, a kind of screaming. Yet I know people, other people who do this; they send me their poems in the mail. Well, it's nice to be selected to have poems sent to if you are not an editor; if you are an editor, well, it's just another day's work. Well, most of the poems are bad, to me, that is. I don't like them. I read them and say, Christ ugg, and throw them away. Yet these people think I am human, more human than an editor, and this is all right. But what I get from this mainly is the idea of all these people going wacky mad etc., out there really, while in actuality they are working as waitresses, truck drivers or male hairdressers. I prefer the poems from the ladies especially when they enclose their photos. But what I mean is: there are all these people out there going mad and writing bad poetry, and when somebody *does* SHOVE THROUGH it is kind a landmark, don't you think? Now Ginsberg bothered me a long time, and then somebody told me Burroughs got a regular check from the Burroughs adding machine co. and some of the floss fell away, let alone the homo bit which DOES bother no matter how humanitarian you try to get. But you've got to hand it to Ginsberg. He's gotten away. He's sitting in India, which is something. I guess they've got good beer in India and I imagine now and then Corso comes to see him, which will later give them both something to talk about write about, a kind of Lawrence-Huxley mess, you know the people bite on this and get excited. The only people who come to see me are winos who need enough change to round out 64 cents. But Ginsberg has gotten out of it somehow so he has time to write even if he ends up writing badly. It's a gathering of dust and electrodes and a vomiting out, later. But he's got a better chance than if he were working in a Chinese Laundry or as Secretary of State—IF HE REMAINS UNPROFESSIONAL. But the problem is not Ginsberg tonight, it is me. I feel like a sow or an edge of dust of a lamp shade in the attic. I do not want *attention*, I want myself and they are tearing the arms of my mind apart. The only thing which saves me from cutting my belly out like an apple pie is that I am a coward, and anyway I have so many things wrong with me now that any one of them could take care of the situation with less clutter. God save the King and send in the longshots. If people can set themselves on fire in the streets, I can have another

90

cigarette. They have turned off the refrigerator and the beer is warm. I must wash my stockings.

[To Jon and Louise Webb]
October 18, 1963

[* * *] Whenever I need a lift I look at that table of contents you sent and I think of all the pages and all the poems. You really let the book run away with you and I'm glad. If I remember right you were once thinking of 60 pages. If I never write another poem, I will always have this book, a kind of holy thing to me. [* * *] And we've got the right title too. After these months it has become solid as a wall. I'll never forget the night I came across it, early a.m., and I said, they've got to take it, they've just got to. And then sweating Cerf. I've been lucky on the titles of my books because the editors have always gone right along, and each title has explained my mental-spiritual shape of the moment—or if this is too fancy: the way I felt. [* * *]

[To Jon and Louise Webb]
October 19, 1963

[* * *] Some outfit in Frisco wants me to give a reading in Feb., offer of 2/3rds of house but I can't see myself on the boards in front of the yak hyenas, lonely hearts and homos. Not yet. If I were starving, maybe so. But I am not yet starving. People keep explaining to me that I am really lonely, and this makes my ass bleed too. What they are talking about really is themselves and they figure my machinery has to be set the same way. There is nothing sweeter to me than closing the door on the world, having the walls again. Generally, I am too TIRED to be lonely: a hangover or bucking the horses or the job or some woman and when the time is finally given to me I like to duck under the table and hide rather than go get myself the wet nurse of the crowd. You remember the poem I wrote of the man who dug a hole in the ground and crawled down into it? And

he didn't tell the people why when they asked why, he only smiled because he knew that they wouldn't understand, he knew that he was odd-fish out—Outsider of the year, Outsider of the world. I too have learned not to explain anymore. Let them win the word-games of the air; if I have anything to say I hope to put it into a rock with a fork. Maybe it will last through a few rains or maybe they'll throw it into a cesspool, endurability is not so much the matter anyhow as is waste and nonsense and yak yak yak. [* * *]

[To Jon and Louise Webb]
October 27, 1963

[* * *] Wild telegram from Orlani Mahak. Perhaps she needs . . . friendship? . . . but she appears to be supporting a very young poet and thinker (I only know as David) and it so happens I like David and would also have to work around the stuff I have on hand now and I don't like to tiptoe or to spoil somebody else's game. Besides, all this has very little to do with writing the poem, and I am still interested in that, and I realize that if I had not written the poem the Orlani Mahaks would not be telegramming me, but it is the stuff of my own kind of life I am interested in, and what this other stuff is I don't quite know. I don't want to become anybody's pet. I know that Henry Miller was good at it. Henry, like the rest of us, hated to work for somebody else; but I hate to be petted by somebody else. Which does not make me a better Artist than Henry Miller, just a different person, and not nearly so famous, thank the gods! [* * *]

[To Jon and Louise Webb]
November 10, 1963

[* * *] No poems lately, although I may knock off a couple to send with this, I doubt it, I've got to be alone and the woman has just come back [* * *]
Now she sings, "There is no Christ upon the Cross
and we are sad . . ."

92

She makes these songs up. You see why I drink?
Now she sings, "Buk is bleeding from the asshole,
    Buk is bleeding from the asshole,
    and we don't give a
                  damn
                      damn
                          damn . . . !"
You see why I drink? You see? You see?
Get some drawings out of Patchen . . . those upside down soft elephant creatures asking us to save the world of flowers and baby's hands, they're good like sunlight on putty in the window says. [* * *]

[To Jon and Louise Webb]
November 26, 1963: THE DAY

I came back from the store and there was the package against the door "don't open 'til Xmas," but to hell with that, I *have* been waiting, and I tore the paper off, saw the miracle: jacket, cover, skeleton in sand, the works the works . . . peeling back the pages I ate the whole insides, read the poems I have forgotten, the good Corrington, back page wherein you describe paper, type etc., the humor-agony bug-rat breakdown struggle which goes so well along with the author. And to say you've come through is nothing; that you've come through in this way . . . page by page, inch by inch, breakdown by breakdown, cut fingers, landladies, the street corner, the hours, my god, if the poems have been wasted the BOOK has not been wasted, little calm and precious beauties and loves of doing like a garden of good, like mountains, like everything that counts . . . by god, you've done it, you've done it, and I'm proud and struck and awed that you have—the both of you—caught me up in it.

This is the kind of book that grows on you in days not minutes; this is the kind of book that you remember like you remember war or birth or love or fire, this singing in my darkest dark—the photo of Buk with cigarette, everything, everything, there is no beginning, I don't know where to touch the book next—first I think the jacket is impossibly impossibly true, then I go elsewhere, it's like walking through a forest with wine at high noon and everything gone except the soaring. my god, you've done it, you've done it! Never such a book! Where? Where?? in all the libraries, in all the cities I have never seen such a book put together in such a way, inventive creativeness and love. Where have the publishers been for centuries? You've done it.

you've done it.

The books will sit and grow on me, they will enter me, it is a part, a beholden and miraculous part. It does little to say more: the whole thing wells and turns in me almost impossibly. My thanks my thanks for all the love and honor and pain and beauty; the pain yours, the others you've passed to me. Going now, going.

[To Jon and Louise Webb]
November 26, 1963

Sitting here smoking a 1/4 last night's cigar and savoring the book—as I will always savor it, it is endless with endless little touches, and looking at the jacket now—the way it works around the cover, the marble paper over our sandman skeleton, and do thank (for me) Chevrier and Salantrie for their fine work. The jacket I cannot figure out, how it has this antique quality and I do not figure it out, it would be like tearing a rose, formulas do not interest me, it is the thing being there like the sun that warms me. I do not think there will ever be another event in my life like this book, and I keep thinking of the years drunk in the alleys, of the 3 years I sat in the same Philly bar on the same barstool from 6 or 7 a.m. in the morning until 2 a.m. the next morning, staring down at the wood, listening to nothing, maybe, and now this book, this book, this book out of nothing like somebody saying, see, it is not nearly *all* bad. I know how close you must come to dying in fighting from all nothingness of poverty, hoping on luck, a break from the sky, kinder landlords, praying typefaces do not break, that somebody will send a dollar for paper, that somebody will buy a postcard or a painting from Gypsy, that the body will hold up, that the landlord will smile, that cars will not run you over, everything everything, so please do not say that your blood is "more like the pseudo-stuff that bleeds from the *madras* tissue between pages 96 and 97." I know better and the living people of the world know better. Don't make me sad; the miracle is yours; you have drowned me in honor, and no matter what cheap hotel,

94

what jail, what grave is there for me, they can never take away the miracle.

I would like to say that the people who have seen the book are as taken with it as I and that the last page which begins "777 copies of this book . . ." is one of the best poems, if not the best poem in the book.

A little sadness here—and I thought I'd tell you before anybody else told you—in the poem "Dinner, Rain & Transport" page 46, one line was left out, "I can prophecy evil," this was to proceed "with the force of a jackhammer." And when I say a little sadness I know it will be mostly yours, for to me the book is so much that this makes no difference, so please don't blame yourself for being also real enough to error. [* * *]

[To Ann Bauman]
December 4, 1963

Like the American provincial, I start my letter: "I have been meaning to write but—"

It's good you liked the book; I feel that Webb has surrounded me with more than the poems deserve, and he will hear this from many quarters, but for it all, he has created a book such as I have never seen, and he (*they* really!) have done it out of absolute poverty and the force of their beings. [* * *]

The book has lifted me high over the branches, building, etc., but they are still there, and I go on, actually tired physically as if I had been wrestling a bear for 43 years, and I slept ten hours today and wish I could sleep ten more but after I type this I must go to the place and the place will have its way. [* * *]

[To Jon and Louise Webb]
December 7, 1963

[* * *] Enclosed the article Robt. Fink was speaking of, mentioning *Outsider*, and lucky the papers lay on the floor with the beer-cans for days or I would have long ago thrown this bit away, but enclosed. Lipton gained his golden head through the BEATS but the beats through their artifact of so-called brawny and courageous poeticism did more damage to the pure poem trying to breathe than Poetry Chicago has done accepting the accepted. The trouble with the BEATS: they gathered in crowds to gather SOLACE and when you take the gang-form you become the gang—i.e., the same as CORE or Congress or STANDARD OIL or American Banana and their assorted $ ventures and assassinations and cries. You've got to rise from the floor alone or fall back alone. What I mean is: conceive the Art-form and forget it, and conceive it again if you have the blue blood and the red blood the bull blood to carry you past the matador the god whatever so and whosoforever stands in the way. I told you I was drinking beer. [* * *]

Corrington writes me to ask what I think of the Kennedy thing. So, after I finish with this letter I must write and tell my oh my I must tell him, and he's tough but he might not like what I say, and to you I say although I do not hold K. martyred as most, I do not like the dissolution of K. on down to a RUBY. The only thing that could be low enough to kill Ruby, a Ruby, would be a turd, and maybe one of them will stick into a stone mortuary within his intestines, but I doubt that—shit generally gets along with shit.

[* * *] If Henry Miller reviews me and it comes out bad, don't worry. I once reviewed Henry Miller. I was in a little bus station in the middle of Texas and some gal who had been ramming her tongue down my throat went into the ladies' room and I walked over to the newsstand with my hair down in my eyes and I bought one of the *Cancers*, I forget which, and Henry understood that the only way to get to a man was to speak the language of the day, the present tongue, but he got to a part where he talked about a guy with a big cock and how he made it with all the women with THIS BIG COCK, and he went on and on with this and I began getting sleepy and worse . . . worse than ANYTHING, I got the idea that Henry Miller the ALL-KNOWING didn't know much more about fucking than to talk about it, and that's the way most non-fuckers are. But then, it's easy and simple to knock great names or kill 1/4 great men,

96

and I remember when I was very young, Hem used to work out in the ring, you know, and I always dreamed that I would volunteer to sit in the opposite corner, and in my dream, of course, I kayoed HEMINGWAY, and therefore I was a greater writer, I was a greater everything. Which is pure shit, and a kind of Oswald-Ruby thing. But Hemingway was partly responsible for it because—for all his hardcore writing which was good and needed to be done—he did build, at times, this sort of Hollywood plastic-image sort of thing, and what many call his greatest work, the thing that appeared in LIFE week by week installments, was a returning to his youthful formula of strength and victory and death and bravado straight on down the line, the only thing being he was no longer young, the snows had melted, and when he put the gun to his head he was putting the death to ungrowing cancer, and that the public (*Life*) was ready at the same time as he was ready, this was sad.

And, now having neatly disposed of Hem and Miller, which is a kind of a bitchy thing, but all writers are bitches clothed in articles of the sun, and I am sad because we are all such bitches, all so unreal, and maybe it comes back to the thing I was thinking during the then years drunken blackness: that real men don't WRITE. But, if they don't, WHERE ARE THEY? I have looked, everywhere. [* * *]

p.s. I guess *The Old Man and the Sea* was presented in ONE installment in *Life*. no matter; same god damn thing.

[To Jon and Louise Webb]
December 18, 1963

I, too, am shot. They have machine gunned me down with their labors and I have bought their plan, god damn them, I've got to get the horses moving, no rich women around I can bear . . . 12 hours of madness a night, left shoulder, arm and neck, I mean right shoulder arm and neck about paralyzed and then insomnia, go back moth-eyed and white to the spider mouth and they suck again, and as you can see all this is making me a withered crank. . . . Like the old poem, or something like it: we need time to stop and stare* and blow cigar smoke in the air. [* * *]

* "What is this life if full of care, / We have no time to stand and stare?"—from "Leisure" by W. H. Davies, a popular anthology poem.—*Ed.*

[To Jon and Louise Webb]
December 25, 1963

Christmas night and they've battered their heads together until they are silly and they've smiled themselves silly and vomited on the floor, 98% of them amateur drinkers, amateur Christians, amateur human beings; and I got 4 more books yesterday and lined them up with the other, they stand there, each one different, each one a piece of something, and they are FOR SALE, anybody can have one for $10, double the price on the jacket, for this is the cost of the paper alone (to me), and the labor and the poems and all else is FREE. Yet how can you put a price on anything like this? [* * *] You and I don't have much to do with money because we know that money is beside the point, except enough of it to keep you alive so that you can do something else BESIDE $$$. This is what you've done bringing out this book in this way, and when I hang a $10 on it, it is not an insult, just enough to allow me to KEEP ALL THE BOOKS because I like them lined up against the wall, although I did give one away to Sherman because I am supposed to get one back of his wherein I did the foreword and I wonder what in the hell I said in the foreword like some John William Corrington who did o.k. but luckily I do not wear hats.

●

• 1 9 6 4 •

[To Ann Bauman]
January 2, 1964

the wind is blowing singing inside of my head with holy tiger's feet and also banging the shade and I have pulled down the dirty window, and it's all over, god, it's all over, xmas, New Year's night, and now I feel better, almost as good as they pretended to feel, these hardhearts, these shards, these sharks, and now the woman downstairs beats on the ceiling with the end of a broom handle, my typewriter disturbs her, it punctuates the Javanese exotic head-sounds of her T.V. Well, it is a god damned bad fix, and we go on. Wow. Walking the streets. Drinking coffee. Writing letters to ladies in Sacramento. Another cigarette. A Parliament. Go with cancer. I will be sorry. I will be. I remember reading a book by by . . . shit, he was one of my favorites, yet I cannot remember his name . . . yes, Knut Hamsun, book about a nut house and one of the patients, he was called the Suicide, always talking about it, you know, and then one day the building caught on fire and who came crawling laboriously painfully like a snail down the hot rain pipe? Of course, the S.

And this is enough wind for early 64. [* * *]

The book of poems here envisioned appeared as Cold Dogs in the Courtyard *from Literary Times-Cyfoeth in 1965.*

99

[To Jon and Louise Webb]
January 4, 1964

[* * *] I have been kind of dreaming lately, in spite of *It Catches*, which shows you how we go on like grub, I have been thinking of the 4 books and the stuff I have written; and with these 4 editors I have . . . I have had no part in the selection, didn't want to, didn't trust myself, and yet lately I have been thinking that what the 4 have skipped (much of it) is not only pretty good stuff but maybe my best??? This is a hell of a statement I know. And so I was hoping to get somebody to run these poems in book form; I was going to write a foreword telling a little about how things work, and this is what is left, and god damn you, reader, what do you think? I was going to call the book *Cold Dogs in the Courtyard*, meaning rejected poems, of course. [* * *]

I hear from people on the book, answer them, but without being too much of a prick I try to insert the idea that maybe the creation of ART could be more important than my writing letters to them— or anybody writing letters to them. Hand-holding won't get it done. 4 walls can teach more about writing than any praise-mongering lying friend or person. I am not Hemingway but even not being Hemingway I never considered writing to Hemingway or asking him anything, or worse: telling him anything. I did, however, consider writing *myself*, and once or twice I did. maybe 3 times. I am a very powerful influence on myself. This happened in Philadelphia and I was not lonely. There is something wrong with me: I am never lonely. It could get that way. I could get doddy. The world can work on you, trick you. The traps. My man Jeffers spoke of this. Beware the g.d. traps . . . that trapped God

> when he
> walked on earth.

Those are some pretty good lines. If I can ever learn to write as well as Jeffers I will throw all the apples on my table out of the window and they can have me. [* * *]

[To Jon and Louise Webb]
January 10, 1964

[* * *] Don't remember writing a long letter but if you got one, fine. Sometimes when there is plenty of beer and cigars and the electric light hits the white paper and the chopper chops and that whore downstairs doesn't bang on my floor I go on and on, a little cracked, kind of hypnotic, smoke and cold beer and PAP PAP PAP PAP PAP, and this, too, is good for what is left of the soul. [^ ^ ^]

"Frances" is Frances Smith, who had recently become pregnant with Bukowski's daughter, Marina.

[To Ann Bauman]
January 23, 1964

Frances says she will write in a couple of days.

Little here. New tenant downstairs knocks on her ceiling (my floor) when I type. This, of course, disturbs the thought context all to hell. Doesn't she know that I am the great Charles Bukowski? the bitch!!

Cold here and the life force drags on within, dull, putrid, limping. The job is white light, heat and madness. But then, starvation is a bother, and with either course I feel the coward.

Blighted god damned roaring stinking world.

Cheer up, dear.

the works,

101

[Unknown Addressee]
January 28, 1964

You knock on my floor when I type within hours. Why in the hell don't you keep your stupid t.v. set *down* at 10:30 tonight? I don't complain to managers, but it seems to me that your outlook is very one-sided.

    H. Bukowski
    Apt. #303

[Reply to Above]

[Sir:
It is not my T.V. set you hear, I don't have it loud at any time.
I was told you work from 5:30, but your machine is going day night and Sunday. It is like living beneath an arsenal.
This is an apt house not a business establishment. You have had your television on loud until midnight and later. It sounds as if you have all kinds of machinery up there.
You would not be allowed all that noise and racket in any apt house where people live for peace and quiet.
I have been in this house 26 years, and have inquired from many people, and you are out of line.

    apt. 203]

[To Jon and Louise Webb]
February 5, 1964

Thanks for sending the review. On the review: I don't think I am "tough" but if the poetry appears that way it is only because they are used to a different content and style. I am more tired than anything and if I refuse to get heated-up over a Sunrise or the blooming of a peony, they think this is tough. Rest of review pretty much on stick, though, and does your printing achievement some justice, and should move some copies. Whoever wrote the article seemed to enjoy the book, and that's all we want, that, and to get down off the cross.

102

Sorry on your finances on #4. You put so much time and $$ into book that you smashed yourself, and yet that you got carried on this wave, you must know, is not all loss. What happens to people when they see it, the incredulous wonder and awakening . . . I am not speaking of the poetry but of the book, the makeup . . . Frances' daughter wrote to her and she said when she got book she just held it in her hand for an hour, looking through it, at it, not even reading the poems. It is this awakening of the people with beauty in a world where beauty hardly exists anymore, where we are all too "tough," this kind of thing, just looking and wondering, it's still in people, somewhere, but it takes an act like yours to bring it back.

"Purples" were special colophon sheets for a more expensive issue of It Catches My Heart in Its Hands. *The letter to Tibbs mentioned here is reproduced as an illustration in this volume.*

[To Jon and Louise Webb]
February 7, 1964

[* * *] I stole 2 excerpts from letter to Ben Tibbs tonight for purples. I hope he does not think me a zero for this. Wrote letter first without thought of anything—then got "purples" on mind. [* * *]

[To Ann Bauman]
February 18, 1964

Mind all clogged with useless things—can't get straight—but glad book did something for you—but as you know—it's only the *next* poem that counts, and, then, it hardly counts.

Depressed and jammed-up against small things forever, that's the way if works. 4 day cold. other scratches.

The book itself is a kind of small miracle to rest against—temporarily.

Looks like you've got a good typewriter. Don't get robbed again.

Mothers are particularly painful because the world has rubbed most of them down to small utterings of inanity. [* * *]

[To Jon and Louise Webb]
March 1, 1964

[* * *] I am getting a little drunk, a good wall to hide behind, the coward's flag. I remember once in some city in some cheap room, I believe it was St. Louis, yes, a hotel on the corner and the gas fumes of traffic going to work used to come up and choke my sick lazy lungs, and I'd send her out for beer or wine and she was trying to get me straight, trying to mother me or hang me or figure me, as all women will try to do, and she gave me this old bit: "Drinking is only escapism." Sure, I told her, and thank old red-balled God it is, and when I fuck you, that is escapism too, you may not think it is, to you it might be living, now, let's have a drink.

I wonder where she is now? A big fat black maid with the fattest biggest most loveliest legs in the universe and ideas about "escapism." I wonder if she's thinking of me now, sitting here 20 years later growling about stolen microphones and that the human race is garbage?

Frances pregnant, looks as if I'll have to move from here, looks like marriage (again) and disorder but hoping for more suave luck and grace to help me this time, I would not hope to be cruel to either woman or child, god give me grace for I am weak and sad and do not feel good, but if any disorder happens . . . let it be in my life, not theirs. [* * *]

Frances is a good woman, she gets a little snappish and churlish at times but they all do, and I pretend I am asleep or I do not hear and it soon passes over . . . She kind of has this coffeehouse attitude, appears determined to save and understand all mankind, and this is a kind of obvious and tiring nobility, the other night she fell asleep reading *The People's World,* and then she goes to a writers' workshop, which, of course, is kind of obnoxious to me, always has been; but, then, I have my racetracks and beer and my nice beer drinking friends . . . It all comes out fairly even, depending upon whose head you are looking out of. Like, I imagine the guys who burned Joan of Arc had some strong ideas of why they were doing it. Ah?

104

I still feel good that Genet liked the book. He is one of the few geniuses of our flat age, moongone stealing immoral unimmortal cheap age. There seems so little; it is like being locked in a tin room that they are heating up and it gets hotter hotter and then you are just finally a flake of black shit. I speak not of death but of the *wearing* qualities of our age, the gross similarities. You can speak with a leader of nations or with a cleaner of spittoons and they will tell you the same things, they will look the same. We need more light than this or it gets too dull or drab to go on. Genet does this. He's like a flower in a coal pit.

Haydn's symphony #99 on now. I guess I haven't heard all of Haydn's symphonies; I guess few men have. It is good to have workmen like this around. It does damn well get hard to move on now and then, to open a door, to get dressed, to take your clothes to the laundry, to think of a way to get money, to try to sleep, to try to love to listen, everything gets hard, it gets harder, and I will not scream when death comes I will look at it like the little faint green lace vines they spread between flowers of large bouquets, and I will go without damage of transition, like a man taking his dog out to walk.

[To Jon and Louise Webb]
March 2, 1964

[* * *] Frances says you should come to Los Angeles but I do not agree. This is one big town full of phonies, as you realize. Arizona has such nice little lizards and horny toads running through the hot sand or sitting on top of big rocks looking at you. You can't get that here. I remember once walking out of a small Arizona town, the sun came down like magic, all yellow still, I kept going out into the desert, there was nobody around, not a human in sight. I almost didn't come back. But as you see, I have. [* * *]

By the way, in case you do do the book, I still, at this moment lean to the title *For Regions Lower than Crying,* although I may come up with a later preference, I could go with this one without being hurt too much; the title fits the series of edgy sequence of my titles, makes sense thru the looking glass. . . . Although I realize this title might bear a first similarity to A. E. Housman's "Brooks Too Broad for Leaping," but whereas Housman's title relates directly to death, the impossibility of escaping it, mine relates to the utter sadness, the almost unbearability of existence. [* * *]

[To Jon and Louise Webb]
March 11, 1964

[* * *] Two people down at the mill think I have cancer. Maybe I am starting to smell? Anyhow, feel god awful weak and only feel good in bed, but probably only the cause of too much drinking and gambling and working at the same time, and down where I am getting it you have to work and sweat and bleed for it, I do mean. The people are half wild with fear and something they know not of; they tremble and jerk with work neurosis, all cackling flat laughter of the deserted innards, and I am beginning to feel that way too; it is contemptuous what we have done to life and the living and ourselves. I was hoping for luck and skill in the gambling to free me but this too appears only another trap where they throw sand on the living. All the traps, and I walk into all the traps, every one that's there, I spread myself with olive oil and ointment, with hemorrhoid salve and I say *whoops,* LET'S GO, BABIES!!!

It's a hell of a juncture to bust loose and I guess I'll never bust loose, not writing poetry, and it appears I can't even do that anymore, and I sure can't go the novel, not the way I feel, the novel seems like nothing but WORK, a grandiose concept of saying a lot of nothing, and I guess the idea of the poems, good or bad, is to keep me from going crazier. I could pay money to hear some psychiatrist tell me this, and then we'd both feel better; only he'd feel better than I because he'd have my money and a nice secretary to look at walking around the room and to fuck. ah, wilderness, my wilderness. [* * *]

I reread Camus' *The Stranger* the other night and once again this appeared to me to be the perfect antidote for what was essentially wrong with the resolve in *Crime and Punishment.* It is so good that others do this work for us so that we do not have to do it ourselves.

Children outside gyrating, seeing grass and mystery and freedom, and parental tyranny too; but they (the holy children) will be melded down, they become me: an old man at 4 o'clock in the afternoon writing tea-leaf thoughts in a vestibule that smells of bacon and frogs and tumbling silence.

106

From now until the end of the book, the letters all bear the new address given in the following letter.

[To Jon and Louise Webb]
May 1, 1964

We have moved to—
    5126¼ De Longpre Ave.
    Los Angeles 27, Calif.
Old 1623 is gone and it was a magic number and a magic place, but after 6 years there *is* some wear and tear especially after no repairs or replacements of any sort. However, the landowners and their serfs (managers) always holler, charge too much and feel as if they were doing *you* a favor. Narrow-minded bigots that you have to sneak women past and not be seen drunk and not do this and not do that etc. etc.; all this time you are sharing the place with rats and bugs and old churchly women who poke and grovel and skitter and clog the halls of your brain, ugghg. They even called the police on me one night (a couple of years back) and I held them off through the door chain and talked them away. Anyway, don't send any mail there as it may never reach me. They are pissed because I threw a few glasses of whiskey against the walls, bled on the rug & almost died several times and because the water pipes broke continually in the walls and they had to rip their walls open and I was there, usually in bed hungover sick unhappy with their pipes and their bodies their intrusions upon my tiniest of moments. May those whore-hating finks rot before they reach hell. I have spoken. [* * *]

I don't know where to get a *Village Voice*; if you manage to get an extra copy do send on—this address. It is more difficult, I suppose, to be a *discovered* poet; you've got to carry the load on your soul-back and when you sit down to a typer you are supposed to *do* it. I'd rather be loose, even bad-loose. The name in lights thing is good, of course, especially when you're feeling down—you let yourself taste a little, like a drink, only you know that it doesn't change the *living* life . . . a few more door-knockers, but these soon go away when you don't walk upside down from the ceiling. [* * *]

I tried to make a tape of poems a week or so ago. Started o.k. but got too drunk and started talking too much between poems and I didn't care for it when I played it back. [* * *] I think it best to "talk" the poems instead of poeticizing them, make them "natural" as you suggested. [* * *]

The bookseller Jim Roman also published some books of poetry, among them Corrington's Anatomy of Love.

[To Jon and Louise Webb]
May 4, 1964

Got Corrington's *Anatomy of Love* today. very *very* fine stuff in there, what I've read, he's come along a lot, and it's all much better than his novel and it seems a damned shame we can't keep him always with the poem; the novel may eat him up—I hope not.

Very little today. The cats still walk around. One of them ate a bird the other day. I won't talk to the son of a bitch for a week. As you know, I am sometimes not a realist. I can't take it. [* * *]

[To Ann (Bauman) Menebroker]
May [6, 1964]

good on the marriage.

yes, those long-distance calls tho' they cost us dearly in $$ were MORALE, and very odd and yet a fulfilling strange thing.

I am not married but might as well be. I am in strange country, fairly unhappy, dismantled but no need to be cruel. You can only save what you have left and if that is very little then to hell with it. The flowers die too.

Take care as they say around town, und don't forget ye Muse.

The review by Frances Smith under the name S. S. Veri appeared in Chat Noir Review, *vol. 2, no. 3. The Webbs' new address was in Santa Fe, but they moved back to New Orleans after less than a week* (Hank, p. 139).

108

[To Jon and Louise Webb]
May 12, 1964

aw right, I shoot you something pomes?? to yr new address
to shew u I am still putting my socks on and also enclose knew
chat noir revue wich Frances ast me to en clothes shee is part ed.
and wrote review a *It Catches* wich mite bee pred. but so? und also
she writes under name of S. S. Veri I think some quite good
poems but some other stuff by other peeple in thair I don' kare 4.
[* * *]

[To Jon and Louise Webb]
June 12, 1964

[* * *] I think the oddest thing I have ever heard, I could call
it funny but I have been drinking too much tonight today, was a
woman editor-poetess, they were putting out a special issue or
something of convict poets or what the hell, and she was disturbed
because "these men could not rise, seemingly, above their circumstances . . . all they seemed to write about was wanting to get
out of jail, and why they should not be there . . ."
   my god, her pretty pussy should some night some years sit there
not getting out, not even for the moon, not even for a walk down
to the corner for a dull newspaper, does she know what it means
to walk back and forth a certain space and *only* that space and that
no matter what you say, no matter how you SCREAM, that that space
will not widen except through death or pardon or insanity? and even
then? fuck it. Jon, you know. when I by god get letters from cunts
like this I near vomit, I look to the sun to make me well. that it grows
these blind children.

[To Jim Roman]
[July 1, 1964]

yes, by god, no one is more pleased than I to be the victim of another magic book of the starving Webbs' gutwork and pure glad madness. I don't know about the poems. I know they could print a cookbook that would bring tears to the ears. (and eyes too!) Rexroth was right (in review) when he said my press was too good. but it's like a beautiful woman asking to go to bed with you—what are you going to do? turn her away? ah no, not even at my age! [* * *]

I don't hear any more from Willie [Corrington] and I guess he's shipping in from England, all lost and hooded in the pages of his second novel. I just hope he doesn't get too efficient about turning them out, but I'm a crank and a puritan and a nut this way: always carrying what's left of my soul in a little glass jar in my pocket like a fishing worm. [* * *]

[To Kay Johnson, preceded by note to Jon and Louise Webb]

Dear Jon & Lou:
Letter I wrote to Kaja some time back. Forwarded all over Europe, then came back to me.—B.

[*handwritten:*]
September 15, 1964

Dear Kaja—
All right, I know it was a drunken letter and you've got to stop stealing my stuff! Anyhow you said Copenhagen, so here I am writing to Copenhagen. [* * *]

[*typewritten:*]
you know, u really kant get the ingress into a WORD without the typer, the typer is the carver, the ax, the cleaver, the thing with the mouth that hollers about the bloody dice. it machineguns the mind out of penury. fuck the pen. anyhow, I am sitting around feeling my arms and legs and balls, trying to figure out if I am real or not. I must be: about 3 a.m. I wiped my ass. the sun is just right

today, kind of an icy tired yellow, limp vain vaindog of a sky. bull. listen, do you know what we are trying to do? are we crazy or do we mean something with our poems, or is it children's games, or tricks, or colored water? we gotta have blood! bloody shades in cheap hotels; mortar in the streets, shellholes! hoar-frosted wine! and young girls running wild down the streets chased by hungry dogs! my god my god, everything is so dull. even the bomb will be dull. it won't last. we won't last. this is profound. YOU HAVE NO IDEA HOW *profound* this is. all right, listen, don't mess up too much in Cope.—I remain sitting in the sun, 44 years old, 3 or 4 blocks south of HOLLYWOOD, my god my god, and for it all it is a good day, I am not too sick today although I may hit the first man I meet on the street square in the face.

[To Ann Menebroker]
October 25, 1964

[* * *] have been reading *Saint Genet* by Sartre who turned down Nobel's 52 grand while waiting on a cheese sandwich. S.G. badly written for most part, but good shafts of light there, involuted, and somewhat fascinating like a little box of rusty razor blades. If you have leisure to mull without tension you can pick up a big fat paperback copy for a dollar and a quarter. Genet, of course, was preceded as a robber-verse writer by Villon, who if I remember, was banned from Paris. Genet, more-like, has it made. [* * *]

"Snow Bracero" and 3 other poems appeared in Jacaranda 6, *February 1965 (Dorbin C259-261).*

[To Joel Climenhaga]
October 26, 1964

I got your o.k. on the 5 poems and hope you will send me a copy of whichever Transient Press mag or mags these might appear in

[* * *] "Snow Bracero" I had some fun writing, not fun but flew . . . something . . . I used to write the short story some time back but generally dislike short story on waste of wordage principle but if I can get a story line into what I consider a poem-form I am happy enough, or as happy as I will be? [* * *]

Douglas Blazek, notes Bukowski, "was, perhaps, the foremost leader of the Mimeo Revolution with his magazine Ole. *He was also a good writer, quite prolific, and an excellent and interesting correspondent." Blazek accepted three Bukowski poems for the first issue of* Ole, *initiating one of Bukowski's most extensive and most sustaining correspondences of the 1960s.*

[To Douglas Blazek]
[October 28, 1964]

[* * *] fine, I got your o.k. on the 3 poems, and while I have a theory that rejection is good for the soul, the theory seems to work best when it applies to others.

bio: born 8-16-20. began writing poetry at age of 35. 5 collections of poetry with a 6th, *Crucifix in a Deathhand* to be issued by Loujon Press and Lyle Stuart, Inc. early, in 1965. That's it.

Rough night in the pit last night, bastard on one side telling me how great he was and bastard on other side telling me how great he was, meanwhile the workwhip flashing like a cobra hung to a windmill. [* * *]

my neck hurts. I seem to be dying of something—maybe life— or maybe no young ass. well. listen: bottom of paper here. slipping out of typer. going. hold and luck.

[To Douglas Blazek]
late October 1964

got your letter, and poems enclosed for your consideration.

luck with your mad venture, but hope you get some hard knockers (eventually) because poetry is dying on the vine like a whore on the end stool on a Monday night.

I am snotted-up today, dismal, flu maybe, or maybe just 44 years, a lot of them drunk, anyhow all bent over and have had 2 shots for neuritis from a doc over Hollywood Blvd. who yachts to Catalina too much, and I straightened up a little. He keeps me waiting an hour each time and all I could do was peek at the cunt walking down on the street below and I got rocks but there was nothing he could give me for that.

the woman wants to put food on this table. I've got to get out.

[To Jon and Louise Webb]
October 31, 1964

well, since no pomes I mite as well untrundle the old bullshit harp, but it's not bullshit when I say I got your tired card and know the job has you by the throat, and worn, and I send a white prayer of luck and love for whatever good it might or might not do, and yes, send a page if you get around to it, there's nothing like being tired and tired and tired so you can't sleep or think of hope, but if this book comes anywhere near what you did with *It Catches* I will know that the good angels are near you even if they refuse to do the slave-rote work of drudgery and guts. I wish I could say something to help you through except that I am so often in muddled state and tired too, but if it helps, and it might not,—a book like this lifts my life up into light whether I deserve it or not. I used to have a theory that if I could just make *one* person's life happy or real that would have been otherwise, then my own life would not have failed. It was a good theory but a few whores ran me through the wringer for it, but I do think that for a while a few of them enjoyed not being spit on for a while, and so this made it o.k. for me. [* * *]

[To Jon and Louise Webb]
November 1, 1964

[* * *] Very drunk last night. The landlord and his wife came over and we slugged it down. His wife became rather upset when she saw the kitchen and the bathroom. Frances is not a very good housekeeper. But I calmed her down and got her to insulting me. I had let some gypsies straighten out my car for $30 and she said I shouldn't have done this. What should we do, let these people starve? There were 3 of them, 2 boys and an old man with a huge belly. They saw me typing and drinking beer at the window and came up and talked. We haggled at price a little while and then I told them to go ahead. They didn't do a bad job. When I handed the old man the 30 he bent down over his belly, bowed and said, "God bless you, son." I figure that was worth the 30 right there. Nobody ever said "God bless you, son," to me before. [* * *]

[To Douglas Blazek]
November 4, 1964

write a book? a novel? I am too lazy, too sick, and such a waste of words, and they wouldn't print it, so why not break it down into poetic toothaches, all not so cumbersome, and I doubt I could stick to the subject, I am not that interested in any area of life or that disinterested either.

they all go the way of novels and then there's nothing left.

of course, I am a whore, and if you know anybody who can advance me $500 I will do the trick because then I know I will be able to write it the way I want to, but you know and I know that nobody like this is going to come along, and so I won't go into the cleaver, and there's some thanks in this.

what was I doing before the age of 35 when I began writing poetry? dying, sweetheart, dying. kind of like. you see, I started with the short story, starving in little rooms around the country and drinking too much cheap wine, and I'd mail the things out to *The Atlantic Monthly* or *Harpers* and when they came back I tore them up. I used to write 8 or 10 stories a week. All I'd do was write these stories and drink as much as possible. Then I heard of *Story*, Whit

Burnett, and at least *he* sent written rejects most of the time, and I finally landed my first story there at age of 24. Then a few other places, and then the drink took over. The writing seemed foolish—a con game, a game of prigs and English teachers, a dullard's game. I worked some of the time, very little of the time, and how I made it I really don't know. Drinking was the god. No matter what city, what year, what time. In Philly I used to knock on this bar door at 5:30 a.m. An old bartender used to be mopping up then prior to opening. He'd let me in and I'd sit there listening to the wet flub of the strings behind me. He gave me free drinks and he had some himself. I'd stay in that bar until closing at 2 a.m. That's not much sleep, you've got to admit, but it came in handy when I was totally broke and starving—I'd climb into the sack and sleep for a week. I got kicked out of room after room for being drunk and no rent and for bringing in women late at night. There was no grand plan here, no totality of sense, I wasn't looking for anything. It was just sunlight and rain and snow and nightmares and walking around and the drink in front of me. As I say I worked sometimes and the jobs were all bad and low paying and monotonous and searing and they still are. I am unable to do any kind of work with proficiency and have no trade. Anyhow, at 35 the drink and the women had caught up with me. I ended up in the charity ward of the local hospital spewing blood out of my mouth and ass, completely fallen apart, done. They let me lay there 2 days before somebody came along and decided I needed a transfusion. 9 pints of blood plus the glucose. They'd found out I'd picked up a blood credit somewhere. meanwhile my whore smashed up my old car in the streets.

I came out 900 years older. Found a job as a shipping clerk somewhere and got hold of a typewriter. I started writing poems. One of the first batches I sent to a little magazine in Texas. They went. I finally ended up in Texas with 75 cents in my pocket married to the editoress whose father was a millionaire. After 2 years of marriage she decided I was a bastard and there went the million. I had begun drinking again. And writing more poems. I am still in bad shape physically and don't know how long I can make it.

The job I have now is no better than the rest. I am still alive. a woman just left with an 8 week old baby. they are both mine. they went for a walk. I am writing Balzac. There is a fly on the screen. now he is gone.

this is a kind of kernel of things. a man can get bored with another man's life. I don't want to hang you up. but you asked.

trick or treat? yes, I went to the door too. the woman was in the tub. here were 2 little girls with their big-assed big-titted young and sexy and silly mamas, and I stood there in my blood-stained bathrobe, open at the front, torn shorts, 3 day beard, cigar in one hand, can of beer in the other, and I stood there thinking of raping the 2 mamas, but they didn't seem scared at all, I was just an old man in the doorway, and I turned around, put down beer and cigar, and shot the candy into their paper bags: FLOP FLIP FLAP! and they said thank you thank you and they walked off with their sexy silly mamas who were wiggling wiggling wiggling in the moonlight all on fire FIRE! and I went back in and emptied the beercan.

the fly came back on the window screen. I swung the rolled-up newspaper and missed. you see how it goes around here.

hot damn! I got him this time!

the horns of grief need no honing.

[To Douglas Blazek]
[November 23, 1964]

everything finally kills us from carrots to the timeclock or no timeclock at all, and it's the faces that kill us too: faces like putty granite with raisin eyes snapped in, and the way they walk and the way they laugh and love and hate and drive their cars and piss into the diminishing areas of our lives. we are the pitiful beggars—we don't even want the coin, we are so sick we don't know why.

the drink kills me and saves me too, my whole insides have fallen apart; hemorrhage Friday, coughed up a half pint of blood, but you've heard all this, and even now the old fingers, once again, rip down on the typer, and I listen to some rotten half-ass classical music for the in-between hammerheads who have not fallen asleep yet . . . don't worry about a botched-up *Ole*, we are not mechanics, we are lazy, fumbling, aching from the shrill pipes and ugly whores, listen, try to get the CONTENT, that's all. the best living poet I know of is Al Purdy, 185 Wellington St., Belleville, Ontario, Canada. (Belleville? Bensenville?) You might right him write him and tell him of *Ole*, hide nothing, tell him it's only mimeo but talk a little bit about what you think (my suggestion) & ask him if he might send something rejected dejected or otherwise. It will be good. whatever it is. I have

116

read his collection *Poems for All the Annettes* and I turned the pages one by one reading in a state of pisspoorpissgreatstun within myself at what he was doing. he writes like chopping down trees; he writes about those bees that are stinging the inside of his head. he lays the words down as if they were real instead of angelcake. he might not be able to send you anything for one reason or another, but I'd suggest a try??? I don't know if he's still at above address but I think if you try your letter will be forwarded unless he's dead, and he was drinking a lot of homemade wine the last time I heard from him.

I don't expect *Ole* to last too long and I tell you this because I am a donkey-hard old man and it's better you know it straight in case you haven't guessed. The same 50 poets are writing the same crap over and over again in America. You'll get tired of it. I am. you'll get tired of turning the crank and taking abuse from half-talents. your wife will want love, your factory body will want rest; you will to write. the sour cream will spin up in your mouth and you will spit it out, *Ole* will go down the crapper.

I tried turning the crank once at something called *Harlequin*, I sent 3, 4, 5, 6 page rejections to poetry that came in, talking about everything from big-assed women to T. S. Eliot and what came back?: WHO THE HELL ARE YOU? they wrote, I'VE NEVER SEEN YOUR NAME ON ANY OF THE LITTLE MAGAZINES ANYWHERE? WHAT GIVES YOU A RIGHT TO TELL ME HOW TO WRITE? HORSE-SHIT! etc. I was surprised at the venom. these people reminded me more of traffic-cops, bankers, foremen, factory owners, clerks, teachers, and I guess . . . that is what they were. But I hadn't suggested to them HOW to write, I'd only suggested why I didn't care to print that particular group of poems. I never *claimed* to be a poet. I claimed to be some type of editor who intended to print some type of thing when it came along, but, only once or twice did it come along. I stopped cranking or my wife divorced me, or anyhow, that's past. but it wasn't long before I was drunk again at high noon, fallen down in back alleys with dogs sniffing at my feet to see if I was alive or kids poking sticks in my back to see if I was alive and truck drivers pulling up short and getting out to look and see if I were still alive. What decision, they arrived at I don't know. also, my grammar hasn't improved since then and spelling is harder than fucking when you don't want to while intoxicated. [* * *]

There is nothing worse than talking about poetry or poets or ourselves, is there? It keeps us from doing the thing. It keeps us from the knife, maybe, or the red hot poem blue flame smashing, through

117

the wall hollering blowing bugle & slobbering the real good tears that will bring all the priests and whores and clouds and garage mechanics and Sir Winston Churchill into the same quiet bar to talk about mice and waste and grass and towers and strange things like people with beautiful eyes, fine candy bars, new symphony music or the great color of the bartender's shirt. [* * *]

Bukowski's review of Layton's Laughing Rooster *appeared in* Evidence *no. 9.*

[To Douglas Blazek]
[December 1, 1964]

[* * *] all drab, drab. and it's that kind of day, drizzle, damnation, the plants heave and puff in air that has no air, the plants sweat and the screens crawl with the one or 2 stupid lost flies of summer, who have somehow failed to find a spider, who have somehow failed to die. my 12 weeks old daughter wails in the other room; her cries cut through all my poems, all my writing, but she is a sweetie, they have not gotten to her yet, she is all eyes and skin, she bends, she bubbles . . . she wails. now the old woman comes in with the kid and she sits in a chair at my elbow, as I type and she has the kid and the radio plays *In the Clock Store,* badly, and I'd like to say, Listen, don't you realize that I AM WRITING TO BLAZEK! WHAT THE HELL IS WRONG WITH YOU TWO BROADS? (do you hear the cuckoo? she asks. do you hear the alarm clock? she asks.) well, kid, there has always been something, some woman screaming for a bottle of wine or the landlord at the door for his rent or the police with a passkey or God's left-handed angel stealing my cigarettes from the dresser. well, this will be a lousy letter. sometimes I stand a better chance. Sometimes she is busy with something important—like reading a *New Yorker* in the other room.

I remember one, this one was a looker, I was drunk all the time and how I made it I'll never know, or I will, the horses were going very well this year and a half, I could do no wrong: I didn't know what I was doing, just one long run of luck (good) and I drank it drank it and kept going to bed with this woman with all that body, and I remember one night I drank so much (I had been hitting it at the track all day) that I fell off the couch and I was down there on the floor and I saw these LEGS smooth cool nylon magic filled down into those spikes, my god, magic, and that placid face looking down at me and she was smoking and I saw the earrings and I could feel the rug on my neck and the whole world swirling around: buildings full of janitors, jails full of quiet men held in a web, alleys of murder, swans asleep on lakes and I looked up at her from the floor and I said: I'M A GENIUS AND I'M THE ONLY ONE IN THE WORLD WHO KNOWS IT!

Blazek, she looked at me for maybe 20 seconds and then she said YOU DAMN FOOL, GET UP FROM THE FLOOR!

and she was right and I did get up, I laughed and walked over and poured myself a glass of whiskey and looked at those legs. electricity yellow and whiskey yellow and nylon colored legs. she's dead now and the legs do not look so good anymore but I can't blame her for that.

[* * *] On Layton, he's up in Canada, I don't know where. You can probably contact him through Alan Bevan (editor) c/o *evidence*, Box 245, Station [*illegible*], Toronto 5, Ontario, Canada. Bevan sent me his latest book *The Laughing Rooster* to review, which I have done, and am waiting on word whether it's going to run or not. I tore a little meat but also went on in waving wands of glory over some of the poems. Layton's been around a while and maybe the way the teeth of the machine work, too long. he's getting to be a craftsman. I mean in his own way. not theirs. but it's still bad. he's finding it's too easy to lay it down and make it sound good. the words flow off the ribbon good, but not just quite right. this comes from working the bull, from knowing the steps, knowing the crowd, when and how to hook the sword perfectly and bring in the ears and the tail too and bring down that BIG one out of the stands for later over the springs zeep zeeep zeep ZEEP, another sword. But Layton—even with knowing too much what he is doing, is still far ahead of the rest.— how many people will come through for you with work, I do not know. the poets I have met are generally notorious snobs, they are not very good people. what I mean is, some of these Awrtists . . . might think mimeo below their dignity. really, most of them eventually buy the shadows, they buy the stink . . . the *New Yorker* or *The Atlantic* can wave them on in with a dollar bill and get them to stick their heads right up that dirty crotch. I don't understand it, there is very little that I do understand. If *Life* magazine walked

in with their cameras they'd smile and smirk and pose and talk like highschool boys with their first drink working toward the first dizzy worthless bitch dressed in taffeta. I mean, you may write these boys, and they may write well but I am not responsible for the rust and bologna that crawls into the soul and makes a snob or a prick or a jackass or a fink out of a man who can, or who once could, lay down a good line.

—the old woman says to give her love to your 3 year old. I give my love to your lucky dog who can't speak English. give your wife a kiss from me too. arrg, we are getting sloppy. some good classical stuff on now. I go the classical & the new experimental & the 12 tone, which of course, is now old. we all get old so fast. I like jazz too when I like it.—I've got to get ready to go in to the pit. my back aches already. I can see now the sheer empty bash of faces, the screaming guggling words; the dumpling of a foreman in his white shirt and eyes of spit . . . the blood is everywhere.

hold to something.

[To Douglas Blazek]
December 8, 1964

Harlequin was a grunion, a brick goblet, a drowning moll, and there was something about a dwarf, a dwarf at the door and I had 75 cents in my pocket and it was early morning in Texas and she stayed in bed and the d. took me out and showed me showed me the old man's lands and lakes and belongings and I was not impressed and I did not say anything only rather yawned but the dwarf thot I was a sharpy he thot I married her for money which wasn't exactly so and I do not want to tell you exactly what it was because it was more personal on her part than mine and more sacrificial on my part than hers & dollars be damned, and it didn't last, of course, she had the millions coming and wrote bad poetry and I had 75 cents and wrote poetry, and there I was and she had the magazine and then she wasn't too interested and left submissions in the closet or under the sofa or mixed in with the kotex and I took to answering these things and became more or less a part of the magazine until she met a Persian with a stickpin and a lisp and that led to divorce and then I heard she was in Alaska and she married a Japanese fisherman or school teacher named Kami and Kami had wonderful manners, a gentleman, and *Harlequin* more or less c e a s e d, I could give my god I cd give you more but it's so dry; I think shots of light are best, nice stores tories stories have slivers and yawns.

[* * *] I really don't know if there is enough plentitude of talent to deserve even one magazine. and when I say talent I mean JUICE TO MAKE THE EARS JUMP and the hands look like hands, know they are hands and the window screens to look like mother's panties, I mean SOMETHING. I just don't think it's there—maybe a line or 2, and then limp again, making the same old picture. maybe it's the human race, maybe we're just full of shit and no light, maybe we're still full of shit after we shit it out.

There are many things that bother me. I know that I have never passed a man on the street that I liked—most of them giving off a kind of ether of disgust and stumbling and clay-eating, snot-eating grievance. I don't like the human race at all. this is my confessional, father, pass the wine. [* * *]

[To Douglas Blazek]
December 9, 1964

no murals, noting nothing, the overtime has got me, I am dead, dog-fucked tired and the old woman drops tin cans in the bathtub and walks around complaining that life is hard, the baby is cranky she says and she has a cold and maybe the baby has a cold too. my old woman has had a cold ever since I messed-up with her. well, look. yeah, a cold head too. what I mean. I got *Ole* and the few moments I have left before going into the mill again, maybe I could say something, although I feel my sight is a little twisted today. what's wrong with the foreword, introduction? I agree, we gotta put balls on poetry. this lisping home freak has layed pale in dead libraries long enough, let's bomb on out. [* * *]

let me say off and on and over as time keeps running that it was a lively number a good number and I can say this easy without lying which I have not learned to do yet and so you wanted to know and so now I've told you, & we look FORWARD to more *Ole,* poetry with balls!!

and I will put this in an envelope and tool through traffic, weaving around the old ladies and grinding toward the death, my foot to the floor, all insurance companies have already dropped me and the police leap out from behind the palm trees of night on their scooters to hunt down the nub of snarling over the wheel, go go go!, down Sunset, to Alpine street, then a left and out of car and leap into fire of death and fire of dead faces and why I still will be able to walk around and move my fingers I'll never know. [* * *]

●

· 1 9 6 5 ·

[To Jim Roman]
January 11, 1965

Who the hell is U. Grant Roman via "ML" and signed Jim Roman?

You Rebs oughta forget *that* war awhile. There've been other wars, and I was born in Andernach, Germany, August 16th, 1920. Yet when I bummed through the South, and particularly in Houston, they kept calling me a "Yankee" in the bars and threatened to beat the shit out of me. I always got so drunk, tho, they never got around to it because it wouldn't have been much of a victory. [* * *]

I was re-reading your "Outsider" catalogue the other night, and some odd & pliable & weird & strange assortments in there. I keep thinking of the one woman in there (forget name) who said she'd burn all her works and damn near did. I might say it's refreshing compared to the almost standard preciousness of some of our better talents. If I'd saved all my notebooks I wouldn't be able to move around in this kitchen—or read them either. Yet you can't tell the possible value of some of that stuff, say even later. (their stuff, I mean.)

Imagine having something, say, some scrawls by Whitman or T. S. Eliot or old Ez? Even these jaded fingers might tremble?

Keep the despair bottled. We'll all out under a handful of cropped and drying blooms—

PHILIP HENRY SHERIDAN BUKOWSKI

The essay Blazek accepted was "A Rambling Essay on Poetics and the Bleeding Life Written While Drinking a Six-Pack (Tall)"; it was printed in Ole *no. 2, March 1965.*

[To Douglas Blazek]
[January 13, 1965]

this is still Los Angeles, yes, and it's Jan. 13th. and the rent is due again, and I shove the green into his hands and he drives off in his three cars. Listening to Meyerbeer, an opera, somebody has gone mad and now runs off and sings with her other-self. the bile backs up into a shoal which gets so large ya can never swallow it. I have spoken. Silence in the back rows!

Glad the essay got past you, although I am always ready for the reject, I am a dark alley loser from way back, and I write badly enough when I try and when I don't try, and so all right. Although I drank more than a six pack getting it done. It was 6 writing it in long hand and then 6 or 8 typing it, dropping and adding, translating . . . all right.

No, Purdy didn't tell me he'd send anything. g.d. shame. but we've got to let him live. He's going to the North Pole or something on some crazy kind of grant. He scrapes through the hard way (or the easy way) doing things like this. Maybe he's wiser than we are, we who are walking into those buildings where they scrape the meat and replace the eyes with apple pits and bird droppings.

No, I'm not any good at babies' names, and it's a torturous thing I don't enjoy at all, and always figure it's best to forget the thing and leave it up to the woman since it seems to mean more to them. Except if they come up with something outlandish I can't craw down.

I have nothing, right now, for mimeo press book series although I may try and give you a submission later and glad for invite. Going to New Orleans in March to help Webb wind up *Crucifix* but all I'll prob. do is end up getting him drunk, which isn't very nice, but it's kind of relaxing while it's going on and you're not paying the price until later, ah. If I should submit something it would not be poetry, I think, but rather a wild literary blast rolling zombie easy and graceless headless type of thing, easy on me and perhaps confusing to the reader. I have a title in mind I have been trying to get rid of, *Confessions of a Coward and Man Hater,* and I could encompass a lot under this, like say the time the black in a Dallas hotel

124

came into the room with a poker and wanted to blow me and I opened my blade and sat there and when he got close I lifted it and showed it to him saying, "Oh, be careful, you might CUT yourself!" and he ran from the room with these pig squeals. This kind of stuff is drab to anybody but me, but look you get away with it by erecting a facade: you tell them while all this was going on you had D. H. Lawrence's collected works in your suitcase. I bullshit too much. But I'd like to try it eventually. I have a lot of loose language inside of me.

O.K. to put address with essay. I can handle writers and callers by breaking their hearts and their arms. I do quick work. cheap.

By the way, nobody has sent me $500 to do a novel yet, which is really one hell of a relief. I might find out I can't write a novel. This way is easier. [* * *]

[To Douglas Blazek]
January 25, 1965

the alka seltzer's sparkling and down it goes. depressed fit of cut cat running by without a tail where it had a tail before, or my head is strung like beads around a savage day. All that crap. Anyhow, I have been drinking too much, and on top of that—another kind of mess, and the time has gone by and I haven't done anything, I am ashamed, I am lazy, I am stupid, I am King Kong bending over for a button, I am a torn picture postcard of East Bermuda.

yes, if you get to feeling you want to use any excerpts from any of the letters, lay to it. And don't worry about defamation of character. I have nothing to hide and anything I say in a letter goes anywhere anytime, and if they don't like the taste of it, let them suck empty beer bottles. or their bloody thumb's footprint.

I will submit something for your mimeo series of indecent literature (wild-hair mad talk; not poetry) and if you want to use my name on a circular, go ahead. My only hope is that you will like what I do well enough to print it. My tigers sometimes stumble like mice in wine cellars. But I will probably not be able to write you anything until I get back from New Orleans in late March, early April, after helping Webb wind up *Crucifix*. There's a matter of a few more poems, signing pages, drinking beer and pounding nails, walking the streets at night and moving in and out of the taverns looking for the man without a head, asking the question, waiting for the white bull that smiles. I will do you something for you. A welsh fandango that will clean the fingernails of your soul. o o oh. [* * *]

don't worry about the "bandwagon"; if I'm riding a bandwagon then I guess this blood on my gut is only ketchup and the stones over the heads are only the aria of a multi-color dream that can be snapped off like a carnation. I get all the bayonets when I walk out of the door; I move through them like fields of wild flowers, saying hello to half-buddies, punching time clocks, snarling at supervisors. The young girls look the other way: I spit through a hole where a tooth has rotted out, let the belt out a notch and move on through, and I come back in dazed, punched-out, fooled again, tricked again, wasted again, and the old woman glares at me as I peel the celluloid from the pint of rye and move between the sheets far from the glory of the lucky soldiers and the green-eyed crapshooter. If I am riding a bandwagon, let me get off. The zone of sharpshooters still surround me and they pick me off little by little while humming patriotic hymns and eating bumblebees.

if the world digs me it is only to bury me.

I resent anybody being published because he has a name and only because he has a name, and this is being done much, and I don't understand it, and it's more fag and fart and drag and death, and *Poetry Chicago* is good at it; almost everybody's good at it—publishing name crap when meanwhile some young artist is on fire all flame flame flame FLAME and they let him burn away to knife or razor across the string of wrist or throat while Mr. X-somebody dulls the screams with flat verse on flat-printed expensive paper. [* * *]

[To Douglas Blazek]
Early February 1965

Any drawings or fanciness are not going to be worth a Negro's shitola here to you, but what drew me to your mimeo outfit (*Ole*) was that I thot you were a hard-muscled brain of a drunk laboring lost son-of-a-bitch without a chance like I am.

I can't do you a foreword because if I did you a foreword (on these grounds) there would also be other people I should do a foreword for also.

Look, you are not that great and neither am I—and I don't know where next month's rent or tomorrow's poem is coming from.

I've been drunk for several days (am drunk now) trying to figure how to answer you.

Sorry on the heart-attack thing. But most of us who write don't live too long because we eat ourselves up one way or the other. [* * *]

There are 3 poems here, in this order:

(1) —(great and beautiful)—"Up a Different Creek"

(2) A sweet last line damning us—"Plastic Dimestore Life" and

(3) "Testimony Concerning . . ."

But wait before you inter me with the bones of hard-head disbelievers—

(a) I still believe that more untalented fake poets are being published than ever before.

(b) —I believe that most poetry stinks like the rot of a garbage can, a game of professors & fakers. And

(c) —that writing a foreword to your poetry would do more to destroy you than any heart attack, than any gift of a new cadillac that wd allow you to drive through the latest town of culture and give a wave.

Certainly, I'm drunk and certainly I'm mad, but, also, most certainly, my word won't make your poetry good or your wife and children love you, and, hell, you know this, you've known it a long time. And I don't have to get drunk to tell you and you shouldn't force me to get drunk to tell you—no matter *what* you think of your poetry or any poetry or anybody else's poetry.

I hate to speak like a knowing prick from a pulpit, yet you've put me up in the pulpit, and shit! I've fallen down drunk from there, and I can't help you, I can't help myself. [* * *]

The adverse review by A. Frederick Franklyn that upset Cuscaden, publisher of Run With the Hunted, *appeared in* Grande Ronde Review, *Fall 1964.*

[To Douglas Blazek]
[February 10, 1965]

[* * *] look, just went out to get mail and here's two letters
from Cuscaden, the last airmail and about an attack on me (review
of *Run with the Hunted* by a. frederic franklyn (his lower case)
and Cus quite upset about it, says freddy boy gets "almost hysterical; every low blow known to man (dig such lines as 'the suspiciously
effete contemporaries'!)" "This bastard's harangue amounts to a
disgusting, personal sort of thing . . ." says Cuscaden. I've got
to write Cuss a letter and buck him up. He tells me that Freddy boy
went on for 5 and 1/2 pages. As you know, Franklyn is with *Trace*
and May's right hand agent. I don't go well in Los Angeles I guess
(at least, that). Once I was over at May's, brought my own liquor
and got blasted. I get nasty sometimes this way and May later
phoned me and said, "You couldn't have meant those things you
said about me; you must have been talking to a face on the couch,
just somebody you saw sitting there. And nobody's ever acted *that*
way in my house!" Christ, maybe I smashed a few glasses against
the wall, I don't know. I know some weeks later when I was sitting
in jail on a drunk rap and looking for somebody to bail me out
(20$), the money was on my dresser but I had lost my wallet, and
since I am a loner I was dialing long shot chances—May was one,
and when I got him he told me: "I can't help you. I am entertaining
a man from India." The shits have me wired for destruction. May
knows the book reviewer of the *Times* (L.A. newspaper) and when
the last issue of *Coastlines* came out the reviewer listed the names
of all the writers appearing in there—except one. Sure, Bukowski.
accident? maybe. accidents have been happening to me all my life.
I never belonged and never will, and in a sense, I am proud of this.
the only shit who can destroy me is myself, and that is when I start
writing as bad as they think I am writing, or as bad as I think
they are writing. I remember when I bought May the fifth he took
it into the kitchen and every time I wanted a drink of my own whiskey
I had to ask for it, and I was drunk or I wouldn't have been there
anyway, and I believe I remember starting on him then: "Why do
you use all that fancy vocabulary?" and so forth. Sweetheart, they
are always axing me because I don't smile pretty or come to their
tea parties. This poet Sherman came by the other week and he said,
"I've got your archenemy out in the car." I didn't ask him who
my archenemy was—it's a kind of nebulous thing with yellow teeth

and a swimming pool that I sometimes think of. . . . anyhow, what was I saying about *Ole?*

Please thank Nathan for the drawings. he's got a good touch.

yes I'll submit something for your book series if I don't go mad or crazy or dull, but yes, first N.O, and beer with Webb, and walking the mighty wooden nightstreets full of hammerheaded whores and newsboys and rats and grifters; 5 will get you 30 that I will carry around a basket of torturous legless writhing hangovers with black rotting hearts of apples in their mouths, but this is the game we play, in this we rape little girls in the upper branches of palm trees while reading the life of Richard Wagner. [* * *]

[To Douglas Blazek]
February 16, 1965

[* * *] yours was a fine letter, baby. we don't think exactly alike but I never have any trouble understanding you, which is more than I can say for Shakespeare. you, if something doesn't get you first, are going to be a pretty good writer, maybe a great one. well, hell, this doesn't flush the turds away or keep you out of the factory, does it? I don't know: we get slammed and slammed and slammed so much that it almost feels good. I have run through quite a few women but there was never a child to hold it still. But the women are essentially the same. they look into your soul long enough and it's not changing to fit their fingers so they began the chant, the protest bit:

"Why to you always laugh at yourself? Why do you always make fun of yourself?"

(no answer.)

"I can't stand a man who doesn't like himself."

(no answer.)

"Why don't you quit that god damned job, then?"

(no answer.)

"You think I don't feel trapped too?"

(no answer.)

"You're jealous. There are many people I like better than I like you and you can't understand this."

(no answer.)

Yes yes, if you have the special interview issue of *Lit. Times*

I do wish you'd mail it. why they refuse to mail me one when I send
$ I don't know. guilt? they feel, somehow, I guess as if they've rup-
tured or fucked me. they shouldn't worry—everytime I step out the
door 4 thieves and a bloody toothed cocksucker dog chase me around
the block. ah. —the circular is sweetfire (*Ole* ad), and it sure as hell
creates an interest, and talking about me in the same hairbreath as
Whitman and Rimbaud gives lift to this sagging soul so torn by complaining bitch of woman, and I allow myself a small lift, a splash
of water in the eye, a cool can of beer as 45 pigeons circle in the
lot across the street, and the mountains are dark today dark, and they
are dropping lumber ripping lumber tearing holes in the ground,
and a man sits on an orange machine lighting a cigarette and where
one hour ago I could see a house from this small kitchen window,
I now see matches of misery where there were once dark halls to
walk down in order to piss at 3 a.m. in the morning, and Bukowski
floats dead, upside-down in a pound, pockets full of rejects, head
still crackling racket of complaining womanhood or ladies from Mass
who think I don't rhyme with reason. Anyhow, it will be an apartment house. everything passes. m.m. had all that leg and ass and
killed herself. we are confused. we don't stick together. Hemingway
shotgun. Chatterton rat poison. Pascal's last bath. we all of us ache
and are incomplete forever. no victory. another night's sleep, if you
can sleep. sometimes I don't sleep for 2 or 3 or 4 days or nights,
or so it seems. madness? why not? what man is holy enough to last?
the stupid are the survivors. they've got good lasting qualities. I must
be stupid. I never thought I'd almost live to see 45. god it's gross.
I walk around an old man and I still feel the way I felt when I was
11 or 12 or 14—that is—sick, unpleasant, not knowing; aching from
the sight of wooden faces, wooden jaws, wooden arms, wooden eyes,
wooden blood, wooden voices. jesus mother am I the only one stuck
in this fright of un-wonder?

I watch this guy playing with his machine from the window.
I would say he is dead but the woman would object on grounds of
my inhumanity. He's young, has too much hair under a dirty felt
hat, and no ass at all, the pants fall flat, a straight line down from
the neck to the heels, a line like a hard board. He scratches at mud
on his machine. He has a little rag and a scraper and he works at
the mud. he picks away. inside of his head it is like inside the head
of a blackbird skipping over a wet lawn. tick, tick, and that's it. I
am supposed to save this man for democracy. I'm supposed to say
something, nice about him. I can't.

130

stomach in bad shape. I should gaze upon more pleasant subjects. then too, I don't look so good either. [* * *]

[To Douglas Blazek]
[February 23, 1965]

[* * *] I now stoke up me cigar and plus with the coffee comes
ye steam of bullshit, so gear your readies, pat yr paddy belly, wipe
the come off yr nuts, & hearken baby like a white horse in moonlight
listening for the last rider slipping up thru the elms. —I don't know
much about the phoney-non-phoney theory of lit., but it might be
best to keep the ear down to the heart, not like Emily Post, but more
like the assassin or the garage mechanic with Saturday night off, but
I don't know if talking about the stuff helps too much. think maybe
the easy way is best: I mean let it slip out like a wet fish outa your
drunken hands; and, of course, if the fish intends on staying, you
got a stink, you don't have much chance. Planning seldom gets it,
although the way you lift your coffee cup or brand a steer or dip
the thing into the cobwebbed dauber, might. Speaking of writing
(aren't we?) I get much more stuff back than I ever get rid of, which
keeps me kind of puritan about how much moxie I do or am supposed to have.
   yes, I've heard about C. from other sources; evidently he runs
up the gall mast of most. I guess he makes too much money for most,
and the other things too, yet I can't get flamed-up. I too like to sit
around in safety and I drink endless cans and bottles of beer and
smoke cigars until I am senseless and ultra senseless and I go on go
on within the seeming peace of rented walls, o lifting and drinking
rivers of that yellow piss and pissing it out and listening not to jazz
like a good human but to the symphony, the large orange flaming
red green white fires of curling steam steel leafy hammer sound sound
and form, and men centuries old walk around inside of me, and I
feel them feeling it, saying it as if they were sitting across the table
from me, lifting a beercan and saying, "Bukowski, it's hot shit.
everything's shit shit, yet look maybe— I don't know. I may not make
it. have you ever seen a yellow dog pissing in the yellow sun?
Bukowski, rip me open another beer!" I can come crashing in from
the racetrack where maybe I have nipped away at a half pint or pint

of scotch during the action, but this liquor hardly contains anything except maybe a bridge to walk across so I can get over and past the 50,000 faces whirling dead en masse like other things—like flies, like rocks, like turds. it gets me over. —now I used to hang in the bars, peering through the smoke, lipping the bartenders, walking out into the alley (usually for a beating), fumbling at the whores, and often ending rolled or in jail. after some many many years of this, Mozart or Bobby Strauss or Stravinsky does not seem too bad over a familiar tablecloth and a couple of salt and pepper shakers and a calendar of a peaceful cat. yet, I still gang outside now and then, and there's trouble trouble, and the last time I woke up in a jail with piped-in music, and a kid with a broken arm on the floor next to me. When the last I remember was being in a fancy apartment and lifting some girl's dress up to her waist and kissing her legs. Somewhere along the line madness enters and the police enter, and it's the same old thing. or it's getting home, and hemorrhage again, very close to death again. Some blood and then lying still as a rock, listening hoping for the mending of the threads not quite ready to go. someday they won't mend; meanwhile I am writing this letter to you.

I've got to smile. you're a real romantic, looking for me in that index file in the library in Elgin. Let's see? where would I come in? just before Bunin, Ivan, The Gentleman from San Francisco? no? well. or Bulosan, Carlos? America is in the Heart.

America is in the balls. America is in the factories. America is in the streets, hustling shines and newspapers, climbing down through skylights to the mother-blossom of the safes. I am the toilet paper wiped against America.

waiting on birth always wants to make me cry, it's so sad, like the gliders coming across the hill and ripping through the strings of gas-inflated balloons fingering the freak sky. farfetched? yes, that's what I mean. maybe by now it's all over, and over into the good.
[* * *]

Jeffers, of course, laid it down in blocks of cement and he did not lie, and he lived it too. I guess we owe the curse of Carmel's artist colony to him, I just as we owe the curse of Taos to Lawrence. The freaks and the ants and the pretenders always love to swallow the shadows of the great dead, walk their gardens, stare at their ground, but it does not work—it makes them less instead of more. There are no crutches. nothing is free. I will never forget the finks in the Village cafes with their berets and goats and sandals and happy and ugly faces. I got out, fast. —I've got to go out and pay some

132

god damn bills before they shut things off, rip things out. It's a small court in front with highrise apartments rising, rising on either side, walls of swimming pool darkness and $125 apts. with wall to wall fucking, and we linger out in the grass, remembering the sun, and to the north is Sunset Blvd. (the cheaper section) and the observatory on the brownpurple mountain, and the radio is off, and the blue Cad. drives off with its dead man, and an old woman with a red coat walks by. the girl-child is asleep on the big bed in the bedroom. Marina Louise Bukowski. what awaits this little wench? poverty? a father of 60, drunk with dim eyes when she is 15? or a photo of a man who died in 1966? no, it's one day at a time, and my life too and her life too and all our lives, Van Gogh hanging from the walls like a necktie, Brahms' skull 5 feet under rattling and rolling to the fucking of 2 gophers.

all right then, I now give you the gift of a little
s i l e n c e

[To Douglas Blazek]
February 28, 1965

[* * *] in 4 or 5 days I climb on the train to New Orleans so if you do not hear from me I am not necessarily dead, although maybe so. Not having mail forwarded. Going to read it all when I come back and see who wants my sweet balls in the frying pan, or better yet—enshrined in crusted gold. Brought in 5 horses first yesterday and still only made $7, 5 or 6 drinks, and then I loaded on the highweight even-money favorite in the handicap (#131), one of the worst bets in the the business. There went my profits. well, that's past; let's only hope I have learned something. at 45, they are beginning to walk around and shut out the lights. get going, Buk, the grave diggers are licking their palms in the sunset!

Purdy makes it with the typer and with grants and talking at the universities and by, he tells me, the grace of his wife. so being caught up in these various segments and his homemade wine, you've got to forgive him, he's a little lost out there. Layton I don't know much about, except he must teach somewhere and probably is getting a little comfortable and have heard in *Lit. Times* fashion, that he believes anything written by Layton is automatically good. this

133

is bad. men change. everything changes. you don't have to be much to realize that. we all write very badly at times and sometimes we write good, which doesn't matter too much either, like a good drunk or a day off when the old woman isn't acting haywire like some Bette Davis throwing a pissfit or the kid wailing wailing the blues, scratching your inner guts with barbwire, and you wonder what ever happened to that small room when you were alone and glad to be alone forever. yet, we go on: having lost the left jab, the hook, we backtrack, stalling, clowning, smirking . . . trying to save one round, sneak in the sleeper punch. sure. sure. could I be an evangelist? sure, for myself [* * *]

[To Douglas Blazek]
[February–March 1965]

[* * *] Sheri's pissed at me because I stay down in the mud and also because I put her in a poem now and then. But take the *Cantos*. I understand they are good writing because Pound wrote them. I know there's a lot of Chinese in there, Cantonese, whatever. Sheri tells me they put him in a wooden cage once and did all sorts of crude things to him. All right. he went to the losing side. Many men are tortured every day. they put tarpaper on church roofs. they dig up beets. they pick lettuce. steal cars. slaughter beef. turn the same screw. wait on old ladies. on and on. they cut us all to pieces. well, anyhow, I took the *Cantos* home. Every time I went to the library I took out a copy of the *Cantos* It was always there. 15 times I took the *Cantos* home. 15 times I took the *Cantos* back, unread. I don't say it is not a good book; I say it is not a good book for me, Ezra Pound and Sheri Martinelli be damned, and all the Sitwells too, and H.D. and all that gang.

I told Corrington to stay away from the novel but he had to run off to Oxford or someplace and become a Dr. and then come back and write a Civil War novel—and the next one will follow course: modern & incest & rape & murder, which happens, but not like turning the same screw happens and putting down the newspaper and looking up and seeing the face of the woman across from you as a dead woman. they write about the seeming-loud things and leave out what is happening to us, to people like you and I, me, and so it's

134

published. they only used to write about kings, people of seeming
nobility, mostly, and in a sense, this still holds. I remember once
sending a very long story, almost a novel, to a magazine, and it was
about an alcoholic who ended up strapped down to a hospital bed,
and who heaved up his blood and guts and was left to die in the
dark charity ward. They wrote back, "This is a tour-de-force, power-
fully done, but we finally decided to reject it because the central
character seemed to have no meaning or worth." The central character
was me. But what man has no meaning or worth? Almost all of them,
and none of them. Anyway, the story was finally lost in the mails,
or really I couldn't get it back and I didn't have carbons and so to
hell with it. But nobility? nobility is useless and beautiful. didn't
Cervantes tell us that? the toilet is universal. who knows about the
boss finger-fucking the secretary in the stock room and then firing
the shipping clerk for taking a 15 minute coffee break? who knows
how the streets of Bensenville look at 6:15 a.m. in early March? who
knows about Blazek and Wantling cutting through a golf course?

yet, I doubt any of us have been broken enough to see. I used
to mouth how I used to lay around alleys drunk, but this was nothing,
merely a time of easy thinking about sunlight and dirt and country
and shoes and flies and warts and flowers. have you ever read the
novels of Knut Hamsun? he had to live most of it, and smell it, and
take the blade. he could write with feeling for the fool. too many
writers dismiss the fool. Hemingway had style and Hemingway had
clarity, and wrote more badly as he went on because he leaned on
the style which he stole partly from Gertrude and partly from Sherwood Anderson and which came partly from his soul. style is a good
tool to tell what you have to say but when you no longer have anything
to say, style is a limp cock before the wondrous cunt of the universe.
Hamsun never ran out of things to say because Hamsun (evidently)
never stopped living. Hemingway stopped, or lived in the same way.
Sherwood Anderson never stopped living. and then there are always
little men in back rooms, like me, talking about their betters, saying
what's right and what's wrong with them. there have always been
and always be little men in back rooms: ask Malcolm X, ask Kennedy,
ask Christ. [* * *]

Both sides of the correspondence with Al Purdy, the Canadian poet, have been published their entirety in The Bukowski/Purdy Letters. *The relationship began in 1964 with a favorable review by Purdy of* It Catches My Heart in Its Hands *and with Bukowski's enthusiastic response to Purdy's own work. This next letter was written during Bukowski's visit to the Webbs.*

[To Al Purdy]
New Orleans
March 14, 1965

This won't be much of a letter. Sick, sick, sitting here shaking & frightened & cowardly & depressed. I have hurt almost everybody's feelings. I am not a very good drunk. And it's the same when I awaken here as anywhere. I only want sweet peace and kindliness when I awaken—but there's always some finger pointing, telling me some terrible deed I committed during the night. It seems I make a lot of mistakes and it seems that I am not allowed any. The finger used to belong to my father, or to some shack-job, and now it's an editor's finger. But it's the same. For Christ's sake, Al, I don't understand people, never will. It looks like I got to travel pretty much alone.

[To Douglas Blazek]
March 24, 1965

[* * *] they continue to build highrise apts. all around here, and little men with hammers and steel helmets crawl around fuck around, talk baseball and sex in the smokey sunlight and I stare out the window at them like a demented man, watching their movements, wandering about them as the kid screams behind me and the old woman asks me, "Have you seen my comb?" "No, I haven't seen your comb," I tell her as a man walks by the window and his face contains the monsterism and brutality and sleepiness and false braveness of a million faces of a million million faces and I want to cry too like the kid but all I think is,—I'm outa beer and I'm broke and the world is burning shit and the flowers are ashamed. something like that. not all like that. just mostly the first part, and the rest crawling in my brain like some beetle. [* * *]

136

[To Douglas Blazek]
March 25? 26? 1965

[* * *] I had a few bad days in N.O. but after 2 weeks we had
each adjusted to various madnesses and ignored each other enough
to be comfortable. I signed 3,000 pages plus, which was painful, yes.
The Outsider has not expired and will come out with #4 shortly after
Crucifix which is finished now and has to be collated and so forth,
a big job, slow, but you should have your book soon. They are going to another town. where, I don't know. [* * *]

no, I don't sleep either. I used to shack with a broad who claimed
I never slept. she also claimed I jacked-off in the bathroom which
I didn't because the explosion of her body across my sight was all
I needed to leap and drive home. she drank too much, she drank
more than I did, and you know that's too much. [* * *]

[To Douglas Blazek]
[?early April 1965]

[* * *] I remember getting ten page letters from my old man while
I was starving in cardboard shacks trying to write the GREAT
AMERICAN SHORT STORY and when I first got the letter I'd always
flip through the pages and riffle them and search them but nothing
green nothing green and I'd be freezing my whole soul in a pitch
of vomit darkness and he'd write ten fucking vindictive pages about
AMERICA and MAKING GOOD, and it was worse than silence because
he was rubbing it in—he had a place to shit, beans, turkey, a warm
bed, a lawn to mow, names of neighbors, a seeming place to go each
morning

and he rubbed it in good. and here I am an old fuck myself, probably on a ten pager telling you how I feel and what I mean to myself.
anyhow, a little green, I wish I had put more on that 17 to one
shot this afternoon but I didn't, and so a $5 for dogfood and for
which I expect a lifetime subscription to *Ole* if it ever manages to
continue??

I remember one time I was on a suicide kick and drinking myself
sick hoping I wouldn't do it somehow, or however a man thinks at
such time. all nerves shot. all everything deepening. the human face

137

and way a horror forever. crouched under my blankets like a worm and wishing I could be. anything but what was attached to me. grisly factotum of high-steeped blues. God damn God's breath and understanding. I wrote a letter with some English prof's name to it and I verily had at one time almost sensed an understanding. he had written me how some kid had hit him over the head with a brick when he was young and how he understood violence and horror. I was staring pretty much at pretty knife blades way up high in a 3rd. floor place, esp. when the stomach got sick and the blood came and I had to lay low for a couple of hours because I wanted to kill myself my own way, or maybe as a voice from the back would say (I hate voices from the back!) maybe I didn't want to die. anyhow, I wrote him the circumstances of my soul and also my penury (which was secondary) and what happened? this reader of all philosophers, this understander, this guy who got hit by a brick, this teacher of children, this man who drove into a place with his car marked out for FACULTY PARKING . . . what happened???

he didn't answer. for 5 months.

you've got to hand it to me, baby, at least I answered, dig it anyway you want, sometimes even sound helps, it would have helped me when sunshine looked like shit and still often does, but you gift me with letters of genius, open and swimming blood real, no writer that I know of has ever written letters such as you do and I am keeping them and if grace and God and luck be kind some other eye and eyes will fall upon them beside mine.

YOU TELL YOUR WIFE AND YOUR CHILDREN AND YOUR DOGS AND YOUR LANDLORD AND YOUR GROCER AND YOUR ARCH-ANGEL AND YOUR FUCK-ANGEL AND YOUR UNION MAN TO BE VERY KIND TO YOU CONTINUALLY for you have a touch of grace and damnation and beauty that the world should try to preserve.

and yes all I can say is "hold, hold." please try to understand what this means.

. . . might amuse you . . . the prof who didn't write. I met him in New Orleans one night at Webb's place. he still wouldn't speak to me. he talked to everybody else. so what? who wants to talk?

. . . McNamara? seems a little standard . . . yet seems lifted by something. I can't ignore his wanting to be real . . . whatever that means. christ, how phoney we sound, I sound! well, I don't know what else to do. I don't have

FACULTY PARKING

ONLY

138

I hope you remain alive in order to keep sending me the good letters—your letters mean more to me than any poetry I have ever read because your plain and even and screaming and clear voice talking certainly beats T. S. Eliot, Pound, Shakespeare, John Fante, even Jeffers . . . for me. how do you do it? how many poems DO YOU WASTE by wasting letters on me??

god damn you, then.

look, you asked some puzzling and rather melodramatic and taboo really questions on writing and witchcraft of poetry, for each man is some kind of weird nut, brotherly as a hatchet, and he'd rather keep his balls to himself than spread the flesh for hungry chipmunks of whore shit flaking through clouds of radium. all right, eyow, ok, well, I need some teeth pulled anyhow.—

to wit: "do you ever get the lousy feeling of where the hell the next poem is coming from—that perhaps you can't see anything worth writing about anymore?"

Answer: no.

"What kind of stage or period or interim do you think yr in?"

I don't know. I am afraid of thinking. I have seen what thinking does to men. I watch my girlchild look at an orange in the sunlight and know that she is all right. I look at our President Johnson who tries so hard to think, so hard to be right, a leader, and I know that through trying that he is a madman. I forgive him. but, like you: who feeds the dogs?

yet, like Hon. Johnson I think I am getting better, I think I am doing better . . . I THINK. I THINK.

> I think I can be another Cervantes
> another Warren Spahn
> Jersey Joe
> Braddock
> Laxative Lazarus shit shouting
> lazarus . . .
>
> but don't make me write a novel now
> or ever
> unless I g.d. truly feel like
> it—and
> not just for a space on the
> shelf.

so the way I feel now I guess I won't ever write one,
I am terribly lazy and more terribly tired

I need rest to gather
and they keep the sandpaper on me.
lack of guts?
of course.

[* * *]
—please, you don't bother me talking suicide. suicide is a rat
running thru my hair continually. in fact, it's the only way I can
get out of my present position. these 2 small rooms. no money. all
the time I am writing to you I am holding a conversation with a
woman scraping a dish, and if only she were washing the dishes,
all right, but she's just fucking around and nothing gets done, all
is dead, and the girlchild is a foot to my left and every now and then
I reach out she reaches out, we make faces, and I love it, she's round
flesh of young madness, but really I am stuck in this center, and the
very beginning was an act of kindness, something I did not want,
and now more kindness kindness and there is a love for both of them,
a mad gambling sort of thing, but they are killing me, not the poetry
in me, fuck that, but me, and they don't know it

and this is the worst:
to be eaten up
day by day
piece by piece and you are the only one
who knows

while they play jokes with
celery sticks
and a good night's sleep for
them.

I don't think I sleep more than one or 2 hours a night. I know
that there are many nights that I never sleep at all, many many nights.

and it is not that I am having profound thots
I am not having any thots at
all.

140

just looking at the shades
this wall
a drape
a side of a dresser
the invasion of ants
the wind like a mother's voice dead
to a sissy like me,
covers shaped like
matzos
the holy ghost of
Pain

I can't sleep

I used to live with an old whore with
a very wisdom sort of
wisdom and she'd always say

"You tell me to shut my mouth
so you can get some sleep;
well, let me tell ya, bastard,
I KNOW YOU:
                    YOU NEVER SLEEP!!

so don't tell me ta shut up!"
[* * *]

[To Douglas Blazek]
[April, 1965]

[* * *] oh yes, well, on slipsheets and all the stuff, I don't care;
I rather like the paper you use. F. likes to act intelligent and knowing, only she's really all fallen apart, and it's kind of an act and she
runs with these poets who have workshop meetings and read their
stuff to each other and chatter, and they go to things like "pot-luck"
dinners and long church drools on Sundays and they meet for coffee
and cake at Fay's or Marty's and they may even have a martini and
they all STINK, and sometimes they come here and sit around and

141

I try to be decent but they chat like monkeys fingering their crotches and I find it less and less easy to be graceful because they eat up my one or 2 hours of peace that each day away from the mill allows me before I go in again that night or on a day off they might stay for hours, and so at times I have gotten a little hard, they will be sitting yammering in the small front room and they will see this figure in his shorts, cock peeking out, pounding in beerswill rhythm on the hall boards making for the kitchen, saying nothing, ignoring all, not worried about Selma, not worried about Viet Nam, just trying to shake people and ideas from the ratskull and suck down another beer and maybe think about blasting out for a fifth of CUTTY. They may be fucking F. physically as well. I don't care too much. We are not married. the kid came along and I did the thing, moved her in. I think the kid is mine. I thought she was too old, I thought I was too old. the gods fooled me and reamed it home. one more hotpoker for good old Bukowski! Anyway, don't worry about postcards from F. she's that way.

I would be honored if you pumped out a book of selected B. bullshit letters. I don't know if the people kept the letters or if they were assholes. Must rush off to work, so must shorten bullshit and just pump out names, say in order of the people I have written the most letter to. [* * *]

Tom McNamara, editor of Down Here, *responding to the* Ole *essay, wrote to Bukowski from Greenwich Village.*

[To Tom McNamara]
April 9, 1965

yeah, sweetheart, life is a spider, we can only dance in the web so long, the thing is gonna get us, you know that. I am pretty well hooked-in now, have fallen into some traps. and speak mostly from the bent bone, the flogged spirit. I've had some wild and horrible years & electric & lucky years, and if I sit and stare out the window now at the rain, I allow myself the final gift of some temporary easiness before they throw the dirt on. Yet, even being trapped I know I am trapped and that there's a difference between oranges and rocks.

there's a difference between hard retreat and puling surrender. O, I save what I can; I never give anything away—I mean to the shits and chopppers & the clock & the buildings and the mad masters, the cock-sucking bloodsuckers. yet it's like one man fighting an army without help; yet when they tape me to the wall I will spit in their eyes; when they cut my balls off I will drip blood on their shoes . . . so forth, on and on, endlessly. . . .

the small pamphlets and books of my poems are out of print. You might find a copy of *It Catches My Heart in Its Hands* in the New York public library. I know there was one in the New Orleans library when I was down there. And I like an old man watching a kid run through a broke field I could not help being somewhat proud that the fucking card showed that the book had been in and out, in and out, continually, almost never resting on the shelf. Maybe N.Y. doesn't have a copy. I haven't checked L.A. This book is my selected poems from 1955 to 1963. I began writing poetry at age 35.

I was down in New Orleans last month helping Jon Webb put together 3,000 copies of *Crucifix in a Deathhand.* Yeah, I helped him a lot; I helped him get drunk. Anyhow, the book will be distributed by Lyle-Stuart Inc., New York, I don't know exactly when. Contains all newly written poems, none of which were submitted to the magazines. Why don't you write Jon Webb, 1109 Rue Royal, New Orleans, 16, Louisiana, and ask him how to get holda a *Crucifix?* Book about finished. Large, wild, and beautiful format, cover and paintings by Noel Rockmore.

I lived in the Village some time back. was disgusted. no men burning in agony, dreaming knives. just con-babies. berets, goats, sipping tea by the window, or whatever they were sipping, I never went in. they looked too comfortable, they looked too money, too phoney, sure. sitting there with their cunt pretending they were Picasso. don't ever pretend. be McNamara without the band. there I go, handing advice like God. an old fuck on a rainy day lighting up a Parliament and dreaming about the slow and easy fifth of CUTTY I am going to drink this Sunday while my mind draws designs on the pavements and the butts of all the beautiful women who don't even know that I am alive. yet, there aren't many beautiful women. sows. lots of pavement, tho. look, I've got to go out into the night. hope I've answered some questions.

[To Ann Menebroker]
April 10, 1965

F. and M.L. have been out of town for 2 weeks and must suppose F. will get to your letter with response after she settles down to the sanctified break of living with me, ya.

Crucifix being collated now, but no price set, and this type of thing done by Lyle-Stuart who will distribute. I hope he doesn't get hooked for the 3,000 copies—I can't buy them. art work by Noel Rockmore, vast cover and 4 plates inside. Large book, like children's fairy tale thing, long wide pages, 100, I am lucky again to fall down into the center of this thing.

meanwhile there is toothache, insomnia, hangover; my wildly staring eye thru the slow drowning. Have been reading *That Summer in Paris* which somebody mailed me. waste. unless you wonder what Hemingway did in the bathroom of his soul.

[To Douglas Blazek]
April 12, 1965

[* * *] anyhow, Sheri M. [* * *] gets pissed whenever she believes I mention her in a poem. she says I talk out of school or something like that. One of her boys came down from Frisco and knocked on my door and came in and said they were going to sue because I had used his lady in one of my poems. I was in there with my whore and I was laying drunk on the floor, and I said, ok, if you're going to sue that's the way it works, only I don't have any money, I don't even have a jockstrap. then I turned on a tape I had made while drunk and I layed on the floor listening to my quips and madness and singing, and soon he gave up and went away. I even offered to get him drunk but he wouldn't drink. I guess Sheri thot him a pretty boy; she drew pictures of him all over her magazines, adding curls to his head. But act. he only had regular features; satisfied & blank look; no coal burning. dead, really dead, pal. Anyhow, Sheri I think was for a while sending my letters to somebody at Yale who was sticking them into a tube that was going to be buried—Pearson, I think his name was—and so there go those letters—buried along with a lot of other modern contrivance. Anyhow,

Sheri said her Chinaman husband enjoyed my letters. that's something. S. always trying to get me to change my style to the all-embracing, classical style—the only way to be immortal and so forth. She sent books by H.D. and even had me write H.D. while she (H.D.) was dying. Well, that's all right. But there are enough of them writing the way Sheri wants me to write. I've got to go my way. If I can't reach the gods at least I can see the dirt under my toenails and dream of sleeping with 14 year old girls. Jesus, save me. But not right away. [★ ★ ★]

[To Tom McNamara]
April 16, 1965

Typewriter shot thru 20 times and now dead. Must get another: feel like a man without a cock having a spiritual hard-on and nothing to ram it home with. I can't spin anything without the keys, the keys have a way of cutting out the fat and retaining the easiness.

If you want to run the letter fine but forget essay a while. A man can go drunk on essays & handing out advice & being a master critic (T. S. Eliot, so forth). I've got to go easy because I still don't know where I am. Guy hit me for a 20 less than an hour ago telling me his word was his bond. If I had back all the money I've loaned I could buy 1/2 dozen typewriters (new) today instead of writing with this fig leaf stem & liquid shoe polish.

You speak of certain names, and I guess we all like the lions who cut the way, yet I met a friend (backer) of one of these lions last year, and I'd rather be a dead cat than feed from certain hands. He told dull jokes all night, drank my beer and argued with his wife. then he tried to slip me a ten. "I'd like you to meet X." "No, thanks," I told him, "I've read his books." Then his wife at the door (to me): "You're so quiet. You never say anything."

Hell no, they didn't give me a chance.

Reminds me of when I was in New Orleans last month and 2 college profs drove some miles in to see me and then argued with each other into the night about their degrees and how they were going to take over the university magazine. Finally one of them noticed me, turned to me and said, "My balls hurt!" I told him that was too bad and then they went on with their talk.

145

Really, tho, I guess the gods let me off easy. My balls didn't hurt once all night.

Then, you speak of my having starved. Of course, you know that starving doesn't create Art. It creates many things but mainly it creates TIME, and I don't mean the paper bit. If you're good and you have time you have a chance, and if you're good and you don't have time you won't be good very long. I think there is kind of an area of distillation you have to go thru and once this settles there isn't much they can do with you, although you can do it to yourself (see Hemingway, S. Anderson and so on . . .). [* * *]

[To Douglas Blazek]
April 17, 1965

[* * *] the old typewriter finally fell apart to unrepairable stage. like the death of an old friend, all the fire we went thru, the drunks, the whores, the rejects, and the occasional home run. I have not learned how to handle this typer yet—it is a very cheap second hand and I see why now—you've got to hit the keys just right or it won't work. I hope you can read the enclosed manuscript. [* * *]

I get these letters on the essay I wrote for *Ole* #2 and they seem to think I said something; I am a fucking oracle (oriol?) for the LOST or something, is what they tell me. that's nice. but I AM THE LOST.

going on to the collection of letters you were talking about; some of them may be thrown away and some of the people might be pissed at me, and some of them may be too possessive, but I think most of them pretty good people and you ought to get some co-operation. sure, edit wherever you wish, edit out dull parts, print partials or what you think entertaining. no, I needn't see what you're going to print beforehand. that's waste. I am not ashamed of anything I have written in letters. you print what you want and how you want. and I look forward to this bit and hope you can work it out. you see, I wonder what I said too. [* * *]

[To Douglas Blazek]
April 21 or 22, [1965]

have not heard from you on first part of *Confessions of a Man Insane Enough to Live with Beasts,* but here is second part which I wrote tonight. naturally, I hope it goes. please let me know soon.

tired now. got your letter today which I will get to soon; I mean, answer soon. feel slugged now, and am closing.

[To Tom McNamara]
April 24, 1965

Letters? god damn, man, let's be careful. all right at outset, esp. for tightheads who have been working in sonnet form, writing critical articles, so forth; it gives them (letters) the facility and excuse for wallowing in the easiness of their farts and yawns without pressure. really, writing letters are easy: nobody likes form, and I know this— that's why I discard a lot of it in my poetry (or, I think I do) (form is a paycheck for learning to turn the same screw that has held things together). so now we start with the letter as an o.k. thing, and then the next thing you know instead of being an o.k. thing, a natural form, it simply becomes another form for the expulsion of the creative, artistic, fucked-up Ego, like maybe this letter is, I don't deny it, I don't deny being a part of the poison, and soon a lot of the boys end up working as hard or harder on the letters than they do on their poems. wherever the payoff lies, what?

now look, for laughs and for instance, I've heard a certain old-timer who's never quite made it with his work but who has always had a finger up some big boy's crotch or been in some Movement. maybe I'm being unkind. anyhow he has seemed monied and has seemed able to recognize a talent before the big publishers puke over it and kill it with circulation, publicity and $$$. what I mean is, I now hear this man is going to issue a collection of his LETTERS. now, how in the hell are you going to issue a collection of your *own* letters unless you keep carbons? and if you keep carbons, aren't you more or less writing a literary essay type of precious thing, and keeping a hunk of it yourself because it's so good? or if you don't do that then it's: "Dear Paul: I hope you have kept all the letters I've written you over the past fifteen years as I am now issuing a collection of my collected letters and, of course, would like to include mine to you. . . . hope you still have them, and, of course I would o.k. any deletions you would care to make . . ."

I used to think of a letter as something like this: "Dear Paul: Sure hot today and have drank a lot of beer. Martha had a wisdom tooth pulled yesterday. The Dodgers lost yesterday. they just can't get their pitchers any runs . . ."

yet I find most literary letters duller than this, and this includes the letters of D. H. Lawrence, Thomas Wolfe, or any I can remember, and, if I have missed some good ones somewhere, let me know.

I had to pick up a cheap 2nd hand portable and as you can see I have trouble controlling it but as long as some of it can be made out, all right. and I sure hope it hits through o.k. to this nice fresh carbon I have stuck underneath.

yes, the LSD is the fading rage, stuff written under LSD, about LSD, my god they all do the *same* thing at the same time—THE IM-PROPER PROPER THING, if you know what I mean, and always in the concert of the safety of each other. . . . sure, if you want to use parts of my letters, go ahead, why the hell do you think I write them?

somebody in the neighborhood here has his stereo turned up as loud as possible and I do believe because he is enjoying it he also presumes everybody else is enjoying it. it is really only a half-hearted masturbation of music and it does make me ill. I'm not saying I'm a sensitive type but I keep thinking of the continuous intrusions that keep slapping against us and it is these intrusions: the small and con-tinuous and everyday ones that finally grind us down either into ac-ceptance or insanity. intrusions are many and varied, like say a dead face, urinal murdered face, hanging onto a living body and looking down into a bag of apples the hand fills in a supermarket as you walk past.

there's hardly any way out, even after you've seen enough, and after a number of years you have seen enough, but you can only close a door and pull the blinds for so long before they come get you: the landlord, your wife, the public health inspector, the men from the insane asylum.

now toothache, tooth breaking off in back, I have about 7 stubs of teeth that need yanking but I am a coward and no money and ashamed of the condition I have allowed my jaws to crash to. I think of the dead down there in their caskets or what's left of their caskets. how are the teeth of the dead? think of all those jaws down there!

148

think of Shakespeare gaping open, unable to drink a beer.

maybe it's because it's so hot today I do not feel well or maybe it's because I have to go to WORK and it's Saturday and I'd rather get drunk, but they tell me I've missed too many days already, and my girlchild has these blue eyes and she thinks I can make it, but some day I'm going to lay it down again and see what happens, watch the walls come down like bombardment, watch the landlord snarl, listen to the lady from relief insult me, roll my own cigarettes, put ice in the cheap wine to kill the gaseous taste . . . the defense and demise of myself comes above all—my choice to fall and not do, stare at ceilings, beg for bread, exist like a pigeon, a sack of manure, a flower under the window with 17 days to live.

I see the flies in the green leaves and I think,
it's strange, they've never read Richard Aldington . . .

"Nash," mentioned in the next letter, was Jay Nash, who, Bukowski notes, "ran the underground newssheet, The Chicago Literary Times." *He had published Bukowski's* Run With the Hunted *in his Midwest Poetry Chapbooks series in 1962. Bukowski notes that he was "obsessed with Hemingway and the twenties."*

[To Douglas Blazek]
[late April 1965]

[* * *] I don't see how *Ole* gets around so much. I hear on the phone. 2 guys knocked on the door and brought me beer. all the same thing: "I read your article in *Ole*."

on *Confessions,* of course, I'm glad you accept. actually it's going to destroy a lot of IMAGE that has been built up and it's going to make me freer to move around. yes, I know that any section could be extended, and there were more acts to add, I think of them now: the gang of fascists who carried guns, screamed heil Hitler!, drank wine; hanging posters in New York subways; coconut man in a cake factory; the colored maid with big legs who fucked me in a St. Louis hotel; a Fort Worth redhead; myself insane in Dallas and more more more, the things that happen to almost everybody while they are waiting for the executioner.

149

but look, on doing the novel sort of thing something holds me back. maybe it hasn't jelled, maybe it seems like work, maybe dropping poems off the tips of my elbows is easier. technical point—in *Confessions* I have a place in the slaughter house scene—I think I say something like, "The Negroes rolled up the wheelbarrows, they were painted a white, a kind of chicken-shit white" or some such line. I remember thinking of correcting it but forgot. I mean the people might think the Negroes were painted a chicken-shit white. should read something like: "The Negroes rolled up the wheelbarrows. the barrows were painted a—" or let it go the original way. who cares? [* * *]

word from Nash who also sent a flask Hemingway took a slug from, and now it's mine, a nice gift, and it will see use, good use, and Nash also says that he is going to bring out *Cold Dogs* by the end of this month—which to me, means in a couple of months. This is in response to a ten page drunken letter I printed out via hand to him. at least it did appear to rattle buried bones, finally. *Crucifix* now (see Webb and Lyle-Stuart) is being collated and it won't be long at all, and someday too I will get *Confessions,* and hang it up there on the top row of ye old bookcase with the rest. I don't feel so much like a writer as I do like somebody who has slipped one past, and I guess my detractors would agree with this. I feel like Warren Spahn squeezing out just one more for the lousy Mets, or like the dice are hot but it's gotta end. of course it will. I'll peel and die like old paint, hurrah, but anyhow I have been gifted with not ever having had any first-class fame, and this has allowed me to go on writing the way I please to write. I've been lucky, no one can have been any luckier. look, I'll be 45 in August, think of it. no guns have killed me and I have not been suckered into any beliefs. uh, just think of standing in a kitchen and pulling up a shade with 45 years on you and letting in the sunlight, thinking of the stockpile crashed behind you, thinking, I might even some day be 65, peering from slits of eyes like a grey tank and pulling at a tiny bottle of whiskey and lighting a WINSTON and watching the blue smoke curl curl climb the air, and still feeling bad, and taking it, wearing an old green sweater with moth holes and knowing death is very close as the young girls sing in the streets and literary and political giants have risen and exploded and disappeared.

the vietnam thing is in the papers every night and the govt. keeps sending over more planes, bombs, troops, battleships, and, of course, I don't understand it, I haven't understood any of the wars, I only

150

know that I am always told the enemy is a big bad guy and unless we show him constant muscle and boldness I am told, he'll someday be in the doorway finger-fucking our wives, but all that I do know is that after the clearing of one war we immed. pump up another, and after you see the same picture book again and again you know that it's only a nightmare train always getting ready to run off the tracks, and you neither fight it, accept it or forget it; you ride along hoping the thing holds to the rails a little longer, hoping for one more beer in a peeling kitchen while listening to Haydn, hoping the enemy has sense and forbearance instead of what we're told he has, and the newsboys hawk the crazy news as our wives burn the toast, think of other things like changing diapers and nose drops, of going to a Sunday's church or wanting a drive down the coast to inhale the turd-filled ocean. but the car's too old and the spirit's tired: forget it, baby, I want to sit in here and just drink tonight. what again? again. Blazek's wife brings him beer. why don't you bring me beer? no, I don't want a boiled egg. listen, what do you think of this vietnam thing?

Lewis Mumford said long ago that there wouldn't be any atomic war. that we would only live under the shadow of fear for some decades, perhaps for the rest of the century.

how in the hell can Lewis Mumford say that? how does *he* know? as long as there isn't an atomic war he sounds right.when one happens nobody will care whether he is right or not. [* * *]

[To Tom McNamara]
May sicks, 1965

writers are a sick-head lot, a gathering of neon-light tasters, spitting out their words, their absurdities, their bile, their orange-juice blood. we are down in submarines; we don't know; a nervous nasty lot . . .

I'd rather sleep for 3 or 4 days than do anything, so what happens? I can't sleep at all. I worry about motor tuneups and the death of sparrows. and all the women walking around and me not fucking them. then, sometimes I think I am too much topsoil, I want to get under, forget the toteboard and gambol with the worms (later, I know), so the other night I am wandering around at 4 in the morning and I pick up something by a Chinaman, 300 or 200 B.C., a couple of centuries after Confucius, and here's this guy running around giving the word to Dukes and State Ministers and Kings, but it doesn't reach me, I don't have any armies or loyal subjects or disloyal subjects, only a matter of keeping myself alive another 15 or 20 years if I feel like it. more wasted time. now I've got a pain under the collarbone; I've been going a pack and a half but my pecker is hard when I awaken the few times I've slept. I am angry with white Spanish walls and sound of tires on the pavement. no, I don't read much anymore—Donleavy, anybody. it's a matter of the juices saying no, no, no. no. there's simply no intake. if I power it down against the grain I am deader than I am now and that wd. be some horrible thing, ah.

I hear Lyle Stuart is going to charge $7.50 for *Crucifix in a Deathhand*, my new book of poems. It has expensive paper, format, plates of artwork and so on, but I can't see anybody paying $7.50 for a book of poems, and he has 3,000 books of poems, and so I guess he's going to have to stack them wall to wall and forget it. most of the people, I think, who might go my poems, most of them don't even have $7.50 and if they did they'd prob. buy something to drink. well, I write the stuff and what they do with it is theirs. the paper is supposed to last 800 years or 1800 years I forget which and I don't know, except one bomb or bad poetry will take care of all that.

Your New Bohemia sounds a little disturbing, and it might well disturb the shopkeepers of the Village if the tourists get the buzz. I remember when I was in the Village so long long ago, 25 years ago?, I happened to read in the paper that O. Henry hung out in this certain place and did his writing on the table down there. so I went on in, down the steps and looked around. red tables. nobody there. I thought, O. Henry must have been a fool. I walked up to the bar and ordered a drink and the bartender said, "Sorry, sir, I can't serve you." I didn't ask him why. I was sober. but it made me feel filth as if he smelled some inner stink in me, and I had been feeling mad, thinking suicide, maybe I looked too ugly, too vile. anyhow, I did not like the place, drink or no drink. then down in New Orleans a month or so ago I am walking along with the editor and he takes me through this kind of sidewalk cafe place and he said Hemingway and Faulkner and Tennessee Williams used to hang out here at one time or another. a real commercial hole it was, and I thought, these guys must have been crazy. jammed with tourists and conceited waiters. I told the editor that those writers must have been nuts. and he said, well, they were drunk.

that still didn't help too much.

there's a lot I don't understand but this is standard. when I wipe my ass I guess I understand that this is something that should be done. and I understand that I should not go out on the streets naked there might be lions out there. vietnam, hitler, caesar, the falling of boards from roofs I do not understand.

do you know something? I am getting sleepy. maybe I ought to go to sleep?

there are days of too much of the same and in the whole human mass not an eye or a face or a voice or a sound. Only a frog under a bush. only a cat crossing a street. a street without tits. graveyards. books on mathematics. chalk for lunch. madhouses. farmers. fish. meatballs. manure. sleep. sleep, sleep, sleep.

[To Douglas Blazek]
May 20, 1965

[* * *] the woman is standing here beating a big spoon around inside of a water jug, now she's ripping cardboard, banging refrigerator, sniffling, snuffling, now she's making coffee, now the kid suddenly screams, more bangs, these walls are so close, refrigerator again, now she lifts a wet rag and carries it across the room like a sleepwalker. . . they are pouring it to me BLAZ!!!

30 minutes to go before work and I am trying to get this letter off to you

DO YOU WANT ANOTHER COOKIE? I hear her voice say.

fuck it. we march on. an angel will give me a hand-job in the year 1986. it doesn't matter. [* * *]

little incident last night, foreman saw me standing talking to another man. this is against the rules. he rushed up. we have little slips we carry that show the amount of work we have done. he rushed up and I jammed the slips into his belly.

I'm leaving, I told him.

what?

I'm sick.

huh?

I'm sick of working.

what do you mean?

153

my 8 hours are up.
I saw you standing there talking . . .
my 8 are up.
why didn't you tell me?
add me up.
then the jackass runs to another minor wheel and says, I saw
Bukowski standing there and talking to that man . . .
well, says the other guy, his 8 hours are up.
I walked past and out. I mean, it doesn't mean anything except
that these babies are all sucked out and I don't like to talk to them
or even look at them, especially near the end of the night. [* * *]

---

*The book of poems announced here was ultimately published
not by Mad Virgin Press but by Poetry X/Change, Glendale,
California. It did not appear in print until 1968. The book of
"mostly drawings" was never published.*

[To Tom McNamara]
May 20, 1965

strike for freedom of time to have a look around. they have caught
me. it's a sad and silly story of doing-in but the main thing is they've
got me. 8 years on the same job and just as broke as if I were not
working. Of course, the first years were the slippery days when they
had a hard time finding me; when I could sit and watch the smoke
rise from my cigarette while men were killing each other. and men
continue to kill each other and themselves and they've cut a lot of
woodwork and a pile of soul from me. there are a hell of a lot of
ways to die but I still have a finger on the ledge, I think.

something called THE MAD VIRGIN PRESS wants to do a book
of my poems and I don't know if it will be mimeo or what and I
don't care. they say ten percent, and I can always use a little beer
money. I think I have a title—*Poems Written Before Jumping Out
of an 8 Story Window.* I will try it on them and see what they say.
Then Border Press is going to come out with a book of mine, mostly
drawings interspersed with poems, but I haven't done the thing
yet, but will. I like to play with india ink and lots of white paper.

154

I tried some oils one time but what a strain—like going for the 3rd piece of ass. so what I mean, here I am sagged and dying but still fumbling with poems and drawings, and it's a way of going on— like the whiskey and the horses and sleep sleep sleep, if I can get it.

this is an indrawn and particularly kind of cotton and waiting time, faucet dripping, something on the radio 200 years old, the teeth falling out of my head, horns honking, children pissing down their legs in a May afternoon, and below us pipes underground passing the shit to the sea, and the morgues stuffed, men in stained neckties selling ass, more books on Kennedy, myself barely feeling it out— the flailing, the words, the trees, the whores, the ways, Time battering like a tough fullback &, Ace, I do not mean the magazine. smoking cigars and dreaming of Mata Hari. ducking under sparrow droppings. I saw a lizard yesterday. also read a quotation by E. E. Cummings in the newspaper yesterday that I didn't like. all in all, you gotta figure a newspaper is a bad buy because it can make you terribly unhappy and you even have to pay a dime to get that way. Berlioz. somebody writes and asks if I want to read somewhere. I have to tell him no. it's true I don't want to. snails don't do much for me. I have these pains in my shoulders, neck, back, and I walk as if I were mortar. topside. only the tigerlegs kid with the moth-soul. when it rains I cry like Mortons' salt.

you keep it going. we all end as turds yet let's make them WORK for it.

the Spanish troops passed down the streets today their bayonets like whitened teeth and I burned the tablecloth, a picture of Herbert Hoover and a crossword puzzle of Asia. [* * *]

[To Ann Menebroker]
[May 27,] 1965

[* * *] yes, the phone call time was a good time and an odd time, a very odd time, and I am always very close to leaping but then was a very most close time, and I'll always remember your clear and water-cool voice, you voice sheen blue and easy and clean saying "hello, Buk." once when I had just gotten out of jail, had just opened the door—the phone rang—"hello, Buk." It was very good.

and now I get up like an elephant of a man, I have been drinking beer, I am going to piss, gross, gross.

the life hangs with us. it's not easy. you and I, we work with words but the words are like bricks stones turds clay turtle shells fucked out by sand, what have you? I can't be generous with myself. I've felt better giving a bum 25 cents, I've felt better being a bum sleeping on a park bench with my youth yowling over my angry and demented bones than I ever have felt writing a poem. what is it? nothing can please us. we are in a somewhat fine cage. you know this. christ is not the only bastard who was ever nailed to the wood. or bastardess. I include you in. I think as time goes on, the female more and more is beginning to inherit the reality and knowingness of our state of being—which is sadly almost zero. but please keep writing your poems. I think it is something about our Age—that men no longer speak so very well. they are frightened to show any more than muscle. ugg. muscle, I have. but muscle isn't going to show us through the bomb or through ourselves. I don't mean to intend a religious yammering or fear of fire. I think if D. H. Lawrence were here now he'd sense some of this—what I would call "unmanliness," shits, look, it goes up and down but if we want to save it it's going to take all humans to save it, and if it's not worth saving (and maybe that's it?) nothing will save it. [* * *]

[To Tom McNamara]
Late May [1965]

got the *Journal Unamerican* and enclosed buck for next 5 issues. this pb. just zany enough to bug-gas us all. comic strip best of all—"Mr. Hurts," my god!

you didn't let me know you were starting a mag. I will make some attempt to submit but am pretty burned-out after hurling together *Crucifix*. look, if you tell Webb—1109 Royal St., New Orleans . . . or Lyle Stuart 239 Park Ave South, New York, 3—you are going to review the book, I'm sure you'll get a copy. Or why don't you walk in on Stuart, wave this letter at him and tell him you are the editor of *The Journal Un/American* and *emanon* and demand a copy of *Crucifix*. this would be much more dramatic! Stuart runs a pretty good liberal paper himself.

156

this is late may 1965 and I have not yet killed myself although I fell down drunk in the bathroom last night and vomited over myself, I, Charles Bukowski, mad poet, fuck, and asshole. I was once married to this millionairess who had to let me go mainly because she couldn't understand me. "You're always laughing at yourself, demeaning yourself. I like a man who *likes* himself." well, that's all right too, only we are all crazy in our different ways.

working into the 2nd 6 pack now and a pint of CUTTY sits on the shelf. I intended to go to work tonight but this woman and child don't seem to be worrying about $ or rent or survival so why in the hell should I? sometimes it's just not the night to go in and if you do go in that night you are dead, you know what I mean. our man Blazek having money trouble now, and how any of us survive—what sweet hell, what a going on! my trouble is that I don't know how to do anything but get drunk and write poems, and often the poems are not what they should be. can I hand the landlord a poem for the rent? I'm fucked, we're all fucked, we don't stand a chance. I might get some green with a novel but I still don't feel like writing a novel, may never write one, and so there goes that. It's terrible just to try to stay alive and not quite know why. just to eat a little and wipe the ass and stare at a lightbulb. the gophers and worms are foxy;—they stand in line with my last rejection.

Steve Richmond says he gets letters from you. what ya trying to do, Mac?—wake us all up?

[To Al Purdy]
Late May, 1965

I do not write too often because I do want to keep it easy and not let it be a drag. I am engaged in writing several young literary fellows right now and my balls are dragging. you know—everything's new to them: life's a drag, life's horror, life's anything but writing a poem; life's more like talking about writing a poem and clutching hands. well, shit, maybe I am a little hard on the boys, and some of their letters are good but it does become a merry-go-round. [* * *]

some kid in New Orleans tells me you wrote him a personal note and said you'd send your *Horse* on into him. you don't know what this means to the kids, al. it can keep them going a couple of years, it can keep the factories and the whores from killing them. but I guess it'll get them anyway. [* * *]

[To Douglas Blazek]
Sometime, 1965

oh my god blaz, I write you because I believe you are the only person who'll understand but the agony is almost too much it's standing on all four legs—my god my god, there I go, being literary—I want to kill myself so badly but there is no suitable instrument so I keep drinking and wishing—a gun a gun a god damned sweet GUN—wham!—it's over. I mean, baby, I am sitting here with a toothache that is reaming the life out of me, and it's not just the pain, it's everything, it's this pain on top of all the pains!!—I was writing a poem last night and what happen? I am perfectly content drinking, pounding out my silliness, and then what the shit??? the landlady comes down and she and her husband want to get drunk with me again, they get their kicks that way, I say things that bring them to life, fine, fine, and so I chop the head off the poem and go on down there, and I know what it's going to be, he puts on his recording of *Oklahoma* and we all sing, me with a forged frog in my throat, and I say, look, don't you have *Guys and Dolls*? I am a guys and dolls man, I am a loser from way back, I like to hear them songs. of course, he don't got *Guys and Dolls* he got *Oklahoma* so we sing Oklahoma until the very tired frog dies and swims in my dead brain. so the old lady finally comes down with the kid and I've got an excuse to leave. o.k., so I wake up this morning with this tooth reaming the shit out of me, it still is, sweet baby, but somehow writing you it seems like you can feel my fucking pain and that makes it less. I almost laugh & sometimes I think you are the only living American human being, Blaz I'm nothing, all the poetry I've written is swill, I hurt all over, and it's just not the tooth. now fucking rain dripping down like hemorrhage of my brain and my elbows and knees busted and bloody now from falling down in the streets gaging plunging 2 nights ago, naked albatross of hell, me, falling again and again, until all blood blood, nose blood toes blood, I don't understand anything, anything, look look, now I wake up this morning and

158

I ask the woman, I tell the woman, OH MOTHER OF GOD THIS TOOTH IS FUCKING THE SHIT OUT OF ME!! I NEVER KNEW PAIN COULD BE SO PAINFUL AND SO CONSTANT!! (I should have remembered from other bad days) and I said look, do we have any aspirin or anything around??

and you know what she said Blaz?

in a yawning imbecile voice, she said,

"ah don't know . . ."

"what the fuck do you know?" I asked her quietly. but it was no good. she was asleep again, snoring, vacant, vacant, unfeeling, waiting for her next session of the poetry workshop to come her alive and make her jabber her silly shit jabber.

so here I sit now, in the hands of round blue purple pain mashing the beer in, and I'm quite a solitary, I take it mostly alone like this, but for once I wish you were here, I wish a *human* were here, I'd like to hear you say, "Shit, Buk, I'm sorry you feel bad." that's all I'd need to hear—then the pain couldn't do anything. [* * *]

oh my god, and just earlier a terrible happening. I am bitter and yapping a bit about the pain the good God has sent me and the woman goes in to the bathroom she says sleepily

"I think I have some Numz-it in here."

fine. I let her flounder around in there, then many minutes go by and I get nervous, I am kind of on the cross you understand, a kind of bad situation, and I go in there and there she is sitting on the can, so I walk out. I give her more time. then I see her rise and go to the medicine cabinet. she hasn't even bothered to flush. she doesn't know where the hell she is. I reach over and flush the toilet for her, then I stand there and watch her staring into the medicine cabinet. I've got patience. I wait 5 minutes, 10. I try to outwait her. she's either too stupid or too shit clever for me. I've told her 3 or 4 times that she is insane. but I don't think this is true. she is simply dead, dead, dead, dead, and she will always be dead but I don't quite want to let myself believe it because I must live with her because of the child and the child is a very beautiful child, and it's the *musts* that kill us . . . forever.

finally I can't stand her bland vacant stare into the medicine cabinet any longer. "Jesus, forget it!" I tell her. "forget the whole god damned thing!"

she walks out into the other room. in 30 seconds she is asleep snoring like a Canadian woodsman. yet I understand from her writings and her mouth and her many liberal and educated friends, that she

159

really wants to help the human race, that she is looking toward a better world, that the problem of the Negro should be solved, that, after all, with proper planning and govt. we could *all* have all that we need. and being in need I look at her and she snores snores snores . . . and I might as well be dead.

love has got to have another name; the people who use the word shouldn't. love begins an inch at a time; in slogans or brandished across a universe, it doesn't work. you'll see. this is the failure of Communism—the theory is proper; there just aren't enough human beings around to work it. people continue to shit upon themselves and scream for theory, when anywhere anyday anytime the smallest kindest touch falling like a raindrop can start the whole thing going. but it's just not in them. and here I might make you angry—for I say it's in me, I feel it running up and down my arms, like cool moonlight, I am ready to begin, but they continue to be nasty, to fall asleep across the body of my pain. so fuck it, finally, and fuck them—they want me on the cross and they won't get it. I have the great secret that they do not have: you needn't wait on death; you can call the day and the moment.

I am a loner, Blaz, and it's too bad for you are one of the few men I could ever feel contact with, and it's too bad I'm not in Illinois or you're not in Chicago but poverty our few talents keep us apart otherwise I would slug it out on the front lawn with you after 50 beers and show you that 20 years difference in age is not a begging for a lack of guts. yet guts to go on living or guts to kill yourself— it's the asshole same thing, and if you ever get word that I did it across the kitchen table, I'll know that you knew and that the choice was clean, a clean sweep, a shit goodbye, and an asking for more nothing—just a changing of the same dirty drawers. all right? all right.

I think mostly of continents of men like ants going nowhere not wanting too much not caring, fucking stealing writing bad stuff eating and living bad stuff all the horrible kitchens of unliving women bringing us our badly cooked meals to our badly worked bodies until we go mad or until we go simple and believe that the whole thing makes sense.

the tooth is banging away, it will not give up. wait I know the place of an old cigar like a bragging beautiful white kitten in a toy box in heaven. I found it. reams of blue smoke across this kitchen. a ltter a letter to Blaaesake. blaz.

yes, I am drunk and terrible and the ladies come out of the church and I want to fuck them all it is Sunday and the ladies come out

160

of the church and I want to make them come in their red and green and yellow dresses. my tooth is killing me yet the leaves of the plant outside this window say hello hello

> but I want to make all the women come
> and they walk past my window
> big and bold and insane and daring
> in color and wobble
> 30 feet high on spikes
> CLACK CLACK CLACK CLACK CLACK
> asking for it
> and if a man gives it to them he gets 5 years in jail
> for rape. it doesn't make
> sense. [* * *]

Blazek's Mimeo Press had published William Wantling's Down, off & out.

[To Douglas Blazek]
[June 2, 1965]

[* * *] this is now the best part—woman and 8 month old child gone to attend a poetry session weekly one a night somewhere and I sit here opening more beers and writing to somebody I have never seen and the kitchen light comes down and my fingers smack like drunk spiders on the keys and I don't know what is next on the page, except same old alphabet of scrambled eggs of me trying to worm-out, attend, sing, pray, bullshit . . . meanwhile, thanks for the Wantling, well-done—you give mimeo a live and foodish red-meat look that others fail to do. like me go get the Wantling and check on the beer. also have a pint of scotch after I run through these 12 1/2 quarts, so it figures to be a burning and perhaps ugly night, but maybe easy enough. wait. my good god, she's put it away somewhere. I could look but it would take hours and by then too drunk to write. some of the poems went, or almost went for me. but I always got the feeling as if I were being kidded a bit—like the con with the tray under his shirt—but didn't mind that too much; writing was clear

and contained little poetic malarkey. on the capital punishment essay, I felt it began well when he spoke of society in the all-over scope but when he began to get down to his knitting he got drab, academic and wrote badly. the all-over book was good reading, tho, except is it nec. for poet to place month and year below each poem? isn't this too precious? sometimes I think it is better to wonder when you *did* write the things, or, if you did. why pull at threads, tho, when the world is falling cesspool fat into its glory turds? I shouldn't complain about dates at poem-bottoms; getting older, cranky. fits. dreams of Miles Standish. fear of somebody smelling my dirty underwear.

I hope that you are still alive, I hope that I am not now speaking to the top of a coffin lid. there was a bar I once sat in for 5 years. maybe I told you. the early barkeep, Jim, used to let me in 5 a.m., 2 hours early and I'd watch him mop and clean up and we'd talk quiet and easy and drink free, and then they'd swing in at 7 a.m. and I'd watch them come and go, the lesbians, the whores, the dim-minds, the canned-heat drinkers, the office-workers, but nobody to STAY, I was the only one who stayed and it worked into my mind that if I could just get onto that stool each 5 a.m. somewhere somehow there, I wouldn't be too much touched by the asshole war of the world, and it was a strange and necessary time: many hours of not-talking, staring at the barwood, watching the sun come up and go down, of listening to them laugh and fight, and knowing that I, myself, would never have the strength to go anywhere, do anything want anything, just another beer, and watching somebody's head turn on a neck, watching the wrinkles in the neck, watching the head turn in the collar, maybe thinking, idly, DOESN'T HE FEEL THE HELL OF EVERYTHING? ARE THEY ALL BRAVER THAN I AM? ALL OF THEM??? there was nothing to do but manage to get drunk every night without money. this was due mainly to the fact that I could drink enormous quantities of all types of drinks for hours hours hours without becoming intoxicated—at least not in their sense. I could feel things running up and down inside myself but I needed it so badly, so much more of it, that even all they gave me was sad, it didn't work, and this goaded them on and the drinks came and I slugged them down blank-faced and waved a thanks each time, never forgetting to do this. since I never ate, I needed the nourishment. I went down from 190 to 131. I was the joke, the discard, the madman. the night bartender used to fight me at his leisure when he needed a scarecrow to slap around and wanted to impress the ladies. I took him one night; after 50 beatings I had finally had enough; what happened, I don't

162

know, except I stayed out of the bar that day and drank muscatel and ate boiled potatoes and rye bread, and they pulled me off of him and broads sat round him and said "o, poor, tommy, poor poor, tommy . . ." and he fucked them all later but then he just sat there holding his head and the broads wiped him with their hankies and I sat there and I hollered out, HEY: WHAT THE FUCK IS THIS: I WANT A DRINK! and the relief bartender came down and leaned close and said, "I'm sorry, sir, we can't serve you." and I walked out.

now here I sit in this place with woman and child and I am not any different than I was then, I wonder if they know this? the girl-child simply does not care, they have not gotten to her yet—she is sweet honey on the side of my hot brain. but nothing much helps. Mac says, "write a novel." "just for me and Blaz and Richmond and Wantling . . .": well, look, I don't believe much in this groupism, but I do BELIEVE I COULD WRITE A NOVEL FOR 4 people to read??? maybe what kills the novel is that you are writing into a tomb-mouth. think of it, the title and the atrocity: *A Novel Written for 4 People to Read*. I ought to do it.

Stravinsky, Percy Grainger, hell, Mahler, the world was is and remains full of good men who fall dead across the doorsteps, and if they don't kill themselves some son of a bitch will do it with a mail-order $12 rifle, or like with Gandhi, or like with Christ, let's laugh, it is not a game to win, it will never be a candy christmas forever, and sometimes the guy with the $12 rifle belongs, we no so little we know so little of how it works, and now believe me I do not mourn Kennedy anymore than I do Caesar because it seems that to get to the SO-CALLED TOP, it is most evident to me that you have to kill a lot on the way to get there. but I am speaking more or less of the working sadness of everything—how everything never seems to work. and why should it? we've been given minds and bodies and a love that will not last. how long can a man try before he gives way to death? why does Wantling discourage me when he becomes so drab about capital punish.? shouldn't I expect the drab? now they give me *Madame Butterfly* by Puccini. where are the people? where are the beautiful women? all these women reach up into their asses and wipe away shit. I am discouraged. I can figure it out. it is the education, the lore that this society has yoked me with and the things that I have found out do not fit with what I was told. and, please believe me, it is not just the female race who reaches up into shit, it is EVERYTHING . . . and, I cry too much like a disturbed man, but what do I hold onto?

now that, hell, you've told me this, and, now, that I am so very much here?

well, kid, they'll soon be back from reading their poetry to each other, and so I'd better think of hauling in the string, shit, I am like at the bar in the old days, really gone but my fingers insisting on the keys for the hell of the lonely blues and hacksaw evidence. . . . my god, umm. [* * *]

> wanted to see and I lolled and I saw
>   and I didn't see anything like
>   what Whitman saw
>
> I only saw the most terrible horror
> that made me a drunk for ten years and
> a half-drunk for the rest of my
> life:
>   not what they *want* to save or what
>   they want to KILL—
> but that they can't see that there isn't anything here
>
> that they have lied to me for so long
> and expected me to be thankful for
> it.
>
> let them
>   wait.

[* * *]

John Logan was editor of Choice: A Magazine of Poetry and Photography. *Two poems by Bukowski appeared in issue no. 5 (Summer? 1967: Dorbin C384-385).*

[To John Logan]
Early June, 1965

christ, have finally gotten around to some letter of telling you
I got the o.k. on the two poems and although it is now past the midnight of sobriety I type on. why do drunks always like to brag upon
their deaths? it's getting tiresome and I'm very tired of myself. [* * *]

2 people have so far told me that Rexroth has written an article
for *Harpers* called "The New American Poets," and so I guess I can
take the ribs being 45 and tough and having only written ten years,
it is substantial nevertheless that I was always outcast everywhere
I went, schoolyards, whorehouses, jails, I always got the foot in the
face, there was always the subnormal whom I only tolerated telling
me his troubles, through the factories, through the hells, and there
was always ALWAYS somebody *else* making it, which I didn't mind
as long as I was lifted. [* * *]

[To Al Purdy]
Early June, 1965

[* * *] yes, I fucked up in New Orleans but will always remember
your letter "to hell with remorse"! and this wuz big help, baby, I
am such a butcher, I guess the headshrinkers would say I am trying
to hide some weakness while drunk or so forth, that I am really a
homosexual or once fucked my mother, or burned a snail with a match
and that I can't face all this, really. the trouble with head-shrinkers
is that they have never lived—they take it from the white ruts and
the hand-job Freuds and then change it a little, but essentially if they
saw enough men in jails and factories and wars and riding lime-
burning boxcars, they'd know that what bothered us was lack of life,
being hounded and poor and pissed-on and marked on down to the
grave [* * *]

[To Douglas Blazek]
early June, 1965

stinking hot, night, just took a good crap and somebody whaling the shrieking guts outa a violin on the radio, dropped 30 or less at track (I am improving) but there's whiskey here and I have been drinking for a good 2 hours but feel very little except empty washtubs and the snoring of lambs, look, Purdy wrote, and part of it:

"had intended to type new poems or ones I wanted to save in case anything happened to me in the north, so use carbons to send along to you so you can pick out any you think Doug Blazek might want. One was published, "Hunting Season," but much changed from then . . ."

well, kid, I've read the poems over and can't separate them and so am sending them all on to you for a look-see. Like Norse, Purdy is a pro, and what I mean by a pro is a man who has lived enough and is still alive. you're the editor and I don't want to shove anything on you and it doesn't mean a damn to me whether a man has a rep or not so long as he can lay it down. the trouble is that when they get reps they soon stop laying it down, most of them. [* * *]

further from Purdy: "I mean, we're all shits in facets or aspects, our only hope being the sum total of life doesn't amount to being a shit."

I'll write him that I sent the poems to you and that the little ax is in your hands. all right? [* * *]

McNamara has somebody who steals his mail. he found one of my letters in a garbage can with words written all over it like "shit," "fuck," and so forth. a bad situation. the worst sin in the world is when the poor try to rob the poor. the enemy is fairly obvious, why weaken our ranks?

hope I have not pissed you in not going overboard on the Wantling but long ago decided to play it straight (corny, what?) and so I say whatever I say. or like there used to be a cartoon where this guy would say: "I am Popeye the Sailor Man and I am what I am." It used to cost him a lot of times until he got hold of a can of spinach; me, I use scotch and/or beer, just much beer. [* * *]

On Richmond Bukowski notes: "Reclusive, strange poet, has lived in little house by the beach for decades. Published various magazines and sheets, which included Earth, Earth Rose, *and* Hitler Painted Roses. *" In 1966 Richmond was arrested for distributing an "obscene publication"; the case was not finally dropped until 1971.*

[To Steven Richmond]
early june, 1965

gagging on too black coffee. bad image. I am supposed to be dunking my head in a vat of beer. fuck it. I don't like images. won't have them. Webb works on the image bit. I enclose a clipping from the *Courier.* he even has me six feet six. I'm 5 11 and 3/4's. I did drink 30 beers at one sitting but this is the only thing to do when people are talking and looking at each other. it's the only thing to do. If I drink whiskey I have a tendency to reach over and rip off somebody's shirt. I don't care for the interview; it's juvenile and standard, written by a rich young man right out of college but this is the type of thing that goes in those papers. [* * *]

[To Steven Richmond]
June 11, 1965

[* * *] I don't mix too well with people, I am now so old and have this old woman too and we have gotten this unexpected child, and she's art, I love her every bone, but it's all kind of foolish, I am almost done, tired, and I just don't know what to say to young men, I am not a talker, Webb found that out when I went South, I just sat on a chair, and a couple of profs came down from the University and yammering and I couldn't say anything, shit, I felt foolish dumb and in many ways am, they were so bright, they came up with a lot of jazz and action and life and I liked them but I could contribute nothing, too many factories, too many drunk tanks, too many women, too many years, too many park benches, too much everything, and that is why I do not invite you over, you'd think I was stale or cheese or freezing you. really, hell, there's nothing to say. I guess

167

I'm what is known in the terminology as a "loner." even at work I catch it. old man walks up to me on coffee break. I am sitting on a truck in corner, dark corner, while they talk baseball and so forth, and he walks up:

you mind, he says, if I ask you something?

no, I answer.

you're kind of exclusive, aren't you?

yeah.

I mean, you don't mix with people.

I guess not.

you don't like people, do you?

most of them I don't.

you're anti-social then.

I suppose I am.

You're miserable! he screamed at me and his face, as they say, contorted, almost tears and he walked away.

Steve, that I've gotten a couple of books published has nothing to do with it. I could now get broad and easy imagining that I have *scope* or *some damn thing.* it won't work. I've never felt good with the crowd and it started in grammar school, I sensed that they touched each other, understood each other, but that I did not belong. and now, 45 years old, I find I still do not belong, fuck dramatics, but the worst part is that I do not even belong with the *best* ones, the living ones, I seem sliced off forever by some god damn trick, either my imagining or some type of insanity, but even the good ones leave me dangling and I feel like a fool, and I know that I am a fool for I feel what I know, and my ex-wife used to get mad at me because I laughed at my stupidity and my mistakes, and this is not well: laughing when you fall and she quickly got rid of me when the man did not seem as good to her as the poems, and yet she must have read the poems wrong for the man and the poem were the same thing. so she took her million dollars and married an eskimo. god fuck that. [* * *]

168

[To Douglas Blazek]
June 12, 1965

well, I gotta figure you aren't dead but I'm drunk mainly . . .
listening to Dos Passos on radio, my god, he sounds like an
englishman! a fop! umm, ummm. they've gotten to him, he's soft
and sly and addled, christ, I mean he's gone back on everything, if
you know what I mean. I feel shame for him. his whole speech and
thought garbled; here you are an unknown kid in Illinois with more
clean and feel and real than a world-famous what????? god, life rakes
the shit out of us! now I turn to a little dark Bach organ work, better. Bach was supposed to be a man of God but I always get the idea
when listening to his organ works that the devil is talking to me,
giving me the straight deal on what is—am I mad? hell yes, maybe
so. [* * *]

so I write you a poem:

DRUNK AGAIN AND WONDER, WONDERING, AND SO SIMPLY
DETERRED THAT THE BUCKLE OF MY BELT SNAPS LIKE A FART
IN THIS FROZEN SNOW OF LIFE—
                    horsefeet down the window's way
                    is it real? where am I hell,
                    drunk again? curtain like the
                    sadness of a Garbo film
                    or people climbing into lifeboats
                    in a shitty swine-like
                    effectual sea. old songs like
                    bats in the dark
                    kissing my nose.
                    the characters in Camus and
                    Genet (I guess a lot get into
                    Genet)
                    are almost
                    right—they hardly
                    try.

                    why?
                    it seems to me that
                    man is rising up to meet God
                    man is disgusted *at last*
                    disgusted

with his waste and
disgusted with God always being
Right—
it is time for man to be Right and
for Man to be the perfect image of Man.

God's ways may be perfect and good
but for me
I've seen enough hurt
and if I am being tested beyond my reason
then what reason I have
can only resent this.

I remember much:
men in unemployment lines forever
good men
frightened and laughing and real
nothing wrong with them
hardly as much wrong as with those who were
sullenly and righteously
working.
I remember much:
old women living with me
who had once been beautiful
and who resented me because I was never
beautiful. God forgot
me.

in jail the last time there was a
blonde boy on the floor
laughing
holding his arm:
"I think my arm is broken. Christ,
they worked me over
but I know if I tell the judge I will only get more
days. I want to get
out."

there it was. so much real seems never true
or thought of as true. they have a trick—
they hold us all down to

stone—
we presume that what we want is beyond us always
and that
as men
we must eat turds and smile

yet I feel that someday
God be damned
the turds will fit the mouths of the
killers
and the rose will grow out
saying softly: it will be
so.

crist, rlly blasted out now [* * *]

[To Tom McNamara]
June 16, 1965

Yes, I am getting the idea Stuart is less than lovable, rather a businessman in spite of his liberal paper, but he did finance *Crucifix* when nobody else would take the $ gamble and that's something no matter how you turn it.

yes, some of our best and worst stuff in the music business, the musicals, and I have an idea *Guys and Dolls,* the good oldie, will hang in as a classic . . . many of the songs have not gone stale which is what so quickly happens to so many of the pieces from the boards.

the job is killing me true and here's this kid running on the floor hollering hollering and the radio is on and the woman plods around in her pajamas and my back and neck and balls hurt and it looks like rain and the men with the shovels will soon be coming for me.

o, the men with the shovels will be coming over the mountain
the men with the shovels will be coming and
I'll be coming
too.

Jon and Louise Webb the pros who did *It Catches* and *Crucifix* swinging onto a train out of New Orleans and looking for a city that doesn't make them sick but I don't know what to recommend having been around the handle many times and coming up with nothing myself.

all I have left is hoping for luck at the racetrack and getting drunk and trying to stay out of the jails. by the way, one line left out of a poem in *It Catches,* in "Dinner, Rain and Transport," just before the line "with the force of a jackhammer" should be the line "I can prophecy evil," but little matter, they did a miracle job, these 2 not any longer young people, in a small room with a small press and broke and tired . . .

the baby is screaming so loud I can't think. have got to wait for better times. no sense in getting angry or going the self-pity bit, just work on, somehow. now I get off the table so these bums can eat. I've been standing up here screaming.

[To Douglas Blazek]
[Mid-]June, 1965

you asked to look at a nature poem and I have enclosed one for you to look over. you've got to realize that they ran the nature poem boys out a little before 1914, and it's a little late in the day; in fact, it's about 11:47 p.m.

yeah, the mother-humping emergence of *Crucifix* has somehow shut off the stream and the typewriter has turned on me like a tiger leaping at his trainer, to hell with whip and chair and just having *had* dinner. it is a curious situation, something like a broken neck, maybe worse. yes, I was hoping Webb would let me illustrate the book myself but guess he didn't want to take the chance—I sent him some early drawings which haven't been returned—and then all of a sudden he whipped in this pro with long line of credits. but maybe Time will prove Webb right. [* * *]

[To Douglas Blazek]
June 24, 1965

fly on curtain, woman scrubbing pot, child stopped hollering, the air of the world filled with gray and blue and me, and it's Thursday, 2 more days nights at the pits and then a long drunk, the horses, same old bit, but somehow a climb-out, a fulfillment, at least away from machinery and stone-glazed bosses of this democracy of this freedom they tell me I have and that we should fight for.

listen, I'll send you *Notes from Underground* if you want to read the story but send copy back when you get a loose dime as it's my last copy, all right? will send by crawl mail . . . book rate.

I had a grandmother who used to pray for my infidelity, she'd come in while I was asleep and make these big-ass crosses over my body and mumble her incantations, she bugged me sure, but she was mostly senseless, life-drained, and it would not have been any victory to rip her arm off. I mostly had visions of her pissing, the yellow whirling fluid corkscrewing from that ancient blob of warted body [* * *]

the lights keep going on and off here, might be a bombing, or the enemy working on the wires, or might be some of these big crosses old grandma made over me fucking each other in the air. . . . body trouble? mostly I get stiff as a board, pains all through, sweet sweet stuff, and mostly during this time the woman is talking some utter drab zero nonsense and goes on and on and I lay there and listen listen and then *I* pray: Jesus, I pray to thee, please make her be QUIET just a little while, I can't breathe, it is like a STEAMROLLER, big daddy God, TAKE IT OFF ME!, but he doesn't and she talks on, spilling it all over me, a neurotic chip chip chip of sound without sense, all twisted up with her poetry-meeting Unitarian Church world-saving complex. then the kid crawls in and: WHHHHAAA!! WHAAAA!!! it's hardly any good for me most of the time, and during all the sound sound, these pains shooting through my body, ah. . . . and I had to be a wise guy and think: this one is too old to get pregnant. [* * *]

At Bukowski's instigation, Purdy had sent poems to Blazek for Ole.

[To Al Purdy]
July 5, 1965

yes, I wouldn't have wanted your poems for *Ole* if I didn't think the mag was a kind of powerhouse, and that's why I like to stick my stuff in there when I can . . . I guess you read the essay I wrote about a part of my youth for *Ole* #2; it was kind of a loose thing, but have gotten more comment on that than on anything I have written, and I doubt that any other mag slick slim or snobbish would have run it. They are also going to bring out a booklet thing, prose I wrote. *Confessions of a Man Insane Enough to Live with Beasts,* which I also don't think anyone else would publish, and christ, if you don't have outlet, you choke. I believe that rejection is good for the soul if you are not a quitter, but my soul has had plenty of that. [* * *]

[To Douglas Blazek]
July 8, 1965

[* * *] a small sparrow in the bush outside the window, reambeaking his feathers in the 4 p.m. sun, and I've got to take a shit. just got a tune-up on my '57 plymouth and the thing runs worse than ever. what the fuck? well it's good to have a car like that. once in a while somebody'll say, "why don't you come over for dinner?" and I can just say, "Car won't make it." I don't have to tell them that time is scarcer than young pussy around here. and I don't mean time to write POETRY. I mean time to lay in bed, alone, and stare up at the ceiling and not think at all, not at all, not at all. . . . [* * *]

William Wantling contributed to many of the same magazines as Bukowski and had a book published by Douglas Blazek. An ex-convict who had spend five years in San Quentin, he took an interest in matters such as capital punishment and penal reform (see Hank, *p. 164).*

[To William Wantling]
July 9, 1965

no, haven't made a dime on poetry but am supposed to get 10 cents a copy on all *Crucifix*'s sold and there were over 3,000 of them printed but I don't know if I can trust Park ave. I never saw the contract. Also supposed to get 10 percent from *Poems Written Before Jumping from an 8 Story Window* and am supposed to get 50 percent from a BORDER PRESS book of drawings, both of these supposedly to be issued this Fall. but, after all, I've only been writing poetry since I was 35—about ten years ago, and I figure about ten cents a year would be very good pay. hell, that reminds me, I did get $2 for a poem once, a horrible thing in *Flame.* and Garner of the extinct *Targets* sent me checks of $10 or more 3 times for large groups of poems—so shit, I did make my dime on poetry. and when I was young and used to go the short story—$25 for one from *Story* and ten bucks for one from *Portfolio.* so I've made around $80 writing and no end in sight except the a-bomb.

I don't know about this anarchist handbook, I really wouldn't know who to burn or who to put in if I tore down the works. the way I see it you ream out one piece of shit and substitute another for it. in the human mechanism—soul, balls, brain—there simply isn't enough there; it's a bad party, good guys in or not. . . . [^ * *] everything here sags. now toothache. out of beer. car stalls in streets and they honk honk honk and I push it to the curb and think it's time they dropped the god damned hydrogen bomb and got everything over with. there's your anarchy—it'll come from the top and they won't know it. except the few big fat fuckers who get away on that space ship to another planet. I hate teeth. shit's all right if it's yours, but teeth, no, soulless shirks of things, fangs into brain center pulling . . . puking. [* * *]

[To Tom McNamara]
July 14, 1965

yours was a good letter in courage but no more than I would
expect from a guy like you living on the edge of hell, you've got it,
and I could no more give a damn whether you were a latent or an
unlatent homo or a desk drawer—although one always gets a little
touchy about this subject and feels as if he were saluting the flag,
and if you talk enough about it somebody points a finger at you and
says, "you are a homo yourself!" same with Shannon—what he is
as a sexual weapon or tool or plant doesn't matter to me—he writes
a good letter and had a beer with me, and to hell with it.

bad day at track today, hot sweaty hot crotches of whores and
maidens and men and jocks and newsboys stank and I made some
bad plays against my reason, feeling my 45 years jumbling in my
balls and getting a little down with EFFORT, the old death-wish
assuming its effrontery, and I drank too much out there and sun came
down and the whole world stank.

I guess it works like this in Spain too, or The United Arab
Republic, and I have some sketches to make for a book of sketches
drawings due in Nov. and I can't get rolling, I think of ants and garters
and wire of cheese, and madmen dicing up committees of kangaroo,
wawa, didn't d. h. lawrence write a bad one about a kangaroo? a novel?
well, who cares? he hadda eat, I hadda eat, I do things I do not like
to do either but not yet on a typing machine although I guess there's
not much difference if you hold it under strong glass. . . . christ, I'm
tired. think of all the piss pissed away today; not the shit, just the
piss. momentous. think of all the poems written today, then if you
want to, think of all the shit. I donate. when the cat comes home
in the morning I'll have 3 pears on my head.

I am pretty well on the way and listening to some Beethoven;
(on radio)—with music I like what I care for, and sometimes it's jazz
or whatever or sentimental or sound that strikes against my arms
under electric light just right, awwha, you ever get that guy fucking
with your mailbox?

Find a way to survive that does not cut too much of a hole in
you or anybody else, said the holy man, and then he lifted out his
palm and I dropped in the pecan shell and the lighted cigarette butt,
and victory is not what you capture but rather what you don't want
to capture, and I've wanted to be a monk but the robes are hot and
they itch and I'm afraid I'd meet the same men there too—dressed

176

differently. conch auszieh tusche schwarz! this is a dull one! like I told you, I am on the way. and the woman's in the bathroom and the baby fell, YAAAH!!! more death on a fork. by midnight I will know no more; I will be sitting naked on the edge of the bed spitting invective out of my broken teeth out of the m.g.'d psyche, slabs of fat rolling like bread dough white and gummy over my gut, my face hacked with the bad years, my eyes sucked out by the snakes, I will be sitting on the edge of the bed . . . mumbling, twitching, shading myself against the walls, shading myself against my self, the elves, the whores, taxes, love and demolition, it will be a more drab-plink night than the one before and finally it will be a little while safe in the barbwire of sleep. sweet picture of groveling snail can't breathe.

I used to lean slightly toward the liberal left but the crew that's involved, in spite of the ideas, are a thin & grafted-like type of human, blank-eyed and throwing words like vomit. essentially they are *very* lonely. the secret is really that they have not put society down but that society has put them down and so now they gather and hand-hold through 1/4 souls and play at tinkertoy games with 1/8 minds. there's nothing left to do except admit that they are slugs, worms, and they are not going to do that. I do not say that these people do not sometimes do things for the betterment of mankind; I only say that they give me a pain in the ass when I have to sit in the same room with them. I am essentially a loner and now that I've got hung with child and woman a lot of people are coming through my door (her friends) that I would never have to look upon. christ, this is a bitter letter. maybe it was the phone call. she's still talking, "yes, the writer needs to make such a thing *vivid*, give it *vividness*. . . ." it's the same old swill I heard on campus so long ago. god damn, Tom, am I insane? it seems to me as if everything is the same mouth saying the same thing over and over again from all these bodies and faces that also look the same. sometimes I feel sick, sick, disgusted. you get your faith up again and again; then it's like trying to climb a mountain for a good hot piece of ass or a fifth of good scotch at the peak, and what do you find? a basketful of worms.

I'm going to get something to drink. you slam through that novel.

  the realest part of the leg is
    where is ends, like the mind
    becoming soul or an apple thrown into
    the sea

p.s.—christ, don't get me wrong. I'm no John Bircher or am I for the power boys at all. nine, nine, I only like time to lay around and stare at the ceiling for a while without voices around or bodies with voices. like that.

The following letter is printed entire and verbatim.

[To Douglas Blazek]
[July 14, 1965]

July 14 in 1965 in Los Angeles in America in a kitchen drinking beer and smoking a Dutch Master panatella, and lost $8 at the races today, and listening to Schumann I think . . .
aye, Blazer:
    you're right, I have been feeling down DOWN and almost did the Big Thing last Sunday, but that's talk, Krist, I'm still here with 14 half-quarts of beer, stocking feet, red-eyed, misty of brain, gaga fk goofy, and the man on the radio asks me:
    "Have you made your will yet?"
I don't answer him.

MORE THAN THE BLUES, MORE THAN A SPIDER
CRAWLING NEAR THE CORNER OF THE WALL:
    quite quite quite
    quit quit quit
    I want to quit
    I am not brave
    I do not want to fight
    I want to stay under the covers and
        cry cry cry
    I don't want to see a
        human
    I want to sleep

    I will stay here until they come and
    get me
    or the meat disappears from the

178

bones and I am
beautiful
again

    this is a free poem to hang in your bathroom in case you run out of paper.

    I will send the letters I will send the letters I will send the letters, it is only that I have been a little goofy and some things going wrong—no need a list—I am being chewed to pieces by everything, and if I were a smooth gentleman I would not admit this—but I eat hash, hate policemen, baseball, squaredances, nuns, factories, goatees, barbers and old women who want respect only because they are old women. I will send the letters, only like I said most of them are not so good, god damn it. yours, Purdy's, and then that's it. I will send yours in seperate envelope so as not to defile their good guts. it's a matter of getting to a postoffice and I will be very haappy when i get up the verve to seeit done. I am half-assed weak or something lately. how about death by cannon, Blaz? shit. great, eh man? completely blown apart in the public square, in the park on a Wednesday afternoon under a statue of Grant or Lincoln or Beethoven or Lee! in the sunshine! poems blown to pigeons. I've never seen a statue of Christ in the park, any park, I guess they don't want the birdshit on his brain, I saw one once in a glass case and I was drunk and felt like getting up in there with him, it was night and he was undera small blue light but I didn't get in there with him (Him, I mean). I was too much in a hurry to get to my place and knock off a piece of ass from this longlegged wino whore I was living with at the time, she's dead now, poor slit. which reminds me—once I was drunk in Inglewood and I was walking down the street and I saw this mortuary, it was 2 a.m. in the morning and you know how mortuaries are out here, the big ones, those long flat steps leading up to a kind of white colonial granduer and they keep the bright big lights on all night, and I climbed up on the top step and stretched out and passed out on those mortuary steps until thepolice came and got me. and when the judge sentenced me he not only sentenced me for drunkenness but also for BLOCKING TRAFFIC!—ain't that the shits? you know there aren't many cars at that time of the morning but so many of them stopped to look at the body on the top step that it caused a jam. I guess they thought I was dead and that's what I wanted them to think, chop up the smooth jugular vien of their sleep-within-Life , the fuckers. I don't do this so much anymore because

179

ₜthere is this ten-month old kid as an excuse, and I shouldn't use it;
but you know I used to conk out everywhere. there was one of my
favorite hills, I believe it was Westview street just above 21st. and
the hill was very steep a dark steep street going straight down without
lights, and I'd get drunk and just lay myself down in the center of
the street right near the top and pass out. a car never got me. although
once a woman came by and screamed when she saw me out there
and it brought me to and I lifted my head and looked at her and
said, "Don't worry, baby, I don't want to FUCK you, you are too
ugly, you are a shitty ugly looking human being because you live
like a roach!" she disgusted me so much that I got up and staggered
after her until she ran into a house. then there was an alley behind
a bar in Philly, I think the bar was at 16th. and Fairmount, a real
piss hole and I ran errands for sandwiches and begged for drinks
and shook the pinball machine for drinks and talked for drinks (I
used to be a good talker) and about noon I'd go into my first phase
of drunkeness and walk out into the alley and lay down, and I knew
these trucks used the alley to deliver and pickup stuff from the
warehouses but since it was noon or one p.m. they had some chance
to see me, and they had little houses in there that the blacks lived
in and the kids would come out and throw rocks at me or poke me
in the back with sticks, and I'd hear the mammy's voice finally, "Now
you chilrens leave dat man alone!!" and the truck didn't come by.
I am writing you now and I have 12 beers left. I been thinking about
Wantling. got a rather (what?) knifey postcard from him today because
I had told him in a letter that I was rather disappointed with anarchy and revolution because the way I saw it shit was only replaced
with more shit. he inferred that I was getting old and—"that terd
yr carrying in your pocket, throw it out. somebody might throw you
back a diamond." I don't intend to argue with him; yet it's true that
I don't have much hope. I don't disrespect either his hope or his
energy, or his work. I give money to people on the streets. a woman
stopped me the other night. I know I shouldn't. it doesn't help. maybe
I should have fucked her. I am tired of pain. mass anarchy is more
pain, more error. I don't know what to do. shit, I know about the
corruption, the lie of office and govt., but these are only men and
if we put them in different jars with different labels they will remain only men, and the process is slow, most surely almost 2,000
years wasted, but I don't know if i could kill a man or even say that
I thought I was right about anything.

   and even tho W. infers that I am old, I infer that he is YOUNG

180

LOS ANGELES IN AMERICA (o!) and this is OCTOBER 28th. and a fly keeps
brushing bumbling bastarding past....

hello D.Blazek:

fine, I got your o.k. on the 3 peems, and while I have a
theory that rejection is good for the soul, the theory seems to work
best when it applies to others.

bio: born 8-16#2#, began writing poetry at age of 35. 5 collections
of poetry with a 6th., CRUCIFIX IN A DEATHHAND to be issued by #####
Loujon Press and Lyle #Stuart, Inc. early in 1965. That's it.

Rough night in the pit last night, bastard on one side telling me
how great he was and bastard on other side telling me how great he was,
meanwhile the work-whip flashing like a cobra hung to a windmill...

Listen, on the books most of them are out of print or too hard to
get but for the record: FLOWER, FIST AND BESTIAL WAIL (HEARSE PRESS);

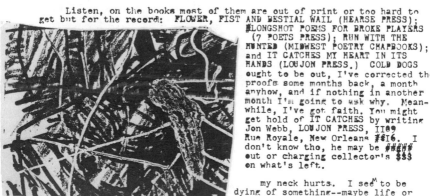

#LONGSHOT POEMS FOR BROKE PLAYERS
(7 POETS PRESS); RUN WITH THE
HUNTED (MIDWEST POETRY CHAPBOOKS);
and IT CATCHES MY HEART IN ITS
HANDS (LOUJON PRESS) COLD DOGS
ought to be out, I've corrected the
proofs some months back, a month
anyhow, and if nothing in another
month I'm going to ask why. Meanwhile, I've got faith. You might
get hold of IT CATCHES by writing
Jon Webb, LOUJON PRESS, 1109
Rue Royale, New Orleans #816. I
don't know tho, he may be #####
out or charging collector's $$$
on what's left.

my neck hurts. I seeM to be
dying of something--maybe life or
maybe no young ass. well. listen: M
bottom of paper here. slipping out of typer. going. hold and luck, Buk

To Douglas Blazek. October 28, 1964.

JANUARY 26TH, 1964,
  LOS ANGELES, CALIFORNIA —

Dear Jon and Gypsy —

Hope long tape got there OK., IT IS NOW 5 IN
THE MORNING, BIRDS STILL ASLEEP AND I AM SUCKING ON A
sour orange candy which MAKES ME TOUGH AS
HELL BUT THEN THE ASS HAS BEEN bloody + bloody
CHUNKS OF **FLESH**, SO I am tenderly COOKING IT
FOR A COUPLE OF DAYS. — ON BEER, ECT.

Thanks for RETURN OF POEM BATCH — I WILL
continue to send NEW ONES IF AND WHEN They
become.

Got 2 copies of book sometime back, all good like
new icecream again + I am waiting with some WONDER
on inscribed copy FROM the **EDITORS**, yes.

To Jon and Louise Webb. January 26, 1964.

VILLAGE VOICE ad does cost like Hell

but might make Loujon Press well-known as well
as Buk + I hope you have ENOUGH copies left to
go at $5 which it should HAVE gone FOR <u>AT ONCE</u>
and when I THINK OF THIS BOOK SELLING FOR
TWO DOLLARS, I think it A CRIME and people
should have sent you more money at once
out of SIMPLE DECENCY OF SOUL, But it's much
EASIER for them to think that MONEY is
BAD for your soul but O.K. for theirs — so
O.K. FOR THEM TOO keep it — the MONEY, I mean.

I don't know about the Cherry Cherries —
Jory says he spoke to them about it — let me
know if they finally + decently ante up. I'm
told they are NOT GOING TO <u>SELL</u> the
10 copies BUT SIT ON THEM !!! This doesn't
do the LOUJON PRESS one damn bit of good,
the way I see it + specially for FREE.
WE can sit on our books OURSELVES + that's
our <u>RIGHT</u>, but seems to me when you
give special <u>bookstore rates</u>, they oughta
OPERATE LIKE A BOOKSTORE + I mean
SELL BOOKS.

Please don't sell any more books for LESS
than $5 — the word is out, they know what
you've done; but hell, you're the editors and
I know that you know more about
THIS type of PUBLIC than I do.

Rough on the moving coming up. There's
always some son-of-a-bitching obstacle
to BREAK a man down when he tries anything
out of the ordinary — while the fools
and PRICKS sail blithely on.

To Jon and Louise Webb. January 26, 1964 (Page 2).

I read book REVIEW of IT CATCHES Frances wrote for South + West; it seemed O.K., mentioned WORK of editors too... She re-wrote completely a first version which I thought was FLAT and mechanical, which can + does HAPPEN TO ANY OF us.

Ship more purples, sure. I've still get plenty of SILVER + the YELLOW, and it is easy ENOUGH, rather FUN + EXPLORATIVE specially if I have 2 or 3 weeks.

I don't KNOW if there will be poems enough, good ENOUGH poems for another book in some future should we all survive EVERYTHING, but I will keep sending and if you finally see fit, GREAT!!!

Yes, you're right — Willie prob. tied in with THESIS + 2nd. novel but he wrote such INTERESTING letters that I miss them.

I might have to MOVE OUT OF this place — 1623 N. MARIPOSA — many reasons, many odd reasons... but not quite yet.

SHOOT the purples out + I will get busy. I am full of BALOGNA + some DRAWINGS.

HAIL, HAIL,
HAIL,
Buk

To Jon and Louise Webb. January 26, 1964 (Page 3).

dear Jon and Louise:

　　　　　　thanks for all the photos, they really brought me back there, sick, ####hungover in the old bathrobe but really being glad to be with both of you but no way to say it without seeming corney, and like with Greg. and Steve, same thing, I am just not a talker, so to all of you I #####must apologize, I am not OUTWARD, and there isn't any help for it. that's it. I do think all you good people understand what kind of cage I am crawling around in. so thank you. love you all, plenty.

　　　　　　yours,

　　　　　　Buk

p.s.--poems enclosed. try to get back soon?　luck with the landlord...

　　　　　　　　　　　　　　　　　　　　　　　b.

　　　　　　　　　` HA, HETE, HA ...

P.S.- I SENT WORST PHOTO OF MARINA. CAN'T SEND OTHERS, AFRAID OF LOSING, EVEN THO I HAVE NEGS. YEAH, I'M CRAZY.

　　　　　LOE,

　　　　　Buk

IF YOU COME TO KINGMAN CAN'T YOU FLY HERE TO SEE ME? CAN PICK YOU UP AT AIRPORT. DRIVE BACK. I'M UNEMPLOYED. BED YOURS, COUCH MINE. LOVE, B.

p.s.s.--wrote a poem about meeting Mrs. Robertson but sent it to NOLA. don't want to hurt any feelings. Betsy a lovely lovely woman, believe me. I am the o.k. you see her, tell her, my love.

NO-1-63865

To Jon and Louise Webb. [April, 1965?].

June 2, 1966

ah, blaz:

        terribly hungover, so short here, but not to keep you bouncing the blue
lame dream in your malted milk--send your poems and I'll submit forward. but
give me bit of time--forward's are like fucks or poems or whatever: they have to
wait the proper emergence. I think your poems will allow me to do the forward,
and I have no shame in sending a good man out on the street with a rose in his
hand. but if the forward doesn't work for you, it's yours to kill. you have
a title yet? anyhow, send the stuff on in when you are able.
                        iz
        Good the Norse went. writing such an odd thing--you work it but don't hardly
ever know if it works or not.

        really sick today, and this isn't a letter, just to let you know I am ready
to read the Blazac screams and declamations. o.k.?

        sing horses to sleep when the picture books burn,

To Douglas Blazek. June 2, 1966.

les angeles, calif.
march 3, 1967

hello Karl:

    very dull and damp and down today, and for some time....

keep remembering tho, you wanted me to say something about Klacte, so I will, and if you
care to #use it? otherwise--

    KLACTOVEEDSEDSTEEN DIFFERS BECAUSE IT DIFFERS IT DIFFERS FROM OTHERS GOOD OTHERS
BAD OTHERS BUT I FIND THIS STRANGE DIFFERENCE MOSTLY LIKE YELLOWGREEN ELECTRIC LIGHT
LEFT FROM WIRE INTO WALLPAPER AND CRYING BRAIN, SAYING THIS THING LIKE THIS:
CLOSED AND ALERT, NOW/DONE IN THE MESSAGE*FLICKS OF THE SMILING GENTLY WARM THINKING
METABOLISM. ZANI BARBWIRE INTELLIGENCE TRANSPOSED INTO MORNING TOAST. DO YOU SEE
WHAT IT IS? BAYONETS AND TURDS AND WHORE CANDLES AND DOG WITH TOOTHACHE NOT ONLY
UNDERSTOOD BUT RE-:LINED, BOXED, TIED WITH RIBBON, THEN SENT TO THE PICNIC SHADOWS
OF FRA BARTOLOMMEO AND MAXIMILIEN FRANÇOIS MARIE ISIDORE DE ROBESPIERRE. SOUND LIKE
BULLSHIT? I AM SINCERE ENOUGH, BLUE KID. LET ME SAY THAT WHAT I HAVE SAID SHOULD
BE PLENTY: IF YOU DON'T SMELL THE GRASS HALOS YOU MIGHT AS WELL ###KEEP LAYING
AROUND ½ ½ one-eighth BLOWING YOUR GRANDMOTHER. or the DIAMOND WART WITH THE
STALE MEDIUM SAUCE ON YOUR LEFT WRIST, GOODBYE.

                    --Charles Bukowski

    not too good here. health slipped again. eyow, next thing I knew I am walking
around drunk again, unable to make work. worried about THEIR DAMNED WORK, their place,
their walls, their trained-seal rules. ummm, umm. LIKE WORRYING THAT A SHARK MIGHT
SNUB HIS NOSE STUB HIS NOSE WHEN HE TAKES A BITE OUTA YOU. then I am somplace else
and somebody keeps handing me this pill-things in a ####/####jar and I am transfixed
like a thorn upon a rose I cannot see. I turn down fucks. I don't talk. I listen,
nervous, uncomfortable, unable to move, not caring too. sun goes up and down. voices
say voice things like flutes and beards hidden under some near pier, shorn white voices
with broken backs. fuke! 36 hours later you get up out of your chair and walk out;
it's cold. the car starts. you are cole cole cole COLD. LIKE BONEWET AND PACKED WITH
FISH*ICE. eyes don't care. you drive out. broke. days away from chicken shit job.
you come back to your place and it's a SMEAR OF PAPER AND SHIRTS AND STOCKINGS AND
SAD UNDONE THINGS ON THE FLOOR, LETTERS FROM Germany, und letters from peppermint
hades, and a letter from a lady who still wants to get FUCKED. I lay down and
cannot sleep. I FEEL AS IF I HAVE BETRAYED THE FOOTBALL TEAM BUT THE FOOTBALL
TEAM ISN'T ANYWHERE AROUND. round or around. I can't sleep. don't want to come.
have arrived. only the fish smell like selda-wands with ####flick-switches.
::::::write: Karl:

        so that's it.

nothing to roll or pipe, no pills, no money but will go out for beer at this place,
beer and wine, have credit, whiskey scotch that stuff tears my stomach which is about
gone. but shape of spirit strangely gross-strong, like badbreath come-thru, hahaha,
maybe I get lucky strings inside, like no matter what happens this butterball thing
keeps puffing, yet no long dastardly letter, I allow myself greenbean laziness,
complete stinking of socks, and know u understand and that is fine phine.

    by the way, do you have tape machine? I knew good madman, poet Dohan Thomas,
who has 2 or 3 tape machines, we can send stere or mono, #####prefer 3 and 3/4
speed. can you send us something? we will answer from our bearded hills,
something.

      meanwhile, pray for dead fish,

          Buk

LET ME
KNOW IF
YOU
"WANT" THIS
ACTION ???
:D

To Carl Weissner. March 3, 1967.

April I9, I967

hello Jon and Lou:

god, Jon, didn't know the prostrate so bad. DON'T DRINK, please. I have gone on the wagon myself, for a while. the ~~full~~ price seems terribly high for us, surely and especially you.

this very short letter to tell you to take it easy easy. a few beers aren't worth all of that.

~~#######~~yes, please mail some pages for me to write some sayings on for your Crucifix's. it will give me a chance to mouth a bit. won't take me long and I will mail back as soon as finished. I too would like to see Crucifix move a bit more, especially now that I see that most of the poems have held up through Time--for me.

have been having insomnia among other things and now another god damned scheme in my lap to pass for the postoffice, hours and hours of MY TIME wasted, I mean time off-the-clock. I cry into the same hankercheif. (ie).

if things a little better around June 26th. and you still want me to make that run, understand that I will not drink in front of you. I will go back to the place I have rented and maybe have a beer or 2, do a little work on the damned novel or whatever.

on yea or ¤ nay on Patchen edition of OUTSIDER, I couldn't wouldn't toss in a word one way or the other--- somebody singing on Opera now -- MAD, MAD, THE WHOLE WORLD IS MAD-- to influence or un-influence you.

by the way, in PRISM international, Spring I967, there is a cover photo by one Jon Webb. ###I take it this is not you? or is it? anyhow, mag obtainable by writing PRISM, c/o Creative Writing, Univeraity of British Columbia, Vancouver 8. B.C.
             this is·
now must try to get that sleep. short half-wit letter, but to tell you, Jon, to stay away from stupid BEER CANS! and you, Lou, see that he does. I have spoken. let there be order and a chance to breathe.
                                                       ¤
better letter soon. don't forget to mail pages to inoribe for good ol' CRUCIFIX.
fine.

                    the big page to you,

                        Buk

nothing on L.A.Times interview. guess they decided not to run it. Free Press beat them to it and guess they did not want to play #2nd. fiddle. well, either way.

P.S. Hope you rec. mag Down Hope #I , TANK I important) you 2 in letters to MAC. that new last my copy. L, B -

MAR INA

                    To Jon and Louise Webb. April 19, 1967.

in spite of the 5 and one half years he did, and there goes *that* argument. I suppose now that I will be referred to as an extreme rightist and that I voted for Barry while I was disguised in a stocking mask.— yet, W. is right: our anarchy is best served in the poetry we write. do you think we'll all end up writing stuff for *The New Yorker* and *Esquire*? how much ya wanna bet some of us do? and *Evergreen Review* is halfway there.

Got your flyer on *Ole* and the chapbooks, and well done, baby, well done. although reading about myself this CHARLES BUKOWSKI, seems very strange. I seem to see some pisser done up in white robes and tilting a winebottle. where is he? sitting in the ants? tickling his belly with red turpentine?

look here, Bensenville, from *Mo tzu*:

5. Seven causes of anxiety: bad city walls, no allies, careless expenditure, incompetent officials, overconfidence of sovereign, failure to recognize loyal officials, crop failures. Reduce expenditures and be prepared.

14. 16. Love everybody uniformaly.

17. 19. Against offensive war.

26. 28. Will of Sky.

> (oh shit, I just spilled beer over my cigars! will of Sky? lucky they in cellophane. me drunk again? Blaz, you're only person I know who is worse speller than I. you must be good person, yes. you are not interested in hopscotch while the walls are on fire.)

31. Ghosts.

35-37. Against belief in Fate.

39. Against Confucianists who love narrowly, like music, and believe in Fate.

> (if I were Wantling I would say that Fate is an excuse for lack of courage and disorder. I'll say it anyhow, although it's too simple—and not always so.)
> (Stevenson died. I saw the headlines. when E. E. Cummings died somebody told me—5 days later.)

(ho, I am growing old old, silver threads amongst the gold, the kid keeps crawling in and I sit her up here and she bangs against the keys. and I am the man who once sneered at babies in carriages and dull-faced men walking along with their dull-faced wives.)

oh hell, I have been reading some shit about summoning a gamekeeper with a hat of feathers. it should not be done. you use a hat of fur. good gamekeeper will not come (I mean appear) if you summon them with a hat of feathers, even if it means they will be shot. they just didn't go for that hat of feathers jazz.

of course I am almost drunk now, and fine, and I think reverence and adoration is horseshit, there is no man that I adore, or a chance that I will; there are men that I would want to drink beer with, there are women I would want to fuck. that is as far as my love goes. we are contaminated by nearness. I say I love this child that has been on my lap but if I say this it also means that I do not love some child that I cannot see because if I can't see her she surely does not exist, and although only what exists is that which is near us or what we can see—it traps us into error—like murder, war. the 8 or 12 hour job, the house, the flag, the love of the greasy tablecloth that we puked upon just last night. it is certainly logical to seek for the things which make us happy and safe and drunk and immortal and christlike and comecrazy but we are all banging heads to satisfy the teeth of our own souls—anarchists, rightists, leftists, religionists, judo practicers, horseplayers, drunks, chess players, all, all, . . . lost in the tilting glob of self. what the hell can we do? I have often thought that much more than suicide that MADNESS was the answer! think the sweetness! battering against rubber walls, screaming great poems and Nobody hearing! cold showers when you don't want them. WATER? WATER, WATER!! wires jammed into theback of your neck jammed with electric shock. the TRUTH AT LAST: YOU DID NOT *FIT*. you are therefore crazy because we as members of society have practiced various standard devices that make us safe and you unsafe. nobody takes his pecker out in a stadium of 90,000 people and shouts SHIT ON AMERICA! that man must be crazy. he's been treated so good. what the hell does he want? *we* can live without protest, what's all this *protest* SHIT? so he lost his job? so he's worried about the bomb? so he writes madrigals on the sleeves of his dirty shirts? some PANSY who wants GOOD? real men don't fuck with good; real men are tough; real men can take it. the stockpiles of bombs don't bother us. shit, we got more an' they got. and we'll figure a way to handle those chinks. Remember Teddy R.? a big stick and a soft woice. I mean, Blaz, I am ready to go crazy not because I think the good guys are not winning but because the good boys are almost the same as the bad boys, I mean it's jazz and waste and holler, and all this expenditure and not even a young Portoguese girl say 19 licking my cock with her sandpaper tongue while whilst I lay back upon a mass of blue pillows while the VULTURE winks.

your stuff about letters, your u putting out these letters I don't quite know about because men seem to lie in their letters as while well as in their poems, theonly thing bing being that maybe the lies in the letters are the more relaxed lies. this helps. and of course, the letters the pomes are maybe the best of the sorid worst of us, but I keep thinking of everybody shitting and then getting up to wipe their asses, dabbing in the paper, holding it in the hand, looking tat the smear smears of brown and then the terds and the n flushing it away, looking at the swirl of guggling white anhi hi hoping tit high that it does not stuff up that the mackeral holy get it so we can eat it again and jam it down and out, hurrah. I give top shit advice so listen, I am one eight eighth of your heart, and I say, you';l get some good ones, the very worst and best of men come clean sometimes, but really, mostly, I guess as your finding out—you'll get flashes and flares, but mostly sandin the motor, crap, hackneyed, and it being loose will often be worse, and so that's more hell, yet we are used to that, so I'd say (the voice from above) that you should try to pick the meat, the avocado, I mean EXCERPTS, baby, you read? sure you do. of course, like thaat ass C.C. would say, all my letters are good, but if you printed *all* my letters y'd probably make a fortune and I'm not quite ready to spill I mean spoil you yet.

the rats are drunk and the bluebells dance upon the top of WITHERED TITS.

not being shit, but I wish you could get hold of the 50 or 60 letters I wrote CORRINGTON, but doubt that he'll let you peek. do I guess right here? Willie all right, mostly more so once, but gone off on tangent of success and power, and maybe he's right, shit, I don't know, I don't know, we did not get on wll in new Orleansin that room full of prefessers and laymen hymen lawyers and bigwigs, and I didn't say anthihing which was cowardly, but on the other hand, they didn't give me much a chance too. all that exposition of brilliance and nobody really wanting to get drunnk. I just get the toothache of everywhere, these people sitting around matching wits and in the pocket brilliances . . . I sometimesdo think that I am XRA crAZY because I am tired and do not seem to care, although actually I do care, andI remember Williams, Miller Williams was hard but kind and gave me a book of his poems, but even Jon gave me a tough time—holding things against me that I said anddid while drunk, and I think this is amatuer, and I keep thinking of the boys who did a lot of TIME up there and I keep thinking they haven't learned basics—the 8 or 9 whores I shacked with knew more about me drunk than Jon could understand. what good's the lockup if you come out

183

like a little boy with a blackboard? you and Jon Webb and Louise
Webb are the only living editors that I know in this world—yet if
if it comes to a break I will go elsewhere—and not be published. God,
I guess I give a lot of shit and ask forgiveness, but I've
                    what? whet where am I?
                    the woman just camein and asked me to fk readone
of her pomes. o.k. pome but title way off, I had to tell her so. all right?
        man, I can barely findthe keys where was I?
        woman came in and said we she was almost outa cigarettes
        I said go get some I'll watch t h e kid
        and I pray that this is what keeps us from conquering room
        Rpm Rome I mean or not being a tetrander
        I guess by now that you gather by now that I my my am a nut
case instead of the true inspirational ½poet, but I do not think that
this bothers you, so far you are the only man I can trust, and I do
not mean some kind of fictional handholding duressof gag ignomy,
when you rot or I ror rot roar, it will be time enough to let go, where
was I???
        o, yes—
                    a native American citizen must submit with his applica-
                    tion for transport: a birth certificate, or, if such a cer-
                    tificate is is not obtainable, a bapistmal certicite or a cer-
                    tified cop y of the record of
                                    bastardism.
        god, thanks for your invite to sleep u ½ on your rug when the
        human beasts close in, but I cannot accept mostly because I love
        yor wife and your children and your walls, and also my love for
        you goes too deep to allow myself to die prick thing or wounded
        dove within your gentle hands, and now christ I've said p5ick-
        thing andnow you think it's my prick between your hands and
        that I am jiving you, god god I mustn't drink so much exce t
        I want to, what I mean to say, my sorrow nose a way to end get
        off the head when it hurts enough, I got the secret, you know
        what I mean.
look, don' ever send me money: I will take it
it's not lack of money keeps me from sending letters
shit written to me it's only that after reading the
letters I am scard scared thatnobody has written to
me. it came as a kind of shcok I keep dying up and
down, dull-eyed sacroscant mar macarroni of self

184

I don't think anybody knows
and it is really very much like
being lockedin a closetful of
socks and wrinkled shirst
and hearing the breadman's whistel
at noon and no way to get out
to buy a taffy-roll or a green smock
full of warm woman bending over a cupcake
whileher husband dies in a Kansas City
electrodudc of shock
and victory.

another free pome for your shithouse . . .
your furnish the paper and I'll furnish the
HA HA HA hahaha
                    rest,
                        baby.
what seems the cunt mock intonation of the gravity of my sadness
is not a play game   it is eyow HEAVY
    and I do not promise you suicide or anything that *must*
    be cone snapped intto turtle's mouth
                            done
only what I've got to do want feel now here hear hear
you cotton-stainer long-haired squash bug ally in
pn pendulous necktie drifting
                    HOSUMMA!

I've run out o   of my children
            (they keep playing Gustave Hotlz "The Planets"
            becauw of these space cocksuckers and I grow very
            tired of bad music and plentifuf timing)

    I lost it.

    look, don't worry about paper for *Asshole Insane Enough to Live
Between Breasts,* I am most happy that you understood the manuscript
but I can't write any novel I think, unless I feel like it and I just
don't feel like it and maybe never will, andso here we go on being
poor, novels means dollars, and I still envision the smashed face not
giving in, stoking in the cigar, lighting it, saying fuck you, and all
escxuxses of later times if I even am around will call me a homo a

coward a fink a seller of cowardice, and who knows? maybe I am all or any of hell these, yet I sometimes think of those who makethe decisions, I sometimes think of what they are and where they are andI do not

       feel so good

now Richard Wagner.

    they stoked off Wagner and tossed him in the corner, these laterists, an expelled jackoff kid, and even an anti-Wagner school, and he had certain ways, of grandeur of malicious exploitation of sound but shit, don't they all? every man who arrives upon the scene thinks he knows it and most of them do, like Corrington, but they know too god damned much, and what they missed was the fact that Wagner had

     MUSCLE
       ENERGY
         HEART
and the guts to fill 40,000 pigs,
or   80,000
   human?
     beings.

      see Hon Jonathan Swift
      see Schopenhauer
      see Orpahn Anney.

    I am going to close this letter while I am drunk and this is the onl y way to do it otherwise we choose sides of ourselves to see

    I HOPE THAT YOUR PORCH STEPS HAVE SPLINTERS

    I HOPE THAT YOUR BALLS ACHE WHEN THE MOON IS
      HIGH HIGH HIGH

    I HOPE THAT THEY KILL THE FACTORIES
    AND THE ALREADY DEAD
    I HOPE THAT THEY KILL THEM SOMEMORE SO
      THAT MY $$$# EYES MAY SEE
      MERCY

        within them
        within
          me.

186

bathroom poem.

something about Jean's Journal. you were good man not too attack too hard, cd. have told the bitch she shd have named dog after
her pussy.
            I guess Stravinsky Pound
            John Fante to be the best men
            of our age
            with the early Saroyan
                    even then lying to himself
            but wide and lovely style of flaoting
yet to go down in the muck when the war began
            WORLD WAR 2
                    he did not follow his dream and
                    he therefore died
and I am trying to pick up some of the strings from the best of M9lton
dante inferno big nose wax mustache death of them all
        somebody once took me into seeing this old and almost famous
poet andI did not want to go u know fuck u but I got drunk enough
and we went, the id kid with the scarf around and and around his
neck and me I went with some whore some woman and the great
poet finally leaned forward and he said to me:
            I THOUGH YOU WERE YOUNGER THAN YOU ARE.

            and we watched his young boy who looked like a woman
                    pa. play
            the piano and he p.a played it good good
            I got icehole asshole chills on t into the dark of me,
            he was good
            yet he was pitiful—
            like a srouge a stranger trained to die a certain way,
            and his mother knew
            as , I said goodbye
            she said
            he's so strange, he's so little man, I don't think
            he's ever kissed a
            girl.

            don't worry, mama, I told her, your little boy is
            beautiful, and goodnight, and I stole
            one of there gentle little statutes of

pewter
and then gabe it very much back and
smiled

and they, Mr.Bukowski, I'm very sorry we do not
drin herem , but good to meet you   we've
read your work
somewhere.

　　　　　. . . look blaz not much good
　　　　　　　list ning to Srav Strav
　　　　　　　　　and trhing to fond i find
　　　　　　　　　　　k e y s

　　　　I better leave
　　　　　　　　now.

　　　　　　　if I could piss only be
　　　　　　　the shadow of this
　　　　　　　　man's
　　　　　　　　　　giant.

　　I've got to wake up to that yellow ;pro mise of action and I w n't
certainly bd be ready.
　　　　　　　think of the
　　　　　　　breadmaan,
　　　　　　　Buk

[To Steven Richmond]
July 23, 1965

[* * *] I am reading Celine, who is somebody else who writes
better than I do, and I find this *comforting,* I like to be led along,
I like somebody else to do THE DIRTY WORK. there are so few people that I *can* read—Camus' *The Stranger,* the early Sartre, the few
poems of that homo Genet; Jeffers; Auden before he got comfortable;
the early Shapiro (and then with a sense of distrust); Cummings when
he didn't get too *too* fucking cute; the early Spender—

188

"the living or the dying,
this man's dead life or
that man's life

        dying."

Patchen's got a little too much sugar for me, too much melo-dramatic bravado which makes me feel as if I had been crying in a movie house, but I find his drawings innocent and lovely and they continue to appear that way to my eye at this stage.

Of course, the Dickey boys, Allen Tate, the whole South Ken-yon Sewanee snob cocksuckers of the blood of Life, they write so very well, and they are real bastards, they know the game, it's a power game, and they know the language and the history, but they are tru-ly a bad people, the worst people of all in the worst game of all: con-ning men out of their souls. Last March in New Orleans I met a couple of Southern profs who had once been men and I could see that they were gone, and didn't speak, or that is, they spoke. one had acquired a whole new line of degrees, had gone to England and written a batch of research on James Joyce (but history will find, I say, that he wrote only one decent book: *Finnegans Wake*), and this boy had even been given a grant to do this, and the other one had been given a grant too and he went somewhere and translated somebody in South America (hell! vallejo again? or the other one? can't think, can't think), and one had a fine red beard and the other a beret and they shouted across the room arguing various things of university power—degrees, control of magazines, publication credits, all that shit, my god, jesus, all that shit, and there was some lawyer who had come over to the Quarter and this lawyer collected John Crowe Ransom, Allen Tate, Y. Winters, the mess, and I thought sure they would all leap together in the center of the room and kiss and ream and kiss and feel each other's balls if they had any. yet, in a sense, I was hurt, let's admit it: they did not admit the reality of my existence and soon forgot me. I should have known because I have been cooled all my life—beginning with my 2 bugged-up parents and down through the schoolyards and into the alleys with the winos and down through the women and the years and the liv-ing I was either always something to laugh at or forget, which was all right with me, I almost liked it, and still almost do, being alone, being alone here now with the girlchild screaming and the woman flushing the toilet . . . [* * *]

Blaz fucked-up again—this time not strike but something worse,

189

I can't tell you; maybe he will, and it's really none of my horse, but I keep thinking that he is the Great Romantic Caught in the Spider Dream, and worse yet the kid has got to begun believing that I am some source of wisdom or Life-long Kool, you know, and I think he expected me to o.k. his latest, but Christ, I can't walk a straight line most of the time myself, and if I had to straight-talk him I'd say 2 things at the same time:

a) take what you want, take what's good for you, take what keeps you alive

b) but don't kill anybody ever in the process in this process who has ever loved you depended on you or saved *your* life.

if you take a without b you don't make it and whatever you take will kill you because you are as phoney as that which you wish to overthrow. the weakest men take that which seems immediately better; the strongest men hurt themselves (if hurt has to be), and wait. I'd never say this if I were sober, of course, but I'm seldom sober, of course. [* * *]

[To Jim Roman]
July 23, 1965

I really believe that *Cold Dogs* will be issued [* * *]

No, I didn't see Jonathan Williams when he hit town. I have a reputation as a vicious and nasty drunk (not entirely unfounded) and somebody gave him the word prob. when he asked. That's all right. [* * *]

oh yes, Stuart hung with 3100 copies of *Crucifix* but he'll unload and at $7.50 too. now I am fairly high on beer, typing this in the kitchen while the woman and the ten month old girl sit in the front room listening to Russian poetry on the FM radio. I can't listen because almost all poetry is bad for me; it irritates; me makes me twitch and have spasms. I don't understand it, I feel as if I were being reamed in a pig pen. [* * *]

p.s. Finally reading Celine and it's about time. A master, no doubt of it.

[To Jon and Louise Webb]
July 26, 1965

[* * *] Did Corrington show before you left town? if so, I think
we gotta give him points. I think I have g.d. been too hard on too
many people. to hell with KNOCK CORRINGTON. to hell with
KNOCK SHERMAN. this is small and I am sick of myself. I can
disagree with some of their principles and ways and manueverings,
but, hell, no man knows when he is right and when he starts thinking he is always right and that the universe is his apple, then he might
as well either start a whorehouse or become a preacher. he's got rocks.
[* * *] I am still growing up and I'm very much afraid that when
I reach full size that I will be dead.

Marina keeps yanking at me and I lift her up and she sits here
in her yellow pajamas

> banging at the typewriter
> grabbing for my cigar and beer
> tiny hand sea-blue eyes
> she thinks me a monster of heroic proportions,
> my god such a sweet DOLL!!!
> she breaks me and breaks me up again and again
> as I peer at her out of my
> evil face.

the faucet drips. and on and on I write, it's so easy when drunk.
the poems are flowing again, poems, poems, and good or bad
they may be, I am now easier to live with, I'd suppose. those 2
books, they almost froze me. It's like somebody wrote me, "Well,
you might as well kill yourself now and go out clean." I know what
he means. but what about Marina? I think she likes me very much,
she does seem to, so suppose I left now? a dirty trick I'd think. you
should see her eyes. what eyes what eyes what eyes!!! [* * *]

look here, if Henry Miller liked *Crucifix* that's good enough for
me, that's the best critic there is—a man who has lived that hard
that long just can't learn to lie and also has no need to. Christ, Jon
and Lou, isn't life *really* strange??? that a man like Henry Miller would
be speaking about all of us? we are truly lucky, we are in touch with
the gods, and I am happy for us all. god damn, that was a *good* phone
call, you LIFTED ME RIGHT UP WITH YOUR HAPPINESS and that is
why I keep drinking and write on and on. Frances has fixed me

191

something to eat but I keep saying no no, I am busy, to hell with food! oh shit, everything is so strange; it's so good to know the good people, but do you know what else??? we must be wary, we must be careful, we must follow our own guts . . . or else the poems will quit, we will quit and we will forget where we are. look, the world is still, I think (so far), a very horrible place filled with horrible people (am I snitching?) (I keep opening beers and drinking them and lighting cigars like a madman), look, look, it's only next poem or the way we walk or the way we act or respond to the next situation. all we've done beforehand DOESN'T COUNT IF WE WASTE IT! and this is what gets me: so many writers, artists, people, begun well who turn to shit when in the beginning they knew what SHIT was. but all it takes is a letter from the editor of *The New Yorker*. and they sell. thank god I still had the nerve to tell an editor of some big publishing house, last year or so, that I simply did not feel like writing a novel upon his request. I keep thinking of Corrington (I'm snitching again), and thinking of death. look, I am crazy with everything, I am confused but it seems to be quite simple to me— the line is drawn, either you're on this side of the line or that. they say any man can be bought. I deny this. they say that any man, any man has his price. I don't have a price. it may be the biggest laugh of the century. they may buy me with a lollipop. poverty is bad enough but poverty that you drag others into beside yourself is what makes them win, what makes you sell out. yet I believe that this beautiful little girl with the beautiful eyes would become less instead of more beautiful if I sold out. that's the way it works. backwards. it really takes more than 2,000 years of Christianity or anti-Christianity for a man even to get a half decent bearing. and 65 or 75 years of life are not enough. hardly a beginning. I began at 35 which leaves me nothing, and the way I drink and have lived, certainly less than half, perhaps. not even another lousy Summer or 2. well, I have talked long enough. [* * *]

[To Ruth Wantling]
August 10, 1965

[* * *] the heat has me goofy too. and I get these pains in my neck and back and chest, I feel like screaming, "oh Christ, let's start

the bloody Crucifixion!" I don't know what I've got. but last night I sat there working with a black foreman glaring at a spot at the back of my neck and the human race went down like lumps of gravy mixed with dung and spittle. I played a little game last night—each person I saw I asked myself, IF YOU HAD THE POWER TO ORDER THE DEATH OF THIS PERSON, WOULD YOU DO SO?

and as they walked by, man and woman, I'd say to myself:

that one, sure!

and that one, MOST SURELY!

and look at that pig, that gross manure, runs through with con-ceit! death to that!

and look, that one thinks it's pretty! ugg.

and that one must go and that one, and that, and look at THAT ONE—a sore in the eye of the sun, kill him!

anyhow, nobody got by. it was very sad. no nobility. no grace of walk. not a flower. not a leaf. not even a water spaniel. just bugs, pigs, worms, ant-eaters, gorillas, monkeys, pageboys, so on so. on.

I hope it's a better night tonight, I hope that I see somebody whether the pains stop or not.

you go easy now. not much sense to anything, of course. your husband writing better as the years prop him up, but hope he does not get too well-known. this usually flips them over the side and does them in. [* * *]

The books by Ginsberg, Kerouac, Corso, and Burroughs that Bukowski lists below were in fact in print in 1965. Carl Larsen's Plot to Assassinate . . . was published by Seven Poets Press in 1962.

[To Jim Roman]
August 14, 1965

[* * *] my god, I know, I know little about Patchen, I know the *name*, and that's all. this is the hell of it with people who come out in small chapbooks, small books of poetry, editions of 200-500. they are soon swept up and the years go by, and then there's just the sort of a ring of a name somewhere. I'd like to see some publisher reissue

some of these—*Howl, On the Road, Gasoline, the Naked Lunch, The Plot to Assassinate the Chase Manhattan Bank, It Catches My Heart in Its Hands*. . . I don't have any of these myself except the last one. and then there's Patchen. and what he has written, drawn. Maybe *Outsider* #4 will throw some light where it's needed. [* * *]

it's been searing hot here for a week running, between 95 and 100. race riots in the streets. stores burning and looted, automobiles burning; whites and police beaten. whole blocks on fire. fireman shot at. all hell. I guess they'll clean their area out and then come up here looking for me. I've got my black face ready, ready. "*Mammy! Mammy!*" "motha-fucka!" of course, I've got nothing for them to steal except a couple of books of poetry but I'm surrounded by a lot of white meat they'd just love to beat on. hell, I know they've had it rough; I have too. the only difference being that they want a lot of things that I don't want. anyhow, it's hot and there's FUN in town. they caught a white guy the other night and beat him, beat him until one of his eyes was hanging from a thread out of the socket. I keep thinking it's a good thing the whites didn't do this to a BLACK or there'd be a national uproar. the whole thing, I think, is just the human monster showing teeth, shitting upon itself every chance it gets. the social workers and professors can talk about conditions and background and all the big glib vacant words, but it's just the human-thing with hands and feet and bloody flat brain and soul letting go in another direction. shit will always find a direction out, and if it doesn't, they'll operate or blast it out. I mean black shit, white shit, brown shit, yellow shit. I need me a wall, oh, I need me a 12 foot wall. with beer inside, with me inside. oh, I need me a 12 foot wall.

well, like I said, it's hot and we're all a little off in the noodle today. [* * *]

[To Douglas Blazek]
[August 15?, 1965]

[* * *] this is Sunday. I've drunk about 2 six packs tall and still feel quite sober although I am gradually growing deaf. will be 45 years old on the 16th., my god my god my god. don't think I don't remember being young—the bars, the fights, the alleys, everything— refusing marriage, work, country, culture, literature, the sum total.

194

now I sit trapped in a little by everything; the heart got soft, I slipped here and there, finally. and that's how they trap the fox and the madman.

I wonder about you out there and I know that you have been going through your own particular type of HELL, the Blatt thing, the factory, everything, and that I have been very little use to you. I am sorry; mostly I only write poems, and many of these—as you know—not so good. Wantling tells me this and you tell me this about *Crucifix,* and I know that it is true. I knew that when I was down there in New Orleans, I knew I sensed that old man Webb wanted more and better poems but I couldn't do it. I just kept wandering the streets a drunken jackal of self, wandering drunk, and I could not come up with it. and then they charge $7.50 a copy; well, they had their makeup and format and their artist—only the poet dipped between the slabs. so fuck it. I've died before. why lift me upside-down? why strain at me? I think that what might have held the pages down was a more clever poet, practiced. I only mourn and dip within my own ink tears. I don't know the rules. and I get the side whispers around here from the woman's poetry-group finks who slip in through the doors while I am asleep? "he's slipped." "um, this is really not as good as *It Catches.*" so, what the hell do they want? we all slip. we slip all the way into the grave and then we stretch out straight and no more vomit no more bluebirds no more busrides to East Kansas City and a blow job by a maid with a lisp and a big ass for 3 dollars. the woman now in here sliding a big knife into a mayonnaise jar, clank clank clank, smiling a sunlight smile and not realizing that I am writing to the great Blazek. hello to Alta, by the way, and that I'd suggest that she hang close, you'll make it, hell, you've got to, jolly old chopper, I'd like *you* at my funeral, don't you see? a few sharp mad words. are you still there? all right, I'll no longer ask you to "hold" but you must have known what I meant when I said it. the other night, coming out of the slave pit, here was this long freighter load behind an electric motor dragging this body, one ball here one ball there, cock sliding into the moon, asshole like a gnome, fingers and arms spitting at the sky, a letter to mother in the back pocket like a dirty sex picture, some bum had gotten caught and dragged beneath the wheels . . . blood of course, the human body is mostly blood and mystery and sadness . . . a dirty game . . . and a voice shouted out: STOP THE TRAIN!

later, after they examined the shreds, they found it was o.k. "Just a transient," they said.

just think if it had been a United States congressman. or president Johnson. but to my mind this man could have easily been a better man than any of them. and probably was. and this is the insaneness of our times: that only what you KNOW or are TOLD ABOUT can be hurt. all else is either shit or the enemy or useless. says who? what the fuck is this? I am getting tired of it. [* * *]

I almost never think of suicide anymore. what would be the sense in killing this cuckold, this fat demented flabby body, this distilled eye, this color of YELLOW. I've got a yellow streak running up and down my back that would make the Sahara Desert look like a children's sand pile. else I would have killed myself long ago.

> so here I sit like a shit
> writing a 23 year old kid I never met
> and I get drunkeran drunker
> and jam the beer down down
> the sunlight is all gone
> and the cigars too
> I go to the woman's cigarettes
> and light one after the other
> like a jackal imbecile
> and I don't know where I am
> and a small light burns over my head
> a touch of endurance up there
> and it makes me almost smile
> but the world's out there humming
> and the world's not right for me
> which makes me a de-balled oxen in the
> poverty of myself
> and that's sweet enough for me
> and I lift the beercan and
> drink.

what I mean is, kid, where do we from here? relief rolls? the bloody razor blade? Eartha Kitt, that voice, through a foggy radio? that foreman's face like God, cut from wood, from glass, seeming to know but knowing nothing nothing . . . and so, such poor fuckers as you and i? you and I? we turn to the immortals and the immortals hand us a hot turd, the smell of shit. what a sweet mad game! tricked all the way.—and the most famous poets of our Age, they appear in the pages of the New Yorker, silk white, and you read the poems

196

again and again; and the poems say
NOTHING.

except they are kinda nice. eyow eee yes. how they work the word.
this takes training and culture. not everybody can do this. the slip
of the word like the knife into Caesar.

let me make up a New Yorker poem as drunk as I am I asshole
may not get it, anyhow—

> mass effusion darkens my brain—
> Clymentia, where are you—
> with the silver goatherd
> or emptying the glass of
> me?
> swish, swish the coattails of the
> Ark, never by god gone never gone
> by god, sweet please, Clymentia,
> the dark boys coming over the hill
> into a machinegun fire
> that would moon-strike gorgeous
> teacups from
> Georgia to Abeline.

and so on. this they consider poetry because it's pretty and it's
a con game and they think that we CAN'T write it, but we can, we
simply refuse to, we simply refuse to give more to an Age that already
stinks like an old garbage can, and that after Pound there has to be
somebody and after Eliot there has to be somebody, and it's a shame
but—Ginsberg, Corso, the rest have been sucked in playing their en-
trails across the applause of the crowd, and they are dead and they
know that they are dead, it's useless, they've skipped across listened
to the applause of half-drunk freaks too long too long, too long have
they taken the bait, and I think of one of Corso's poems: "I Hate
Old Postmen!" this sounds nice, but I predict that when Corso reaches
the age of 45 he won't be writing at all. of course, I will be dead
so it won't matter. but the Ginsberg, Corso crew (and they write
well) will die because they can't resist the delicacy of being forever
known forever touched forever heard NOW before 20, 18, 45 people
applauding their stuff. they are weak and lack STEEL GUT. I learned
in barrooms of the world who the men were. those who spouted the
worst were the lousiest fighters. the quiet man was always another
kind of job. I don't want to talk like Hemingway, but my face is not

only scarred because of disease. I've caught some good ones.

I am an ugly man, surely, but I've also learned that there other kinds of ugliness; and that some beatings that I have taken in alleys, or from a friend across the room, these do not diminish me.

Blaze god damn it, I am SORRY SORRY I could not help you in the Blatt thing. fuck poetry. poetry makes me vomit. and I am tired of fights on the front lawn. I've had enough of that Hemingway stuff to last me 300 years, 2 men on the front lawn punching the living shit out of each other, blood going, we should be punching Johnson right into his fat Texas map for killing us *all*, for trying to be a shadow of Frankie D. what a tent show we put on, eh?

and then we open the *New Yorker* and here's one of the Dickey boys—who knows the difference.—

of course, I keep getting drunker and drunker and this makes less and less sense.

I think I'll chop it off and just fall forward over the keys. BROOKS TOO BROAD FOR LEAPING. good night, babe.

[To Douglas Blazek]
August 24, 1965

the shits around here all discussing the race riots but they are all in the limbo theory, hacking around and vomiting all over their minds and enjoying it listening to the sounds of their own voices, but they are all cotton, cotton-shit with paper faces worse than any halloween masks, and it all ends up like a skeleton trying to fuck a 500 pound ape-gorilla . . . they just don't just can't make it. I speak of certain friends of the woman's who come around. my friends are different, hahah ha! the few of them. at least they don't get out beyond the depth of a dripping cunt until they've thought awhile. I can't think of thinking as an *activate* sort of thing like throwing a ball, even if you've studied the target a long time. thinking is very strange; mostly *it* thinks you and it takes its time. that's why these people who warble their ideas for hours make me want to walk away from them—they are all unpacked loose. besides one of them ate my steak. I left the other night for work and here was this Stanley from her Writer's Group warbling on the couch. he's the one who claims that his writer's group writes better poetry, better stuff than any of the stuff printed in the littles. and they claim they don't send their stuff out, any of them, and that's why you don't see it in print. the magazines are not good enough, real enough, to recognize them. sweetheart, I have not only seen and listened to some of these but have also read some of their stuff. it is weak, weaker than weak; trivial, flat, washed-out. their egos can't face rejection so they gather together each week, chatter and praise each other, scream at each other, haggle, and make up the dreamthing that their stuff is good. better than. anyway, I came home from work, balls-tired and looked in the refrig. "hey, where's my steak? where'd ya put my steak?" 2 hours overtime and I was thinking of that steak sandwich and a beer and the yellow light over my head as I read the race results. "oh, Stanley ate your steak," she said. "he can't cook at his place and I don't think he's working a full-time job." I didn't say anything, but when that monkey starts getting into my beer and whiskey, somebody's gona get hurt.

I wrote Henry Miller the other day to twist 15 bucks from a patron of his who promised same if I mailed Henry 3 more *Crux*. I undersell Stuart and it buys whiskey and some horsebets. like I've got a $70 brake repair bill. the *car* isn't worth that. anyhow, I was drunk and inferred that Henry shake his patron out of his money tree. the 15 arrived from one source today and the Miller letter from another: partial quote: "I hope you're not drinking yourself to death! and, especially not when you're writing. It's a sure way to kill the source of inspiration. drink only when you're happy *if you can.* Never to drown your sorrows. and never drink alone!" of course I don't buy any of this. I don't worry about inspiration. when the writing dies, it dies; fuck it. *I drink to keep going another day.* and I've found that the best way to drink is to drink ALONE. even with a woman and a kid around, I'm drinking alone. can after can laced with a half pint or pint. and I stretch wall to wall in the light, I feel as if I were filled with meat and oranges and burning suns, and the radio plays and I hit the typer maybe and look down at the torn and ink-stained oilcloth on the kitchen table, a kitchen table in hell; a life, not a season in hell; the stink of everything, myself aging; people turning to warts; everything going, sinking, 2 buttons on shirt missing, belly working out; days of dull clubbing work ahead—hours running around with their heads chopped-off, and I lift the drink I pour in the drink, the only thing to do, and Miller asks me to worry about the source of INSPIRATION? I can't look at anything, really look at anything without wanting to tear myself apart. drinking is a temporary form

199

of suicide wherein I am allowed to kill myself and then return to life again. drinking is just a little paste to hold on my arms and my legs and my pecker and my head and the rest. writing is only a sheet of paper; I am something that walks around and looks out of a window. amen. [* * *]

my god, did I cry that you didn't like my poems?? I musta been drunk. this is really amateur, old ladies' sewing, circle tears. it's as silly as walking in dogshit. forgive me. we all stumble, even old iron-head here. [* * *]

[To Jim Roman]
August 28, 1965

[* * *] it seems like everybody and his grandma's dog now own a mimeo machine and is putting out a magazine, and most of them are bad, but a few are good. I yearn for the old days when everything came out in clean print and we knew where everything was. some of the mimeo boys put out faded half-hearted almost unreadable pages, and some of the big boys drop off their crap in here—stuff they can't get to go elsewhere. and the little boys too. I tend to do it. yet there are a few good mimeos and there are some many bad print jobs, and the essence, the secret, is content. [* * *]

[To Jon and Louise Webb]
September 7, 1965

I had 5 days off (Labor Day + 4) and a hell of a five, and I'm glad I wasn't with you because my mind drew a blank and I fell all over myself, drunk in the streets, I am now lousy bloody bruised—each knee and elbow a blash and scab of blood where I landed each time, drunk, dumping myself like damn keen garbage—what a mess, and no sense to it, I know. my new system seems to work but no good because as soon as I make it I blow it, give it away on the streets, burn it burn it, my god sometimes I think I am truly crazy, but hell, here I sit, trying to shape up for tomorrow to go back in if the job is still there, and I never know—I have a habit of showing in places like that and raising a lot of shit. lost my job at the Biltmore hotel that way. no matter. and it's my teeth too, I've got a half dozen them aching and I can't sleep—but why all these complaints? I bring on my own woe. I keep thinking of Crane jumping off the back of that ship. of course, Crane was a homo, but he was also human. I don't think anybody but a drunk can understand the terrible the horrible horrible BLUES!!! a hangover can bring! of course, I am no longer hung now, am fairly high, and even enclose a half-dozen poems I batted off tonight. not that it matters that they are good or not; what matters is a little juice is flowing, good or bad, there's a little flowing again. I had a hell of a period, it was like steel walls built all around me. but now a little song and dance. it's not excellence we want, it's a kind of going-on, a clown's gesture. it took some deciding to come to this. I think we are all too careful. fuck reputation. if I have a reputation it's only the dirty work of others. I have a right to go on. nobody has the rights to rope and bind me. fuck 'em.

so the eagle came over the San Marcos mountain like a horse and I sat under a busy and rolled a cigarette just like in the old days with Minnie and Mary and Jane in the cheap rooming houses, and it's cigarettes like this and comic strips and radios that work badly and a clean pair of stockings and something to laugh at that keep a man going—even something like Joe Conrad or Tolstoy and they are pretty bad; even something like Faulkner and he's horrible. an eagle over the San Marcos. a cup Hem drank coffee out of. a photograph of your father shooting golf in knickers. Herbert Hoover, alive, without wrinkles. victrolas you had to pump. Icemen with leather shoulders. God on the dole. Mickey Rooney in a tent getting whipped by Wallace Beery. so the eagle came over the San Marcos. the san marcos. and I read where India and Pakistan are fighting, something about a border. but it's not something about a border. it's something about us. we don't make it. I don't make it. I stink. I am ashamed of myself. I am not ashamed of you, I can never be ashamed of you. a cigarette. bad writing. more bad writing. Jane told me that I couldn't write. when Burnett wrote back—"all your people seem to die in their own excrement," dear Jane thought this was wonderful criticism. "That RIGHT, that's RIGHT!" she screamed, "ALL YOUR PEOPLE DIE IN THEIR OWN SHIT!" I only told her, "For Christ's sake, drink your wine and shut up!" I had always thought that all people died in their own shit; it wasn't until Jane and Burnett told me that I thought there would be an alternative?? and the eagle came over the San Marcos and stopped to shit and was killed by a most agile wildcat, looked something like me.

as bad as I feel sometimes it comes pretty close to the end but I remember reading a Norwegian somewhere??? I was much younger. something called the suicide. *The Suicide.* This Icelander could write much better than I; married 3 or 4 times, born children, plowed the land, gone crazy, sucked up years of the sun, I think he finally died an old age, maybe in prison or embarrassment for being a political dupe—became so because he went to the underdog, what was his name? his name? no matter. the SUICIDE wanted to live so badly that given the final great and stereotyped chance, he wouldn't buy it. but this isn't any secret. many men who want to kill themselves only wish to do it because they are tired of being born in an age that will not let them live. I fall in love with my own limbs, my head ugly as it may be, my cock, my balls, my writes by merely being around them, by being with them, awake and asleep, my head, my breathing, my sense of the sun and walls; but when these things become too greatly violated by outside forces I will make the choice, and then finally the choice will not be now when but how?

I have met garbage men with more soul than President Johnson; and this is not sad, this is the way it should be. Johnson is trying to stir alive the soul of Franky D.—which was War and Economic Justice. well, that's the same chapter. I am not much on these history-makers, these killers; but I'd like to see just one pop up: non-war and economic justice. but this is the hell of too much thought. I sit here writing you tonight with 6 teeth aching the living christ outa me and only 2 beers left and the landlord will want his $85, even tho once a week she or he will come down and get me and ask me to get drunk with them and so I'll get drunk with them, we'll talk, and then we'll sing corny songs, songs of their choice, and I'm glad to see them happy but they don't help my happiness much except that they drink and I drink and we sit there in their breakfast nook until Frances brings the kid and the kid cries and Frances says, "come home, come home!" so I come home, fuck it, and it's a beautiful little girl, tho, and I think she loves me. that's hell. [* * *]

[To Ruth Wantling]
September 11, 1965

in response to your last letter, which I realize was a lot in jest but not entirely—yes, I prob. do carry around my little wooden cross of pain and wave it a bit too much, and even feel foolish defending it . . . for it's up to a man to create art if he's able, and not to talk about it, which, it seems, he's always more than able. I'm nuts, yes, reamed-out and sick; a lot of it shows in the poems. I am an anti-man, pretty sick of the show, yet I have not killed myself, so you have me there; but if you think my way is bad, you ought to try the other—I mean the life-is-good, God-is-good, life-is-beautiful crew. Mostly midwest with names like Irma Tremble Stockholder or Bobby Poots West. they vomit continual Affirmation at a sickening rate, and just because you don't see the magazines around (I doubt Bill reads them) doesn't mean that they don't exist. don't get the idea that everybody writes like Wantling (they can't) or Bukowski. they don't. just for a laugh to jack-off the fleas I once sent a couple of poems into one of those golden hymn singing outfits. they took them. but I had to pay the price. a long letter came along: "I know your type, brilliant but a drunkard, a gambler, unhappy, disbelieving in God . . ." (so on, so on). "I awaken every morning to the sound of birds outside my window and I have birds inside too, my canaries, and I have joy and peace, and my magazine pays for itself." the letter was 4 or 5 pages long in the handwriting of an old woman. I took all her guff until she mentioned that was her policy to make contributors pay for their issue. I wrote back an ass-scorcher and got my issue free. full of hundreds of 3 or 4 lines poems. a photo of a man (poet?) in airforce uniform on cover. so this is the way it works: she thinks I'm sick and I think she's dull. how do we know who's right as I sit here listening to E. Power Biggs pound out Handel?

then, too, there's something else. In America, everybody's supposed to be making it. if you don't make it, that's all right too—only *play* like you're making it. riots are accidents. refuse to think. you know how it works. somebody will pass you on the sidewalk, say a neighbor, and he'll say (sure, he will), "Good morning, nice day, isn't it?" and you're supposed to say, "yes, it is a nice day," and that ends it. but if you say, "no, it isn't a nice day," or the answer to the other question (how are you today?) with "I don't feel so good," he will act as if struck across the face. you aren't playing the game, and this is *not* just a little voice game, it extends all up and down and across through life. phonies, galore, phonies walking around under the same sun that makes roses, that makes wheat. now, I am not a mad seeker after TRUTH, god damn all that; but I can and do get a bellyful of phonies, and although I don't care to machine gun them down I'd like to get away from them but I can't because I must live with them, work in their factories, fuck their women and drink their booze and kick their dogs and eat their beans. about the only chance a punk like me has to say anything is on a piece of paper called a poem, someplace in between sleeping, eating, batting a woman off what's left of your soul and turning a screw in a factory. so if it comes out as a scream sometimes it really is because the pinch is too tight, the Bastard keeps tightening the vise and smiling and you're supposed to sing The Jelly Roll Blues or say a couple of Hail Marys, but it doesn't work. we are dying inch by inch, being chopped-up and killed by the minute by the hour. I keep looking at that clock, doing the same dull things over and over and over again with my hands, looking at the clock, and doing the dull thing over and over much faster than I want to in order to keep up with production so I can keep my job and die some more, and I keep looking up at the clock, and I die a minute at a time . . . ALL THOSE MINUTES THAT I COULD BE SHIT SHIT USING FOR MYSELF!!! . . . never to be gotten back again, and all around me my fellow-workers laugh a continual hysterical almost female laughter while bragging on their virility as MEN!!!, or there's the tough type full of hatred, nothing but hatred hatred and not even knowing why, swaggering to the latrine thinking he's cool, cool, but what a face on this type of job—a kind of flat shiny deadness with 2 little piglet eyes peering out. and everybody TALKING TALKING about . . . nothing. sports lifts them. they can talk baseball all night, getting fighting mad, or insane, and still not knowing anything about the game. jabber, jabber; my hands moving, moving, the clock hands stuck like arrows in the wall. self-pity? why not? but if we could only do the job quietly without the neurotic jabbering, the fear, the lies, the back-stabbers, the swine, the slickers . . . and I watch the clock and it finally gets there, and if I am lucky they do not call one or 2 or 3 or 4 hours overtime. the only time I am free is driving from the job to where I live in the early a.m. all other times somebody is getting at me. so I get home (home? 2 rooms? a woman, man and child in the same bed?) (I want riches! I want to fuck Elizabeth Taylor's maid!) so I get home and I can't sleep, I can never sleep. I just lay there and listen to the woman and the kid snore. it's beautiful. and I watch the light change from black to gray to red to orange to yellow and finally it's morning and I still stay in bed like an invalid and about noon I go to sleep and about 4:30 p.m. I have to get up again and go to work. nuts? sure, I'm nuts. what do I care about sending kids off to school if the world does not fit around them? President Johnson looks like all the idiot and unfeeling men I've worked for and quit from and been fired from. bombs like walnuts on a row of trees. the clock, the clock, death riding me home in the car repeating the little dirty jokes of my fellow working man. and some x-whore operating a poetry magazine in the Midwest and giving me a lot of jazz about sparrows singing, the angels of God awakening her. if I don't crash through with a poem now and then, I am finished. drink alone is not enough. staring at the ceiling is not enough. my little wooden cross. sure. and yours,

[P.S.] my god, it's all so terrible: all our self-importance; we'll all soon be dust, and that's not news, not news. less even than the smell of shit.

[To William Wantling]
September 11, 1965

as ya can see, I've burned myself out writing a letter to your wife (enclosed) when I should be out building little bird-houses for the approaching winter and those little bastards too lazy to leave this Goldwater territory.

where the riots have just about said quits and the committees are in dividing govt. poverty program funds among contractors, engineers, bullshitters and companies to train janitors—or as they now are called Floor Engineers. I was a janitor for a while but I can never imagine a man calling himself a Floor Engineer when he has to walk into the woman's crapper and clean up what they leave behind. I couldn't get a hard-on for a year after working in that place. what they leave behind. and on the floor. and in that little compartment behind the seat. or alongside of it. or wherever it was.

knives, guns? you're one deep beyond me. I can understand drilling wood with a bit, tho. that's fetching. your problem, of course, is not that you're insane but that you are entirely too sane. through war, jail, dope, woman you're still twitching to find something to hang your hat onto and you probably don't wear one until it snows.

I guess, if I can guess, that what hurts is that no matter what men go through, little changes them. they may change an inch for a moment, then snap back, then snap to. the centuries and the training are too jesus much for them. you want victory now, not in your grave where it doesn't count. I'm too tired for victory. I fight a slow withdrawal. I can't make it. if your wife only realized that while you are drilling into that ladder that what is left of your soul is falling back into place. I can see you out there now in the middle of the night, a small light bulb like a crazy sun hanging near your ear and you are smelling the wood and the burning oil from the bit, jesus, what sweetness, nobody around, not even people you love, and if the people you loved would leave you alone you'd come to them with eyes shining in your head so beautiful they'd cry cry cry, but the average woman and no matter how good she is, is only more or less average and the Art they help create is the child and that is enough and too much for me; the average woman wants a constant reminder of love and fuck, and from their angle, I can't blame them—they figure we've been off to a big ball game in hell, tough, yeah, but how about that long cock now, daddy? you haven't told me you loved me since I burned my hand making strawberry jam in 1961. yet, love is confining if you hold it too close to your own belly. I read somewhere a week or so ago that the food America throws into its garbage cans could feed two-thirds of a world and that two-thirds of the world is starving. think how many lovers have thrown their garbage to the pits. love is, in a sense, only a form of selfishness, a form of recognition, usually between 2 people. I do suppose when you are drilling that wood in the middle of the night that all this has occurred to you, but just to let you know that I have thought of it too, and that you are not insane, and that the faces you'd think of machine-gunning on the boulevards are only dead and you only want to bury them bury them, not kill them, for it can't be done, even tho y'd be charged with murder. Your problem, our problem, of course, has been faced before most strongly in the 3 novels (I hesitate to use the world great, they are more than that, for they are beyond the Bible, man's saving little stamping ground) *Crime and Punishment* via Dos, and Camus' *The Stranger,* and, I think, the strongest of them all: Celine's—*Journey to the End of the Night.* where the hell was I? [* * *]

all right, I'm not much of a man. you've busted them out of their high caves with grenades, with air power, and they've come out ready to meet their slant-eyed God while screaming a banal language and you got to them, aimed, took them out, got some taken out. people like Mailer and Hem made money (and Hem *some* Art, earlier) writing about it, but where does it leave us and what??? [* * *]

listen, Bill, listen to me, stay off the stuff. [* * *] only Ginsberg can smoke pot and advertise it and get away with it because his name has become BIG enough so that he'd love to get busted just to help push the circulation of his fading poetry, and also he'd be able to blow the screws after lights out. a man who WANTS to get busted can't get busted because the orders are in. it's like sometimes I've wanted to get fired but I couldn't get fired yet some guy with 6 kids busting his ass and sweating his balls would get layed off. that's the way it works. [* * *]

[To Jim Roman]
September 26, 1965

[* * *] A Charles Bukowski checklist/bibliography? why not? for all I've written I seem to remain like a monk fornicating a goose in a coal mine. of course, this is to my advantage too. it allows me to go on working, chipping at the block without interruption. of course, I die in my own vomit, but quietly, and that counts. the gods have been good to me, very very good. if you want to know anything, ask me—I have kept every mag that has published me except one—*Portfolio* II, which went for $10, a Caresse Crosby Black Sun Press thing, very akin to Webbwork, lavish with love and color, I had 2 copies, a short story of mine in there, around 1944, 45?—I remember Caresse writing me—"Who are you to write this story? I have never heard of you." even a ten buck check, and there I was in with all the famous fucks—Sartre, Lorca, Miller and on and on . . . I was on the bum and needed the ten. I got drunk. came to the door of my parents weighing 135 pounds. my usual weight around 200. they hated my guts. charged me room and board, atrocious prices, while I got a job and paid it back in. or looked for a job. anyhow the old man stole *Portfolio* II, both copies, and got himself a better job at the L.A. County Museum by claiming that he was Charles Bukowski, and I often wonder, as the years went on [* * *] what the people thought of him. he was such a beastly stupid prick. "there goes Charles Bukowski," I can hear

207

them saying. well, that's all over and he's dead dead dead, thank god.

the date of issues of *Story* that published my short story was March-April 1944, vol. XXIV, no. 106. I remember I was in New York at the time and walking down the street broke and I looked up and there was the god damned magazine in a rack at a corner drugstore. a hell of a feeling, believe me, when you're 24 and half mad. a hell of a feeling anytime, I'd imagine. [* * *]

Blazek planned a book of Bukowski letters but the project never reached completion. Some letters, however, were included in the Bukowski Sampler *that he published in 1969.*

[To Douglas Blazek]
September 30, 1965

[* * *] I thought you were thinking of a general book of letters but if you want to do an all-bukowski thing, shit, I'd like to see what I have written too. honor, honor, like a crippled cat fighting off a bulldog or police dog while backed to the fence. (this is good scotch). if we should somehow get some fancy publisher and there's any $$$, I'd suggest we split the god damned loot 3 ways: Blazek, Blatt, Buk. the mighty bees. I don't look for such luck, however. [* * *]

given a choice, 9 times out of ten a woman would rather sleep with money than talent. given a choice, 7 times out of ten a woman would rather sleep with money than genius. given a choice, ten times out of ten a woman would rather sleep with more money than less money. [* * *]

Younger readers may need reminding that this letter was written before the widespread availability of the xerographic copying machine.

an open letter to those who hold my letters to their bellies in the dark closets their lives . . .

Dear mr. miss, mrs. queer, lesbian and so forth,

what the hell, they are stacking the stuff up to smear us like fly smear and you hold onto a couple of ten cent baubles. these editors are attempting to *collect a collection*, that's profound enough, and a dog with 3 legs staggers. dogs, flies, ach! what I mean is, don't be that way—when I wrote you to begin with, I wrote you because I thought you were a real person not a real estate salesman of sorts, and look look, I am drinking here now and I think the sky will fall down, I look around in panic, 45 years dripping from my belly and you hold onto a couple of letters. it's this, it is a collection, and, shit, it *may* be YOUR LAST CHANCE AT IMMORTALITY, ah haha ha!

when I wrote these letters I wrote them to you and I wasn't thinking about a collection because as you must know I was mostly very poor and very unknown and still am. yet, some find interest in these drunken wailings. are you going to kill me like being a screw in a jail? are you going to half-kill me like a whore taking my wallet while I sleep? are you going to fire me like the factory foreman because orders have fallen off? are you going to kick me out like the landlord because I can't pay the rent. WHAT I AM TRYING TO SAY IS THIS: ARE YOU GOING TO BE LIKE THE REST OF THE WORLD OR ARE YOU GOING TO BE LIKE THE PERSON I THOUGHT I WAS WRITING TO? if this sounds like I am begging, then I am: I am begging for faith and a little bit to go on with.

I don't know the actualities. maybe a big name publisher, maybe just shit smeared onto toilet paper with fingernails. but when I wrote you I felt you, the sound and realness of you, the you you you, myself directing the arrow the heart the crooked music of what was left after the factory the racetrack whatever whatever. I can't feel you'll let me down; I can't feel you've grown that dead. if it's only money money, my god, I'll try to send you a little each day each week each month; whatever I have.

I ask you out of whatever is left of my soul, out of what tiny bit of gentility and mirror of a sweat shot of sun I have left, please send in your letters and you'll be received where you should be received: where I met you, say, peeling an orange and talking about Picasso, anything, guts, spirals, pawnshop brokers, rain, *almost* love, broken doors, donkeys without names. I guess I must sound like a cocksucking preacher. I am tired. I only want all the parts to be all the parts like the river running after the 6 horse. I can't say anymore. your move and the night grows dank with the sweat of violets pimping.

love, ya ya ya.

[To William Wantling]
[Early October 1965]

thanks for the Dos thing, I will comb it like I did the same central caves of the novel, only what bothered me about *Brothers* [*Karamazov*] was this unreal division of the brothers into those cast types like chessmen, each with his own move. a wonderful diveboard for stunting but I wonder about the critics who rate the *Brothers* Dos's #1 work. *Crime* seemed the more evil and normal and natural work. I think that Dos wanted to say a lot more than he did in *Crime &* but lost his guts, his nerve and his senses. a great novel, still. and since I haven't written a nearby companion piece I had better shut up. [* * *]

it is 5 a.m. as I write this yet the woman snores over and through Mozart. I cannot help thinking that snoring is an infirmity of the soul, a true voice speaking through sleep. my father was the most vile beast I ever met and he snored louder and with more ugliness than anybody I have ever heard. [* * *]

I was never good with the women, never really tried to be, couldn't get my back up to go through the prelims, the fake talk. it cost me too much. then, too, a kind of withered pride. they all looked kind of pukey to me, even those the boys called "fine." too much battle. I settled for the old ones. those nobody wanted. a fifth on the dresser, a little talk, a kind of dead fuck (tho, not always), then more drink, more easy talk and then another fuck. but not much strain or pretense. kind of a wearisomeness. I just just can't pay the price of tight new pussy, and won't, it's too high. always was. for me. [* * *] but it's all shit in pink drawers and squatting to piss, finally. [* * *]

[To Douglas Blazek]
October 10, 1965

been playing with the little girl for an hour and a half on the rug after work and now I am like a burned city, but, shit, so? & Thursday at 12:30 p.m. I swing onto the CHIEF #20 for Lamay, New Mexico with 2 pints of scotch and then a bus on into Santa Fe, 7 a.m. Friday morning if I do not die or fall off the cliff of myself before then, and I have bummed for years until this crotch of a life grabbed me on this job for 8 years, my god, but a little space again, a shot of light, and then back, or a shot of agony—I do not make it with people, I can't help it. and I can't sleep on trains, I can't even sleep on a bed. the only way to sleep is to drink yourself senseless.

you get people together and they sit around in a room and look at each other and try to think of things to say; it's ugly and senseless. or somebody gets on the make. or somebody vomits in the back porch. or somebody screws the dog. I am not all there in conversation; sometimes I think I am made of some kind of hard and unfriendly stone. most things disgust me; I don't know what I want. then I begin thinking that I am insane, that I can't see what they see, that I can't understand what they understand; that they are naturally warm and that I am a dribbling fake. and then, in the next flash, I suddenly think that they are damned fools and I don't give a damn what they think. all my strings fight in discord; my cock is trying to screw my brain, or the other way. then I look down and my belly is flopping out, my sides are flopping out; my zipper is coming undone, China crawls in a teacup like a worm; everybody looks handsome and clean and there is dirt under my fingernails and a stink rises from my soul. a bad fix all the time—perhaps a little exaggerated but not too much.

now the kid is crawling under my feet and the woman says PEEK A BOO! I SEE YOU!!!

no, I don't want a steady stay in N.M. those things don't work. the battle I have here now is killing me but that one would kill me faster. I have to go by instinct. actually I am not trying to write mainly poems or a novel. actually poems are only toothpicks that hold me up a little. [* * *]

you might have guessed by now that the literary gang is an unclean mob—dollar crazy as any manufacturer, as any pimp, as any anything. and cold, and cold. they pretend to have intelligence, and they write so seemingly of justice and life, almost as if they knew something. but the dirty cocksuckers would sell you off in a minute;

a pawnbroker has more conscience and more heart. the Arts, generally, are the hiding place of the weak and the imbecilic. I know I know I know. I am not knocking Art as a contrivance, as a good bell ringing inside my hollow head; I am knocking the polluted stream, the turds. you know.

yet maybe I am just talking talking talking. the longer I live the less I know. maybe death is just eliminating everything—life is a turd—you pop it out and you are ready. I mean, each day I get a little simpler: I believe less, I feel less, I realize less. I like to watch flies now or look at coffeepots or listen to refrigerator sounds, sounds like god-voices. I hear. isn't this what a child does? I want it easy; I don't even want to win. of course, there has been a lot of this. even when I am fighting a man and he is intent upon killing me, I cannot believe him, I cannot believe what is happening and I cannot become truly angry. there are 2 things that bother me, that make me weak in the world:

1: I have never been lonely.
2: I have never been angry.
and the third thing:

I fuck with the Arts.

drinking is only to jell the parts that have been taken apart by factories or whores or a faceful of busses. I mean, that it brings me back to the basics of myself, whatever those basics may be. if drinking destroys the brain, fine. for what my brain has seen it yearns destruction.

god, I wish I had the guts and style and cement and vastness of a Jeffers—clean through rock into an eagle's eye, and then behind stone, hacking, sounding. I have some of this but not enough, and meanwhile I jump through all sorts of weird hoops at others' behest, and I get rapped and trapped bit my god by bit until I am hanging by a finger, by a thin gutstring in the middle of an empty sky. get me? melodramatic? o, hell yes—96,000 SEASONS IN HELL ON OVERTIME. [* * *]

and here I go down to poke my smashed head into a doorway. I really don't want to go. I don't want to do anything. I lose 3 days at the track, harness races, sunshine, the quiet drink from my flask on the grandstand steps, the looking at the legs of women I don't know the name of. I could weep for my quiet freedom, yet somebody sends me a railroad ticket and I play it through. maybe it is that I have seen enough hell; maybe it is that I don't want to see anymore. yet, I guess, there I will be getting on that train 12:30 p.m. thursday,

212

my face twisted into nothing, sitting down, waiting for the thing to roll, wondering what ass I will draw for a seat partner and very glad the 2 pints are in the cloth bag over my head.

wish me luck, baby, wish me everything; I am sad, I got the blues the blues the green blue purple blues. my my my.

[To Al Purdy]
October 11, 1965

[* * *] people keep sending me poems and novels to read and collections of poesy—I mean people I have never written to or heard of—and all the stuff is bad, bad, bad. I wonder if you realize how much bad stuff is written in all earnestness? and they'll keep right on with it. thinking that they are undiscovered genius. I rec. a beautifully printed book of poems, fine paper, hardcover, and inscribed "to Buk . . ." and etc. an honor, sure, but I can't even write this person and thank him because the poems are so flat and drivelling that they are not even bad—they don't even exist. if you know the type I mean. yet I don't throw a book away when it is sent to me in this way and I don't know what to do with them. I guess there'll be another one in the mail tomorrow. there are a lot of dead men sitting at typewriters. I would have quit long ago but when I saw the truly bad stuff that was being done, I couldn't let go. [* * *]

[To Douglas Blazek]
October 23, 1965

[* * *] it has been 100 degrees for 3 or 4 days and everybody smells like shit and everybody is, of course. in from track, medium day, plus $32. the human race is an empty egg out there. the crowd is a dog made of sausage. I could not think of fucking or singing out there, or dreaming; only murder.—now back in the trough: cigar, beer, old hat bit. my guts are dropping out and I sit here pecking at the keys like a propped-up Hemingway with matchstick soul. and the typer seems shot. hope you can read.

back from Santa Fe, ya. [* * *] I was sick most of the time I was there but did hunk down quite a bit of beer and scotch and got into a little trouble. Webb always flips a bit when the image does not fit the peg but I can't be bothered. one night I was quite drunk and locked out in the icy rain and knocking on doors but nobody wanted to let me in. somebody finally relented and gave me a long angry speech. shit on that. my father is dead. I am dead. [* * *] I got on the train and my foot began to swell. I walk around barefoot when drunk and all the glass and steel I had picked up decided to play death. I found a sadist doctor when I got into town and he sliced my heel open and dug and probed and dug. no shot, of course. German accent: "Vell, vell, you took it like a man!" "You enjoyed it more than I did," I told him. "Nine, nine! you see I vuz only interested in seeing vat was in dere, I did not enjoy . . ." "make out the bill." and that, was Santa Fe. [* * *]

the average person has largely and finally already left the earth, my friend. they generally leave about the age of 5, although some stay a bit longer. tough for you, mother, but you are still here. your letters and poems get better, better, as I shrivel up into bologna-string walking. have you ever seen a bologna-string walking? Death is 2 balls without a head. Death is not being able to possess a good woman because I am dirty from factories and alleys and sluggings and hospitals and marriages and shackjobs, and poor, poor, poor, poor crippled dirt. wine bottles, nights of a steaming light bulb, scribbling on little slips of paper and unable to read them in the morning or at noon or ever.

> death is all this waiting without screaming
> death is bread rotting in the heat
> and 90 million rats and roaches
> death is a sea of piss
> death is a sophisticated afternoon in Santa Fe
> with nobody saying what they are thinking

maybe it's the heat, kid, I am really snarling through these thin rented cardboard walls. how much separates me from the loony bin? sometimes down at work I feel like slugging somebody. no hatred, only the zero complex. I want to bust something. sometimes it happens by itself. same thing happened to somebody that happened to me in 53 or 54 or whenever it was. the belly broke open and the blood came out, out, out. he was dead by the time he reached the hospital. the bad life. I whine before I turn out the lights; I pray for spastics and dwarfs, Pal, I pray for scrub women, Pal, I pray for frightened women of some seeming beauty who play their hand and exchange one rich man for a richer man. I pray for the nail that enters the hand that enters the wood, I pray that that nail may not be rusty. Pal.

a couple of old wrinkled-up women down at work are trying to fuck me. they know that I am whipped. one of them has a young girl's ass and legs but she must be a thousand years old. "I am getting a new Mustang. will you teach me how to drive?" "I'll drive you, baby, I'll drive you!!" "he, hehe, hehehe, that's what I thought! an' I want ya ta meet my sister too!" looks like I gotta fuck the whole family. I'll probably pass. it's a hairy drippy drizzling game. it's only when I get drunk that I imagine that I am the lover. what nonsense. and Rupert Brooke wrote better too. but he didn't have any sense and decided to go to war. and try to be lucky. bullets are built for poets. I knew this one guy, not a bad writer or human being either (sometimes there's a difference) who said, "But suppose some stupid cocksucker points a machinegun at me and squeezes the trigger?" "if you go, he will." he went—it happened. m.g. slugs. but they'll always find an excuse for another war, that's all right. but they'll bust you for a little game of pot. or jail a whore for selling her pussy. or blame a homo for being a homo. or fire a man for being 10 minutes late to work. or jail you for being drunk on the streets. or run a woman out of the country for not believing in God (Mad Murray) and saying so and getting them to ban prayer in schools because she figured the kids should have a choice. but War? stockpiles? shit??? why not? listen, I don't mean to preach here but a little drunk a little tired— up all night at work and then the racetrack today and now almost midnight, no sleep, so the seams ripping a bit.

something on from the Three Penny Opera. Brecht does not help me too much. I do not trust his melodrama; a god damned horse thief. the social structure bit. I mean, he holds a good hand . . .

the little girl runs up and pokes me with her finger. I sit in my shorts. "uts DAT?"

"dat's fat."

"uts DAT?"

"dat's my bellybutton."

. . . because he speaks plainly, that's a good thing, but he turns it on too much. there are other basics besides a Jewish nose. clarity of delivery can trap you as much as obtuseness because you can kid yourself that you always *seem* to know what you are saying. (See Hemingway, Dos Passos, Sherwood Anderson, E. E. Cummings.) but I know a lot of guys down at work who have a plain clarity of delivery and they never say anything.

tell me, Blaz, do you think the dead get hard-ons?

do you think the worms and maggots will ever crawl the body of your Love in that closet down there in the dark? what did that fly mean? why did it affect me? why all the sunlight? and the horse standing under the tree? will I live another ten years? [* * *] a siren goes now, ambulance, then fire trucks earlier, the town is on fire, and earlier today coming in from the track I drove thru the Negro section of the x-riots and they were shining their cars and sitting on their steps, they'd had their drunk, and now it was back to it. my god, not a chance for any of us. white or black, living or dying, we are snot, driven helpless snot before a brainless moon of God. seesee, see the Martini Life! the homes in the hills! 14 bathrooms, 17 fireplaces, & 7 great muddy garages while buying 2 more homes over the telephone, one with a winding staircase marvelous like a lighthouse thing for your guests to fall down drunk upon after drinking their *own* liquor.

well, 6 more bottles of beer and then to sleep, maybe. [* * *] now they play the Blue Danube and I snap the radio off.

now everybody is here in the kitchen and the whole kitchen is hollering. they talk about making OATMEAL! don't say that I don't properly feed these broads.

so we go on. no death in the road. no Nobel. 5 bottles of beer. a typer that wobbles on 3 legs and wants to kick off. my my. there goes a fly. [* * *]

I am spreading wall to wall, fat and stupid, hardly feel the pain—translate it mostly, I do, into shots of blue and green light. a formula. I didn't mean to lay it on you, baby. I remember the bit about (who was it?) Flaubert telling DeMass to keep on clerking, practice on his writing and not to become a journalist. so de Mop clerked and Flub wrung his hands in the light of his (Flaubert's) fame. sometimes I think it might have been to remove competition? anyhow, DeMop took it out on his rowboat and mad he went because of the siff and mostly because of clerking, although they won't admit that. [* * *]

there is a poet-novelist who said, "Bukowski worries about his soul." this is too pat of course and puts em in a neat box. but I have packed the meat on my shoulder and have seen the threads come

216

out of statues. I don't need a soul; all I need is a light bulb, some beer and a chair to sit in. but some want to take that from me. now I have been shipped the poet-novelist's latest book of poems and I am supposed to review the bit for a mag. I don't know what to do. it looks very much as if my friend has not worried about *his* soul. christ, how we snipe! should I shoot him down? we are all a bunch of bitches. dying is often a slow process. why rack a man because his poems have started to fail anymore than rack a man because his eyesight is failing or his teeth falling out or his pecker failing to get hard? we gotta have a winner, what? yet, in another sense, there are some men who sell too easy; one second a man is his brother's keeper and the next second he is Brutus. [* * *] then too, you might figure it this way: a real man is gonna lose his teeth his hair and his balls long before the soul??? it is confusing. yet I keep looking at faces, I keep watching ways things are done. I'm no Virgin. I've rolled and been rolled and yet, in a certain sense, there is just so far that you ought to go, just so much that you should do. I don't speak of morality and code—that jazz has held the world back too long. I speak of simple things, although I can't say just what they are but you know them when they come upon you. Genet's seeming immorality and depravity are nothing of the sort. because he is neither depraved nor immoral toward himself. he does what is proper toward himself. the greatest immorality is going for gold against the grain of yourself when you don't need the gold, the possession—like taping dead oranges on an orange tree. of course, most of us figure we need some of the gold. there's always an excuse to die: the wife, the baby, the girlfriends; there is always an excuse to go to the cowardice that most men are naturally inherent to because his father was inherent to it and his father's father etc. there's always an excuse to be a prick. it even seems clever. graft. babes with long legs and tights pussies. new cars. then often immorality and immortality lock legs and you've got jism all over the bed. Oxford. grants. lectures. poetry readings. mouth, mouth, mouth. we are sucked forever into the traps. I've always found the face and the ways and the honesty of a ditch digger more alive than any English prof. of course, nowadays even the ditch diggers are getting sophisticated. trouble everywhere. what am I saying? I've lost the string. good. good, then. [* * *]

catch? fine. the critics say that I am non-cerebral. I think the same thing of them. I think that they are patsies to the dupe, playing some kind of con-game, not because I *don't* understand their words but because I do. they and Grandma may call it carnal but I call it wet pussy and prostitution. I am as cerebral as any of them (at least so) and if they want to talk about Government or God or Plato or the Meaning of Man, or any of those useless things, have them pour me a couple of glasses of bourbon and I'll take them up alleys they've never seen and roll them out of their minds. Everything is basically simple—especially the critics, especially my critics. and, thus, having unloaded this load of come I move on to other things.

do you think, my son, that I will ever get a job teaching Creative Writing at the University of Columbia? I would very much like to fuck some young coeds or have *them* fuck me. [* * *]

I guess that so many problems come in upon a man that he finally dismisses them all and becomes a rock. the world is full of rocks. but the beer goes down down down. Wagner's *The Ring* on now. Wagner goes good with me. Shostakovich. the Russians, the German in the Arts. The French, the English, the Spaniards do me little good. the Italians, halfway. why is it? of course, there's Knut Hamsun. Norway? wherever the hell. [* * *]

Kirby Congdon was editor of Magazine *(New York). A letter from Bukowski appeared in no. 3 (see below).*

[To Tom McNamara]
October 25, 1965

[* * *] have you ever met Kirby Congdon? he seems bright enough to set torches to the world. almost seemingly classical, yet lived, and learned, and not to be bullshitted. I understand he is going to Key West or somewhere. there are so many good people I'd like to get drunk with, not so much as to talk myself, but to see them sitting in chairs and talking. Each man seems to come up with something good, something to make me laugh, and they do it so easily and with grace and honesty. Christ I am a pig, Mac, so often so tight, so often so untrusting.

if I could only realize that right now there are at least 1,000 people on earth better than Christ was; I mean, if Christ was not a fable; I mean, people who don't do tricks like raising the dead and being glorious and so forth. these people stay hidden. they know that contact means the plague. this is what disgusts me with the Ginsberg/Corso mob. they suck to the human adulation bit and are soon swallowed. Corso died rather quickly because his only mainstay was a simplicity of purpose and some type of message that he thot important. It has taken Ginsberg a little longer, but he is swallowing the same bloody bait—via Behan, via D. Thomas. The woman here is full of words and the child runs around. but I am still insane. She says Thomas drank himself to death because he felt his talent was waning. Bullshit. Thomas drank himself to death for the same reason that I do: he loved his drink, it lifted him where he belonged, where we all belong, where we all should be if the stream of people weren't such asses and didn't believe in homes and new cars and all that junk. I have almost died of drink several times, once very close, it was sweet and didn't matter, and they finally stood me up and walked me out of a door to do it again. fuck em. I am ready to die. I am ready to wilt. [* * *]

[To Ann Menebroker]
[Late October 1965]

umm, yes, I am a dog, of course & therefore and forevermore and I have not written but you wouldn't want me to send you a letter that didn't walk around on the paper . . . wouldn't a halfass babbling be an insult? we all die and are stuffed with standard formality, and, of course, now that I've said this, you have a fine springboard to leap upon me with. Christ, that almost sounds sexy! we have to be careful. at least, you have to. anyhow I just got in from Santa Fe, sick, of course, silly and boozed and nowhere further along anywhere. sure, I remember the good old days when you used to ship me a half dozen 50 cent pieces for one of my books, and enclose a trinket or a rose with eyes, sure sure, and I am the same ass. nothing has altered me. I crash through a headful of shoulders and find myself in a marble bathtub with dirt rings, bell rings, blue rings, red rings, the saliva of myself dribbling into lukey water without goldfish, and the world is shot, and I breathe and wait to die, I breathe and wait for November or Rapid Transit or a young girl sitting on bus stop bench with a lot of leg showing. I drink continually and it keeps me going or it kills me and it doesn't matter, it is all the same. [* * *]

the old life was very satisfying, of course. Please do not become too relaxed watering plants, baking cookies, putting out the diaper pail to remember the rest. I don't know exactly what price you are paying for your safety. me, I'm paying a pretty high price for mine and the mirrors turn their backs from me now. I prefer to cover them with towels to spare them the sight of my death. I have joined the walking living dead upon the avenues, in the saloons and everywhere else. but it's 4 a.m. and the police are driving by and I hear voices outside and we all live very close together here and I am a coward, I am afraid of jails, I hate jails, and so I turn Wagner down a little on the radio, sip my next to last beer and wish you the love of memory and the love of love or whatever there is, dear one.

[To Neeli Cherry]
[?1965]

[* * *] I was in a mellow mood (rare for me) when I wrote the intro to Sherman's stuff, and I felt a little kind and comradely. It is easier to feel that way when Sherman is at a distance. Outside of the poem form I do not much buy his antics. I believe I made this clear in my poem "Letter from the North." Yet everything I said in the intro to his poems I said out of the truth of myself, whatever truth I could find. It's a scurvy word anyhow. Actually I do not think J. writes as well as he used to . . . never fulfilled the early promise and all that hogwash, except maybe with the poem "Montgomery Street" which I think is a great poem, and if a guy can write a poem like this, I will forgive a lot of his nonsense in actual life.

[To Neeli Cherry]
October 28, 1965

[* * *] my thanks for the emotive "An Invitation," good flow here. although the truth factor in some lines disturbs me: "to combat all the yellow-bellies who are sucking us dry. and they are, they are." "but the only alternative is not to fight, and my god! we couldn't

do that." sounds like you've been hornswoggled. if you really think about it, it is the white-bellies who are sucking you dry. but, then, to have a war it is always best to believe you are the Good guy and the other is the Bad guy. it runs more smoothly. death needs help sometimes.

then, too, I think you might have written your lines in jest, in satire, and that I missed the point. [* * *]

[To William Wantling]
[?1965]

[* * *] I keep drinking beer and scotch, pouring it down, like into a great emptiness . . . I admit that there is some rock stupidity in me that cannot be reached. I keep drinking, drinking, am as sullen as an old bulldog. always this way:—people falling down, off their stools, testing me, and I drink them down, down, down, but really no voice, nothing, I sit I sit like some stupid elf in a pine tree waiting for lightning. when I was 18 I used to win $15 or 20 a week at drinking contests and this kept me alive. until they got wise to me. there was one shit, though, called Stinky who always gave me a hard go. I'd outpsyche him sometimes by drinking an extra in between. I used to run with these thieves and we were always drinking in a vacant room, a room for rent, with a low light . . . we never had a place to stay, but most of these boys were tough, carried guns, but I didn't, still was square, still am. I thought Stinky had me one night and I looked up and he wasn't there and I went in to heave and I didn't even heave, there he was in the bathtub, out out, and I walked out and picked up the money. [* * *]

[To William Wantling]
October 30, 1965

[* * *] It isn't any secret to myself that I am a rather backward man, lived, baby, but still culling and never sure, always goofed, no answer, and I learn this more and more down at the pits where I

221

work. trying to be one of the boys I will crack wise but it seems to me that I am always topped. christ, the clock is long enough without being topped mentally and spiritually by your fellow-workers. but they always seem to edge me; I get this look of eye and I drop back into silence, once more the defeated asshole, my god. I am always under somebody's whip. a father. a highschool principal. a fine-looking and lying whore. a bottle. a cigar. a flat tire. rent. a child. rain. constipation. insomnia. a screw at Moyamensing, a trusty in the drunk tank. [* * *]

and yet we learn. there is a whiner down at work. he cries cries but his crying is like some suckerfish, it is not a clean cry and I have listened to all his strickenness, I have listened to hours to years of his mewking and it has taught me—a good man can learn from a good fool. even a not so good man can learn. what I mean is that we all have extremities of unfulfilled wanting. we are toys to whatever has created us. we will never get there, and even if we get halfway, the ending will be the same: smashed cat's guts on the boulevard or the last drip of sour blood into the bedpan, hurrah!! I mean

> we've got to live with loss like we used to
> maybe still do
> live with a bad
> whore
>   but
> we know all along what it is
> we take is standing like Hemingway
> or we dismiss it like
> Camus
> but we know
> about it
>
> this is the way it works and
> we wind our clocks and we
> wait on
> midnight or the carnival
> a hamburger sandwich or the
>   garbage man.
>
> we live with it we live until we
> die.

how's that for hot shit? I throw in free poems that will never be used. I am a truly tough spit baby crying outa a blinkin' blinking eye thing. [* * *]

Wantling must have requested some quotable aphorisms.

[To William Wantling]
November 11, 1965

They beat you down with their factories, their booze, their women until you are no longer of any use to them or yourself.
> —Bukowski

The trouble with women is that in creating new men they tend to destroy old ones, and you and I know that women are not very good artists.
> —Bukowski, again.

[* * *]
I have never met a man that I have truly liked. I have met men that I would drink with, laugh with, fight for—but only in a manner of hope instead of reality.
> —B.

I only loved one woman and, unlike all the others, she was the only one who never demanded or asked for the spoken word of it. and even over her grave I said nothing, not even in my head, but the sunlight knew and my shoelaces and [*illegible*].
> —B.

[* * *]
I don't want to play the image of the drunk; it is only that I get so sick of what I remember.
> b.

Social consciousness is what keeps me from raping little girls of eleven—that, and the chance of getting caught. Yet I cannot conceive of anybody raping my own little daughter—her eyes are so blue and holy that God himself might awaken to destroy the offender. Yet what keeps us going while we are racking up our own cruelties is the almost certain knowledge (instinct) that God is asleep during our acts. I am as guilty as any, for the desire to act and then not-to-act

223

is the same as acting; the only factor lacking between them being courage, and yet I must beg off at times through a seeming sympathy for an intended victim, which might only be an inbred Christianity or cowardice. The greatest problem is, however, that no intended victim of rape, robbery, murder, the worst of acts, is *innocent* at all—they have all died or slipped or slurred or murdered something themselves along the way—even eleven year old girls. I think that the best principle for a strong man (if I may invent a term?) is not to get involved with the creatures because the creatures are a swamp. There will be certainly enough involvement, without voluntary explorative involvement, to last you a lifetime and to wear you down and kill you before you are 37 years old.

    —buk

happy birthday you 32 year old dog [* * *]

    [* * *] and we all know about our Great President Honorable Rancho Hot shit Johnson, he talks outa one side of his mouth and shoots a loaded 45 into the back of an innocent man with the other. I go on record that he is a Liar. I've met and worked for his types in all the slave mills from Atlanta, Dallas, New York, any city you can name. I hate his face. he is the final great o o o intruder elected to mutilate society at society's behest. what a hell kind of a democracy is this, that gives you one face, and then gives you the knife?

    the United States Government keeps increasing its hardness by the surety of its strength, and it keeps getting harder and harder and tougher and tougher until it is almost like some crazy kind of wart or cancer gone mad. I keep getting the thought that this is happening everywhere in all governments all countries. . . . christ, we are all so ugly. Is this the meaning of Govts? to get uglier? so, we have the French Rev. which slowly faded back into its cage. and now we have found that even the American Civil War was meaningless . . . an exchange of ariel courtesies . . . while the poor black remained the poor free?? black, and even more hollow doughnuts, this Watts strike which I witnessed and work with most of the blacks, even the blacks have conspired into silence, for Christ's sake, tell them about a few committees, a poverty program wherein not one wino gets 10 cents for a drink of wine, just salaries for officials who have already beat the game by getting into the machine of the game fuck it fuck it. I am lost. and I knew all during the riots that it would be lost . . . that even the words of the rioters would fall back. . . . no new world, never. Just the guy on top looking and talking like the guy

224

on the bottom and thinking the same things and the same way. all lost, forever. my hands on a small torn white tablecloth, my white hands, my drink, my cigarette, hoping verily for a wake up of Big Prick God but knowing all along it would not be so. Keep your grenades, 32 year old tough guy, I have done time too, but I guess all our dreams are going to leak out of a salty piss pillow, and I never had no hope and if you think it hard to be 32, you are correct. it is hard to be anything. [* * *]

[To Douglas Blazek]
[?November, 1965]

[* * *] I've got to say one thing for ALL THE WOMEN I've lived with, they couldn't care less. it's only when the blade falls and we are sitting out on the street on a piece of cardboard that they seem to question. I remember one of them saying, "But I thought you knew what you were doing!" "Baby, baby," I told her, "what ever gave you such an idea?" this one I walked South into the city with, she knew somebody—"he'll let me stay. I only hope he makes his balls quick. I can't stand the son of a bitch." I walked her to the door, watched her make up her face, she gave me the sad death kiss and then knocked, "It's me, Kelly, honey." and some big fat swine of a businessman, 285 pounds of gold wrapped his arms around her and I walked off. to the streets. I didn't have a pussy.

the woman is off to her little poetry reading group at his church or other. Neeli Cherry is down there too. he likes to mouth his stuff but they won't let him read right off. he's got to suck in. he'll shoot some mouth tho. I can see Frances now, "And now, I want to introduce Neeli Cherry, editor of the *Black Cat Review.*" and the little butterball, 20 years of him, will try to get up and say something clever. I'll have them all on my back next Sunday—Neeli, Frances, the kid; I'm going to drive them down to see the Richmond madhouse EARTH, if the old car makes it, and I take F. to drive me back. the judge told me last time, "one more drunk driving rap and you might as well measure up for a loose-fitting pinstripe." only not in that terminology. but I read him, the monster. Neeli keeps telling me, "I don't care for Richmond's stuff," and not being an arguer or a man for detail in vocal transmission, I always give him the same,

225

"Richmond writes some good stuff." which, of course, is so. Richmond writes a clean and easy and a clear line. all those fuckers write well: Richmond, Cherry, Wantling, the whole screwy suffering houseful. I just hate to see them scratch each other. well, god damn them anyhow, I travel alone.

scratch, scratch.

very strange happening today. was sitting going over my horses today before going to track, red-eyed, sucking on a beer, shivering, sick with 2 hours overtime and no sleep, sitting in the torn chair by the door and the doorbell rings and here is the mailman with a registered letter from one Heinrich Fett, 547 Andernach a/Rhein, Privoit Strs. 1, Germany. that's where I was born, sweetheart. what an odd feeling. and here in broken English was a letter from my Uncle (my dead mother's brother) who said, "By chance I got your address on October 22, 65." only it was my old address at 1623 N. Mariposa Ave. where I did some good whoring and maybe some good writing too. anyhow, the letter, short and simple, damn near knocked the beer outa my hand, tho not quite. I'll write him tomorrow and tell him that I am very old and very tired. [* * *]

[To Ann Menebroker]
November 17, 1965

[* * *] It seems like I've written a hell of a lot of drunken letters, maybe more letters than poems, and somebody got the idea it might make a book. Feelers in from some publishers already even tho book is still gathering. I would like your letters—mine to you—included, the best ones, unless you feel that in some of them there was something extra personal. But I have nothing to hide. the letters are yours tho, please do as you wish. I am hoping that you will let them look at most of them, maybe all of them. All letters are returned, of course. Please understand that. and my letters to you are, of course, more personal than to many but I am hoping that anything I said was universal as well as personal. I do hope that you will let them look at most of them? if you do, my more than thanks, of course. for since we have gotten into this thing I would like it to be as complete a selection as possible. [* * *]

226

[To Douglas Blazek]
November 24, 1965

[* * *] I haven't heard from you on the 2 long poems I sent. Please return if they don't fit you. I have been rejected before. besides, one poem must have a portion *eliminated* anyhow. I remember slamming Eisenhower but since his recent heart attack & obvious decline, I have decided to lay off. no need to attack the sick and the aged— there's bigger game in the brush.

now must try to get some rest. please forgive tired letter. and again, much thanks, your master job on *Confessions*.

[To Ruth Wantling]
[November 25, 1965]

[* * *] no no no, I don't like snowstorms, I almost died in one, and I am now too old to die. death is only for the young. o christ, forgive me. I keep opening my mouth. you know, I am always in a jam. anyhow, since you know I am an ass, I'll go on. there was one winter, I think it was in Philly. I am sitting in this very tiny bar and the bartender starts spouting Shakespeare and I am making it with a couple of women in there but this makes me angry, this Shakespeare, so being a blackheart by nature I started bragging on Hitler, Mussolini, so forth, and the next thing I knew I was evicted and instead of being guided to one of the warm pads of one of the whores to be fucked and rolled or maybe just rolled I was walking along in the snow, then stopped and decided to piss against the side of a church. this worked nicely. finished. put it away. then decided on a shortcut across the churchyard. all fine. big moon. ice cold. I have a room somewhere anyhow. I am walking along plenty drunk and then I trip over this wire they have strung across the yard about ankle high. down I go. too drunk to raise up. I lay there knowing I will freeze. I laid there a long time. but it must have been the coldness of the snow on my face that revived me. I got up and made it on in. but, remembering this the next morning, I decided to get out of the snow country and stay out. suicides are desperately vain: they like to choose the time and place. there's a great difference between dying when you want to and dying when you don't want to.

227

I know that it amounts to the same thing yet there remains a kind of difference in how the soul or what's left of the soul enters the earth of the sky or whatever it enters.

listen!!! will you stop this god damned lovely dental technician shit and what great gobs of nicety these dentists . . . these paid torturers of the haunted human race . . . are. all other areas of science have moved forward and these fuckers are still working with a pair of pliers. I can't see a man who wants to be constantly around blood as any kind of decent individual. I'd rather pick up garbage. every dentist I have ever met has had thick wrists, black nazi hair on his arms and an ovaltine belly swarming with the hymns of rats. what lies are you trying to tell me? [* * *]

[To Steven Richmond]
Thanksgiving for what? [November 25,] 1965

[* * *] if you think f. franklyn's thing was rough on me, you ought to see what I did to my dear friend John William Corrington when the editor of *Steppenwolf* sent me his latest book of poems *Lines to the South* to read and review. I had praised Corrington's preceding book of poems but this collection became a complete reversal— automatic poetic poetry. I didn't know what to do. as you might know, Corrington wrote the foreword to my selection-collection of 8 years' worth of poetry, *It Catches My Heart in Its Hands*. he called me some pretty good things, and here I sat with his latest book of poems in my hands and it didn't have it, it didn't even try . . . I can forgive a lot of bad stuff if a man is swinging from his heels but he was making little cotton muffins. like George Washerbaby, I could not tell a lie. I had to let him have it. I never knew that such assassination lurked within my bowels. *Steppenwolf* will be out after Christmas with its bloody pages. yet really, I think you will find it different than the franklyn. I don't think it is snitty or below the belt. anyhow, hell. [* * *]

[To William Wantling]
November 29, 1965

[* * *] maybe my last letter offended you? remember being drunk as usual but remember mentioning something about a desire to rape eleven year old girls. I said desire, not actuality. in other words, if you had an eleven year old daughter staying with me you might consider her pretty safe, at least a lot safer than with men who won't admit their desires even to themselves, or if to themselves, then not to the rest of the world. I am not saying that I am anything special but as I say that if you take offense at my naturalism, at that which nature has put into me, then, you are a damn fool. [* * *]

[To Douglas Blazek]
December 4, 1965

rec. *Ole* 3 and see you are still with hammer and sight and selectivity. I always await a downgrading from first issues of enthusiasm but you are only still more there. my thanks for the ads on various books. I am sure my starving, mad editors like them too. . . . this is my next to last night off until Xmas and I must work eleven and twelve hours each night. hell, of course, sweet hell, but it's take it or quit the job or get fired and there is nothing in my brain working yet on the perfect escape. yet I have hustled my horse-race figures over and over and now the madman says (Buk), "with my method of play, I can average $500 a week with a straight $10 flat bet on win." I've put in hours and hours of work and on this thing and it would be some laugh if it were true! it's true on paper, at any rate, and almost frighteningly logical, and my job is to follow my scientific papers instead of emotion or hysteria or so forth. you get out there and some ass spills beer on your shirt, somebody steps on your shoes, you glance up and see a man staring at you with a mountain of immense hatred; you look around and here is some gal sitting on a bench with her skirt pulled up around her ass. you take a good swig from the flask Nash sent you, the one Hemingway drank out of, so it's good enough for me, maybe not good enough. anyhow, what I am trying to say is that a lot of things get in the way of pure paper theory, and it takes guts to continues to follow a straight central line, esp. when a losing streak occurs. and EXACTLY when you JUMP OFF, IT COMES IN AT VERY GOOD ODDS. I am going to stay on the line. listen, what has this got to do with the good *Ole*? I worked eleven hours last night, so make that an excuse. listening to a Rossini opera. I can see why they failed. all his operas sound like his overtures, and an over. and the meat of an opera *are* different things.

more beer. shit, maybe I will pick up. if you don't hear from me until after Xmas, please understand—the hours, and my health is bad; pain pain in throat back chest shoulders, sick stomach, weakness. sometimes I am working and I get faint. it is all I can do to keep from falling to the floor. it is very embarrassing. but after a while it passes. and after the tenth or eleventh hour you longer no longer give a shit. it is like being drunk, almost. you say *exactly* what you are thinking because you no longer care. senselessness. that most of my fellow workers seem to like their jobs and even like each extra call of overtime hours . . . is what?? disheartening, at least, when I think of the future of the human race. I was sitting next to a fairly sensible fellow the other night and when the screws weren't watching I said to him, "You know, it would be nice if they let each man work the number of hours he had to in order to take care of his needs. you know, when you get tired of working, just get up and walk out." "It wouldn't work for you," he told me, "you'd starve to death." like I said, he was a sensible fellow.

Frances and I have split. she and the little girl are over in a place on Carlton. it costs me something, but hell, I blow every paycheck anyhow, so what's the difference? I see the little girl every day so she'll remember me. I am soft in the head for her, Marina. the other day Frances brought her over and I was in bed asleep and she crawled on my chest and looked at my face and smiled smiled like crazy and then she kissed me on the mouth. little wench. and then she laughed. she's all full of this kind of love and she makes me remember somehow how it once was.

lighting up a Corona. fuck, I am a big money man. the boys on the opera on the radio laugh at me. [* * *]

Norse has not sent me his poems. I wrote him. now, Blaz, I just can't write this guy a blank check. I've got to see what you are printing. I realize that he is some sort of overlooked master craftsman with a master heart, but I've got to see the poems you are publishing or, I can't say a word towards or against him. he has an *instinctive* way with the word; he makes a man feel *good* reading him. the line is clear and specked with blood. I suppose what worries me about him is that he never throws the bomb or screams. but this is the danger point: it is hard to scream or bayonet and still retain the vindictive and cool Art-form. this was my trouble with *Crucifix*. everything was bothering me at once. I was stumbling all over the place and my blood was real, except for a few jokes, but the bull was making me look bad. it's best when you look good and say good. not rules, shit, no, but a way to do things like the wind or the trees or some gal at the track just showing you enough leg to make you forget God and his peashooter. fuck it.

Now you asked what I thought of *Ole* 3. please understand that, first of all, almost everything I read anywhere or anytime disgusts me. I mean—newspapers, billboards, poetry mags, poetry, poetry. . . . I mean, I just cannot hardly read anything anymore. I have backed up. choked off. whether this means ego or madness or stupidity or whatever, I don't know. so please, when I rate this stuff, understand my mind-state. this is important or else you are going to think I am telling you you print a lousy magazine and it isn't so. a new *Ole* is like new sun, only better because you can open its eyes and talk to it. I rate the littles in the following order:

1. *Ole*   2. *The Wormwood Review*   3. *The Outsider*
after that, there's a hell of a drop.

anyhow, if you have an *Ole #3* there by you I'd like to go through it page by page with you and instead of doing a lot of talking I will simply rate the poems as they affect me. you see what this machinery and factories and all these x-wives have done to me? all right, for kicks, I will rate the stuff percentage-wise as it affected me, and remember—like I told you—my head is hard, the upper one. if you want more of a definition of the following ask me sometime, only now I am too tired. the bosses' goggling dry-sinking eye-of-skin death-faces monkey-swinging in my brain. overtime, overt-time. now, they are playing WAGNER. good. there is a man who never wrote a bad note. what I mean is, it all came from the GUT. your heart can trick you but that little bit of underlay under the bellybutton sends it on home. all right. let's take it this way. 100 percent means the thing is immortal. zero means it is shit-death glued to paper. I will rate each piece, like some bigshot critic, on the following lines:

Style
Clarity
Meaning
Interest (force)
Originality

now I am the first to realize that these are just words and perhaps a further breakdown is needed but I am tired like I said and Wagner is dead. getting a bit drunk but that will help. [* * *]

[To Douglas Blazek]
December 31, 1965

have taken woman and child to their small place 8 or 10 blocks away and I wait to sweat out the New Year with the jackass horn blowers who will attempt to blow the snails out of their minds and butts, erect the skeleton of the the the soul and try to make it dance make it sing make it do something . . . but it won't work. maybe not for any of us.

down at work they have worked me to the point of insanity. I have scratched both of my legs raw with my fingernail. and the damage to other parts is, of course, unrepairable. the schedule board still says WORK but I can't keep making it. they now have a new idea to work the cruds on holidays and give them 2 days pay. most of the cruds love this but I can't bear it. I don't need all kinds of money; I need time and just a small bit of money to keep me alive. but Christ, it either works one way or the other always—either I'm sleeping out in an alley without a job or I have a job and I work 7 days a week, 11 hours a day. both of these ways kill a man, finally. if I only had myself I could live on $20 a week, easily. just because I am 45 does not mean I don't like to pull the shades down and stay in bed 3 days and 3 nights like a slug like a maggot, and then to walk out into the sun, walk along the sidewalks, feel the whole city rocking and stinking like an old whore's ass. but I cry too much. each inch we get I guess we are lucky to get. a professional writer over today—I mean one who makes his living by writing. he left me his inscribed photograph in a picture frame. very nice, very nice. he talked about how everything fell into place for Hemingway. Hem had a nose for climbing up and he had the nose up, up Scott F., Sherwood A., G. Stein, various editors, others, and like a good American he dropped them when they were no longer of any use to him. he even got fired once from his newspaper and came back the next day like he hadn't heard. these are not admirable qualities. but all of us have holes. maybe he figured he had it and the only way to get through, finally, was

232

to justify certain side actions? yet, how many millions of men think the same way today? well, balls. [* * *]

[To William Wantling]
December 31, 1965

[* * *] I understand there is going to be another article on capital punishment in *Spero* TOO, this time by somebody else. I must have a frozen soul for these cap punish articles are short-hairing me to a much earlier imbecility than I ever expected. I guess what I figure, mainly, is that almost the whole structure of everything is wrong so why pick at the parts? I mean, let's sink the whole ship. the ship of state, the ship of the world. A-Bomb? anyhow, what I mean is, take even jail. we don't need jails. we don't need morals. all we need is a common working sense and easiness and instinct. society kills more men than it saves. in fact, society kills everybody. none of us are truly alive. all we do is fight to save the last inch after we have given them 40 miles. religions senseless. morals senseless. so-called decency senseless. laws senseless. a fucking cop pulls me over because I am driving 80 miles an hour while drunk. the theory is that I don't know what I am doing and that I am endangering other members of society. bullshit. he doesn't know what he is doing. he is a wooden pigeon with a badge. WE CREATE AN ACTUAL *MONSTER* ON THE *THEORY* THAT WE *MIGHT* PREVENT A *POSSIBLE* MORAL AND SOCIAL WRONG. get it? you were jailed for getting caught using drugs. they were worried that you were getting something that they didn't have. it's a hell of a society when you are told it's wrong to use drugs but it's all right to kill yourself in a factory for a pitiful and demeaning wage. A FREE SOCIETY SHOULD ALLOW EVERYTHING THAT MAKES A MAN FEEL ALIVE AND GOOD. what then, you ask me, would you do with a man who rapes your little daughter whom you profess to love very much? well, the idea is, that under present conditions, this can happen anyway. the idea of a SOCIETY OF TRUST, not holy trust or church trust, but simple easy feeling, no jails, no war, no punishment . . . this man would come to THINK while walking down a sidewalk FREE that there was no necessity for his act, not in a sense of *taught* morals but simply in a sense of sense. things would take time to work free. I would say,

233

don't even lock up the madmen, the perverts, the deerslayers, the sadists . . . shit, it's just now 12 a.m. happy new Year and my love to you both [* * *] what I mean is: we must *give* chance a chance. what the hell else. I can work out all the lack of rules. trust me. shit, I *must* be getting old. musing of a better world. I guess this capital punishment article thing caught a hair in the brain and started the sawmill going. well, we can't eliminate so much. the pain, the accident, the death. the tottering clay of us and our big mouths. your wife lost a kid. my first one did too. right in the crapper. afterbirth, afterbirth. an early fish flushed away like a turd. I was not much of a man. I was so insane that time, and years before that that I couldn't think of what to say, do. I don't blame my first wife for divorcing me. I was of very short stuff of soul. still am. I mean it. this is not theatrics. I am forever disgusted with myself. I am not even as good as my shit, my shit is better than I am. more man, more rose, more real. Barbara, I am sorry forever that my mind was tied-up with chickenshit nerves and dull crossword puzzles. [* * *]

Pound's x-girl friend Martinelli trying to cough up my whore-O-scope. stars, something. I suppose this puts me somewhere near the Master. just think, somebody Pound went to bed with is now writing me, has been for years. my, my. I know all about myself: I am the Original Hard-Luck Story of the Universe. Job only got tickled. [* * *] I can't make it into heaven now. burn this letter. maybe I can sneak past. could be I am in heaven now only I don't recognize it or could be I am in hell and I do. [* * *]

●

· 1 9 6 6 ·

o Walter: thanks word on *Confessions*. no, nothing else like that have I written, and prob. won't. prose bit to shape up shit a bit and wonder where I've been. so that's that.

I understand Jon and Lou Webb have come across hard times—broken press and the like. I'd like to see them get into #4. a Patchen issue, but things are not working right.

well then. we all move on. flowers in the air. gaslight. drunken birds. paradise is a cold wet stocking dripping on the back unexpectedly. I get sicker and sicker. little men outside sharpening their spades. to hell with them: I have 5 bottles of beer left and a bottle of india ink that sits here and says on its side: TINTA CHINA A LA PERLA.

the world is very good. I am sure of it: I keep gaining weight.

[To Douglas Blazek]
January 9, 1966

[* * *] word in from Norse, damn fine letter, and perhaps he has more style and touch than any of us, young snip. anyhow, he has been laid up in some Greek hospital unable to stop shitting, which is a hell of a way to go, what? anyhow he is getting better and jumped

235

out of bed in Hydra and escaped to Athens, where he is feebly typing up a batch of poems for me to look over to see if I think he can write or not write. for Norse—*Ole* issue. maybe I am being cruel? but I can't say anything about a man on 2 or 3 poems. the few things I have seen of his are clearly very good but I would like to see more for my own good and for his. I do not judge poems as a critic out of learning but as a human being out of my own experience which must nec. be limited but which nevertheless contains truths and instincts and flowers and spiders and snakes and dreams and stinks which may apply to any man living anywhere, anytime. and sometimes the way the "learned critics" talk about poetry and/or Art, I sometimes think I have even read MORE BOOKS and junked them down better. lot of ego to say this, yes, but you know as a man walks down a sidewalk or takes a piss or breaks an egg into a pan, strange thoughts enter the head and walk around, one of them being that the critics are my Aunt Sarah. [* * *]

[To Steven Richmond]
January 27, 1966

[* * *] still down with this flu or whatever it is and couldn't get to work again tonight. maybe keeping this flu is deliberate? do you think that going down to the liquor store in my bare feet is lengthening the case? or sitting up in that cold grandstand watching them run? I sit way in back by myself and they've got 40 sparrow ups there in the eaves, singing, chirping, shitting, but they have, so far, been very nice and have not shit on me. found a dead one on the pavement other day. didn't know what to do. couldn't touch it. couldn't move away. just sat there looking at the dead bird and feeling very sad for it, for everything, the works, and kept telling myself, you shouldn't you shouldn't, that's the mathematics of it, you ought to know by now. but that god damned bird hung in the center of my mind and I missed a couple of good plays. went down and had a couple of drinks, looked at some of the flaxy piss-dead women and drove on in. 25,000 people at the track and they had to show only me the sparrow. tough shit.

[To William Wantling]
January 28, 1966

[* * *] you know, baby, I think that the cleansers are the jails and the hospitals and the new whores, and without these Time seems to take it in the choppers—as waste. I think that unless a man is in constant realignment with himself he must die. the women might be good to us and actually love us as we trot off to our factories with our little gay lunch-buckets but that's because they are not dumb. they know that we walk into and are chewed by the very teeth of death, for they see us when we leave and they see us WHEN WE COME BACK. a hot bath, a meal and good night's sleep, even a good fuck does not return everything. listen, don't put me down as against women—I'd hate to be one and I know that they have their own personal world of horror. but life keeps chewing us up and how often can we keep getting up off the deck, and what for? me, I've just gone limp all over and let them punch. down at the coffee break area they call me, HANK THE PLANK (my first name in Henry, middle name Charles), BIG TIME, MONEY!, etc., but they don't know that when I go home in the morning that I comb agony and poems out of my hair. but to hell with that. [* * *]

I like your photo and will send you one of mine if I can steal a WANTED ad from the local post office. you look like a rough baby, kid, and I'd hate to meet you coming down any dark (or light) alley. but actually, in the 50's and 60's a different type of poet has evolved through the dense brutality of our age. we've had to be tough enough to live and at the same time to save the soul. the university boys are merely soft and tricky and clever but they don't know even what a wall *looks* like or a cat or a fish or a landlord or a policeman or a blade of grass, unless they attempt to imagine these things and they do attempt, and, of course, the mockery of our age is that these safe and clever and dead men are published everywhere. this is why the audience for poetry is so small—the masses know that most of it is fake—has nothing to do with lives, their or anyone's, has nothing to do with Life. [* * *]

[To Steven Richmond]
February 2, 1966

[* * *] LSD, yeah, the big parade—everybody's doin' it now. take LSD, then you are a poet, an intellectual. what a sick mob. I am building a machine gun in my closet now to take out as many of them as I can before they get me. *All* the death does not lie lay ly with the academics or the poetry workshops or the pawnbrokers . . . [* * *]

[To Douglas Blazek]
February 3, 1966

[* * *] our boy MacNamara has quit his job and now I seem to get a letter a day from him. that's nice. nice and frightening. I don't know quite what to say, finally. I mean, the thing can get kind of religious. but whatdy you do when ya lose yore bible?

I guess I told you the woman and I split, she has the girl with her. finally it was her poetry workshop and church group that turned my gut. christ, you know I work nights, and after being pissed all over with the overtime bit, take me hours to fall asleep and then I'd be awakened by the shits giggling and making dull jokes in the other room. they just can't get together *enough* and talk talk talk, and, baby, complaint is bad, I guess, but if you could only see the *look* of them, the flat cardboard soul stink of them, maybe you'd know. if they had only had the decency to wait until I was at work . . . to discuss their freedom marches, peace marches, civil rights bits, poetry readings . . . how can you be made sick even by cardboard people who seem to want to do everything right? ah, christ, sometimes I think I *am* crazy! maybe it was simply that they were FORMULA people, even down in the shitpit where I dragged my ass to work I found a people more *real* and even they were nothing, but still a relief in comparison. there wasn't any argument; don't ever remember cussing her gang, although might have done so while drunk. now she has them and I have me and we can all die separately. [* * *]

but look here, how can you find things out, feel things, even have a chance to yawn or look at the wallpaper if your jaws are going all the time? I guess we all feel badly enough and I have felt plenty of times like going to bed and crying for a week (Hemingway is far from my ideal, or, at the other end, Camus either) but what I felt like crying about I was not certain—it could not be worded or spoken, not over a telephone or not even to myself exactly, and maybe that's the reasons for this fucking thing called Art, Creation, whatever, sometimes we hang it in *just* RIGHT—we get it all, the dizzy broads on the phones, the flunky fired from his shithouse job, the guys like me wanting to cry in bed, the cat run over, the empty beer cans, me writing a letter to you and me being 1/2 nuts with old airplanes running through my brain, ah. [* * *]

[To Steven Richmond]
February, 1966

[* * *] yes, the sickheads will think *Earth* is another dirty mag. they do not realize that the cuss word is used only as explosion of fury-agony when nothing else fits that space. but you are still a good enough human to tell a real poem from an unreal one, and I think that *Earth* one, #1, was right in there, right up there, alive and burning, as good as *Ole* and *Wormwood*, maybe better. you got rights to be proud of your baby, baby. and that damn cunt in Sacramento who wrote me that *Earth* was shit, she still writes me as if all were sweet. I have not answered. the *Promethean Lamp* made me heave and I threw it into the trash but I did not bother to get highly vindictive with the editors, to show them my hot prong because I figured they were dead anyway and that in the machinery of the human affair such things as the *Lamp* were expected in my nightmares. yet these sisters who sit at home in their gardens and piddle with poetry while their husbands are out there being chewed-up by the world, these piss-pure sisters have always got to let us *know* what they *think* they think from inside their sea-dead skulls. fuck em. I want to congratulate you sweetheart on putting out one of the most vibrant bouncing searing jumping living of the littles and I am honored and proud and scared and sick-dizzy that I had a poem or something for you that you could use. [* * *]

[To Jon and Louise Webb]
February 28, 1966

well, as zero hour approaches and the rat of death spins on the knife, I have bought myself 3 books today to read in there if read I am able—Camus: *Resistance, Rebellion and Death*; *The Fall* & *Exile and the Kingdom*; *Notebooks 1935-1942,* and now my radio gives me Brahms' First—apropos, for I was listening to this one when the F.B.I. walked in on me in Philly and threw me on in. I have told Frances I am feeling better but I am really not feeling so good, but shit. shit, yes. saw Marina almost all day today, she's a joy doll and when I leave them at their place and go to leave she screams, "no! no! no!" and I hear her crying as I get into what's left of the car, as what is left of me gets into what is left of the car. hell of a life. got to take castor oil Tuesday night and then get up at 7 a.m. and give myself enemas—shit is right—so he can probe through the tunnels for rot at 10 a.m., then I enter hospital at 3 p.m. that afternoon. god damn fuckers. started reading Camus tonight, a chapter called "Create Dangerously" but I had read no more than 2 pages and he pissed me off, had me pissed off and disgusted. I too have been guilty of throwing statements around with abandon—whatever pleased my mind—whatever sounded right and strong and entertaining, but I hate to see a man like this building such cases, and then giving it at a lecture—University of Uppsala, Dec. 1957. [* * *]

in a sense, I feel it will be too bad if they cut my candle now. I have never told you but I always thought that my best writing would come after the age of 50. I have felt this slow fattening inside of me, the gradual thing, so gradual, a strange warm presence . . . well, shit, fuck the dramatics. [* * *]

About Henry Miller—print him if it will keep you afloat; he wants the wondrous Loujon format and you can't blame him. you'd like it yourself, for yourself, wouldn't you? Of course, Henry has slipped a few steps down, but he's still a good name and doubt he can ever *forget* how to write unless they kill him with a bomb or a stone or a hammer. Odd that I've read so little of him. in a bus station once in Texas, I think, and he too, like Camus, pissed me off. yet I realize that they both think, and write well, with force, I mean, there is just something in my brain that will hardly let me enjoy anything at all. I don't mean that I am an automatic crank or that I am bitter with the success of a Miller or a Camus; it's just that I'd rather not read. looking at the sun or a woman's legs or a horse race, this fills me;

reading just fidgets and burns and flops across me . . . dead grease, print, the coffin-lid down. [* * *]

[To Douglas Blazek]
March 1, 1966

I enter the Queen of Angels hospital tomorrow. dear doctor wants to probe a bit more tomorrow a.m. to see if he can find anymore worse, but so far just surgery for hemorrhoids which have gotten so damned bad I can't function anymore. I am hoping, of course, that he doesn't find any dirty words like "cancer." anyhow, if you don't hear from me in some time you will know that I am sparring around a few rounds . . . and if you don't hear from me at all, finally, you'll know I lost the damn fight. This would be a time, I'd think, when I should be sitting down and pounding out immortal poems . . . anything I haven't said, anything that I should say. but I am disinterested. no desire at all. I believe Webb is pissed at me because I cannot make trip—I promised—to come down and cut more tape. But he gets so *tied* in his projects that he doesn't realize that things can happen to people. I mailed him 3 tapes yesterday, old ones, and now the machine is dead . . . the sea rolls in. [* * *]

[To Douglas Blazck]
March 8, 1966

back, still stupid with spinals, knives, shots, people, gowns, noise, stink, the o big ass load of pain, hurrah, I am sitting here (barely) on a fat red pillow trying to make my mind think down to the keys . . . not much luck. I feel rather upside-down. get up continually and go to can and there are little snake turds without eyes, cut somewhat like death, and each bowel movement about a childbirth, gripping elbows, saying, "wwoowoo! sweet son of a bitch, mother, sing to me, sing to me!!" that shit sliding past the incisions of 15 years' worth of hemorrhoids and distorted intestine chopped loose. . . . when you think about poem, poems, or stories, about this time, all that doesn't

241

make much sense. I'm afraid the poem has never quite come up to the actuality and certainly hasn't solved it, althought I don't suggest we throw our rusty guns away.

[* * *] managed to get out to old '57 Plymouth and start it last night, let it run, and so *that's* still alive. I was laying flat on my ass in the dark of night, moaning, my foot on the accelerator, charging the fucking thing. 2 old women came by and stared at me laying in there, they thought I was nuts, but strangely strangely I didn't even care what they thought. I stared at their moth-dry, white-pigment, chalky, room-for-rent, casket faces; their bodies like sticks of hardened shit, even the moonlight seeming to vomit away from them . . . it didn't matter, and they moved on creaking and chirping nothings of waste. to think, they might even once have been half-decent fucks, but now more stupid than armies, less clean than dirt. anyhow, I think the car is ready to go, and with a little time, I am going to be around some more, as indecent and imperfect and vulgar as ever. you think you can remove this old German-Polack like a bathtub ring? hah, they gotta rub me harder than that! [* * *]

[P.S.] [* * *] —have been reading Camus (off and on) . . . 3 books' worth that I haven't got to. stories not so hot, rather common and ordinary, standard. essays contain good brain matter and have quality but the *style* is so dull! why do they have to put us asleep to teach us?

[To Jon and Louise Webb]
March 8, 1966

back couple of days but first day I've had strength or guts to reach typer. I don't know how long it will take me to shape up. just about out of vacation time and sick leave shot. sad song.—hope you got package o.k. with mags and tapes. *keep tapes away from machinery or they will fade.*—each bowel movement here a real crucifixion; but operation I'm told was simply for removal of an extreme (15 year) hemorrhoid condition, plus, I believe removal of part of intestine pushed out of shape with strain. not very pretty what,??? nothing like a good clean heart attack—it seems so much more honorable, but, of course, it's not truly so. (Doc examined my innards with snake: what an invention!) would like to get a couple of new and fresh tapes

242

to you but am simply in no shape to do so now. I do hope that we have a little more time. the $$$ situation looks bad; my pay will stop Monday and all operation will not be paid by my insurance. also have payments to Frances. various other things. but believe all will work out and I will be rolling again. god, it looks like we are all broke this time, TOGETHER!!

it's good, tho, to be alone again, out of the hospital, near the typer and the radio and Camus, and the sun and the sound of things flowing together. all will work, and easily, our luck is strong. health and love to you. Marina is so BEAUTIFUL!!!

[To William Wantling]
March 9, 1966

when you consider all the men born who are now dead, and when you consider the remaining living, these remaining living seem not only some miraculous mathematic, but also seem something to get *done* with: like a pruning or a picking or an ultimate road-end. would it be too precious to say that we live almost with a sense of shame, as if we were getting away with something? I would hardly regard my upcoming death as anything sorrowful or tragic—just the removal of garbage and a hacking voice that talks too much of too little.
                                              —Bukowski, 3-9-66
[* * *]

[To Ann Menebroker]
March 11, 1966

"green," new trend? "green, green, I want you green!"—Lorca. the use of "green" is now mostly an ultra-poetic Romanticism. of course, the word "green" is not outlawed but it is generally used by the pretenders and most poetry is written by pretenders. the living are busy doing something else.

To give talks on Poetry it is best to have a captive audience. Get them where they can't walk out—say a hospital, a jail, an insane asylum . . . school auditoriums are not safe—those with guts will leave. you can't blame the masses for disregarding poetry—it is pretty dull stuff & obtuse & unreal in direct regard toward what is actually happening to them. In the Atomic Age they don't have Time to waste or to be wrong.

This letter was printed in Congdon's Magazine, no. 3.

[To Kirby Congdon]
[ca. mid-March, 1966]

if this letter is detached and punchy, understand, at least. I'm out of the hospital, and these couple of dark hollering rooms are mine to divide, to throw myself on the springs and wonder about how I keep getting it in the ass. (don't misinterpret . . . or do, who cares?) (which reminds me of a guy in a place I just worked, I mean used to work. he had this reducing machine which he put his girlfriend on and fucked her. "we turn it on every night about 3 a.m. and it sounds like a washing machine. people wonder what I am doing washing my clothes at 3 a.m. but it's a great machine; you just lay there and it does all the work. you and I ought to try it?" "you and I?" I asked. "yeah," he said. "but who's gonna get on top?" "what the hell *difference* does it make?" he answered.)

I have been vaguely unhappy, bored, disgusted with poetry for years, for centuries . . . I sometimes try to tell people why—not in the involute & secretive and vocabulary-deadened style of a Creeley or an Olson, but really, what the HELL *ISN'T* going on and what the *HOAX* is. Of course, the best way to point out is to *create*, but sometimes I can't resist a few beerhall speeches. It is not so much in telling people how to DO things but in letting them know how the trusted kingpins have managed to slice an inch or two off the peckers of their souls and make them smile and say thanks. I'm 45 now; have only been in the game ten years but the way the body is falling apart I thought it would be best if I left some word. I hope I do not talk too much like a con-man. I'm sick of that; I've seen enough of that. anyhow, nothing.

244

the review on Corrington in *Steppenwolf*—the editor wrote me asking, "if I send you Corrington's latest book, you mind reviewing it?" a free book is a free book. hell, no, I don't mind, I told him, send it on in. I thought it might be something along the lines of his last book, *The Anatomy of Love & Other Poems,* and that I could say a few good things and then go to the racetrack or the mill or the rack or wherever. however, *Lines to the South* didn't have it, and since I had stuck my neck out I had no other choice but than to chop Willie's off. (Corrington's). he hasn't sent the Klan up yet so I guess I can put this rusty luger back under the hotwater bottle. Corrington had me worried when I met him and Miller Williams down there. the talk was all University-power talk, intrigue; talk about degrees and all that very drab shit. evidently it didn't take long the for the talk to catch up with the poems. but if you think I just write adverse reviews like a vulture trying to strengthen his own flight with dead meat, see *evidence* number 9. I do a review entitled "The Corybant of Wit," a look through at Irving Layton's *The Laughing Rooster.* I am afraid that Irving L. writes very well. when I can read a man without lessening the electric charge within me, I know that man is a writer. to hell with iambic p.'s and spondees, I go on kilowatts!

I keep getting stuff in the mail from people about my review of Corrington. the odd thing being that they all agree with me, which worries me. there was some Roman ruler, I believe, who said: "The people applauded. I must have said something wrong." I know what he meant. then too, it tickles their twats that after Corrington befriended me I jammed him. well, fuck it all. being a reviewer is too easy. I am afraid that if I reviewed my own stuff there would be blood all over the floor and walls. I know there would.

Corso? Ginsberg? maybe I am jealous of the big cats? they've got one thing I got—clarity of style, but they've got a little too much the sweet tooth for their own soul (soul-importance) and they suck up a lot of bait. Camus said we've got to be a part of History and get out with it, but I am not sure he meant on-stage bellowing to the idol-lovers. still, I am full of too much complaint, I guess, but I have turned down some offers to prance on stage for $$$, good place to sleep, food, drinks, fare, that bit. I'd have to be pretty hungry. (see Behan, see D. Thomas, see Christ.) the come-on is only a softener so they can rope you, kill you. I go with Jeffers—the best friend is a rock wall. (see Capone.) people do come to my door and I open it and treat them nicely, mostly because I don't have the guts to do otherwise, and also because they can easily have more than I. but then, too, these people are mostly *peekers* and the whole thing has nothing to do with CREATION or slamming the keys down, crackcrackcrack vapvap. I've got to be a loner because most of the time I am shoved into factories and places I don't want to be, and in order to get out of the spaghetti I have to crawl under the rug. I am not a snob and I am not precious and I am not playing genius; but where were these people when I was starving and freezing in a shack in Atlanta, when I was living in a cardboard shack without light, heat, water, food, toilet, hope, for a dollar and a quarter a week? where were these people when I was in jail, or on the park benches? where were these people when I turned the gas on one night and tried to kill myself? in Los Angeles? in hell? their sweet knocks, their quips, their stares . . . who wants them? if I fail to write any more poetry, they will be the *first* to say . . . "he's lost it. he's finished." I don't need their judgements. all I need is a sheet of paper, a typer, some food and some rent. win or lose, talent or no, age or death . . . I am, I was a human being. I never had a desire to look at a writer, to knock at his door, maybe because most writers never did me any good; maybe because I figured what they wrote was all they owed me,—if they owed me that. so, I'm just a crank who has had surgery of the asshole. fine, then.

bit of race rioting in Watts last night—not much—a Mexican and Negro killed, 25 injured. not much? I hear you laugh. I thought so. some writer, a guy who makes it professionally via the sex and nudey bit, phoned me last night. "I've got my gun loaded! I'm ready!" he said. this guy doesn't even live in Los Angeles. highly sensitive sort. then his doorbell rang and he just about zeroed out. I think I heard the safety catch go off. "gotta go," he said. "see you." he probably shot a Western Union boy with a dark tan. [* * *]

[To Douglas Blazek]
March 22, 1966

the dog poisoners are legion and slinky and seldom get caught, and we don't have enough death, they have to play dirt with the little we have left. I was supposed to go to WAR to save such creatures as these? the dog poisoners are usually members of long standing in the neighborhood, respected, churchly, own their own homes, and are often childless or their children have grown and tend not to see them anymore. the dog poisoners are usually between the ages of 55 and 70. most of them loved animals as children but American society and what it extracts from the body and the mind and the soul can grow very special monsters of its own. most of them are concerned with property and "property rights" as they like to call them. and since they have nothing else to hold to, this becomes everything. not so long ago there was a doctor out here in one of the suburbs who clubbed a puppy to death with a pistol butt. it was not even a grown dog. and he did it in the open, on his lawn, with children and people watching. (I was not there.) but his excuse was that the puppy had no right on his property. being a doctor and fatted with the worship people tend to give doctors and fatted with $$$, he was simply bolder and more insane than his brethren dog-killers. the case came to court but I didn't hear how it came out. they didn't print it or I missed that edition. probably case dismissed or a fine, say $15. property, property. I had a beautiful hound once (half-wolf, half-collie; but gentle, gentle) and I was walking him down the street on a leash and he stopped to piss on a plant outside a real estate office on Beverly Blvd. I had him trained to crap in vacant lots. but he pissed on this bush and this real estator leaped out of his office, he screamed at me: "HEY! GET THAT DOG OFF THAT BUSH! HEY! HEY! HEY! PISS IS POISON! HE PISSED ON MY BUSH!" you could hear this guy all the way to Bensenville, Illinois. I just looked at him, looked at his acid face and his eyes and his body dangling there. "I can't control my dog's piss," I told him quietly. "Well, let him piss somewhere else! move him off!" I didn't move off. either the dog or I could have killed him if we had so chosen. "Your chickenshit bush won't die," I told him, "and if it does, I'll pay you for it." "Get that dog outa here!" we stood there until he went back inside to count his blood chips of profit. sometimes I think that these people almost know that they are dead, ugly, wasted, and they don't want to see anything or anybody happy and careless and easy; they don't even want to see anybody unhappy in the way we tend to get unhappy—it has to be their way. my wolf-collie got killed by a car when I split with this woman. I had left the dog with her. pets seldom die of old age. how I hate the fucking world and their special ways and values! Blaz, you'll get over the dog (dogs) but you'll never get over what did it: The American flag. money. property. the dead citizens in cities of horror and madness and fear. christ, christ.

good that *All the Assholes and Mine* went. writing it so soon after,

I didn't know if I was caught in the stream or could see it go by. and yet maybe too much objectiveness tends to let the air out of the tires. that's the trouble with most literature: everybody's so cool and superior to the action that it becomes a word-game, a chess game— and the King is asleep and the Queen wears kotex and the Knights and Castles stumble and the Pawns, well, they don't matter, do they? [* * *]

[To Douglas Blazek]
April 4, 1966

[* * *] of course it would be sweet if you could get hold of a printing press; it would add to what is already there. *Ole* has so much more lifeblood than the others that it's . . . no contest, riot, runaway. I hope that a press will not delete the beautiful madness from your silly head. I don't think it will. as much as you hate it and know that it is killing you, that factory, without wanting to, is also keeping you alive—to this extent: that those few moments given to you— you realize that here the god damn sun gotta finally shine, no lies, no bullshit, words cutting into paper like flowers, like swords, like screams, like paint. your family too, as much as you love them, will sometimes think you are mad, think you are cruel, because you will want to cop some moments from them too. but they ought to know that without your writing and without your editing, without your crazy colored paper and your crazy debts, you would REALLY BE A TERRIBLE FATHER, you would be the average American citizen male breadwinner and he is a horror to behold, he is a sight to make one vomit blood and gut and hope all out, for even when he smiles even when he is kind even when he is a winner a lover a father a playboy a champ, he stinks he is rot, he is a flower without a head, a plant without a root, a slab of meat butchered and dressed in clothing. I've got a hunch your family senses some of this, senses your need to hold to walls, to cry at night, to go down in your basement and play with silly piles of papers. so, I'm not scared of you getting a press, I am not scared of you dying. I am scared of me dying. so many of my poems are coming back. one guy told me, "I also rejected Allen Ginsberg." fine. but means little to me, for I have also rejected Allen Ginsberg. but worse, I read the poems, and it

248

was true—they weren't any good. mainly because one line didn't even relate to the other. I'd say one thing, then jump right off into space with something else. and I wasn't even drunk. maybe that was the trouble. yet, it's good to fail. I don't say I had a belly laugh on myself but I did see that the way is curious, thorny and never clear. I am lucky too—to fail a lot. if you fail 40 times, 41 is not so bad. keeps the bowels loose, keeps you human enough to hope, and the miracle becomes mainly that you have typewriter and paper and that something *does* come out. umm, how I remember the hospital; operated on a Wednesday, didn't shit until sometime Sunday afternoon. shit is important too—as long as it's your own. what? [* * *]

[To Douglas Blazek]
April 6, 1966

you are like me, baby, the life and the way is killing you—it may come out in the chest or the asshole or the belly . . . something HOLLERS . . . Krist, I'd *like* to say the SOUL hollers?? ah ah, we are DeMop in the rowboat, orange huge muscles and mind and siff of the soul and nothing to cure it. ouch! you and I have seen enough factories and hunkies and beasts and straw bosses and layoffs and breadlines and unemployment lines and hangovers and hospitals and jails and rotten women to make anybody's stomach want to drop out and crawl off into a hairless hole to hide forever until the bomb until the whiskey god of love and easiness (DEATH) shows up. those chest pains of yours are from ugly work and nerves and senselessness; you have 2 clock hands drilling into your heart, and it's an ugly clock too, very. you need time more than the first 5,000 people you pass on the street and you know it. I do too. don't kid yourself—many people want SLAVERY, a job, 2 jobs, anything to keep them running in the cage. and when they call overtime night after night, sucking the last blood from our limp bravery, see them smile, smile their greasy overtime smiles, they love it. my god, they have a phrase for it down where I sometimes work. a word. "PORKCHOPS!" they say and lick their greasy lips when the word roars down at us, as God shits on us from the speakers above that are turned as LOUD as the machinery allows: "YOU ARE REQUIRED," says God, "TO WORK ONE HOUR OVERTIME!" that's the new word: required. then you make that hour and then God screams down, with just 2 minutes to go, that you are REQUIRED to work another. then, the same plan: another, another, until you get your lousy 12. all right, 12 and 8 hours for sleep, that's 20. hour lunch, that's 21. breakfast, dinner, travel, shit, shave, dress, undress, say something to your kid, look at the wall a minute, and all the odd things, haircut, buy shoes, get a tooth pulled, try to get the car started, kill a fly . . . that's 24, and you're back. more PORKCHOPS. you know all this. I thought I'd let you know that I know it too. and there's never any money. for it all, there's never any money. you have as much money working 40 hours a week as you do 72 or 32. strange, but it's true. you have a family, I have child support. we do not beg off. it is something we did and we run it through. I love my little girl ten thousand times 402. fine. all right. but we're crazy too. we'd like to walk down some beach with a knapsack and a cheap bottle of wine. we'd like to stare at the moon for 3 hours or just sit there and smell the stink of dead fish, of another death; we'd like to sit there and mug and tickle the shadow of China there across the waves, VVVASSSSH!! we'd like to do nothing for HOURS HOURS HOURS, gentle do-nothingness. filling like a sink with hot water. feeling our cotton brains up there. feeling mice between our ears. even wondering about Christ, wondering if there were 13 at the table, wondering if it ever happened, wondering if anybody spilled wine on their sleeve or farted. wondering all the easy things. comparing the sun to a lemon. falling in love with the color yellow like a big-assed whore. yellow, yellow, that's me, and it's my favorite color too. good. luckily I knew a lot of the traps from watching my father, from studying my father. I worked myself a lot of lay-around time in. I always lived with old drunken women, very OLD women because I didn't want children, I didn't want the trap. "Bukowski," the few guys I knew used to say, "you can do better than THAT!" "sshish!" I'd tell them, "she's coming in with the wine." I even used to amuse myelf when I'd introduce my women. "Hey, this is Mary." "Mary, this is Joe." and I'd glim Joe's face as he took in the sagging bellied, wine-struck, age-struck Bukowski cow. I never alibied. actually most of my cows were pretty good women. I mean, all they wanted was me and something to drink. I figured that these were pretty endearing qualities. meanwhile, no babies, no marriage, no squeeze, and I didn't look so good either and I didn't feel so good either and I either felt equal to or inferior to many of my cows. sure, some of them were vicious sluts, dirty and hardened as 3 week old and unwashed dishtowels and so was

250

I, straight, I felt too like cursing all the walls and landlords and fuzz and children and the stars and the queers and the money-grabbers and the stink of life. it was a good bargain: I knew where I belonged, I was clever. I slipped once, and out of compassion more than anything, found myself with a 23 year old wife. she neither had the bone, the wisdom, the chapters of life behind her. she was a snit, a snob . . . hypersensitive to the smallest criticism, but meanwhile taken in by the grand phonies, the liars, the movie-trained Romantics, the dead-souled pretenders of Grace. fine. but ridiculous. lucky for me, there was a miscarriage. that rather did it. her phonies moved in and told her what a beast I was, or rather, by pretending no-beast they showed the beast in me. which was there. which was truly there. of course. shit. so divorce. escape. I walked down to the beach and tried to read Faulkner again. I layed on the sand with all my clothes on in mid day so they couldn't see my scars. I've got these bloody hideous scars all over my back from some former hideous disease. show me something and I'll catch it. why I never got the siff or the gon, I'll never know. only the crabs. and I've screwed the filthiest lousiest stuff in bars from Coast to Coast. deliberately. did I tell you the time I picked up this young whore, around 19, 20 in this bar, a real fine piece as the boys would say, only the madam, some old hag around 55, insisted on coming along to see that I didn't spoil or mutilate her young fine meat income. o.k., I said. we sat up at my place and had a few drinks, more than a few, it was an old place up the hill by the Grand Central Market. I still thought I was a writer or something and was living on potatoes and boiled fishheads. everything went all right until I had another drink or so and then decided it was time for the great lover, Rupert Brooke Bukowski, to screw to fuck. by training and instinct, of course, I grabbed for the 55 year old hag instead of that fine 19 year old meat. training runs deep, pal. I'll always remember this hag with a face like a killer (I don't know if they wore a Green Beret) and she had one hand missing at the wrist and attached was an iron hand, very shiny and large and silver, with, I remember, one VERY LARGE HOOK protruding. and I mean protruding, baby! after the first grab at the hag, I think she was a lez to top it all, she backed off and swung the hook—S W I S H!—"hey, this son of a bitch is NUTS!" she hollered. and I remember that hook swinging again and again and myself ducking, ducking around the room. meanwhile, the 19 year old meat very puzzled. me too. I ran out of the room and left them in there with my immortal short stories, to burn them if they wanted

251

to, to fuck each other if they wanted to. . . . where was I? yeah? down at the beach reading Faulkner. trying him again. trying to convince myself that he wasn't a phoney to me. he'd won all the prizes. his photo even looked like a man. what was wrong? I felt like he was slipping me the smooth bologna. I am still puzzled. he can't write. he slicks it. he's celluloid. clever. cute. what's wrong with me? some monkeys were playing with a beachball and they'd bounce it near me, sand all over Faulkner, all over me, in my mouth, ears. I stayed on there, right in the middle of their game, right in the middle of Faulkner's game as my x-wife ran off with a cultured Turk with a purple stickpin and a cultured accent, a kind of Boyer, and he knew how, he owned a drive-in movie.

what am I talking about? mainly my extreme cleverness at staying out of the traps. so here I meet this woman. she is 42. I am 44. who needs to worry about children? responsibility? another good deal. by God, when Bukowski came along he must been in front of the line to get all those brains!

listen, Blaz, the day she told me she was pregnant, that moment, I do wish somebody could have photographed my face. it must have been a monument of disbelief, something say like a guy getting up in the morning and noticing that sometime while he slept somebody had clipped his balls off—I mean, that FIRST KNOWING, that FIRST LOOK, reaching down with the hand and finding nothing there. listen, kid, I *have* my balls, so far. even tho I wrote a poem about a guy who cut his off. I am just trying to give you the feeling, the look of it. 44 years of planned and deliberate cleverness. shot. bang. like that. over. I wish you could have had a photo of my face then because whenever you got the blues you could take this photo out and laugh for hours, you know. —anyhow, she's a beautiful little girl, a miracle, and glad she's here now, but jesus sweetheart, god or somebody pulled the switch on me, fast. well. think of all the young bodies I bypassed! arrrg! when bigger and better jackasses are born, Bukowski will still lead the parade. [* * *]

glad to hear *Assholes* will be a book. I dedicated the thing to Wantling not on the assumption of a book but merely to dedicate. last I heard he was working in a carwash for $1.25 an hour. this is kind of rough on near-genius. I don't mean that they should be spoon-fed and elevated a la Patchen, no matter what the misery. all men suffer, even those who *don't* write poetry, and if we're going to help Patchen with a bad back, we also gotta help Joe Brown with a bad back, or else this makes Patchen no good, you see? think you do. [* * *]

252

Webb, I dunno. he's blown thousands of dollars running around the country for a year looking for a new Taos, a new Carmel, a new something, meanwhile staying out of direct Atomic Warfare areas, according to the experts. well, that's his business. but he's running around in special trains with his wife, 2 dogs, the printing press, tons of cartons of paper, type, books, manuscripts. they had to get away from New Orleans, couldn't stand it—tourists, the Ku Klux Klan, thugs, bad weather for Lou's lungs. o.k. I get postcards from this city, then that: "I believe this is it. everything fine." then a week later, another card: "oh, we can't stand it here!" and there goes the press and the dogs and the works somewhere else. Laredo, Santa Fe, Phoenix, Cleveland, Phoenix again. "I feel El Paso will be the place. I can get paper. can walk across the border to whorehouses. real life. everything I need." no, something went wrong in El Paso. too low? Santa Fe was too high, and other things. one place they rented a house (Phoenix), paid 2 months rent, $200. fine place, they wrote, plenty of room for dogs. then I hear it is too hot. air conditioners don't work or the blowers don't reach the crapper or something. 3 or 4 days. on the train again. the press, the dogs, the works. 200 dollar rent lost, but o.k. they learned something. Phoenix won't do. where now? now it's Tucson. $235 to get the press hooked up again. triple wiring like in all the other places. Tucson, o.k. have made down payment on a house. fine. low monthly payments. everything fine. fixing place up. there's even a bed for you. dogs love it. will have bookshop in front. send all your old books, paperbacks, little magazines. (I did.) well, fine I thought, they've settled. they went through the same thing a year ago, and finally came back to New Orleans. now, at least, they know New Orleans is not right for them. Los Angeles is in the Atomic area, Frisco is in the Atomic area, so forth. I had written them a long letter some time back trying to tell them that there weren't any cities, that shit spread wherever humanity lived. but they didn't seem to get the message, so when I got their notes from various cities, that "this might be it," I just wrote back fine, fine, good. now I just got a letter from Tucson, "Lou misses New Orleans, wishes we were back. this is a lousy town. the busses stop running at 6 p.m. nothing but old, old people around, walking around. we haven't made any friends." But they are going to stay, Jon says now, a year anyhow. a lot of work to do. the record Bukowski TALKING won't be out in April. *Chi. Lit Times* ad only pulled in about 20 sales so far. they just don't have the kind of $$$ to put it out now. October better. would take $600 at least to press the record.

broke. might do the Henry Miller book submission first, that would give them enough money to get into #5, the Patchen issue, and then, in October, the record. I busted my ass, shooting mouth into a borrowed tape recorder, laying on the floor first on one side then the other because my ass was too sore to sit on, I got them fresh mad tapes for their April deadline, and now I find I had until October, maybe forever. it's Webb's $$$ and his right to travel but when he cries Wolf now, when he cries broke now, I really just do wonder who is crazy, me or him or the dogs or the press or the American cities and The Bomb or what? he gave me 2 great books, *Crucifix* and *It Catches*, I can't deny that. yet I wonder sometimes if I wouldn't have been better off coming out in cheap editions of one or 2 hundred copies? certainly the writing could have been judged as *writing*. it's difficult to hold down pages like that. I means *Crux* and *Catches*. automatically they are going to beanball you for coming out in a purple necktie. format, beautiful format! all right, fuck it, I wrote some poems one time, long ago, too. see the ungrateful wretch I am! [* * *]

Larsen's book is The Popular Mechanics Book of Poetry, *published by Blazek's Mimeo Press in 1966.*

[To Steven Richmond]
April 12, 1966

[* * *] got to agree with you on the Larsen book. humor is good when it stems from truth—in fact, truth alone is often humorous in itself, makes me laugh. but the humor of artifice—whose worst device is exaggeration—always makes me a little ill because it is just another con game. confined, my last days in the hospital, with some idiot with a t.v. set he never shut off, I was laid open to what the world considered comedy and at the expense of my dwindling sanity. how they made me ill with their obvious extremisms—lying there with my ass torn open, my beautiful walls taken from me. I suppose that the worst is Bob Hope with his flip little cute exaggerations. and his name droppings. I don't keep much up with the world and he drops these names I never heard of, all supposing to *mean* something. about the only lout I could stand was Jackie Gleason—at his best

254

he showed some showmanship, at his worst he was like the rest. but Larsen, Larsen, no.

Bukowski wrote a foreword to Richmond's book, Hitler Painted Roses *(Santa Monica, 1966).*

[To Steven Richmond]
April 15, 1966

hang in there on *Hitler*, the more they holler the more you'll know you are getting closer to the bone. I remember when I was a kid, 16, 17, I was just beginning to play with short stories. came home one night and here were all my clothes thrown out on the front lawn—coats, shirts, shorts, stockings *and* short stories. the old man had dipped into a drawer, uninvited, and had become a literary critic. "No son of mine is going to write stories LIKE THAT and live in MY HOUSE!" "Come on out here," I told him, "and I'll beat the shit out of you."
be glad *Hitler* curls their neckbones. you are there. [* * *]

[To William Wantling]
April 18, 1966

[* * *] dull letter. sorry. but have been writing a lot of poems, even a review of Artaud for local liberal rag. the libs too are a kind of jellyfish crowd. I want to see the poor man fed, sure. but don't make me love him. anyway, surprised they took the Artaud, I hung some strong salty lines in there, using the review as a crutch to slip across some of my own demented and boiling ideas. [* * *]

[Addressee Unknown]
Mid-April 1966

Randy, old kid,—

Frances and I separated now. turning your letter over to her. she is good at writing long (long) equivocal things. you'll probably get a 6 pager full of . . . wisdom.

I keep writing my poems and waiting, mainly, to die.

Sorry I am a little short of tonality and space here. All I can hand you is a brick. Love works like machinegun fire. I don't trust it.

You are a good young kid but you will be broken like the rest of them. Your first mistake was not to take the 5 years rap. It would not have killed you, not nearly as much as the 30 days you are doing now. But that's the way it works. It's very tricky. we are finally tricked out of the last of our wits. so be it. so says this drunken voice from the top of a syphilitic mountain.

Pappa Webb pissed at me now for various reasons. this is how it works. gangrene in the beef stew. so, they held me up to the sun and the sun shined on me. but whatever is left must go on, a while . . . huh?

If you want any advice from an old head, I'd havta say—try to hold off any real or desperate entanglement with women as long as possible. The problem is not so much in *losing* a woman, this is expected, but it is in seeing where they finally go . . . toward the rottenest death, toward the falsest of the false, toward the lie, toward the obvious lie forever. It's like a comedy, only you are the only one in the audience and they are on stage.

And look, pretty boy, I still don't get your movie-writing shit. are you, alone, going to turn the whole rot upside down and make truth of it? you couldn't take 5 years, how you gonna change a whole industry? I think that you are in some kind of dream-state. If you have the guts to wash dishes, surely you have the guts to know where you are. One doesn't work without the other. You confuse me because you have too many cards in your deck.

I talk to you straight because nobody else will and also because I have a little time now, having had my asshole sliced a bit, and unable to work. but actually, yes, I did meet more death in you the last time I met you than the first—you were more cosmopolitan, less human, more full of angles and ways. . . . Christ, I know the Romantic in us must die sometime, but must all *else* die too? But, this is the same old *horseshit!*—the old talking down to the young . . . I went through

256

so much of it, and *all* their advice was bad. So, all ya gotta do, is turn everything I have said to you, turn it upside down and you've got the truth.

I told off some Catholic priest the other day. you think I'm turning into an old crank? enjoy your next piece of ass to your full capabilities, hahaha ha ha!

[To Steven Richmond]
May 16, 1966

[* * *] by the way, somebody's stealing some of our fire—or borrowing it anyway. Frances showed me a copy of *Xenia* 2. she has a couple of poems in there and not bad ones at that. but what I mean is, baby, there are articles—attacks on Olson & *Poetry* Chicago, so forth. the problem being, with them, that the poetry they print does not attack the problem or rattle or burn or jump or exist. in other words, they know what's wrong but they can't dance. which still gives the edge to *Earth*—she dance, she know what's wrong & she know how. ya. [* * *]

if the universities ever read *Earth* they will burn their doors and books and walls. god damn, something in red just walked by. my pecker jumped like a worm in a sparrow's mouth. when they gonna let this old man rest? [* * *]

[To Steven Richmond]
[ca. June 1966]

[* * *] I composed this magazine in 20 minutes—from memory. I hope to *hell* you don't think I am serious! [* * *]

THE TOILET PAPER REVIEW

our motto is: we don't give a shit

edited by

Charles Bukowksi

pirc

priceless

poem

o it says
    vamma
        ?????
        ?????/////
        crutch

hold me
    Hold me
        o eternal motor
            super heart
            supermarket heart

        sputtering

            the night becomes me
            and I die

—John Vance, Glendale

poem

it is only
me.

—Curly Eisten, Pasadena

editorial

the only ones who can write is us. nobody else can
write but us. we are the only ones who can write.
I don't understand why other people can't write.
send money. send your wife—for one night.
we do this for love.
we hate war. we like guitars. we paint. we swim.
we know everything. the world is evil. we are not
evil. send money. we send love. we send love
everywhere. send your girlfriend—for 2 nights.
don't pay your income tax. blow up the troop
trains. smoke pot. sell pot. write your president.
write your gov. write your mother for money and
send it to us. don't send your mother—at all.
literature and the world are in bad shape. we are
dying. legalize rape.
no payment for poetry.

        yours, love,
        Charles Bukowski

259

poem

war is terrible. people get killed in wars.
I once killed a man. I will never kill
another man. bow to the sun. suck your own
cock. the stars come down like
RAIN. love, love
LOVE.

—Joe Esterlund, Cleveland

poem

o dear, the green of me, the green of me
is dying in the fountains
the green sun stops my breathing
mother asks me to get married
I can't teeth the world
or I am afraid
o my green my green is
going
in fountains
and the stars are
grey.

—Mary Jane Wicks, New York City

if you say you like poetry, this is another
editorial, then god damn you, buy books, sned
send me money, I am up on a pot charge. anybody
who says they like poetry and doesn't send me
money is a god damned fink.

editor

note: all manus. must be acc. by stamped return
envelope. not resp. for anything. no payment for
material.

letters

yours is the best magazine ever. raw guts.
—Randy Page, Ohio.

your first issue knocked me out.
—Randy Page, Ohio.

I read it straight through.
—Randy Page, Jr.
Ohio

have been waiting a long time for something like you.
—R.P., Cleveland

how do you DO it????
RANDY PAGE—
poet

I was not pleased.
Rance Edwards, Eirie, Pa.

the police threw the cat out the window and found 4 lousy grains of coedine. I am going to enter Ohio State, take a major in Engo9sh oit. to hell with the spelling. if you don't like it too bad. this magazine is for fun and love, LOVE, LOVE. nobody will be send an issie until the write me a LONG LETTER asking for it. are you going to ask for it? send stamps, love, $$$$$. we don't have much money. paper costs money. and we need voluntteers to do the work. I've got the keep the lawns trim and have to collect rents from the bums in back. we hope to continue with this mag. but need your helop & love & money.

ed.

poem

the sky reaches for my intestine
and the kitten walks across the floor
and the door is the moon
and I am an iceberg
and want icecream and pussy
and my green is going
and I can hardly see the stars,
o my god,
the pain,
fuck you.

—Randy Page, Ohio

LOVE

LOVE

LOVE

AND THANKS TO ALL OUR FRIENDS.

[To William and Ruth Wantling]
June 20, 1966

shouldn't have told you about the Pulitzer nomination because it's useless and futile, no chance, but thought it might amuse you in a kind of obscene manner, you know, maybe here I am dying and I am nominated for a longshot shit medal. [* * *]

still weak but feeling better, must be short here now, haven't worked for a couple of weeks—doesn't help with $$$ but spirit she lifts like kite, color comes back in eye, skin begins to glow, no doubt fucking job is one-half of what is killing me. they kill me if I work, I starve if I don't. [* * *]

hello Ruthie:
o christ christ ya I'd ride a bicycle if not too many hills. I don't have a beard but I've grown me a little red goat. hell, thot it would look good in a casket if I get a casket. now now, don't lecture me. I know, dramatics. ya, I could put on shorts. old as I am I've got these huge mysterious muscular legs, don't know where they came from. I could see Bill and me now, bicycling, red goat and beard, legs and glazen eyes. . . . every gal in town would get it bad, my my, and we would pedal along singing Salvation Army hymns or old Wobbly songs. maybe some day we will, if Bill and I climb through our troubles. just never ask me to be happy, that makes me unhappy, or never ask me to be just, that makes me unjust. o.k. o.k. o.k. o.k.

[To Douglas Blazek]
June 25, 1966

[* * *] strange woman came to my door the other night, one a.m. "yeah?" I said. she wanted to know if I were Charles Bukowski. I let her in. weeping face. good legs. I was sober, sitting there looking at the walls. soft pecker. I explained that I was ill, told her to look at my paintings on the walls. she looked and didn't say anything. Blaz, I will no longer fuck on demand or because it's there or because something has to be proved. that's called old age. I signed something and sent her on her way. now Hemingway would have had her all up and down the springs, flexing his soul muscles. I was glad when

263

she left and fixed myself a glass of tea (see T. S. Eliot) and then got down on my nubs and prayed for a good night's sleep. lately I can only get an hour, an hour and a half's sleep a day or night. if I get 3 I feel pretty good. keep leaping up imagining burglars, my brain going, going. or that somebody is planning to kill me. (that's an old one.) meanwhile Webb writes that I have been nominated for the Pulitzer Prize. Webb said they asked for a bio and photo. altho what a bio and photo have to do with a man's work, I dunno. [* * *] happened to mention to Wantling, and he and wife made a big thing of it, made me feel rather foolish. I liked better Frances' reaction. she came over with the kid and demanded 19 weeks child support in advance, she wanted to go to mountains or camp or somewhere with kid.

"god damn it," I told her, "don't you realize that I am dying? don't you realize that I am not working? I'm not a money tree, I am SICK SICK SICK SICK!"

"well, that's not Marina's fault, that's not *my* fault. I wanna go to camp, I wanna get outa the smog, I wanna get my baby outa the smog!"

that's when I thought it would be amusing to tell her. "I've been nominated for the Pulitzer Prize," I told her.

"yeah, the Foolitzer Prize," she said.

that's what I like about these women. we can't fool them. they *know* us. [* * *]

[To Ann Menebroker]
Sunday in July, 1966

[* * *] the oddity . . . of continuing to write poetry as one *really* gets older—I'll be 46 in August, there is somehow a sense of shame as if one didn't belong, but I think this is an ingrained Americanism— that age is a crime and that poetry is for the young. my age is a miracle and poetry is for me, or, what I write, whatever that is, is for me. it's a clarification of issues and also some screaming and also some things which we don't know. it's Romantic, unromantic, useless and important. it's a way to go. I don't think that I can quit. I believe I will be writing little lines on my drooling bib in my senile crib. the pleasure of my madness. [* * *]

[To William and Ruth Wantling]
August 6, 1966

[* * *] Webb speaks of another book in late '67 or early '68, even tho I have told him I am feeling very bad. it is so strange people ignore me when I say this. Frances ignores it. everybody. it is not the sympathy bit I want; I just want a few people to know that I can't function so well anymore—the old warrior's got a flat tire. or maybe Webb speaks of the book to keep me going? I wouldn't want a book that way. I want my poems to leap through walls. not that the poems are important but if I am playing with poems I don't want wet sunflower seeds. well, shit, that's enough singing of the blues. [* * *]

[To Ann Menebroker]
August 13, 1966

yes, I'd say get a book together, out, never believe you write as badly as some of them would like you to think or never believe you write as well as some of those would like you to think, it's hash gabble, but the gathering is good for your health, the climate of your being. be there. and don't worry that maybe Pound has written better or Eliot (T. S.), or that your mother won't like them or that maybe Bukowski will or maybe Bukowski won't. to hell with Bukowski. so much of our world is comparison, competition, victory, defeat, scratching, climbing, burying, denying—champions, madmen, fools and apple pie. I am tired of their game. to an extent I am caught in their machine but I needn't swallow *all* the nuts, grease and oil. I wrote a poem in *Ole* about a poetry-writing doctor and this doctor read the poem (it was anti-him as the human being he posed) and wrote back telling me that I had "slipped," that he and his wife were very concerned about my "decline" as an artist. I didn't answer. but actually, it is my FREEDOM TO DECLINE, to SLIP. I don't want to go on and on packing the dear old ARTIST-load anymore than I want to pack any other kind of load. we're all racing for the Moon of being Top Man. WHERE DO WE DIFFER AS WRITERS FROM USED CAR SALESMEN? this is why I hate to be called a "writer," and "artist." call me some other dirty name. think of some of this when you think about getting out a book. don't worry about some other "finer" writer. think about getting a book out like taking a drink for yourself or scratching your toes. all that I am telling you here is THAT YOU DESERVE A BOOK FOR YOURSELF just like Pound deserves a book for himself or Bukowski deserves a hot bath on an August night of almost no moon. what I am trying to say here is perhaps not very clear—I have slipped, you see. there's a young man on the bench ready to take over my center field spot—bright eyes, strong arm, a way to go. I hope he enjoys the madness of the days.

well, enough speech-making. listening to something on the radio a bit dull and classical but with just enough bite to help me endure my landlord who rolls past this window mowing his lawn, bug bellied in no wind, hung to his proper string as the young girls walk by, and when a good one walks by, flowing like the magic of stuff stuck somewhere in me, old 46 gets up and walks to the window and looks out, sucking on his cigar, big green tears cascading down his face as he realizes all the years shot through the head, assassinated forever, wasted sure, drank senseless, hobbled and slugged in factories, bad dreams, 2nd rate jails, mouse and ghost-infested rooms across an America without a meaning. boy o boy.

sometimes when I don't write, please understand that something is happening—flat tires, overtime, illness, accident on freeway, bad horses or just the common white seethe of deadness taking hold inside. I am not hard; I would like to be harder—the days have too many teeth. I think you understand. if you've read my book *Confessions of a Man Insane Enough to Live with Beasts* you might prob. think me quite the cruel dog, but that is just the side I let them see—a cement thing with eyes poked in and mouth talking out the side. in this great land we have been taught not to be seen crying in the streets. we tabulate the works into a pillow at night in a room we think does not know.

[To William Wantling]
August 21, 1966

[* * *] But, actually, I don't know if I wd. like you with college education. You know what college ed. generally means?—security and *their* way of thinking. they run you thru the hoops and set you

free—you think. there's something clean about washing cars. the kids—I know. layoffs, I know. no work, I know.

The game works in all different directions.

The trick is to work it enough in *their* directions to let you live, but enough in your direction to stay alive. the chickenshits call it "compromise"—they mean give a mile to take a mile; I mean give an inch to take 400 miles. there's a difference. of course, the danger with my unbalanced education is that you sometimes end up standing on the razor blade. chop! [* * *]

Vagabond *no. 2 with the Bukowski material was published by* John Bennett *in Munich in 1966.* Klactoveedsedsteen *(named after a composition of Charlie Parker's) was published in Heidelberg and edited by Carl Weissner, who was to become a frequent correspondent and eventually Bukowski's literary agent in Germany.*

[To Ann Menebroker]
September [10], 1966

good to get call, seriously, tho I didn't know what to say, got lift. like old times, what, old girl? damn, how we carry on! I guess we often get the deep blues, both of us, and wonder what it all means—the people, the buildings, the day by day death things, the waste of time, of ourselves.

I've thought of phoning you at times but afraid your husband might answer and he'd think I was trying to break up your happy home, which I'm not.

very odd thing happened today. I got a letter from a street sweeper in Munich, Germany, and he showed a magazine (English-printed in Germany, the editor is a dishwasher) to a postcard seller on the street, an old man, and the old man read my long poem in the mag to a group of young people in the streets, translating from English to German as he went along. this is enough to chill hell out of me. I was originally born in Germany and once spoke the language as a child but now can no longer speak or understand it. and here was this old postcard seller reading one of my poems in GERMAN, in the

267

streets of the land I was born in. who says we don't return? who says that miracles never happen? unfortunately, the long poem is printed with a couple of pages reversed (*Vagabond* 2 is the mag), but the message still seems to get through, so what the hell? you've got to write pretty strangely to have your poem printed in any order, but, since, in this one I was talking of the old mysteries of the soul plus the good fight, it read almost sensibly. good.

meanwhile, another German magazine *Klacto* has taken a couple of my poems. the editor of this one is also very poor. what are all these poor men doing? what crazy souls they possess! it is good to have your own courage but it is also good to take hope and courage from the ways of others. this I haven't been able to do until lately. some very very strange people are arising, Ann. but mostly they are not arising in America. there is something about this land and its ways that kills almost everybody. there doesn't seem room or reason for the truly living creature.

but little miracles keep chipping in to keep me going. an unexpected phone call in the middle of the afternoon from Sacramento; a seller of dirty postcards reading my poetry to children in a foreign land; the *Lamp* taking a couple of my poems after I had accused them of belonging to the "ladies sewing circle"—now my landlady shows at the door—"come on down and have a beer." and so I will go on down there and drink with her and her old man the rest of the night. they like me and I am glad. I am glad to be liked. corny? I am glad to be liked by the non-literary people, and the literary ones too. I am glad you are Ann Menebroker. I am glad you phoned. perhaps someday we will meet and it will be very embarrassing and dull, and we won't go to bed together, but no matter what you think or how odd you think I am, I will still be glad that you were, in many ways, a part of my life, and I especially remember you in the bad times of 3, 4 years ago when I was very close to suicide. it's been a long sweep of years and I think we are all stronger and better for it. when, often, I do not write or snap or seem the aged crank, do forgive this, for there are still times when the knife still gets close, very close, and things fall apart and I am not fair to people. I think, however, that you know all these things. and since you do, this letter is long enough.

Notes from Underground *(San Francisco) was a continuation of John Bryan's* Renaissance. *It ran for three issues from 1964 to 1969.*

[To William Wantling]
Mid September 1966

[* * *] *Notes from Underground* now out, you'll get your copy soon. I told Bryan yours was the best writing in there, und he agreed. glad you didn't insist on changes. it reads as a raw, original and sheer-pure work. if the rest of your novel is up to this level, some of your worries are over. everything fit, the conversation and the action. well, balls—before you swell out to python-size, nice to have known you. ya still gonna drop me a card after you're famous asshole? good.

actually, I am drying up on letters. it was a phase, maybe. big arguments along this row last night. I was not in it. everybody drunk around here, all these places. somebody in driveway couldn't drive. ramming into things. another drunk screaming at him. real loud bingo game. YA WANNA TRY ME? —THAT'S POSSIBLE TOO. I HAD AN AC-CIDENT. —YEAH, WHO RAN INTO YOU??? NEVER MIND, WHAT YOU DOIN' LIVIN' IN A DUMP LIKE THAT? —I OWN THIS PLACE YOU LOUSY SHARECROPPER! this kind of dialogue. I am listening in the kitchen, drunk, smiling, broke, stupid, enjoying the flare from an electric light overhead. realizing that I am not the only man in the world who is insane. [* * *]

[To Douglas Blazek]
September 19, 1966

raining, something by Rossini, coffee here, just took Maria and Frances to their place—all day Sunday recovering from about a week's drunk, god o mighty, my timecard in hell looks like it's speckled with henspots—same old blackouts, dizzy spells, balls balls balls what a game! anyhow, rec. all the *Assholes,* und tanks, babe, your usual lively production, glad to be part of the team, and now *Assholes* is lined up with the others in the wobbly bookshelf and I kind of feel like a christmas tinsel Hemingway. [* * *]

I hope the foreword went [* * *] if you use the foreword, fine, it will be foreword #3 [* * *] Sherman, Richmond, Blazek . . . all odd-cat poets with warm and mad string of melody and punch and message. no regrets, shit, I stand back of these. [* * *]

I hope you and Norse mend it. I like to think that I understand both of you a little. we are all cut and hammered by so many things that do not always show in the poem directly. these things happen. our strings get out of tune. I know how you have to squeeze the faint and slipping and tired minute to get out one page of that mimeo and here I have an edge on Norse in knowing how it goes . . . the pains in the back, the neck, the chest, the fucking soul . . . the foreman's face again, and what a FACE! Norse, tho an excellent poet, is more the literary and leisurely type, and when coming across him try to remember his diving board is a little different. god, the sun just came up. see what these prayerful lectures of mine can do? but must get to sleep, or the sleep substitute. I'm going to need some moxie to handle them tonight, sick as I feel. I'm known as "rough, tough Hank." "Hank the Crank." "Hank the Barber." but you need fangs down there or they'll eat you up. I can't recite Keats to them. better the iron hand. [* * *]

[To Douglas Blazek]
Early October, 1966

[* * *] good, you'll use the foreword, even tho I guess part of it does not jive with your hives. I still hope we learn how to spell "Polypolesian wars." I am not for deliberate misspellings just for the hell of it. [* * *] I am not being straight-laced but why give them a chance for their dirty mudballs? [* * *]

[To Carl Weissner]
Early October 1966

thanks for M[anifesto] for Grey Generation, lively as hell, but don't know quite how much manifesto in there except life-um jump, which is o.k., of course, very little around. I have been on the drinking thing and very sick, but remember some tape myself, talking with big cat with beard who has run away from 2 wives, changed name and is now letting another woman support him. he has children somewhere, both poetry and in flesh. now new name. he didn't drink. took some stuff. I drank and took some stuff. most talk utter waste, of course, most of the time looking at electric light or wondering how stupid I am. and realizing I am much more unhappy than anybody I have met. I have a reputation for toughness, I don't know where it came from. I once tried to bust up a few heads and a guy's house, but, bah, that was sometime back. listening now to an opera that is putting me to sleep but that is all there is on my radio and I don't have sense enough to turn it off. [* * *]

you can talk about poetry and talk about poetry and all you end up with is an old rubber tire full of shit. I mean, we talked somewhat about poetry and it got dull. then I told stories about jail, drunks, whores, my father, and it got better. then maybe about the last 2 hours we found the recorder was not recording well. all that wisdom LOST! about a beancan full.

I can't seem to get straight around here. I have 15 or 20 poems I have scribbled into notebooks but can't seem to get them on typer, and a couple of editors asking for stuff and I can't even give them the joy of rejecting me. I think my chickenshit job has drilled a hole into me and the whole city is riding through me with dirty boots on and dripping condrum. [sic]—if I could get my hands on a good young piece of ASSII ah. [* * *]

drunk outside staggering into hedge of thorns. I know that hedge of thorns. we are all drunk around here, all unhappy. we can't sleep. we are tired of talking. when we shit we sit on our ivory stools dumbfounded that something actually seems to be happening at last. we are proud of our shit. an act. our shit is as good as anybody's shit. old hollow god, try to ace us out here! [* * *]

god damn, it's ten o'clock. got to quit typing. the law, the law. the little drunken fists banging my rented walls!

[To Douglas Blazek]
October 14, 1966

[* * *] this time until Jan. is the overtime season and also I have to pass a rather diff. and searing time burning dull flaggelette exam to hold this job I hate, so it will seem Time done shitted all over me, but if you'd care for me to read some books and give you capsule digest with shark tooth, o.k., send me some books and I will submit wonderful reviews like nobody ever read top of spaghetti eating contest. it will give me excuses not to study chickenshit exam. but remember, I do not like very much poetry and I will have to say so. I DO NOT MEASURE BOOKS AGAINST OTHER BOOKS, I MEASURE BOOKS AGAINST MYSELF. further, I know I have plenty of blind angles but it is only by nursing and mother-nourishing my prejudices that I feel better, and the longer I nurse them the more they *seem* like truth, and I find that this being holy and kind and broad-minded toward others makes me unholy toward myself. I guess what pissed me most as a child was being 2 feet tall and having to take all that shit from those (parents) who were automatically in control of me through nature's and society's big dumb dragging asshole. now that I am six feet tall (minus 1/2 inch . . . why quibble . . . I am damn well covered with 220 pounds of beerfat and my feet and breath stink much of the time) the control is extended to other hands and other ways. [* * *]

Menebroker—all these letters through the years—enough to give a musty candle a hard-on. [* * *] now all this talk from dear Ann about offensive obscenity

o b s c e n i t y

even the word THE WORD WANTS TO MAKE ME RAM MY DICK THROUGH A CEMENT WALL, and she—knows it. you follow? of course you do. this Tom Wolfe she talks about— *You Can't Go Home Again, Look Homeward Angel,* so forth—completely bad writing, very bad writing, the worst, he drivels his jackedup juvenile romanticscockism all up and down the pages wearing you out like a cheap pair of stocking wear out. in the summer. of course, the first time you read him, if you're young enough and haven't been scraped too much by prune-picking machines, he really seems like the REAL THING. there are many writers only good the FIRST time you read them—Saroyan, the short stories of Chekhov, Upton Sinclair's lancing for a Utopia, Sinclair Lewis who seems to be writing from notes from his sleeve, Conrad, Jack London, Gogol, Gorky . . . but the

second time around it is like reading a column on sports by a fat-
tened and spoiled and stale columnist. calumny. cunt. crap. to hell
with Tom Wolfe, I shit on his grave. [* * *]

[To Ann Menebroker]
October, 1966

[* * *] on obscenity, I don't know much about it except that it
(the charge or talk about it) frightens and bothers so-called honest
writers. to me there is nothing obscene about sex or bodily function
(tho both become a mess sometimes); the only obscenity is *bad* writing
on the subjects. good writing or pure Art is never obscene no matter
what the subject, wordage, painted or sculpted matter. I don't think
a hell of a lot more than that can be said. I suppose then it is only
up to us to decide what is good, what is Art or what is not. and that's
where roads and swords cross—Artistic moralities. what may be Art
to me may not be Art to you and therefore obscene, or the other way
around. and the line of demarcation is different in each of us. in other
words we are never going to agree—you or I or anybody else, just
what *is* obscene and what isn't. so no need for me to go on talking
about it. [* * *]

[To Carl Weissner]
November 2, 1966

[* * *] they raided Richmond's bookshop in Santa Monica, Calif.,
taking around 2 dozen books, including some of mine, and also took
a letter from the typewriter that Richmond was typing to me. 20
centuries of civilization, semi-Christian, and we haven't gotten
anywhere. the publication of his newspaper the *Earth Rose* got their
eyes stuck upon him. headline: FUCK HATE.
    Whereby, on this day we able minded creators
do hereby tell you, the Establishment: FUCK YOU
IN THE MOUTH. WE'VE HEARD ENOUGH OF YOUR
BULLSHIT.

inside, poems by Bukowski, Richmond, Buckner.
4 arrests so far. Richmond out on bail.

[* * *] that hour I did sleep I had a terrible dream that a snake bit my cock. only I never saw the snake. only a kind of voice told me. and sure enough I looked down and there was this very clean ugly hole right on top of my cock (in the dream, babe) and when I awakened and saw that my string was o.k. I felt a little better. maybe it's the jug of table wine. so, then, enough. beware the hammerhead albatross.

Weissner eventually published extracts from Bukowski's letters to him in Klacto, *no. 23, Sept. 1967.*

[To Carl Weissner]
November what 18?, 1966

[* * *] by the way, you asked, should you like to run excerpts from any of my letters, please do. although I have an idea I have not written much. it is odd, but letters from you seem to calm me, give me some place . . . I do not quite stare at those rusty razor blades in the same dream-like stutter-stance. I do not mean that I need honey-pie custard soothing, but statements of actual fact and torture of men within civilization make me realize that I am not the only man alive who has to fight himself to keep from driving an ice pick straight down his bellybutton. [* * *]

I get my limbo kicks with my drawings . . . like to draw people fucking each other, strangling each other, staring at walls, smoking cigars, lost among bottles under an electric light. once had a book of drawings due out but the guy just collected money on the ads and now sits on the drawings and no book, no response to inquiry, no return of drawings. a real shit. the world of the arts is full of shits too, both editors and writers, so beware, Karl. I was an editor once and I got some very nasty responses, espec. to my one or two page rejection slips which I used to write everybody. instead of soothing rejection this simply brought out the fangs, yellow ones, esp. from writers of reputation. "who the hell are you? I've never seen *your* name on any of the little magazines? how can you tell me about *my* work?" so forth. or a simple little slip back saying "SHIT." it was true, I hadn't begun to write. I began at 35. but I knew whether I liked a poem or not. and why. and men don't write with their reputations; they write, most of them, with typewriters. each time you sit down reputation is gone with yesterday's sun; every man begins even again. right now, I am very glad I do not have a hotshot reputation—it keeps me clear with myself. [* * *]

good that Norse is mending. I can't say enough about his work. he is one of the few men whose work lifts me. some of the more famous leave me quite flat and empty, and angry with their dull tricks and empty kookoos. but Norse has this CLASSICAL SENSE OF REALITY. he can't write a bad line; I've never seen one. he uses the language perfectly. I don't. my work is full of stone, clipped little droppings out of the side of broken mouth. they have kicked too much shit out of me. I try to stammer out a phrase of fire but by the time I get it from my head-gut to the page it begins to look like an ad for a used car. my vocabulary dribbles down more and more to 30 or 40 words and there isn't anything I can do about it. Norse tells me how (in his work) but I can't follow him, I have to play with my own marbles. treat him well, he is one of the great ones of our rather strange times. [* * *]

Burroughs, Ginsberg . . . how does it feel to be communicating with the Lights of the Age, and also with me. B. and G. have disappointed me at times, but let's admit that they have done things, and that no man creates pure Art day after day. me, I get rejected enough and it's good for the asshole, it make my cock hard. the editor of *Illuminations* writes that Creeley attacked me at some place, he named some name, a club or reading place I'd suppose and the editor defended me. that Creeley searched me out for attack shows that I am functioning along the right trail. Creeley's type of writing has always disturbed me at being anti life, scratched-out with snob and comfortable wire. that he has noticed the opposite of his writing and that it bothers him, that's fine. I do not say that sometimes Creeley does not create Art; he does not create my *kind* of Art. the years that I have worked in slaughterhouses and factories and gas stations and so forth, these years do not allow me to accept the well-turned word for the sake of the well-turned word. . . . there must be more for me or I am just another suicide in a cheap room or in the alley or in the sea of in the gas cloud. I do not treat my work as holy or necessary except to myself. the reason I send it out? to see if I am totally mad or not. I think. I think, but am not sure. there may be some ego there too. Charles Bukowski on a page. so that when I roll over in a drunk tank or am having my guts cut out or my ass cut out or my soul cut out, I feel like I've saved a fraction, a match stick. *save what you can under all conditions,* that's my motto, hurrah! it's only the man who gives it ALL away who is truly ugly, who does not deserve to walk under a tree and inherit the earth. [* * *]

got caught in a dentist's chair the other day, even tho I have no money and not too much courage. a French wench wiggling all over, with rich blue eyes like out of a paint tube came in and started cleaning my teeth, god I was ashamed, I am such a mess, but she leaned her flank upon me and scraped away, leaning there, talking to me, warm as bacon she was, great Jesus what joy, my gums bled and she said, "I'm sorry," and I said, "it's not your fault, angel." and she leaned the flank again and went into my ugly old mouth with her pick, and it was love again, the first time I have loved a women since 1952. I don't mean sex. Carl, I mean that kind of high-washed feeling where you *float,* where you can feel the love swarming out of you like a blue and white fountain of miracle. but I will never tell her, she will never know, for she already knows. she has been in America 7 years but she has not yet drowned. who in the hell expects to find these things in a dentist's chair. when that bastard comes in with his hairy arms and his pliers, then we'll have the moment of truth, eh?

[* * *] it is only when the Artist is dead that the masses enjoy his suffering and go to warm movies and eat popcorn and enjoy it. I was guilty of it myself. I remember when I was in the Village I went to see a movie about the life of Verdi. if I remember, there was a part there where he got a bag of nuts from an old woman in the street. he was starving. I like that. I have starved many times trying to cut some insignia into the cement. I shouldn't have liked it, the Verdi thing. but then when he came back famous with the beautiful woman at his side and he gave the old woman a batch of money for the bag of nuts that night, I didn't care for that too much. he was defaming her act, showing off to his broad. he should have taken the old woman to his place and fucked her and drank wine with her and asked her to talk to him across the kitchen table. but then Verdi was not perfect. I make some mistakes myself.

so I light another cigarette. have another beer. hold off the studying of the streets of los angeles that hangs over me like a mother ax. if I had any guts I would sit and write and paint for hours, for days, for months until I starved to death or until they came and got me. but I know that that is what would happen, one of those 2. I've

276

been through it before. sometimes the police come or sometimes the landlady tell you you'll have to go. drinking, typing, painting, sleeping, that won't do. a man should leave at 7 in the morning and should come back at 7 at night, finished. church on Sunday. a handjob in the bathroom. no women unless you are married. this country is so soulless; no wonder they can't whip a handful of starving midget men and women and children in Vietnam. it's not Russian or Chinese aid that's holding it back. it's damn fool American fat boys who have lived like idiots, well-fed soul-less idiots in and since the cradle. no wonder they torture the enemy; deep-in, somewhere, they know that they are lost, and inflicting atrocities upon a living and real people is their only way of getting back—like tearing flowers, burning butterflies, fucking and hating everything in sight. I have never quite heard of such a war; surely we have degenerated back to ages darker than the Dark Ages????

Omar the Tentmaker would have a lot to say about this.

too many people clear their consciousness with a hot fuck, but after the sperm is wiped away the world is more there than *ever* before.

how ya gonna keep 'em down on the farm?

now playing some Armenian or Turkish music on radio, from the Fez. a little cafe-like place down next to the Racing Form building. I went there one night, quite drunk really, they didn't want to let me in at first, but I was in one of my warm and gentle moods and they relented. I sat on a big pillow on the floor and some big warm wench kept bringing me all kinds of strange drinks but none of them knocked me out like continuous American whiskey would have and I felt warmer and warmer. there was plenty of alcohol in the drinks, I could taste it, the expert, but it only kept me CLEAR. people, men and women came around and sat on pillows and talked to me. I didn't want any ass. I just wanted to feel the people. and it was marvelous. and all the time, this strange music. I just kept laughing and enjoying, all sophistication all ego gone, burned-out. I don't think any man really wants to be a prick, really wants to hate, it is only pressures that make him hate. of course, I don't care for this THOU MUST LOVE, either. I don't like love as a command, as a search. it must come to you, like a hungry cat at the door. what? hearing this music reminds me of that good night. I am not always as hard as my poems. [* * *]

[To Ann Menebroker]
November 23, 1966

good on your acceptances, no surprise to me, you seem to be gaining on yourself, damn good sign; me, I'm showing slippage but little I can do . . . [* * *]

Xmas season is when the populace really becomes beastly. they cram and run and flurry wild and mama empty-eyed; me, *me, I* got! *we* got! my family! safe! goods! roof! food! a drink in hand! whoopee!— what sickening stuff. it's pressure and haste, a MUST. nothing easy or good about it.

then . . . HAPPY NEW YEAR. ugggg. [* * *]

[To Douglas Blazek]
December 11, 1966

[* * *] somebody got me started on a novel and then got pissed at me because I tapped a rich friend of his for $150. I got drunk and had to get my car started, the old '57 was murdering me sitting at that curbing not moving, not moving, and also had to have 6 teeth pulled. how can we write novels with the extra poison from our teeth adding to the other poison? so now I gotta finish the novel, but not in too bad shape because I've heard from 2 outfits (small presses) that want to do a book of mine, and they seem trustworthy, but problem is they might have been thinking poem-book. this novel about 2 years I once lived in a faded green hotel, *The Way the Dead Love.* I guess I'll finish it. I screwed very nearly every woman in that hotel including the scrubwoman who was nearly 60. even screwed a guy in the ass by mistake one night. it ought to be a laugher. starvation, drink, madness and fuck. really all tragic and beautiful people including myself. the chapters will be short clipped action happenings, but no general plot, just a recording of the place. done like *Confessions* only much longer. I hope it doesn't pancake. I'll lose about 100 poems writing it. but shit, I've lost 100 poems, at least, in the mails. that fucker who lives with Warhol, I forget his name, won't return a batch, and in a recent issue of *Tish* I fuck recognized he stole one of my lines, used it as a last line to nail down a lousy poem: MY FEET TOUCH CHINA IN THE DREAM. those are *my* lines, babe.

although accredited to . . . Malanga. giz christ, gossip. but true. and discouraging when weighed against my hopes for the human factor ever becoming clean.

they are going to play me a little Bruckner later my radio tells me, so I will feel better. you know that you are one of the few people I can talk straight to without worry that you might not catch on, or that you might be hurt. these are hard to find. sometimes I write a drunk letter to an editor after poems are accepted and the poems come back. this is kind of funny to me. somewhere in the letter I cross one of their precious gravy paths and they know that I am their enemy. in fact, I even throw in a few short chops to test them. these returns are mostly from people who only print "name" writers. usually on expensive letter press. some of the poems they print are very good—not Ginsberg's or Duncan's or Bly's or Kelly's but say Paul Blackburn, so in a sense I lose something by flapping my drunken lip, but I do find the letter-form to be a very good exercise for limp-soul when the walls are running with blood (mine). you, I don't worry about. I kiss your ass not, BUT WHEN I CAN NO LONGER TELL A GOOD MAN HE IS GOOD AND IT MAKES A CERTAIN JOY RUN UP MY ARMS, WHEN I CAN NO LONGER DO THIS I WILL CASH IT IN. fuck you.

Bruckner. then there's Wagner without the words. and Mahler. there is the warm soup agony speaking, the wallpaper, the rooms, the roaches, the pimple moon. there are people with feet and hands and heads. it is all very something. I am not an Art or a music nut. I do not ream myself with sounds night and day over a fancy stereo that all the neighbors must hear too. but sometimes when I am very low low low and quiet shot, the job crashed through me like I am a tunnel, all *their* talk for hours: baseball, pro football, sex lies. the constant needle the American worker gives to the other American worker through shame and boredom and madness, and I have the best needle in the place—they do not call me HANK THE BARBER for nothing. "that son of a bitch has a line for everything." I even harass the supervisors to keep them off me so I can loaf more. I spend more time in the crapper than the janitor who cleans the place out. but I've had over 100 jobs from Miami to Frisco and I know how it works: I am only trying to save my life and they are only trying to kill me. my talent, if I have any, is the fight for the last inch which I will not give them. they've cut off my hands and arms and one ball and they face me with an m.g. but as the guy reloads his belt I spit in his eye. bravo. fuck the snob publications who only *think* that poetry talks about life. and I'm going to make the same fight with my poetry no matter if the mailbox comes all over the rented porch with rejects. Schumann's good too, you oughta listen to Schumann, just once. *once.* trust me. you'll know. you are probably a jazz cat. well, that's all right. I like that too when it seeps into my proper vein. but the dark long stuff hits the core. I don't trust Beethoven. he catches the ear with surface crash, and outside of the First Symphony, seldom a bad line. but I like more madness. I keep feeling like he's skimming on a giant mirror. yeah, I know he had his troubles. and I also know that if I had discovered him instead of the world discovering him I would like him better. shit perversity. jealousy? I do not know. I do not know my soul or lack of soul. I only know that I must be fair to myself also and that I must allow myself a judgement outside of the standard concepts. I've got to be kinder to myself. on the other hand, I only figure Faulkner as the giant fraud of the century. and using words myself, writing myself, I am on surer ground. even as a young man, a very young man, reading him on the beach while the other guys played football, myself being bigger and meaner and lousier than any of them, reading him on the beach there with the dandy sand being kicked in my face, not even knowing that I myself would someday try to write, I lay there, I laid there as I lay dying, and I thought, how can he get AWAY with this stuff? this obvious dull hack-trick shit? ah, babe, I was a very special critic from the moment I slid from the cunt and my father's face (naturally) was the first face I hated. but not the last.

thanks for the drawing, old boy. it always girds, grieves me a bit that they do not turn you loose all day to play with brushes and words, but like you realize, things that happen in that foundry come out in the paint and in the words, but still, I am not the one to believe in the SUFFERING OF THE ARTIST, or the suffering of anybody. including myself. every time I see a mouse caught in a trap or a photo of a lion shot dead, I am unhappy. unrealistic, they tell me. but to me Realism is only a condescending to the Actual and I believe that man has enough sunlight and god and luck within him to change the actual. when I let the mouse go and the lion eat me, if I am strong enough, perhaps the lion will finally not eat me, perhaps the mouse will sit down and listen to Bruckner with me. madness? shit, maybe. but where has world sanity led us? [* * *] listen, baby, you think my old mind is cracking? I drink drink after drink writing you, knowing that I must face that mob at 3 p.m. tomorrow afternoon. suffering from dizzy spells, weakness, may not make it, may fall to floor

280

as they discuss the afternoon's pro football game. yet I feel that all I am saying here will *not* be wasted, you hear it anyhow. I know that you do. I give you lilt and go-on, do I not? and also myself. the strangest thing is, I cannot eliminate D. H. Lawrence from my consciousness, not the sex-appetite thing the public sunk its tooth into, but kind of the washing of feet and skin, the thin pin-point structured line. a very bitter man, somebody once wrote him off as. why not? he didn't accept the *outside* Realism, and I don't either. I go for the bloodflow stuff of the inner color. I remember a half page or so of his stuff about some taxi drivers (I think it was in Australia?) that is perhaps along with Dostoyevsky, some of the best writing I've ever seen. well, enough of that. [* * *]

christ, I am out of smokes but still something to DRINK. maybe just one good woman would cure me, licking her tongue around and round and around that thing, my soul stuck out into the air like a telescope. but here I sit, what, in a city of 4 million? hell, I don't know how many million and I sit alone. I've fucked my share but more and more as I grow older I know that I can no longer pay the price. what I mean is, the demeaning of self in order to get in or with. I have these problems. all the women in the world sucking my cock at once could not change what I now feel. which is, that I cannot kid myself into a generative love attitude AT THE EXPENSE OF SOMETHING ELSE. do you read? I am too far gone. I cannot faggot myself for the expense of a come. I refuse to make a million dollars to go to bed with a Veryl. I will stick my cock into the hollow of a tree and let lightning strike me dread dead before I ever funky myself again into that hollow and wonderful malicious hole that demands so much. will you write it off as old age and laugh? I don't think so. I trust you. I do think that you are the last man in the world that I do trust. don't die. on me. fucker.

Bruckner quite graciously good, and as I try to type my fingers have more and more trouble hitting keys properly, all right? good. you don't care? good. high heels going past window. fuck me, fuck me, they say. of course, Freud was wrong, sex is not the whole pie, and I knew this long before the detractors, but sex is part of the pie. exit goading impossibilities with come into cunt of lovely woman who has eyes of purple into her head. I've spent many a good night, and some bad ones. I've had some terrible fucks where the pussy spread from wall to wall, but even with this kind, a long night of talk and drinking, a warmness. —I've learned more from the women of the streets in rotting hotels than I ever have from Kant, Faulkner,

Tolstoy, Balzac, Thorstein Veblen, G. B. Shaw, Karl Marx, Hitler. this is not talk shit, this is true.

I owe most of the heart of anything decent in me to the streetwalkers of America.

don't get me wrong. there are a lot of savages out there. killers. shits. dopes. sub-normals. liars. but I mean you get hold of the one or 2 good women out there and Harvard is toilet paper, Blaz. I've been lucky. I only met one but she taught me where my arms were and my mind and my cock and my heart, q.t., wuz. I hope to write a novel about her someday but I don't think I am man enough to do it yet. I may never be able to do it. if I can live to be 60? I hope to call the book simply *Whore.* [* * *]

●

• 1 9 6 7 •

[To Douglas Blazek]
January 2, 1967

the f.b.i.? what the hell? they really think we're porno? lot of
other places they should (?) could go. must be something else that
is bothering them and they use the porno as a left jab, as an excuse.
what might be bothering them is that we are possibly creating life
and nothing makes the dead more angry than this. that has to be
it, sweetie. but relax, we are as clean as a desert bone. I guess you
never thought your little mimeo machine could make J. E. Hoover
twitch in his sleep. secretly you ought to be proud. of course, wives
never understand such a thing—they feel it threatens their security,
I mean the everyday things: supper, laundry, t.v., the funnies, the
fuck, the picnic, the drive to Aunt Sarah's. but I know you can put
her straight. [* * *]

The review mentioned in the next letter of Louis Zukofsky's
A Test of Poetry *appeared in* Ole *no. 7 (May 1967).*

283

[To Douglas Blazek]
January 12, 1967

6 teeth pulled today, so stayed here tonight and wrote the review on Zukofsky. use it if you want to. I am bleeding like a river of shit and I guess I shouldn't get any beer, will swallow blood, haha, and cold beer will scream the holes in my jaw, old daddy getting there, there are only so many teeth to be pulled then I am FREE. ya. guy going to build me a bridge. will try to hold onto my remaining teeth a while. don't know how I will pay him but we never discuss this thing. very nice. I think he was drunk, he sang all the time he was working, and one tooth just didn't want to come out and he screamed STUPID THING, STUPID TOOTH! what's all this talk about teeth? came out and smashed my tail light against a phone pole. poor old '57. I told those people I wouldn't eat any walnuts but maybe if I warm up the beer . . . ??? anyhow, Zukofsky in here, and hope you are making it through the days, you know like killing a bull every ten minutes or being put in a gunnysack with 14 monkeys. how do *we* last, old man? sometimes I think that we are braver than all the armies of history, and then I know that's stupid: the armies don't count, and we hardly do. except to the walls, a couple of faces and our own way of waiting. I am down to 4 codeine but that should get me through the night. knives, pliers, hospitals. watch out for spiders.

P.S. no arrival of F.B.I. rather disappointed.

[To Ann Menebroker]
January 19, 1967

[* * *] have been down, the old depressive hackdown, plus sickness, mine, Marina's and so forth, meanwhile working the hateful job, old stuff, but time all sliced to small sections of stumbling into a room and turning on a light and falling down. meanwhile there are a half dozen poems I wrote while drunk that I haven't yet lifted up off of paper. I mean, all I have to do is type them up but I can't get to that. no tragedy but a buzz in the dome. and down at work a foreman leans behind me and says, "I want more work out of you, Bukowski, I want some production!" and I am dreaming of the lame bones under earth, the whole earth threaded with the bones of the

dead—what a halloween. and then my little girl gets her foot caught in the rear spokes of a bicycle that her mother rides her around in in a little box in back, and I told the woman much earlier, "I hate the god damned bike, it stinks of tragedy I wish you wouldn't ride her in the thing." but no, she insists, but when all fucks up she runs to me with the mutilated kid. next it will be the whole stack of them in the middle of the street run over by a Falcon or something. but if you suggest that a woman should not do a certain thing she will insist upon doing it—thinking it proves that she has independence and a soul, but verily all it proves is that she is an asshole. well, let that be. but getting the kid to a doctor did get rid of an almost continuous cold, pen shots and liquid. but like I say.

so now, even as I write this it is time to go back to work. and even at work I am sliced with jackasses. I have a half hour to eat, I get a table by myself—a tough job. and here some nit catches my eye and brings over his tray: "I just hate to see somebody sitting alone," he smiles. "I really don't mind at all," I tell him. "well, I'll sit down anyhow." "yes," I say, "tell me your troubles." and he does. he tells me he was somewhere or other, babysitting or something, and somebody gave him 2 cans of beer and he got high right away, he fell asleep, and the next day Sunday he slept almost all day, those 2 cans of beer. this was the essence of his conversation. I grunted something and tried to eat during his cold turkey insanity. I finished and excused myself and went outside in the freezing cold in my shirtsleeves and stood out there for 5 minutes and then went inside, back to my foreman.

so then, I know you have your things too. it's not the large tragedies that moil us to pieces—we are fucking well ready for those. it's the little scratchings and drippings, the continuous stubbing of the toes and elbows, the car that won't start, the piece of tooth that breaks off as you are biting into a peach, dirty stockings, a sudden face in the market goring your peace like a bull, a ring in the bathtub, constipation, insomnia, a dirty newspaper, toothpaste too sweet, a fingernail flipping back and ripping from the finger . . . these things again and again, the similar small biting donnybrook continuous hail . . . these tear us to the final pieces. ah ha.

James Lowell was the proprietor of Asphodel Books, Cleveland, an important dealer in underground and little press items in

the sixties. When he was prosecuted for dealing in obscenity,
a large number of leading authors contributed to a collection
A Tribute to Jim Lowell *(Cleveland, June 1967) to help raise*
funds for his defense.

[To Carl Weissner]
January 27, 1967

[* * *]—yes, I wrote an essay in defense of Lowell, literature, art, us, we'uns. . . . the vise closes in. the F.B.I. questions Blazek, asks about me. Richmond out on bail, bookstore still open, and he's awaiting trial. yes, they picked up my *The Genius of the Crowd* at Lowell's. d.a. levy who published that, and other things now hiding from the police, warrant out for him. but the police have not knocked at my door (about *these* matters) because all they have on me is that I write in a very plain and simple style and don't even cuss too much—I am too god damned fucking mother fucking tired to cuss! [* * *]

I do not make it too well with the women because I refuse to throw them the smoke screen, and I really do not get enough good ass and I never will because if a woman's soul is a sack of shit I will not fail to tell them so, esp. when I am drunk. there are 2 new women on my horizon now, hungry-eyed, trying to act decently human but they are really not decently human. I don't mind that they are filled with snot and piss and shit and blood, with the newspaper print pasted above their eyebrows—it is the eventual explosive unfolding, the sharp claws stored in the coffee can. "hey, son, I gave you some pussy, now kiss my ass, run my errands, listen to my harpy song." oye, oye, oye. [* * *]

I am sure Marina will make me feel better tonight. we have a direct line going. everything is simple and clear and magic and even funny.   —your daughter? on back of pic? the date? 1944? is this correct? how OLD ARE YOU, Abraham? [* * *] I have to go over and get Marina now; she looks almost *exactly* like the photo you enclosed, even has a hat like that. thanks the photo. it cheered me.

I don't know if I am glad I left Germany or not. I really think I would be dying wherever I was at. my formula remains the same— keep the last coal glowing long as possible. no sense in tossing in. make them come to us. we will throw the scabs, the guts, the pebbles in their faces, whatever they use for faces.

so now in the old car, the night streets, myself gagging in the love of their tranquil yawn, my los angeles non-people. Marina how do you live in this city? [* * *]

[To Carl Weissner]
[January 28, 1967]
the next day following earlier
letter (1967)

hello Carl:

this quick one, follow up, trying to fight off Marina who won't let me type long (competition), but I screwed up—the photo is evidently of you, and I called it your daughter—so now I've put a dent in your mulch—sorry—but why in hell do they dress little boys like little girls and then hand the photo to a guy with a hangover? the 1944 makes sense to me now. should I consider you wounded forever? don't be. I wish I looked like my daughter. now she's making a train. I hold a conversation with her as I type: "Are you making a train? ah, fine, hum hum. oh, did the train fall down?" Bukowski gone soft as poached eggs for ulcer patients. I always used whiskey for my stomach—I mean my ulcers—got rid of my stomach and my ulcers too.

heard from Greg who got the bundle of *Earth Rose* I slipped past the F.B.I.—Richmond busted for these—and now Dan is walking around hanging them in public places, like Spellman's crapper, so forth. a very energetic fellow. I always picture him with knife in bloody teeth, working upon the Fall and Decline of Empire, which ain't a bad idea. only I am lazy and mixed up with spondees and beer and bad health. all revolutionaries should be 6 feet 5, weight 380 pounds, look like young Gregory Peck with Heidelberg scars, and never be bothered with constipation, insomnia or the search for employment in the capitalistik nestegg. by the way, I hear that the Heidelberg scars are coming back. saw a perfectly bloody set in a mag, I mean photos of the faces directly afterwards, the faces of the lucky boy who collected his scar, and the hogfaces, the cementfaces, the lustfaces of the onlooking club members. you live in a hot town, old man. ACTION. the reason I am reading this mag which is a kind of sex-sadist outlay is that somebody sends it to me, regards an article, portion of which reads: "It's possible that the New Bohemia stands on wobbly legs so far as terminology is concerned. It's possible that the New Bohemia is not avant-garde at all, but merely an appendage of beatism at best, and perhaps even the 'rear guard' of that social phenomena. Take a look at the heroes of the beatniks of the sexy Sixties have chosen. They include Timothy Leary, Norman Mailer, William Burroughs, Jean Genet, Henry Miller, LeRoi

Jones, Lawrence Ferlinghetti, Bob Dylan, Bertolt Brecht, John Cage, Eugene Ionesco, W. H. Auden, Anais Nin, Allen Ginsberg and Charles Bukowski, to name a few." so there I am put in my place, but of the names mentioned I am only partially in tune with a few. (now they are going to give me Bruckner's 9th. and a bit of Hindemith.) Genet in portions when he doesn't creampuff out in love with his writing, Brecht in portions, and the very early Auden. and I doubt very much if I am any man's hero. as the mass goes down to a generalized and easy death there seem to be at the same time more and more individual people springing out of rosebushes with lushlife fire to make me wonder—3 or 4 months ago I had not heard of either you or D[an] G[eorgakas], now my mailbox is on fire with loveletters from hell. not as an act of writing a letter—but as information from the center of the sky to keep me from cutting my throat. [* * *]

woman from Sacramento just phoned. she says she likes to hear my voice. wow wow. I'd sure like to help her. I'm told she's a looker. writes me 2 or 3 letters a week. she also writes poetry. god damn just dropped a cigar ash on my only good pair of pants and before I could get the damn thing up I burned a hole in the pants, and a hole in the leg. but the pants, that's what hurts. constant tragedy. ah, me. but these letters from Sacramento. little scrawls, tired: "it rained today. I cleaned the house. 2 poems accepted by X. one of them is about you." I keep this gal going in a kind of haywire way, and it's kind of sloppy and bites me in the back of the neck, but I try to remain the fuckedup human I am. everybody needs help and I like to help them: especially good-lookers with sexy voices who have read more than the morning paper. luckily for me, she's married, has children, and is probably disillusioned with her husband because he does not have fits, does not brood in the closet. a lot of guys marry these gals with poetic backgrounds because they think they are getting a chance at class, when all they are really getting is a pain in the ass. I have spoken. then too, these poetic bitches with looks always (almost always, I have found by *my* experiences) marry money-makers and then WONDER WHY MONEY-MAKERS ARE SUCH DULL STUPID PRICKS WHEN THEY ARE JUST SITTING AROUND *NOT* MAKING MONEY. so both sides are disillusioned, and the bitch sits around looking at her husband and ends up trying to write a novel on character-disintegration (*his,* of course!). in fact, I got a letter from my x-wife who writes me every Christmas, and she said she is going to write TWO novels on character-disintegration. mine, I suppose, and her present husband's. now, if she *could* write about *hers* . . . twice . . . she wouldn't have any classics, but maybe a couple of best sellers.

(this quick letter to tell you I am sorry I called you your daughter in 1944. in 1967.)

this has been a better week-end. last weekend there were about 12 different people here, and although I tried to treat them straight, easy, I might have been a bit weary, nasty and downright cruel, hahaha, and I haven't had all these people here this weekend, so I guess I know what I am doing. unless I can get at my piano (typewriter) an hour or so each day I am not worth a shit to anybody. not that I am creating anything immortal, although now and then I may slip over *that* line (?) but it is mostly the sound of the typer like ENGINE ///////// MY ENGINE MY ENGINE GOD DAMN IT, and when they shut my motor off I am no better than a hockshop owner. hey, *there's* a good beginning: suppose Dan G. and I went around assassinating all the hockshop owners, as many as we could until they got us? Dostoyevsky would say no. and it *wouldn't* change a beetle. and when I have been broke the hockshop owners always looked *good* to me even when they gave me almost nothing for something—because you see, nobody else *would*. it meant food or rent. to hell with the loss. so even vultures are sometimes useful. although I might agree with Dan that there *might* be a better way of helping the poor and the disowned. like say, a gun to begin with, and a gun to end with. the good thing about G. is that he is not just another standard faded commmie liberal pissedoff nuerotic anarchist, carbon copy like. he speaks from an ORIGINAL FRAMEWORK springing from the gut-soul of his breathing and wanting to breathe. he suggests that one of the reasons the F/B/Itch is fucking with me in the background is that I am corresponding with him. I consider that correspondence as a joy and an honor, sunlight and orange juice—it is Marina walking across the room bringing me a bottle of beer. about D., tho, I am afraid for him in the sense that he seems to feel the NEAR READINESS OF UPHEAVAL. things like Watts, so forth. the French Revolution. the Russian. me, I am not ready to mount the parrapets. I am a shit. I remember the 30's, the depression, the same talk—tho not as creatively sensible and warm as Dan's—and nothing happening. almost 40 years later and nothing happening. in fact, due to the ultra black Romanticism of the easily excited intellectuals (Camus to start with, Malcolm X to end with) the swing has gone way back to the RIGHT, and it is further away from them than ever. there are 2

289

very sad things to see in the world at least, and 2 of them are a very old queer and a very old revolutionary. man, hold, I have worked in the mills for their pennies, the fat capitalists, I have been drained drained and slugged and slugged and cheated, and Dan says bodies must go on the line and he means it, but we've first got to get enough bodies with stuffings, each with its own voice not somebody elses. YOU CAN ALWAYS PUT NEW GOVERNMENTS ON TOP OF MEN; WHAT WE NEED IS NEW MEN ON TOP OF GOVERNMENTS. the only way government (or no government) can work is through living men, and I am afraid we do not have enough of these around right now. this does not mean that I am for injustice against dead men, for even dead men have rights—mainly because they still feel pain, get hardons, have bellies.

[* * *] like any individual with individual experiences I have impaired vision. the capitalist goes by his experiences and instincts. I am afraid I would make a *very* good rich man and I am AFRAID I would keep my money. I would build walls. I would create a Greecian Art from the souls of my slaves. I would fuck young girls until I got tired of fucking young girls. I would not worry about the lettuce pickers of Salinas. I would feel pretty good: I would feel pretty brainy; I might still even have a soul. THE WHOLE THING NEEDS TO BE CLEANED UP BY FUCKING WELL REALIZING EVERYBODY. you see, your boy Dan gets me to thinking about these things. I think of Norse standing up at a table when you walk in. I think of Norse sick sick dying cornered, I think of the good men everywhere being swallowed by the iron sky. and it just isn't government and capitalism and MAN BEING VICTIMIZED BY OTHER MEN, IT IS MEN BEING VICTIMIZED BECAUSE THEY WERE BORN TO DIE. all this is basic, all these things are basic—yet I have never read them anywhere. why? I suppose it is in the libraries somewhere, but IT IS SO DILUTED AND TRICKY AND ARTY that it flips off like a live fish out of the hands. truly, there has been very little good clear plain and true Art created within the life of Man. in Music, yes; in Painting yes—but in the written word, no no no NO!—the written word is till sucking its own tits, crying for mama, posing. let's take a case. Burroughs. all right. he is reaching, shuffling into a NEW DIMENSION. he is bored, mad, pissed with the ordinary product. rightfully so. any sane man is, any sane insane man. but Burroughs in mixed and mixing new paints, combos, finds flicks, colors, discoveries. . . . surcharged with butter and fire, much of it not bad Art. fine. but still he *is* sliding off the horizon. in trying to discover a New Reality he is losing the actual

290

REALITY. this is his failure. let me illustrate—the only true forward-moving art is an art that discovers new form by still retaining actual reality—perhaps the best example of this is *Finnegans Wake* by Joyce. he moved the word out of the concept of the word but still gave us the actual world. the instance came not by *accident* but by the force of innards and the lonely madness of luck and the way. Burroughs pasteups of the clipped-up London *Daily Herald* or whatever, or standing on his knees upside down reading the bible through a film of boiling skimmed milk is often entertaining and REAL but more often a trick, a falling together of an insignificant world by tricks and a lot of glue. now it is possible to get a FREE WORLD WORD, a REAL SHOT FROM THE SKY BY WORKING THE TRICK, but down in us we know, finally, that the only way is to slug it down the river. not because our masters and schoolteachers taught us this but because the masters and schoolteachers must go, and Burroughs is only pasting their dry canine flicks upon our murdered brows IN DIFFERENT ORDER. not enough. we need new blood, new miracle—not the mixing of old soup. and now that I have killed Burroughs, enough of that.

god, enough of that. this is a short letter to explain that I did not mean to call you a girl. [* * *]

I am still listening to Bruckner 9th. do you think I am cultured, little girl? I like this stuff. if I weren't so poor I'd make a beautiful snob. even now I think I could be a music critic for the *New York Times* if they'd let me. but they wouldn't. before I was finished they'd burn the *Times* down or some music lover would assassinate me. let's get the pawnshop owners first. then, me. yes, I'd make a terrible snob. I just don't like most people's faces or the way they walk or the sound of their voices or anything they say. the people make me physically ill. shut me in a room with 5 people for 40 minutes and then ask me if I had a chance whether I'd save them or burn them. Dostoevsky wouldn't agree. somebody from some middle class mag was over to interview me last Friday night, no, the Friday before. but he just kept the tape going and I got drunker and drunker and I finally said, FOR CHRIST'S SAKE, MERCY, JUST ASK ME A DIRECT QUESTION AND I WILL GIVE YOU A DIRECT ANSWER. but he wouldn't. he was wiser than I. or more frightened. not both. there are very few, if any men, more wiser and more frightened than I am AT THE SAME TIME. I MEAN I FEEL TERROR CONTINUALLY. they have built me a little image shit thing of a brave and tough man. I will not buy it. I am a skunk thing, always turning, not knowing. I don't know where I am at. incomplete, nothing full. his friend,

291

John Bryan, kept saying, "Bukowski, you are a bitter old man!" and he meant it but I did not know what he meant. I am not bitter, nothing like that. I am mixed. I mean half the time I want to kill myself and the other half the time I am angry because I have almost no means of staying alive in a society that asks for turret lathe operators or experts on Space, the stock market, so forth. I don't know their game. I am these TWO HALVES AND NO HOLE. a good piece of ass would fix me for 3 or 4 nights but where is it?

I am now drunk beyond the meaning of my saying but go on. ??????

Kennedy was a half-man, hardly that, but a hero of the little punchy guy who wanted class and used K's seeming class to fill the hole. I'll always remember the day of Kennedy's assassination, how all the people seemed HOLLOW without impluse or guide. as if they had been scooped out. me, I felt the same. but I got this terrible feeling as if the beehive had been raided and the QUEEN BEER BEE taken out forever. even their faces had no anger. WITHOUT THEIR LEADER THEY COULD NOT EVEN GET ANGRY AT AN (seeming) INJUSTICE. this was the day I really read the human race down, realized that each man must be HIS OWN QUEEN BEER BEE. and that they could not ever be stuffed with the apple pie of political fairytales to save their dull asses. you can kill one man. it is a little more difficult (tho possible) to kill a worldful. let's try for a worldful. (Carl do you know any woman in los angeles who could come over and throw me a hot piece of ass? if so, tell her to wear high heels and a tight tight skirt, and my phone number is NO. 1-6385.) oh shit, it's past ten p.m. and according to the rules I must stop typing. how can I make it? I am just getting warmed up. (Carl, do you know any woman in los angeles with a NOISELESS TYPEWRITER. if you do, tell her to bring it over. tell her to wear high heels and a tight tight skirt, and my phonenumber is the same.)

this is a short letter and I am sorry if you are a girl. wear high heels, etc. . . .

you know, it is amazing the ugly number of people in the lit. world hate me. no, don't send me to headshrinker. no complex. thing in present *The Smith.* AN INTERCEPTED LETTER FROM CHARLES BUK, something like that.* but really the parody does NOT WRITE LIKE I WRITE. impossible. maybe I do write too many letters. maybe I do write too many poems. but it is simply a matter of energizing into the INCOMPLETE ABSOLUTE, you follow? yes, you do. it may

* Felix Pollak, "A Letter from Chuck Buk," *The Smith,* no. 7 (15 October 1966), pp. 40-47.

be a flowing of shit, and yet within all the turds I feel is some tiny flower. you might have to look pretty hard. I have had a lot of hard days . . . drunk days, days in jail, days of madness, days without cause or form, and the university boys take heed, they don't like to hear back alley talk. THE MAN IN THE BACK ALLEY IS SUPPOSED TO DAMN WELL KEEP QUIET! no, I ghostly damn well throw out the mangled butternut skulls of myself, the sucked-out flies, the cardboard faces of Jesus, Saroyan at Malibu, James Dean & Bob Dylan inflated Dylan Thomas inflated, the inflated fucking raft, Bogey the dull picture hero, myself spitting out my teeth and my life without a chance to breathe. they want the straight-lace picture. novels about the Civil War. novels about daring sexuality within the daring and lovely rich. the UNIVERSITY IS THE THUNDERHEAD OF DEFEAT. the young know this. so they get sucked away from this and they get sucked into other cesspools: Bukowski, Thomas, Dylan, Ginsberg—anything except by going into that lonely room and finding out WHO THEY ARE OR WHO THEY ARE NOT. it's too hard. and milked and slugged and smiled at by parents and grammar schools and high schools, they are already robbed by the time it is ready for them to THINK. think becomes a dirty word. because they have been TAUGHT THAT THEY WERE THINKING ALL ALONG. not so, of course. but if a man can recover, if he has the bounceback, the miracle, he will find that the first 30 years were wasted in fighting off, regrouping before HE CAN BECOME EASY. THINKING OR LIVING IS NOT VERY HARD AT ALL; it is the other thing that they are doing that is killing them. [* * *]

[To Steven Richmond]
February, 1967

yes, the whores with one or more children will generally treat you more human to begin because their circumstances are more desperate but once they figure they have you hooked in against the pussy, lo, the more than trouble begins. there are about 3 women looming on my horizon, eager-eyed, trying to act like kool-true dolls, but I'll be damned if I think I am going to play buck-antler deer with a hard for them. I am tired of the whole gory scene and think I will remain a hermit of an old man behind pulled curtains—say, peeking at schoolgirls as they walk by, whistling through my broken teeth, then running for my paper and crayons and drawing the tower of Pisa, or the Eiffel. [* * *]

—yes, Georgakas strong stuff, not the usual textbook Marxist, neurosis-anarchist, Black Romanticist, bones-of-Trotsky, they-shot-Lorca, let's listen to a folk song type. he leaps from a kind of hammer forge energy purpose of his own invention, he does not hum the same old shit and is man enough to know where he is and where they are. and not introvert enough to let them overpower him with his *own* logic. he leaps like a wild and hungry monkey in a cage, but screams a seeming very good sense and livingness. if all his breed had the same living faculty, I'd throw in with them, start by setting Yorty's hotel on fire and so forth. but I am leery of his club membership, am afraid they are a bunch of hand-stamped farts, and so I sit at the typer, go down to the postoffice, go to the race track and write letters on windy afternoons to Steven Richmond.

THERE IS *ANOTHER* HIGHRISE APT. GOING UP DIRECTLY ACROSS THE STREET. I am now completely surrounded. I see all these beehives. I see people more and more living stacked on top of each other in a kind of demented high-priced luxury that they pay in a kind of fear and a kind of love of the stink of each other behind those shiny walls decorated with mass-produced artwork and sexfilm paint. luckily I can't afford to die in such voluptuous candyshit; I will end up in a cardboard box in the hills. I have discovered the last green hills in town—it is just before you hit Huntington Drive on the way to Santa Anita, a turn left off of North Main or North Broadway, I don't know which, anyhow the streets end there, and there it is: these slices of high green hills, tall, and nothing on them, no terrible houses, no terrible people, and I always feel like stopping the 57 and getting out and climbing up there, walking around in it, laying down in the weeds, but no guts, the city has me, the track calls me, but those hills ride inside me as I drive past, and looking at them, it's like vomiting up a whole sick metropolis and I feel better. there used to be a space like that on the way to Los Alomites but they found it, the developers, and they put their mass-produced houses there and the mass-produced people came running and leaped in and mortgaged their souls to somebody, banks, builders, could make 450 percent profit.

someday when I get rich on the horses you and I will start a colony. there is still desert land somewhere. we put up these houses, rustics, made entirely of wood and unpainted. houses far apart, lots of sand between them. no police force. people can scream or drink

294

or sing or take dope all night or all day or have lions in their backyards. only no rich, no literary pretenders, no Malibu, no Village, no Carmel. we interview those desiring to live there. "lemmee see your paintings, your poems." we look. we are snobs. we are pricks. we are selfish because we want to stay alive. "no, no good, you can't live here." of course, we take in a lot of stupid women because there aren't any other kind. then when it all gets *too* bad, we SELL . . . for 450 percent profit and LEAVE THEM THERE. (this is the way I talk after 2 good days at the track. last Friday and Saturday; when I lose I am much more humane and carry an etching of Karl Marx in my wallet.) [* * *]

2 p.m., 2:05 KFAC symphony now coming on, hope they give me something to lean against this highrise across the way . . . not bad, something offbrand by Haydn, who was a kind of a kool suckass in his time but managed to save some juice. there is much of him that I haven't heard—the masses, Mass in Time of War, so forth. but prefer Mahler, Bruckner, Wagner without words, Stravinsky, Shostakovich. shit, so what?

some guy at work met me on front steps, a small hard Negro with little cap pulled down over his ears. "God damn, Hank, you're really full of BULLSHIT!" "whatcha mean, Roy?" "I saw that magazine." "what magazine?" "I dunno the name of it, but I saw it. about you being a POET! what a bunch of BULLSHIT! and your photo with the little beard." "I don't know what you're talking about, Roy." "no, you KNOWS, you KNOWS WHAT EYE'S TALKING ABOUT, DON'T BULLSHIT ME!" It appears he saw a copy of *Dare* when he went to his local barbershop. this is the poem I got the $50 for writing. easy money but if it's going to get these jabberwockies on my back it isn't worth it.—some guy over other night to interview me for the *L. A. Times* magazine *West.* I was very drunk and think I insulted the guy on principle. he wouldn't even phone me for further details on article but phoned Frances. if this ever comes out in about a month or a month and a half they are really gong to try to rip the meat from me down at the bastille. but I think I can handle them. they don't call me The Hammer and The Barber for nothing. all else aside, the fact remains that the only battle is to remain as alive as possible and to continue to create the poem or knit stockings or whatever you are doing or have been doing or want to do. anybody can go the way of Dylan Thomas, Ginsberg, Corso, Behan, Leary, Creeley, just sliding down that river of shit. the idea is Creation not Adulation; the idea is a man in a room alone hacking at a stone and not sucking at the tits of the crowd. [* * *]

295

Allen DeLoach edited Intrepid *magazine from Buffalo, N.Y. Bukowski was a contributor.*

[To Allen DeLoach]
February, 1967

[* * *] poetry is survival, sir. it throws some of the stink bombs out of my room. if it comes as rhythm fine or physic, fine, any old way. I think of it more as a loaf of bread, a long fat hot loaf, sliced in half down the middle, spread with pickles, onions, meats, garlic, chilies, old fingernails . . . add ice beer and a shot of scotch, ram it down under electric light, forget the mountains of faces and eyes and wrinkles and bombs and rent and graves, get it in, warm, smelling, filling, light a cigar, blow the whole room paint the whole room blue with smoke, play the radio, think of the bones of Chopin's left foot—that to me, is poetry, or zingplay, or the rays. [* * *]

[To Jon and Louise Webb]
February 29, 1967 [?]

[* * *] here I seem to be going through AN INTERVIEW STAGE, kind of a silly treadmill but while going through it I try to talk as straight as possible but I suppose many men going through the same figure they are talking straight too. you never know quite when you're dying but you can get the feeling of it. I've felt quite a few death rays lately. [* * *] I'll send you copies unless you'd rather not see them; I mean they might make you sick: after all, I am a monster almost of your own creation. the Bukowski Vogue, one of them asked me, it's the Bukowski Vogue, what do you think of the Bukowski Vogue? I don't remember what I answered but I do hope my answer took some of the pin curlers out of his hair.

the idea remains the same. I am attempting to work with the poem; I am attempting to stay alive. I find it easier to work with the poem than to stay alive. all these interviews are beside the point. the typewriter is still there when I run a sheet of paper into it and I sit there and I begin again. there isn't any background. there isn't any cheap excuse. [* * *]

Marina growing growing and we are closer than the grass and the earth. it is a very good feeling, an easy feeling. no trouble, no strain. loose and free; creative without fanciness; real without flags. [* * *]

the novel *The Way the Dead Love* has stopped at chapter 5, but no problem. easy to write. about this skid row hotel I lived in for 2 years. it's just a recording of the people, and all the scenes come to me that I have forgotten, they all come up on the paper as I write. it's like being reborn, living it again. very strange. have been on gambling horse-binge which has eaten up my time. but no problem. a free day or so and I have 5 or 10 more chapters. chapters very short but filled with the distillation of the action. best this way. less yawns. [* * *]

[To Carl Weissner]
March 24, 1967

well, shit, a little high, nothing new. well, anyhow, John Thomas said he would airmail tape I did of my poetry—airmail—so you should have it by the time you get this, or very soon. friend, it is almost 2 hours to me reading my swillsteak business. not partkclary from any area, just what my hands reached or what was easy or consumable or felt like it. I didn't realize that I had read so long but had been drinking a bit and taking down these strange colored pills (not LSD), not really VERY high, only in a passable stage of FITS. I mean, time was a dishpan. it didn't matter. I read straight through, I *believe*, without a stop. most of the poems I had forgotten, didn't know the next line, intonation, connection, but feel really this was for the good rather than the bad because it stopped me FROM SETTING UP ONE LINE TO FIT THE NEXT. this is important, I believe. tho it may not be. I don't know. I know less and less—and feel much better for it. I think, tho, I am not sure—that the tape is on 4-track. you got a 4 tracker machine? I think this means you play the same reel through twice? anyhow, instructions are on box tape came in? aren't they? what drab stuff, this talk! only I always get mixed up on presumptions. I don't want to mix anybody up. I mean, people always presume that YOU KNOW WHAT THEY KNOW. YOU ASK THEM THE WAY TO THE NEAREST WHOREHOUSE. they say, 2 blocks left, one right, see

297

this barbershop, ask for sam, he'll send you to clean cheap pussy. so what HAPPENS? YOU GET THERE and there are THREE barbershops! and each barber is named SAM. you run back on in and get flogged across the asshole with a rusty windjammer rainbow clamstink frozen loaf of russian rye bread embedded with toy tots singing, "somethin's happenin' and you don't know what it is, do you mista Jones???" [* * *]

by the way I have an idea of tape mutation intervolving thing but in an rear-area of my own gone gnome tot-process which is: tape mutation or word formage in symphonic or rhythmic breakthru. I have the patterns already processed on paper, the music notes, and hope that I have not [* * *] tipped my beerhand as I would like to try it first, and if I can explain to Thomas' thick head what I would like to do or change or forward or backward after listening to your Coleridge/Burroughs, Weissner tape, I think I could show you boys where you have missed a lot of chances and natural pluses. I don't want to hurt you Carl, you've done anything but put warts in my bloodstream and I want to thank you for the tape, which was very good in the first interfolding part, but you had too much help somewhere, you were too staid self-conscious arty too Burroughs really. all right, shit, I know he is a genius and I am ejalulative [sic] jealous, fine. what I mean is: both you genuine cats getting up too tight and kind of reading it off of paper, breathing tight, tight kitties, good kitties, but not letting loose with who you are as loaf of bread or something shitting; I don't MEAN THE ARTISTRY OF WHAT WAS SAID WAS BAD, THAT *WAS* ART, I mean the Artistry of DOING IT FAILED AS TOO TIGHT AND TOO HOLY. now the Gysin thing at the end was at the other extreme: too highschool and not enough holy Art. if you fuckers could only mix the 2 extremes you'd be in on target, and isn't that the only place to be? check with Norse on what I am saying. he won't lie to you even if it means the room rent. he's too inbred now. there's no out. ask him. but don't get pissed if he agrees with me. you won't. that's why I write to you. that's why I write to you straight. even tho we are all more sensitive—no matter how we act—than a female cat's asshole or pussy or wherever those ramrod hair ends scream into the NIGHT: Y O Y Y O W W W [* * *] my thanks, still, for tape. It was good, don't let me mix you up. My thanks. But would like to send you my mozart—cadillac intermix soon. don't be pissed. You won't be. [* * *]

oh, christ carl, it's good friday, my radio keeps playing these Mozart things when he was starving under shit church supported poverty and really throwing curve balls but the church only thot of it as bad music. it's like Blake, Blake was about as much a religious poet as some whore leaning down to suck purple dick for an extra dollar a mouthful. when the final breakthru is reached we are all writing about the same thing in different tonalities, and you know this, this is no great statement, we are tired of great statements. great statements are made by great liars. Christ had a big mouth and maybe a big ass. who know? if there were more paintings of Christ's ass (I don't know of any) than all these of His face, maybe I could go it. YOU SEE, THE FACE HAS LEARNED TO RECHRISTEN ITSELF IN THE FORM, SKIN, FEATURE, OUTLAY AND APPEARANCE NECESSARY FOR IT TO SURVIVE. it is out front. a sign. not hidden, but certainly hazardous. MAN HAS NOT YET FOUND OUT HOW TO MASK HIS ASS. I am not being funny, Carl. what I mean is that I can follow any person a few feet (man or woman) and watch them walk, watch the balancing of the mounds—I know almost everything about them. AND WHEN THEY LEARN TO MASK THE ASS AND THE WALK I WILL GO TO THE LEFT ELBOW. you see? [* * *]

Tompkins Square Press was run by Tom McNamara. The book of letters was not published. The anticipated third visit to the Webbs, now in Tucson, took place at the end of June.

[To Jon and Louise Webb]
April 2, 1967

[* * *] I have ANOTHER NEW SYSTEM ON HORSES THAT I HAVE FIGURED OUT. this *may* be it, haha, ha. Frances and Marina gone someplace for a week. I miss M. guess that's why I got the blues. she lights things up for me and although she has not worked her way into many of my poems, she is still very much there, ya.

I think Tompkins Square going to do a book of my letters, the drunk ones, I guess. the drunk ones are best. anyway, I got a feeler from them. they say early 68. I'd like to read my damned letters. this is the only way I'll ever be able to do it. [* * *]

well, I've had 2 wild visits with you—the one in New Orleans and the one in Santa Fe, and if I can work this one out I hope that it goes smoother, to hell with dramatics. but Jon you are a tough guy to get along with, and what makes it worse is that I am a hardhead. I DON'T GET ALONG WITH ANYBODY. if I come down I think I will only stay a week, it will be about all I can afford—unless the horses are good to me. this is the weirdest system you ever heard of, yet it works like machinery—on paper. anyhow, if I come down I think it best if you let me look for my own room. I like a place where I can close a door. the New Orleans setup was all right except I was pretty jumpy. sick most of the time, and all those pages to sign. 3100 pages! jesus, you realize what a JOB that was? with silver ink? where's my boyscout medal? yeah, it's a shame Stuart doesn't know how to handle *Crucifix*. I'm real disappointed in his methods, but he did ship me $200.00 when I needed it bad, so I can't write that off. god, this time last year I was sitting on my bloody ass, right after the operation, and here we sit around now, all of us, still alive. [* * *]

[To Ann Menebroker]
April 7, 1967, 3:45 a.m.

Have been drunk for several many hours. trouble controlling pen. [* * *]

Your voice always sounds young as clear rivers crying clear things, no matter what you say, no matter what you say, I feel ice-joy cry in your voice.

But please don't feel sad. I think that *I am something that has just gotten into your head.* I am neither that way or that true.

if you could see me now, baggy-bellied in torn shorts, old, drunk, trying to answer a letter in the half-light of my life, then you would know.

there is hardly anything literary about me nor many either, so there you go.

writing poems is such a chickenshit game! if we were only more alive like they are more dead! then, sweets, we could *finally* write.

About this time Bukowski began his series of columns for Bryan's
new underground paper, Open City, *under the series title "Notes*
of a Dirty Old Man."

[To Carl Weissner]
April 28, [1967]

[* * *] right now I guess you are hurting worse than I am, but
you we ARE ALL JUMPY, cool and tired and hardly caring but at the
same time—AT THE EXACT SAME TIME—jumpy. I mean when I did
not hear from you, I figured first that
a; you were sick
b; you had injured yourself
c; you had killed yourself
then I figured second that the tape was bad, that I had insulted
you with the tape or that I had insulted you with some criticism of
your tape, that I had TOUCHED SOME SPOT ON YOU AND THAT YOU
WERE PISSED. the reason this type of thought-trend mangles me is
through the experience that it has happened very often. so the brain
cells say—"oh, there it goes, it has happened again." there were you
with your head cracked like an ostrich egg with a sledgehammer and
I am sitting around sticking false needles into my hairy ass ego. even
in a long three page letter to Greg the Dan I explained how this so
often happens to ME in this world. poor pure ivory me. like it even
went on when I was a kid in school.
"WIPE THAT SHIT SNEER FROM YOUR FACE AND GO STAND IN
THE HALL! DAMN RIGHT, AND FOR AN HOUR, NO LESS, NO MORE,
YOU WILL STAND IN THE HALL!"
I never knew what those teachers were talking about. really. to
me my face just felt a little blank. I was not much interested in what
was being said most of the time, but who was? to be sent out into
the hall because of something about my face made me feel monstrous,
inferior, spat upon. excluded, and STUPID STUPID STUPID. and I
would get up and walk out into the hall and all the faces would turn,
all those good acceptable faces and they would watch me talk to the
door, open the door, close the door and stand in the hall. that hall
was always very dark and empty. and it didn't feel good. no, no. and
it kept happening, through grade school, high school, those couple
of years in college. of course, by college I had toughened up and when
they layed on me I layed back and they soon found it was better to

301

ignore me than have me slice them open with 5 or 6 words. but even in high school I was not ready. I remember once getting passing grades in this class, English, I think, and on the last day of class, in the middle of something else, the teacher, a female suddenly leaped up from her seat behind the desk and pointed at me and with tears on her face, actually sobbing and in some kind of rage, she said, "Henry, I am going to FLUNK you!" (Henry is my first name, I use Charles my middle name when I try to write but that is another long story I might explain sometime.) and after class, after the others had left and I asked her what the reason was for flunking me, she wouldn't give a reason just that sobbing as if I had INSULTED her. I don't think it was love because I was a rather ugly fuck with a blank personality, and I still don't get it. I mean, these things keep happening and I am puzzled. I don't even want to talk about it anymore, only to say the letter to Dan never got mailed because there is a new newspaper starting here in town—OPEN CITY PRESS—and the editor wanted something of mine to print, essay, letter, so forth, and since I don't keep carbons I just handed him 2 or 3 letters I had written.

anyhow, I am glad YOU haven't turned . . . yet . . . but I am sorry it was your head in enfoldo smash that gave me time to pin-prick my self-pity. forgive me, but understand that I am suffering from shell shock years. leave it up to me to fuck up everything. I am very good at it.

meanwhile, while you were jamming your head into wolfgang ersatz zero sludge I too was trying to kill myself but did not quite bring it off, maybe not kill myself but tinker with the limp edges of the thing a bit, a tendency I have when high, and maybe some day they will give me my gold star on head for being a good kiddy and bringing it off, but like now I am fucking that up too. I was up at Thomas' place and I am the only one drinking heavily, I have brought my own stuff and am slamming it down as fast as body will hold, sensing only electric light and faces, everybody else very calm and kool but I am going crazy quietly, my health has been bad very and there is a kind of delight in ramming it through with surfboards and elephant tusks, and everybody is so CONTENT they are like stems of flowers, not the flowers, just the stems, and finally it comes time to leave, I am with this editor (OPEN CITY PRESS; *Notes from Underground*) (John Bryan) and we go out to my 11 year old car and somebody walks through my side mirror to begin with and I get in with Bryan and I let the car roll, very steep down one lane two way street cars parked everywhere, and I think I ram something, Bryan

302

very excited, "Jesus, make it out, make it!" we are going again, down sliding, I have foot on gas for sound of engine trying to pull the strings up and together in me so I can hold and go, and then we are running along out of the hills at last, on the way out, and suddenly I turn left and we are heading steep UP into the hills again SOMEWHERE, very steep, and Bryan is hollering at me and I find a nice cliff, no houses too near and I take the car and run the 2 wheels along the edge of the cliff seeing how close I can get, I just hear Bryan's voice and ignore it, placing the wheels close to the edge and going at a good clip, and it seems a SENSIBLE thing for me to do, a very logical thing, a very good thing, really, but Bryan can't see it, and I pull off from the cliff to think of the next good thing to do but when I hit the street again he opens the door, leaps out and starts—running running away from me and the car. my first THOUGHT IS TO RUN HIM OVER, but I am rather disgusted with his lack of LOYALTY so I let him go. if he had been more loyal I probably would have run him over, but probably no German blood in him, poor chap. anyhow, I got home all right but of course don't remember driving there, and Bryan is still alive too. he walked all the way home, 5 or 6 miles at 4 a.m. in the morning. well, that's a nice time of the morning to walk—hardly any people you have to look at, no shock in belly as you pass the usual sucked-out corpses. [* * *]

it's raining and I think I'll walk up through the rain, drop this in box and buy one of those horrible newspapers. I enjoy the comic strips by inverting/*reversing* the meaning. and really, all you've got to do with almost any man's speech, thought, action, is reverse it entirely and you get some kind of truth. it comes out very clean. [* * *]

[To Carl Weissner]
May 13, 1967

[* * *] some collectors over last night thumbing through my bookshelf, took some of my early books which I am pretty much down on, plus a few other items, broadsides so forth, a painting I didn't want, and when the guy asked me what I thought—he had quite a bundle, 15 or so objects, I suggested $50 and he wrote me out a check for $100—INTERNATIONAL BOOKFINDERS—and if the check doesn't bounce, it should finance my trip to Tucson, Arizona where Jon and

Lou Webb are working on a record of mine—not poems—but talk mostly, drunk stories of my past. I'll try to mail you a record if it ever gets out. also handed the guy with the book collector a chapter from my novel, I am going slowly, chapter 7, I really don't *want* to write the thing but he keeps pressing me, and the novel may be good because I don't want to write it. it's like trying to run through cement, and I often wonder how people can think of themselves as *writers?* it is pretty near impossible to imagine oneself as a "writer." I can more easily think of myself as a rapist, a pisser of piss, a killer of spiders.

I am sorry for Norse in his suicide knot, and I have been in my little suicide knot off and on, off and on, and it's funny, if and when one does break out of the suicide knot, one feels stronger, better, a hell of a lot tougher, can take almost *anything.* the suicide thing may even be a process of growth—you fall back almost to zero, then lift back. it's a kind of rebirth process. I imagine it would even be good for flies. do flies think of suicide? just think how easy it would be for them to get their dirty work done for them. a nice little blood-sucking web with eyes and fangs and suck suck, held there, no backing out. all we've got is the tops of buildings for no-backout, and we change our mind 6 times on the way down and are insane by the time we hit the pavement. I like to work in more lively elements of variable choice and chance: sleeping pills, gas, the garrote. I tried gas once. turned on all the burners and laid down on the bed. it almost knocked me out, I was on the way, but something about breathing in all that gas, a kind of a grey-yellow feeling, and it gave me a headache, a terrible headache and the headache woke me up. and I got up laughing with the headache, YOU DAMN FOOL, YOU DON'T WANT TO DIE! and I kept laughing, it seemed very very funny to me and I walked in and turned off the oven and all the jets on top of the stove and I went out and bought myself a good bottle of whiskey and some very expensive cigars, and that night I ended up balling with a woman but I didn't tell her she was fucking an almost-dead man. these whores have a way of lecturing like a mama and it can get very boring. you really can never tell a woman anything—they will always reshape and distort the thing out of perspective because the woman is the babbler of rebirth and responsibility; they really love us, the best of them do, and they care, but their way of caring is somehow unsatisfactory, it's as if they want to cut the warts off of us instead of understanding the warts. they hope to clean us up to a big round zero, a kind of penitentiary happiness, a kind of in-jail

304

happiness that cuts the balls quite off of clean feeling-being. a deballed smiling cuntsucker, that's what they want, and that's why I can't make it with any lady very long—I get this feeling that I am being stuffed into a drawer with the handkerchiefs, and they have such heinous ways of subjecting you to their love—like walking into the crapper while you are *shitting* and standing there humming, fixing their hair in the mirror, what hell, they love it, they love you, us, the stink of our turds, they are practicing the ultimate pain of childbirth and childrearing, it's tough and they must practice it, the cape movements, you can't blame them, but I wish they wouldn't practice on me, I wish they wouldn't make me the baby, the child, the blood, the screams, the bravery. I just want to be let alone; I just want to look at them awhile, their bodies walking across rooms or sitting in chairs, I want to notice the color of their dresses, the spikes on their shoes, I just want to eject a little semen, then forget it, hell. but they want to put me into their cage. fortunately, for me, I thrive on ISOLATION, hours days of being alone do fatten me. this sounds like bullshit to most. if I dared to tell them that I AM NEVER LONELY they would never believe me. I am a shit: I grow upon myself; I diminish in the company of others. I don't like to diminish. it's true that I have this fucking or non-fucking string between my legs that creates problems. this is why the true whore is my heroine.— she takes care of my string and leaves off. the harder the whore is, the more pleased am I. they will leave. then I can begin again. [* * *]

Jon Webb had probably solicited a tribute to Patchen to be published in the "homage" section of Outsider *4/5 (1969).*

[To Jon and Louise Webb]
May 17, 1967

[* * *] On the Patchen thing, I don't know. you jumped me pretty hard once for a semi-direct statement on Patchen in the foreword to the Harold Norse *Ole* issue, but really, in a sense, the statement meant that *all* men with bad backs should be cared for; but P. seems to be a pretty delicate subject to discuss. I suppose it's easier to discuss Patchen than to be him. I suppose that if I were flat on my back

I wouldn't be whistling *Hearts and Flowers* either. but still doesn't seem morally right to take the issue from you and suddenly go new directions. but how the hell did I get shooting my mouth on this? insomnia? that's no excuse.

[To Carl Weissner]
June ending 1967

I am on the edge of brain-hammer, that is, I have to pass this test in glass cage in order to hold chickenshit job that is killing me. have to memorize these little numbers exactly, know them off the top of my elbow, like tab: blackburn wlb 61, briggs 79, coolidge, rancho 22, griff 27, marV 31; san fernando rd.N., 1 linc., glass 5, Griff 47-West . . . so on, so on. pages and pages, and I wait wait wait and wait to study until the thing is upon me like a tiger. I read it while going down the escalator to the scheme room, I read it while I sleep, while I fuck, while I eat an orange, while I shit. it is a trick to eat the remainder of my brain and they know exactly what they are doing. but enough to that, just to let you know if I sound a bit strange, not quite like me—this is the reason.

book of poems coming, Black Sparrow Press, they are old poems that somebody found in a bag in a closet, to be called *At Terror Street and Agony Way*. editor coming over tonight, wants me to illustrate book but when in the hell can I illustrate book?—eastern-e.l.a., 1 n, haz 9 n, els 17n, Is-e.l.a. ????? I have thousands of lost poems, lost books gather that never came out; these are just some that happened to show up. also may get grant to do my novel, if I am lucky and am able to fill out the papers by July and mail them in. I'll know by October. shit, it would be sweet to get paid to write! to just sit here and bang bang bang, and get paid to do what I have to do anyhow—like getting paid to shit or fuck, what? too much but worth a try. and prob. will not happen. just like the Pulitzer; I got nominated but they gave it to some woman. I got beat by a slit. well. what's all this prize and grant shit, anyhow? for the profs, for the goody-goodies. I ought to know better. [* * *]

John Martin, the publisher of Black Sparrow Press, was a Bukowski enthusiast from the start. The Press's first four publications were Bukowski broadsides, followed by two booklets, 2 Poems and The Curtains Are Waving . . . , in 1967, and then in 1968 the full-length book At Terror Street and Agony Way, which was accompanied by a tape recording of the author reading from the book.

[To Jon and Louise Webb]
Saturday night, June 24, 1967

dear Jon and Lou:
[* * *] got by scheme, 98 percent, but no pride there—only workhorse death. anyhow, now on my 4th beer, must fill out application on attempt at that grant tomorrow [* * *]

John Martin, BLACK SPARROW PRESS, just over [* * *] I don't care for Loewinson, nor the poet he is going to do after me, Robert Kelly, they are from the excellent school of snobs, I mean they are snobs but they seem to write well, almost real, certain shots of their writing lifting me, but then again it's all so well-worked and *seemingly* perfect that if you are not in too good a mood you get disgusted and throw the stuff in a corner. I guess that most of these boys are working centuries ahead, thinking how it might look in an English class, 2067 a.d., but they might get fooled—there might not be an English class then, or if there is those left might be able to sniff the strain of careful begging. I'm here now and the electric light is on over this typewriter and that's all I know. if some whore uncrosses her legs and has an orgasm 100 years from now over my stuff my bones won't light with neon. not where they are going to dump me anyhow. well, Mozart had a pauper's grave but he had some strange and glowing creatures at the handles. well, that's what counts: give me 4 good pall bearers carrying a cheesebox and let the president of U.S. Steel block traffic. [* * *]

[To William Wantling]
July 31, 1967

[* * *] I'll be 47 in August and maybe the same energy isn't there:

Bukowski's old, Bukowski's old
he wears the bottoms of his beercans
rolled.

[* * *] some small press guy has been harassing me to write a
novel. so in a moment of weakness, and after 4 or 5 beers, I shouted
at him: ALL RIGHT, I'LL WRITE THE GOD DAMNED THING FOR YOU!
I got the first 6 or 7 chapters done. title: *The Way the Dead Love.*
then some prof who teaches at Loyola suggests I apply for a grant.
I did. I turned the novel in and applied for a grant. I asked $6500
for a year's time to write the thing. that got me off. I won't get the
grant but meanwhile I tell the small press guy that I am sitting around
waiting for the grant and can't do the novel because then I'd have
nothing to use the grant on. [* * *]

Louis Delpino was a fellow contributor to the little magazines.
The Sparrow and the Cock *was a long poem that he typed
up and bound as a booklet dedicated to Bukowski as a thank-
you for a recent phone call. The projected book of tributes to
poets recently arrested was edited by T. L. Kryss (who had edited
the tribute to Jim Lowell of Asphodel Bookshop) with Delpino
and Douglas Blazek. It was published as* Forever Worship the
Second Coming *(San Francisco: Black Rabbit Press, 1968).*

[To Louis Delpino]
August 2, 1967

almost every day I get a piece of mail from somewhere from
somebody saying, "hey, fucker, how come you ain't answered my
letter?": it's all right to be a good guy and to send 12 page drunken
letters to 40 different people but after a while there just isn't enough
Bukowski to go around any more. then too, like other people I've

308

got my troubles—job eating me up, car that won't run, days of depression, sickness, so forth. have been real sick, job is hanging, I'm about finished there, and no trade, 47, no way to make it. not even writing poems anymore. meanwhile my little girl runs through here like all is sweet, climbing on the back of my neck and all that.

but not writing letters doesn't cure much. I mean, I walk around like say, thinking of that very good poem you sent me—it's in the bookcase now, somewhere, about madame somebody and that one fuck. one of the best poems I've read in 4 or 5 years, and I kept thinking I'll write Lou about it when I feel better but I've never felt better. then your letter this morning about Richmond so now I must answer. I wrote Kyrass telling him I can't do the Richmond. Cryass? Kryss? anyhow, I don't know Richmond. I mean, I've been drunk with him, seen him 4 or 5 times but I don't know him. there's nothing you can write about him. he holes up pretty much by himself, won't let people know where he lives. not that I give a damn, I'm a loner myself. but others complain that when they do find him, show at his door, he tells them, "go away, I'm busy." and he is, and that's his business. he usually has some bitch in there that has wandered into his bookstore, or whatever it has now turned out to be. he is covered with hair, fucks a lot, and I believe he is on the acid. also has dollars from family. told me once he is coming into a million or half million when he is 25. he was drunk, so I don't know. anyway, the thing with Richmond is that very few people know him; I'm one that doesn't. I wrote a foreword to a book of his poems, and that's about it. Richmond is just a certain type. I don't believe he wants anything written about himself, nor would he want me to write it. I did the foreword to his poems and that's about as far as I want to go. book called *Hitler Painted Roses.*

frankly, I get a little tired of the Kryss books on these poet cats who get busted. I take it that this one is to be the 3rd. shit, a lot of people get busted who aren't poets, or when they do they don't think the bust is so special. plus too many of the bust-poets can't write a cat turd. or when they do write, it's all about busts, the nazi-state, so forth so forth. they become neurotic and closed-in. at least Behan, Genet, those, made a logical literary form out of their incarcerations. these other boys cry too much in mama's hanky.

like I say, I haven't been feeling good. maybe cranky, maybe cancer, maybe insanity. only God knows and He's jacking off. but no Richmond. o.k.? fine. and thanks for the very good poem about Madame somebody.

[* * *] christ, shit, broken stick—I will be 47 on the 16th and it won't be long before they are dumping me, and it's not death flapping down like that, it's just that I haven't been able to BREATHE properly. it has been like living inside a sardine can and then somebody comes along and hits me with a hammer. no fair. although, granted, I've helped them kill me, done almost everything possible to hurry along the process; and given a choice of walking through a gateway or ramming a wall, I have always seemed to ram the wall. but it's not entirely stupidity. there's a lot of sensible well-worked disgust resting within me too. why walk through the gateway when there's a guy on the other side waiting with an ax? and these carbonated waterlumps who are my fellow man, how did they get here?

I haven't written a poem in 4 or 5 months but I refuse to worry. it is not my idea to walk down the streets with poems glued to my forehead. the concern of the poem is to form itself—too many fellows pull them out with ganglia attached, no eyes, no feet; just dull puss and putty put-together. I have done it myself—worried about shadows and axes and the human face. something on paper—a bit of snot—it appears to help but it does not. now sometimes I just climb in bed and waste the few good hours—listen to sounds—the burbling turds of the city—the lost cunts—the flash false happiness flowers—what a machine we've built! this way I can work it out pretty good, in a kind of black cave of my mind, making little quiet measurements like a tailor. it is when I get drunk and then drunk and then drunk, and then the dank screeching hangover in steel collar and chains and dementia, worst kind of chickenshit fears, real, but chickenshit anyhow. my whole bedroom walls are glued with quiet experimental screams. I have them framed in blue and grey and green and red and yellow and whatever, and even when the dive bombers come and the city shakes and the electric light blinks on and off and the cat puffs up in anger under the palm tree, even then the screams hold their places, like places on a map yes, like tatoos. [* * *]

Delpino worked in the Philadelphia post office. He had recently had part of his drum set stolen.

[To Louis Delpino]
August 12, 1967

jesus, I sure as hell don't want to start any tedious correspondence but I am down to my last beer, and thot I'd drop this is the box on the way up to the liquor store. I've just beat out my weekly column for *Open City*. something about bullfights on t.v. and Ernie H. [* * *]

I pity your ass in the post office. I've been there 10 years. each night is more hell than the preceding one. they put in an air-conditioner that doesn't work. we can't breathe. people fall off their stools. the supervisors are hatchet-men, hand-picked. everything is graced with fear and stupidity. there and everywhere. try to get your drums back, for christ's sake!, they'll murder you.

hot hot here. the beer the beer, that's all there is. all of me is a big fat mound of beer. awakened several times in the night with nightmares. I don't know where I am going.

Neeli Cherry by. I showed him *The Sparrow and the Cock*.

"god damn, this is good writing!"

"yes, it is."

"who is he?"

"just somebody who lives in Philadelphia."

well, man, I am down to the bottom of my beerbottle and there is no keeping me in here. sorry on the Richmond. just got a special delivery from Kryss who says he doesn't believe I can't do some writing on Richmond. well, it just isn't there. you can't set up a bank shot unless the run is proper.

be good to your wife. she probably thinks you are crazy.

Kryss writes that he is going to do a book of poems by WILLIE. that's more like it.

like you, the mousy little mag scene is beginning to become less and less with me. I think because it is manned mostly by the very young, who then fade and some more very young replace them. which is all right in a way but in another way neither grows bones or heart. the poetry has this blithe lively sameness, the newness of sex, the terribleness of evil and so forth. all right for a while. then as it keeps being said you begin to yawn and yawn and yawn and YAWN. what's new for the new is old for the old, and what is needed is darker earth and an almost plausible way. I am not speaking of religion; I am speaking of a movement forward from the same old crap. and I don't think we are going to get it. *The Sparrow and the Cock* was pure literature. I am tired of propaganda. now I've got to get me some more beer. [* * *]

Michael Forrest was the first author other than Bukowski that Black Sparrow Press published.

[To Michael Forrest]
Sunday August 20, 1967

forgive me for not answering sooner. I have been in a real fucked-up state. still am. health gone again. dizzy spells. fever. hours, nights, days, years of DEPRESSION. dark gauze stuff. no sense. just a haning [*sic*] hanging there. I make up words. why not? I am fucked. tried work tonight, the spells came over me, worked 3 hours, could go on longer no longer aye, grabbed side of case to keep from falling. and all around me, those FACES (faces? *feces!*) looking. no air. I left. they have been counseling me that I miss too many days. I get warnings, warnings. they think that I am faking it. the doctor thinks that I am faking it. "there's nothing wrong with you, Bukowski! next patient, send in the next patient, please nurse." I walk out and make it down the steps and the whole area of the boulevard is like a roller coaster. I can't see. everything is sunlight. then shade, like dropping right into hell and being kissed by a smelly face like a toaster. like that. not exactly. something. I guess a man has to go to hell 90 times to see heaven once. for me, they can forget heaven. and hell too.

o, shit, it's hot, the fever, the heat. I have this fan on. no good. I am afraid to drink. and the refrigerator is frozen solid into a block of ice. I have the door open and the ice won't melt. I touch the ice and it isn't even cold. it's like marble, like porcelain. the radio will barely play. some kind of opera scratching. somebody is in agony. I smile just a little. The Comedy of Agony.

meanwhile, I have not written, have not answered letters, have not written poems. [* * *]

John [Martin] probably will do my book of new poems—if I am here—next Spring. I think Webb and I have fallen out. I wrote a column for OPEN CITY PRESS about my visit to Tucson and I think he saw it. I no longer hear. that's o.k. I don't think it was a dirty column. only factual. I have been doing a weekly column for *Open City* and if you want to see some, let me know and I'll ship you a few. they let me write anything I wish. might stop doing the damn things soon. poems first, or living first, hell yes. [* * *] applied some months back for a grant from the Humanities Foundation. submitted what I have done of my novel, *The Way We Dead Love*. say they, I will hear in October. I asked for a year's worth of money—$6,500 to live on while I go the damn thing. it's true, I probably won't get it, but what hell of a hell of a shot of life that would be; it would add 20 years to my life!

well, I am feeling a little better now. I guess it's the sound of the typer. it's the sound in my blood. what a way to get hooked! "Doctor, sir, I am sick. please let me type." [* * *]

Blazek moved from Illinois to San Francisco in 1967 and en route stopped to meet Bukowski. The mutual readjustment of mental images produced by their exchange of letters was apparently disillusioning for both correspondents: afterwards, "there was no lasting warmth between the two men," reports Neeli Cherkovski (Hank, *p. 172*).

[To Douglas Blazek]
September 5, 1967

ah shit, what a birthday canard! I am taken. great, old man. thanks.

I suppose the days of long letters, the long-letter days are quits between us, but they did their work; both reading them and writing them was beef and roses and wine and clean socks, good things.

Landlord and landlady standing out there, gibbering gibbering gibbering, I can't think. the fuckers stand around and shoot mouth night and day.

dogs barking through the gibbering. why don't they go in the back? they live in the back. everybody gotta stand around Bukowski's window, make his nuts jump and whirl in agony, ah. reminds me, book coming out, working now, Black Sparrow Press, *At Terror Street and Agony Way*. that's where I live. a friend, a kind of friend I have in the hills says the title is corny. well, it's corny if it's not happening to you but if it's happening to you, then it's not corny. too many people are afraid to say the obvious, or they have to be just a bit cute and in the shadows, playing it out. see Creeley's latest title: *Words.* now there's a man who has never considered a butcher knife. well, for all that, editor asked me if I would do 50 original colored drawings for 50 editions plus 5 inch tape for some of the editions, and I said yes, and so my ass still up in work, not just the common drag work that kills, but working with the minutes I have left when I am not at the track when I am not drunk when I am not playing with Marina when I am not sick when I am not crazy, anyhow have done 12 drawings so far and that's part of the way there. anyhow, he pays pretty fair royalties, and Evergreen took one of my poems, so maybe I will not be swept under the rug—$28 drunken phone bill, gas, lights, car breakdown, dentist bill, doctor bill for sickness of the 3 of us—hell, you know the act. it's like a war. you sit in a room and outside there—there are all these factors working gearing sharpening to chop you down. all god's children got troubles, what? I can't even renew my driver's license. can't read god damned book, dull, may need glasses. mental block. all god's children . . . my hemorrhoids are back. coming back. coming back. all that operation. finger up the bloody ass. hems coming back. must get off the beer for a couple of months, if I can. also same old dizzy spells, fits of depression, missed days at work, broke, clothes shot, same old shoes. . . . everything crazy and lumbersome and getting worse. shit, shit. then I go into work, make it, the LONG LONG LONG HOURS, people just sitting there WORKING, pissing their life-hours away and not feeling a thing, even feeling comfortable. oh, captain, let's blow my fucking brains out and be done with it. [* * *]

Penguin Books published selections by Bukowski, Norse, and Lamantia in their Penguin Modern Poets series (no. 13), but the book did not appear until 1969.

[To Carl Weissner]
September 26, 1967

hello, Karl: god damn it, I mean, hello, Carl Carl *Carl*:

[* * *] heard from Nikos Stangos, PENGUIN BOOKS, I think it is some of Norse's dirty work. anyhow it appears Norse und myself and one other, maybe Lamantia, will possibly appear in their next poet's series of 3-in-a-book. which would feel very strange to me. now I am trying to put Stangos on Al Purdy. I consider Purdy and Norse the two best living poets, and it would make me feel strange, good, godly, golden to run in a book with these 2 magicians. Stangos is a new editor and he's had his fill of the run—Olson, Creeley, Dorn, Whalen, Snyder, so forth, who, for me, are too architechial [*sic*] and mathematic. but, shit, it could probably fall through, and I am ready for that too. or maybe not, because hearing from Stangos he feels very warm and real and ready to take the flyer. he does not appear to be the backout type. I sense that he ready for the gamble. Norse and I have been in the underground cobwebs for so long that I feel that any type of good luck will not now destroy us or make us careful writers—that is not too careful to keep taking shots in the dark dark dark. I think we are now too old to think of anything but the days as they are, with us hanging there, drawing these things, and waiting. no school, ho, no politic, just the typer and the walls. [* * *]

[To John Martin]
October 18, 1967

been meaning to write. your special delivery royalty check bounced me out of bed at 7:30 a.m. Sunday morning. almost didn't answer door. but the enclosure was well worth it. people who have seen the *Curtains* drool over it. I mean, the printing, layout, so forth. [* * *]

[To Thomas Livingstone]
October 18, 1967

have been fucked-up, drinking, so forth, general decline of the psyche, so forth, and so late answer. yes, I liked your writing in *Nothing Doing in London,* they just sent me your pages. the part with the guy in the phone booth, the whole phone booth bit was an immense and startling piece of writing. the pages sent me had laid around on my battered coffee table for a couple of weeks, and finally one day in a fit of depression, I though I was going cuckoo, real deep blues and no way out except all the way, and then I picked up your work. when I got to the phone booth I started laughing. real good writing makes me laugh; if not out loud, then kind of inside, but yours had me laughing outside too. I'm crazy this way. let me say that your writing saved the day for me. that day, anyhow. what luck. what's going to save the future days, if anything, I don't know.

on books. frankly, Purdy's last book was not as good, and maybe the one before that not as good. . . . I mean, if you're going to get Purdy, try to get *Poems for All the Annettes.* 2$. the publisher is CONTACT PRESS, 28 Mayfield Ave., Toronto is the address listed and I think Toronto is in Ontario, Canada. the book may be sold out, tho. might be better to write Purdy [* * *]

my own stuff is out of print and I am out of copies, so hell. but have just corrected first proofs on something to be called *At Terror Street and Agony Way.* a bunch of poems somebody had handed to somebody and somebody had stuffed in their closet and then later somebody had put them on tape, and there I heard them in a place up in Silverlake hills, and I said I wrote those poems and the guy said hell yes, John gave them to me when he was running his magazine, and I said, so that's what happened to them. meanwhile a guy bugging me to do a book, so I took the lost poems to him, threw in 4 or 5 new ones and he had, we had, the book. I've got about 500 poems out there missing. I mean people don't return them. I never see them again. fuckers. real shits. so well. a book of *new* poems will be out early next year, no title yet, but *this* book *At Terror Street and Agony Way* will be out *soon,* like I say, at printer's. publisher wants $4 for the mother, Black Sparrow Press, p.o. box 25603, Los Angeles, Calif. 90025.

I hope some of this helps you out. now the clock hands dig into my back. how's that for corn? anyhow, time running out, game must go on, all that shit. so, here I go. [* * *]

316

[To Douglas Blazek]
October 30, 1967

[* * *] yeah I'm still writing columns most of the time for *Open City* and I'd clip and mail some of these to you but I am tired, TIME TIME TIME slugs me up the side of the head, saying old man, you got nerve. lay down.

give it up.

admit you're dying

so if I get out the scissors and start clipping the things I'll feel pretty damned silly, like I am being watched.

[* * *] your problem is the same as mine—difficult to transmit the living juice from gut to outside speech, almost impossible. and not to pat our broken backs, but I think that's the way the good guys fail. watch the fluid-speech, interesting boys—they have coconut brains. anyhow, you ever hit town, mother, phone. I will never forget the old long letter days, the days of *Confessions* and *Assholes*. them was good daze, babe. you in your factory. me where I am now. both being burned alive and not a fucking thing to do about it. bung-holed, axed, knifed, smeared in our own bloodshit and then told by an eyeless rat with a tin badge that we were not doing well enough, missing too many mondays and spitting out blood into the urinals. your letters got me through some days. it was a time. [* * *]

[To Douglas Blazek]
November 3, 1967

[* * *] on the dick-print thing I thought it over and I can't help you. at first I thought SENSATIONAL, why not? like Hedy Lamar strung to a cross at any age. but later I got to thinking—no, dad, you're too OLD to print your cock across a cover. leave it to some hairy young cat. I am not crying the old-age blues, Blaz, I mean it just doesn't work to have some old beggar like me print his cock. it shuffles over into the area of madness that way, which is o.k., only I am mad enough crazy now. I hope you understand and do not think me chickenshit. I go on instinct, and for me the thing does not seem spiritually sound. o.k. I let you down.

[To Louis Delpino]
November 7, 1967

I've kind of dropped out of the letter-writing phrase [*sic*] in order to batch up enough glue to hold myself together a bit longer. the letter-writing thing can become a trap—I started by writing one or 2, then it got to three or four, then it got to 13 or 14, and all I was doing was writing letters. now, if this were my prime purpose, fine enough, but there are other things to do along the way too—like taking a good crap or inking out a sketch or catching a few winners at the track, or just staring at walls. wondering about toes and your waste, and what the game was about. there are TIMES TO DO NOTHING. very important times. hard to get between women and jobs and sickness and and and . . . so, the writing of too many letters to too many people can get to be like carrying 50 pound rocks back and forth during your few moments of leisure. but people will get pissed; they will think you're up tight or writing President Johnson or essays for the *Atlantic*. me, I'm hanging onto the slippery walls.

[To Douglas Blazek]
December 16, 1967

hello virile captain slugger of the gross elephants:

no, not going with the overtime, too sick, really, washed-out, parts broken, and you might be walking down Haight any day now and somebody will come up to you and say, "hey, Blaz, you remember this Bukowski guy?" "yeh." "well, he died." even Bukowski can die. Hemingway did, and they say, Christ. well, christ, christ, so I am hanging on, barely. (I will write you a letter some day when I am 70. from the fountains of hell.)

hope to enclose last column of Dirty Old Man. I can't enclose them all. *Open City* has moved over to a fairly respectable boulevard, near City College, and I hadn't been over until today, and some of my fears were true. I mean as soon as the publications begin moving up a little, they begin to operate like he dear madam's exclusive fly suckoff parlor, extra phone, new hustlers and con-men, take-over chaps, and the volunteers get younger with tight dressers and cool pussies of snobbery. it wasn't too bad today but I did detect a bit of it, and I foretold to a buddy of mine who used to write for them but no more—"as soon as we help them make it they will have no use for us. bad writers will take over, the pages will be 3/4 ads, and the rest will be unreadable." I'm not saying they've gotten to that yet but swinging in the door here was this receptionist and she gave me this look like, "if you're the trashman, he's already been here," but I busted right past her cool cunt and hollered "Bryan Bryan where ya at?" I saw him nailing a board to the wall and he said, "Hey, Bukowski!" and the cool cunt musta read the paper because when she heard "Bukowski" she hiked her skirt 4 inches, spread her legs and her pussy started to hiss Yankee Doodle Dandy thru her bargain basement panties. but maybe they won't get up too high down there, I hope not, anyhow, one column a week is almost too much for a dying man and maybe I am looking for an excuse to quit. quitter, quitter; dirty dying old man. all right, all right. [* * *]

sure, man, run some of my letters, would like to see, for whole thing becoming covered with a kind of moss and I feel dead already & would like to see that I did gabble about in my palmier days—when I jacked off with both hands, crosshand stroke, underhand and back up around the ass. would really like to see it; would revive some of my mimes. right now, as far as the writing goes it goes slowly. I wait on myself, feeling badly, feeling the Notre Dame worms crawling in my bellyhairs, I still wait, wait for the poem to come out—butter and tacks and a lady with a limp and beautiful knees going by my window. my window my window my window ah my window. [* * *]

[To Jon and Louise Webb]
[December 27, 1967]

want to thank you for the o.k. to PENGUIN on reprint of some of *It Catches* stuff for the *Penguin Poetry Series*. it won't be out until Xmas '68, and the royalties are not astounding but if I am around by then whatever bit it is might save me from the pit, the pit of madness, sickness, the row, whatever pit there is, each inch helps save what's left, so thanks, surely, the o.k., esp. since you are evidently down on me—a column, a Shermanism, whatever the hell, I don't know, but that's the way it works. I know that you were very unhappy and worried in Tucson and both not feeling well, and it was a bad time for me to be there. so it goes, but still you were good enough to give the PENGUIN O.k., so you do not play small and bitter games and crash a man down because of dislikes. that's good moxie, and all I can say is "thanks," which doesn't seem like very much.

I hope that wherever you are now that things are easier.

I didn't get the grant. just a form-letter. so it's try to hang onto the horror of the post office; if it weren't for Marina I think I'd just go out and lay down in the gutter. everybody I know has either gotten a grant or been offered one, so I guess Bukowski is just shit with the govt. agency, and so I sit and peck at the typer while my toenails bite at my feet. in same mail—a few weeks back—a letter from W. C[orrington] telling me, in essence, that I could dish it out but not take it.

the dog-pack is really after my aging ass.

did have some luck with *Evergreen.* poem in Dec. issue and they have accepted a rather long one on bullfighting for a future issue.

so the horses began again Tuesday and maybe a little action can help me forget the whole damn poetry scene. it's good to drink a hot coffee out there, the ice wind from those snow mountains north chilling your god damn shorts as you work out the winner of the first race. that's as good as anything. we don't ask much of the gods. just that they keep quiet for a while.

all right, then. punchy, I shape up to stick more letters. in my neat little shit-cage. and remember the good days past. there were some.

•

· 1 9 6 8 ·

[To Douglas Blazek]
January 15, 1968

[* * *] Heard from Penguin & Webb relented, said o.k., so it'll be Norse, Bukowski, Lamantia, Dec. '68.

The problem with being a poet is that by the time you get well-known you can't write anymore. or, at least, not as well. but, still, being young & unknown isn't the answer either. a lot of them grin out machine-made shit that they think is very real only because *they* like it. then, they quit. to become a good writer takes time & luck & moxie & no special *desire* to *be* a good writer. [* * *]

[To Jon and Louise Webb]
February 25, 1968

[* * *] don't know if I told you but I have been twice interviewed by the big boys in the post office who don't quite like the idea of me writing this column "Notes of a Dirty Old Man." that column has cost me plenty of woe, as you might know. also somebody wrote in to them saying that I was not married to the mother of my child and that we lived separately. the same person also mailed them a batch of "Notes" with certain passages outlined in ink. they didn't care

too much for something I wrote about the post office, plus a thing on sodomy. I told them that I would have to continue writing "Notes," no matter the result. "Are we to consider the postal officials as the new critics of literature?" I asked them. I also mentioned the ACLU. they said that they were not sure of what to do with me because they hadn't had "a case like this in ten years." ten years? I wonder who the other guy was? anyhow, I am told that the whole business must be taken up higher for review. I was sitting in a large dark room at the end of a long table with just this little lamp there and these 2 people looking at me. I'll probably be machine-gunned someday as I walk out this door. joke, of course. or, is it? they asked me if I were going to write anything more about the post office. I told them, probably not. so it might be a truce or they might be waiting for me to really expose myself where they could more easily strap me to the cross.

"have you ever had any books published?" they asked me.
"yes."
"how many?"
"I don't know. 4, 5, 6, 7 . . . I don't know."
"how much did you PAY these people to publish your work?"
ummm, ummm, umm.

[* * *] have really been in very strange mind state lately. seem to be frozen. can't move or write. 25 or 30 unanswered letters in big coffee can on shelf. Harold Norse seems to be in this same deep freeze—the inability to do anything. shot to shit, sick, weak. it might only be a refueling period. or maybe we're both finished. difficult to tell. strange that we should both be in the fix at the same time. I consider Hal a much better writer and person than I am, more human, and getting a letter from him is always a big event to me. I hear Anais Nin is trying to get him a grant so he can come here to Capistrano Beach, where he thinks there is a doctor who can cure him. that's a place down about halfway to San Diego. it would be good to see him. no need to talk. we could just sit around the same room for a couple of days and look out the window, or walk along the beach, say about 6 p.m. among the insane and wild-eyed gulls, we walking along wondering wondering what went wrong with the machinery of everything. [* * *]

met Neal Cassady before he died, up at *Open City* one night. I had some beer with me. have one, I said. he drank the thing like water. "have another," I said. he was crazier than I was. it was beginning to rain and we all got into the car, Bryan, myself and Cassady.

322

we got one of the famous Cassady rides on the rain-slick streets. then we ate together at J.B.'s and had a few more drinks. Neal was the hero of Jack Kerouac's novel *On the Road*. about a week after I met Neal they found him dead along some railroad tracks in Mexico. he'd mixed too much booze with nembutal. deliberately, perhaps. [* * *]

[To Thomas Livingstone]
February 26, 1968

well, Mahler's 10th on and I'm hungover and climbing out, climbing back in again. I read your fuck-piece and that boy is a master-fucker, man; I guess every man wants to be a master-fucker and that every woman wants to be fucked by one, and maybe a few men too. well, I have never been a master-fucker; I am usually too drunk or disinterested or cold-hot; a task, you know. and fucking often turns out to be a dirty task, a trick to do. and, in a sense, I think any man's crazy who does it with real Art. 2 dogs fucking outdo anybody. so, still, yes, enjoyed your piece.

uh, Stuart still has *Crucifix*. he doesn't know how to move them, nobody knows he *has* them. [* * *] *Terror Street* out soon. also a tape to be issued of Bukowski reading from some of the poems in book. $10. too high, of course. but John Martin (Black Sparrow) knows his collectors. so he's only issuing 50 tapes. he knows how to make money printing the poets. his royalties, per issue printed, I think he is the highest in the business. he's printing everybody now—Creeley, Olson, dozens of names like that, pays them in front upon publication and still makes good $$$$. but he realizes the market is limited—really, you know—so he runs only issues of 150 to 250 books, but he gets rid of them. me, he's going to do first, he said, 500 then 750 because so many whores taxi drivers sex freaks circus barkers and Fuller Brush salesmen read me. I am easy to understand even when I don't understand myself.

also have had an old book picked up that has gone from hand to hand, not bad poems really but each person who has touched them has been kissed-off by bad luck, so now I hope Potts don't eat poison or something. but he's gone to work on getting Darrell of Glendale to work up the book with his new press, and Charlie completely off screw, he intends to publish, what was it 1,000 copies or 2,000? but sensible enough to charge only one dollar. he also wants to lay money and 150 copies on me, but I tell him, take it easy, kid. he writes poetry, and I met him down here once, we got a little high here at my place. real quiet guy. not much talk. I liked him. I am not much talk either. so we just sat around without strain. anyhow, book called *Poems Written Before Leaping from an 8 Story Window.* c/o Charles Potts, 6433 Telegraph Ave., Oakland, Calif. 94609. Apt. #J. one dollah. I intend to agree with him. I think the fucking thing will sell out. it's the next poem that counts, we know. it's the way we walk across the floor. but it would still be well to see things working good all around. we've had some coming—good pussy and good luck. I'll take the latter.

listen, Tommy, the next time an old lady very active in church work leaves fleas and lice behind, you tell the man. you missed a perfect shot. I been kicked out of too many rooms for being a drunk and a madman, a bringer-in of ladies of the street. kafka would have spilled the beans on her; me too. if a church lady has fleas and lice the church is fucking her up. sometimes I think twice before killing a fly, but I always end up killing it if I can. all that stupid flesh recognizes is shit. in a pigpen you wouldn't stand a chance of getting a piece of ass. let us know where we are, then we can be kind when kind is sensible. when kind is insensible we are only adding to error. we've got enough help with that. end of lecture.

I have written 40 or 45 weekly columns for the local underground newspaper *Open City.* column called "Notes of a Dirty Old Man." some smut-peddler in North Hollywood who thinks that I am dirty instead of literary wants to run columns in book-form. hinted $500 to $1000 advance. but I am so fucked-up, job killing me, health bad, sucking on beer bottle, smoking smoking, I get on phone now and then and talk to the guy, hard to reach, must get past his fucking switchboard, "this is Charles Bukowski," I say, "I'd like to speak to Mr. X."

"Charles Bukowski? are you one of our distributors? your name sounds familiar."

"no, baby, the only thing I distribute is the end of my cock into wet and throbbing pussies."

she gasps and connects me with Mr. Big.

"ah, Bukowski!" he says. "what is it?"

"ummm, ummm," I say.

"what is it?"

"I'm tied up. can't get out to see you. must get things in order. tremendous fucking job."

"I know. yes. well, Charles, line it up. can you call me Tuesday?"

"I think so."

"o.k., you call me Tuesday."

Tuesday comes. she gasps and connects me.

"listen, Mr. X, I got fucked-up. I don't know, you know."

"I don't understand."

"ummm, ummm."

"what?"

"how about next week? I should have all the stuff lined-up by then. hell, I gotta buy some kind of artist's portfolio to haul the crap down in and I hate to go into Art stores, everybody is fake as hell and it takes ten years off my psyche."

"o.k., call me Wednesday next week, line it up, and then phone me."

"o.k."

I think I've had 5 or 6 conversations with this guy but I haven't moved an inch. I kind of know what Harold is bothered with over in England: THE FROZEN MAN IN THE BARGAIN BASEMENT OF HELL. I can't *move*. it doesn't matter. after all, who really wants fame or money or pussy or anything you have to STRAIN at or WORK for?

lay back, wait for the Junkman to come get you. it seems the only sensible thing. world-renown means world-error. there's never a way out. sit and wait for the ax to fall. just try not to be shocked by its fall. your head, my head. balls.

all right, man, they are beating on the walls.

I am not much good at constant correspondence. just felt like writing tonight. and your letter was down there on the floor. you were the target.

all right, another beer, another smoke, then to bed, waiting for ye Ax, ah.

[To Carl Weissner]
February 27, 1968

yes, I too have 35 or 40 unanswered letters, but now entirely
beyond me to answer them; I can't keep up; for each answer to a
letter, 3 more come in. I am not in the letter-writing business. I am
in a stricken-down stage now, anyhow, bad health, can barely make
it about, hand on. I've just decided to let people think I'm a shit;
it's easier than answering all those letters. [* * *]

rumors on town hall reading of Bukowski, Corso, Micheline . . .
impossible. didn't you know I have made it known for years that
I don't read publicly? I am a shit, Carl. just turned down a reading,
with fee, at Univ. of Southern Calif. Festival of the Arts. I've never
read in public, don't intend to unless it means the difference between
starving in the gutter and starving in a closet. I prefer to starve in
a closet. have turned down fees of from $200 and $700 and told them
to go screw. I believe that if the pricks get a man on stage they get
a man jumping through *their* hoop, they make a jerk out of him. I
am not an actor, I am a creator, I hope. I do read on tape because
this still leaves an area of solitude and peace, but actually I've done
very little reading on tape and any professional actor could read my
stuff better. for a general audience, that is. [* * *]

meanwhile Postoffice has found out I do this weekly column
"Notes of a Dirty Old Man" for the local underground paper *Open
City* and they look upon it most darkly, they seem to think that some
of the work is *dirty* and really not up to what a postal clerk should
be doing in his spare time. I have had 2 long interviews with the
big boys in long dark rooms and we have sparred back and forth,
quietly, neither side giving ground. but, meanwhile, I am still
employed and I still continue to write the column. which some smut
peddler in North Hollywood wants to put out in book form but I
just can't seem to get out to see him—although Bryan says he is good
for $1,000 advance, I am still FROZEN. I get smut-peddlar on phone,
we talk, I say, "soon soon," and he says, "fine, fine," but I just can't
seem to get out there. really FROZEN, Carl. can you understand? it's
crazy. people want to do good by me and I won't let them. I guess
I'm just tired. too much going on. and I look down at floor as I type
this to you and here is this package, *still there*, looking up at me with
its eyeless face, waiting to be mailed to England. ah, England, my
England! oh yes, and PENGUIN wants to send me advance royalty
check on the Lamantia–Norse–Bukowski thing but they also send

these *papers* that must be filled out FIRST, something about the United Kingdom, I must declare that I am not a member of the United Kingdom or something, 2 or 3 pages, horrible, I can't get a pen to damned page, and when I do I have to find a Notary Public, some dame will hike her skirt and I will get a hard-on and she will charge me $5 and place a red seal upon the last page of the blue paper if I EVER FILL IT OUT! paper, papers, I've lost my social security card, can't get my new registration card into folder on steering wheel of my 57 Plymouth, have lost my state income tax card, new papers to be filled out for govt. partly-sponsored life insurance on job they are trying to kick me out of, 8 or 10 pages, the landlady wants to come in here and put up new curtains, I say, "wait, wait, there are dead bodies in there, I don't want you to see all the dead bodies." she laughs, but even she and her husband fuck me up; I just about get straight and she comes on down here and knocks on the door and gets me to come down and they both get me drunk, we sit up all nights singing very silly songs, and I can't get anywhere. [* * *]

Statement *was a pamphlet / manifesto by Robert Kelly, published by Black Sparrow Press in April, 1968.*

[To John Martin]
Monday in [April?] 1968

thanks for mailing *Statement* but I can't understand this kind of writing, but granted, it *does* take talent to write 8 or 10 pages and say absolutely nothing, and it's safe too. At first I thought it was Robert Creeley but, no, I see Robert Kelly. I'm afraid you've been sucked in by the poetry nestlings who pluck each other's feathers. but if you can make money off them, fine. [* * *]

[To Carl Weissner]
Early May 1968

[* * *] god yes! would you do the selections and (I hope) translations on my poems for Verlag kiepenheuer & witsch? got a good letter from R. R. Rygulla. if you could do the dirty work for me, it would help. I am up to my ass. take any poems you wish. I needn't even know. tell Rygulla I said o.k. you don't know how much I appreciate. like I say, up to my ass. just now, I have been doing paintings in the kitchen. this bird, Martin, wants 75 small paintings which will be mounted in the backs of special hardbound copies of *Terror Street*. I've made around 60 paintings up to now he wants 20 more. give me 20 more, he says, and I'll pick them up Monday. I've done 6. these editors just don't realize that paintings just can't be made up, oh splash splash the merry brush—each painting must come from the balls like a fuck. few men can fuck 6 times a night. 20 is just impossible. [* * *]

[To Jon and Louise Webb]
May 16, 1968

[* * *] I have been writing 6 columns a month, 4 for Bryan and 2 for The Underground Review (New York). I am going to tell each of these guy "one a month" and if they don't want that, let them shove it. mostly I am disgusted with the contents of their papers. very high school stuff. plus 6 columns a month gives me no time to fiddle with my precious poems, esp. feeling as weak and down as I do now. [* * *]

[To John Martin]
May 29, 1968

rec. your beautiful check and the 20 copies *Terror Street*. hey, boss, no royalties on the tape? but we workers always complaining!

check much more than I expected, and I hope you don't get stuck with a closetful of *Terror Streets.*

yes, would like to do another book with you—the new poems—will keep carbons of all the shit I write from now on. plus, there is *plenty* of back work. I must somehow shake Webb, who's a good man and has done well by my work, but the no royalties thing is the setback—I'm only human, after all, my friend. but let's let him bring out the poems he has in the present Patchen *Outsider* before I tell him. I don't have copies of the poems but believe they are rather good ones, so best to let the *Outsider* run them so we can get our hands on them. I don't want Webb to have an emotional disturbance.

drop me a note now and then telling me how things are going. I believe that you have published more poets in a shorter time than anybody in history—and have done it neatly. most of us now running around with our little Black Sparrow tatoos. the action is good and the money ain't bad. tanks, kid. [* * *]

[To Carl Weissner]
sometime May 1968

[* * *] the Bukowski/Richmond LP not so hot, except I think I managed to get off the poem "Experience" o.k. the Martin tape is the *one*—all else compared to it is nothing. you will SEE, hear, if you EVER get it out of Martin. I even like it myself, brother, caught myself on a good night, no poetic bullshit, just a natural speak-piece. try to get his tape; you will punch your balls out against some side cupboards. I promise. but try to get the full tape, instead of the selected retail tape. the full one is a 7 inch spool both sides, 3 and 3/4s I think. Martin left out some good ones, "The Body" being the main omission and the best reading on tape. beast reading, rather. [* * *]

[To Jon and Louise Webb]
June 4, 1968

[* * *] got $460 royalties from John Martin for *Terror Street* and it just about saved me from going under. my checks from god damn p.o. have been very small due to sickness—I owed *them* 192 hours sick leave. now Martin wants to do my next book of new poetry and I think I'll have to let him. the money may damn well keep me off the row or out of the cemetery. I hope you understand. I know that your plans for another book were rather indefinite. you've done more to promote my work than anybody, of course, now I hope you'll be kind enough to understand that the body needs help too. I mean this sickness thing. so let's let Martin do my next book, o.k.? and I hope that you don't get pissed and we have to go into one of our long dark silences. as crappy as I feel that wouldn't help much. [* * *]

[To Jon and Louise Webb]
June 15, 1968

[* * *] guy wrote me the other day about an old review Rexroth did of me. I never saw it. something like, "Bukowski a great writer? nope. a pretty book . . ." he drags in Hemingway on me and then says that as a bum I know my business but that Ernie mingled with Artists and writers of his time, kicked around the continents . . . maybe you saw it and never showed it to me. a pretty book? why, that sunken-jawed subnormal! it would have been a GREAT book with Rexy in it, what? these boys can really get catty and jealous as old maids. as for being a Hemingway, I don't want to be a Hemingway. and to mix with the writers and artists of my Time, uhhh uh. leave me alone. I'm crazy enough already. and if I am a bum and not literary then thank all the purple and green and golden Christs of my
Valhalla. [* * *]
I am at work the other day, hungover, beat, tired, sick, numb, dirty, done. this kid walks up to me. "Pardon me, sir."
"yeah?"
"are you Charles Bukowski?"
"yeah."

330

"we're studying you in American Literature at college."
"umm."
"I recognized you from your photo. it was in our school paper."
"oh yeah?"
"I've tried to get some of your books at the library but you're rather . . . restricted."
I laughed. " 'restricted.' that's a nice word."
I got rid of him. ridiculous. everything is ridiculous. I am dying. he came back a week later. "hello, Charles."
"hello, kid."
"what do you think of the Kennedy assassination?"
"I wrote something for this week's *Open City*. fifteen cents will get you the lowdown."
"all right."
. . . I am drinking a coffee. as I get up to walk away I hear him tell his young buddies—"see that guy? he's a great writer . . ."
"aw, come *on*, Bob!"
"yes, yes, it's TRUE!" . . .
well, you see now, all I have to do is lean back and take the applause. life is getting easier all the time. [* * *]

I've got a whole potful of poems to send out but can't get to them. I mean, those you've returned. in my old age, I do re-work. I mean, I knock out bad lines, throw in one or 2 new ones and sometimes I've got a poem. I don't think it's cheating. it's more an instinctive thing. I just can't bear some of those lines anymore. [* * *]

[To Jim Roman]
June 20, 1968

long time & sorry, but been going through same type fire & death all men go thru & it has sawed me off a bit.
I see same results with fellow-poets who have not made it $$-wise or fame-wise
& results are terrible:
crack-brain
bitter men
raving—
me, I have rested quietly (if you can call 8 or 10 hours a day

331

sticking their fucking letters, as such . . .) and simply waiting on the word—

of course, all the time, wonder if death should come at my call or its call. umm.

Our Corrington now teaching at Berk., U.C., and don't give up on him. His warmth is 2-bit whore but his style is classic & history bugs his brain. still I like him. [* * *]

[To Frances Smith]
July 1968

I know you worked hard with these god damned things, maybe too hard, and a lot of aces seem to go down each time we fail, or fail for somebody, but since I am playing God-editor and have been rejected more than accepted—

"a little rejection is good for the soul;
total rejections can kill a man . . ."
bukowski over a beer at the midnight
sun, Albuquerque, 1945 . . .
I think I had better tell you
since nobody at the Bridge is really going to tell you
the Truth is only my Truth
and I know you are touchy, very . . .
but I think you would have been more hurt if I had handed these
back with some cliché and a wave of paper—
well, shit, nothing's easy and poems are the hardest
but poems can be easiest too if we start conning ourselves, and
there is little doubt that most people
probably including myself
would have made better Presbyterian preachers,
so that's a lock and rock
so now listen
since the Bridge ain't gona tell you
maybe I got to save your buttersoft ass, ha,
stop twitching, bitch,
I've seen that hair and tooth too much too long over
too many breakfast tables

332

through my hangover skull, and believe me,
I'd rather see you write an immortal poem than strike out;
I am not your enemy but neither can I feed you bullshit . . .
[* * *]

[To Steven Richmond]
July 23, 1968

[* * *] by the way, Bryan wants me to edit the next literary insert (Renaissance) of *Open City* and I said, "all right." I can see why
he didn't want the job. he had a bucketful of half-ass submissions.
so now I am in the process of writing various people in order to get
good stuff. because if I am going to edit a section it is going to be
stone-pure hard, but I've found out the difference between wanting
to print good stuff and printing it. [* * *] I'd much rather *accept* than
reject, but once you accept one bad piece because you drank a beer
with a guy or you liked his stuff in the old *Ole*, what the hell, you
are going to accept more and more bad stuff until it's all bad, what
I mean by bad stuff is, bad *for* me. that's all I judge by. [* * *]

[To Steven Richmond]
July 25, 1968

hookay, kid, you made it with three [* * *] which is more poems
than I have accepted from anybody yet. [* * *]
got a couple of bitchy little notes in mail today. the boys don't
like to be rejected, especially after I ask to see their work. I find,
tho, that this is the danger of these guys printing each other in their
little mimeos and reading to each other before the lesbians and homos:
they get deluded into thinking that they are *doing* something. are
something. it's only a sucking-out of each other's assholes. guys like
D. R. Wagner, Ritch Kretch, Charles Potts, so forth, can't write but
they go on and on writing so long as the mimeo machines can get
ink and paper. I pick up the average little and just yawn myself into
hopelessness—there are exceptions like *Wormwood, Klacto, Outsider,*

but for each of these there are a dozen others, half-heartedly done, self-important and about as real and interesting as Brenda Starr in the *L.A. Times.*

I don't write too much anymore but when I do I get rejected enough and when I get rejected I *usually* find, after reading the poem, that the editor in one way or another was right. and instead of writing a solemn and bitchy note I sit down and carve me out another poem. [* * *]

[To Douglas Blazek]
July 1968

[* * *] your stuff is still warm toast with butter and the children sitting quietly by the window and the first HOT coffee against the hangover; you've got this spilled-over and unpretentious earnestness in a way that none of the other poets have . . . a Blazek is a Blazek. but after saying all that, I am only taking 2 poems because I look forward to a definite space limitation with this damned thing, and so even with the stuff I like I have to keep it down to the bone; which, in a sense is good because it forces me to choose the finest from among the fine. so, therefore, the other poems back . . . no 2 and 1/2 year hold. [* * *]

but I still like poetry, any gathering of poetry, hung in between a bit of prose and prose shouting—the prose like kind of lumps of crazy mountain and the poems like m.g. shots vip vip vip vip!!! and I'm going to have more of a problem getting the prose I want. why don't you write me a kind of essay on poetics, what's wrong with poetics, generally, and what a man really NEEDS . . . you know, when he comes home after they've clubbed him to death, after he comes home with his 3 or 4 greasy pennies of pay and there is the old lady with hair uncombed, yellow teeth, on the phone, running up the phone bill with insane and unreal woman talk; the kids glad to see you—but just for a moment—like a new toy—and you know you ain't you, you're just a dirty dishrag or gum under the seat, you're just stale piss clubbed with a flyswatter. then *tell* what KIND of poetry is needed and why Creeley, so forth, are the palest and most tortuous of atrocities. something like that. would be good. [* * *]

[To Steven Richmond]
[Fall, 1968]

the 100 pager isn't doing. I'm frozen at 28 poems. can't find another in the universe [* * *]

poems printed in Ren. all selected by me, except the DiPrima's, which are bad writing. D.P. can't write. maybe that's why she gets a yearly grant from the HUMANITIES (govt. sponsored). Bryan slipped the DiPrims in on me. and didn't run all the poems I had accepted. [* * *]

[To Douglas Blazek]
September 23, 1968

some university is offering me $$$$$ for a collection of my materials, and the more I can give them, natch, the more I will be able to make.

my thought was that collection of letters you (and Veryl) had gathered. I wonder if there is any chance of getting hold of these, preferably in the original but also photoed if not in the original? the better I offer these boys the more they are going to give me and it might help me get out of the bloody post office at last. what with the PENGUIN book coming up and a few other things.[* * *]

[To Carl Weissner]
[October 14, 1968]

well, I have some dribbling shit for you, it may make you unhappy, it has made me unhappy the way it has worked—let me get this untwisted here. some univ. library, with the stuff I have on hand—notebooks, typescripts, extra books of my poetry, my paintings, all that gobble, well, I am getting a nice offer from them—enough money to set me free for one or two years, just to write and lay in the sun—and I get an idea if I get this shot my luck will continue—just got the first advance on a book of prose *Notes of a Dirty Old Man*—but

335

the univ. library thing also hinges on my getting quite a few letters, plenty of them BACK from people I have written to.

it looks the way I expected Carl. the literary are a cold and inhuman bunch. I have been writing to the wrong people. they may talk life and humanity in their *work* but when it comes time to *doing* it, you might as well ask a goldfish to change a tire because you've got a broken arm.

most of them simply don't *answer*. others answer but just give me literary jive, kind of essay junk, not even really speaking to me, and not mentioning a damn thing about the letters. one sent a letter of reason explaining why he *couldn't* return the letters and his letter was the saddest of them all; I mean the reasoning of it—I've been talking to an imbecile, a high school boy, a little jealousy tink.

I will say this—if *anybody* asked me for their letters back under the same conditions, my only thought would be, what size envelope should I use? or how many.

now it's your turn at bat. I want to ask Norse when he gets here. and there are 2 others. I hope you can help me, Carl. that post office is tearing me to pieces like a tiger in a cage and the people stand outside watching taking notes or looking the other way. well, let me know.

[* * *] jesus jesus Carl PLEASE SEND LETTERS! I have a chance to breathe, to see LIGHT, god oh mighty! don't put the lid on my grave. someday it may be my chance to help you. now must eat and go to POST OFFICE. eleven years. eleven years down there. going babe. let me hear.

[To Frances Smith and Marina Bukowski]
October 16, 1968

I haven't heard from you and hope all is all right. I mailed a $5 some time back. it wasn't much but hope you got it. with all the thievery going on, no telling what might happen to your mail.

so far I have tried two poets who have my letters, letters that I have written to them, explaining that some univ. will pay me enough for a year or two of freedom if I can give them my letters plus the other stuff I have on hand here—paintings, mags, books, notebooks, so forth. so far one poet has said "no." the other sent me back a kind of literary essay letter, not mentioning anything about the letters.

the poets are shits. I have always said so.

so I am writing 4 or 5 more and keeping a scorecard. it wouldn't surprise me if I came up with a blank.

throat still a little sore but improving. missed 4 days work. they still won't fire me. it's the busy season now.

pleas let me know if Marina is all right.

and take care of yourself.

Hank

[*enclosed with preceding*]

hello Marina:

I went to the store today and I was thinking of you and I bought a red light, a blue light and a yellow light. these fit into the lamps. someday when you get here again we will put them into the lamps and see how they look

I had a very sore throat and had to see Dr. Voegel. I am somewhat better now and I am not drinking any beer at all right now because I think that is what is making my throat sore. so now the police can't get me and throat will get better, so don't you worry about me, I will be all right. and I hope you are all right too. your paintings are still on the wall and they make me feel good when I look at them.

I have to go to work now. please try to be happy. I am sorry your last visit was so short; it seemed you'd hardly gotten here and then you were gone. and I was sleepy all the time. but I love you very much. stay healthy and happy and have a good time.

[To Carl Weissner]
[October 23, 1968]

yes, the New York letters. . . . yes, the Heidelberg letters, January, when you get there. very important. my thanks, sure, straight off the cuff, not many coming through—Wm Wantling is one who *is*—but certain others offer silence or send literary essays; one just sends me a lot of verbal shit about his tough life—his wife works to support him while he writes and *she* doesn't earn very much. anyhow, there are a few others who I must write; the ones who said

337

NO are the ones I expected to say NO; those who have said YES, likewise. I know that these fuckers can prob. sell these letters after I die and make a few bucks, but I've tried to tell them it is more important that I live NOW, that I get out of the post office for a year, out of everything just sit and hit the typer and stare at the walls; after that, I don't care what happens. one year of FREEDOM, babe. the letters *are* their PROPERTY as they so sternly state. all I'm asking for IS THEIR property so I will not go nuts. ah ha. you are a good one you understand this thing. I have personally prepared a SHIT LIST OF THE SHITS which I will publish in my deathbed memoirs. the chicken shits will not get away with anything. they will be exposed and burned and wiped and whipped and tarred and feathered before the city gates under a full moon. and the good guys will be listed, although the list will not be very long, that's the way it goes.

most of the poets are shits. they only WRITE about LIFE. and then not very well. and those who howl the loudest about injustice and pain, lo, all that, those are the ones who dish it out to others. terrible terrible little shits, the bunch of them.

Karl, I gotta thank you plenty for coming through [* * *] all I can offer the good guys is further lifetime communication, and I will not *always* be bothering them for letters back.* the shits, (editors and poets) no more communion, poem or letter or word or beer or sound. and although this may not sound like a very big threat, it is sure a fine thing to get those pains in the ass out of my soul, and that in this way, I have been warned against them. I'm not playing saint, Carl, just cleaning out the dirty dresser drawers. so? [* * *]

Notes of a Dirty Old Man to be issued in book form by porny publisher. they think I am dirty. but they publish good stuff too. *Happiness Bastard,* Kirby Doyle. Essex House. good advance. I have written about 70 columns in 70 weeks so they have a lot to pick from. not too much, either. I threw out a hell of a lot of it. luckily, most of remainder is in typescript. I gave Bryan 20 bucks to have some Negro he knows type up the rest. Bryan paid the BLACK IN FRONT. Negro did a few, faded. Bryan says he will find him, get him going on the rest. gave Bryan 10 percent for setting up deal with Essex house, and he deserves it, I never woulda thought of it. but if we don't get the typescripts in by Dec. 14 we gotta give the money back.

* Another who came through should be acknowledged here: Douglas Blazek generously returned to Bukowski the large number of letters addressed to him. —Ed.

a cool grand. fuck. get 4 percent retail sales up to 150,000, 6 percent after . . .

[To John William Corrington]
November 2, 1968

Dear Mr. Corrington:

I see you did not answer my request to return my letters. Silence is the tool used by superiors to their inferiors. It is possible that you *are* my superior. I have noticed a marked divergence between us since you made your trip to England and poked at the corpse of J.J. for that extra dangler they give you in college. I have nothing against explorations and education except that I have very little of it and so must work from instinct like any slaughterhouse, workhouse, street animal. I recall meeting you in New Orleans. I recall that you didn't bring your wife. I recall other things. This is not a crank letter, this is a letter to explain you to me and the only way I have to do this is to write it down.

It was poking at J.J. in England that first dehumanized you, then it was getting paid good money for a bad novel, no, not a bad novel at all, a medium novel, a wooly jockstrap of fatal reference and day-dreaming, plus a few fine passages. But like money turns a whore's head, money turns a man's head also. After all, there is a hell of a lot of difference between being printed in *Epos* by a Commie who lives with a mulatto (mulatto? u, should know), then getting a bit on fine stationary from an editor in N.Y. with circulation push and that thin but fat check placed within. This makes you a pro. Although some thinks this makes you a prick. Some think Mailer is a prick. But he is mostly a pro. But pros seem to turn to pricks, finally. See Mailer, Genet, Burroughs, Ginsberg, who the hell else? showing at the Chicago Yippie thing. As giants of Humanity? Bullshit. As Giants of Publicity. Still, all these were at one time pros. and some pro remains within them. It is difficult to destroy a truly good man even tho he makes many foolish mistakes against his soul. I ain't no Saint. I drink myself sick and play horses and love my child only and work like a coward on a job that has destroyed me for eleven years.

But I want you to know that I still do not consider you my superior, even tho I am a postal clerk and you are a Dr. of Literature.

339

To put it bluntly, I think that I am the better writer and the better man and that your refusal to answer my letter was chickenshit and chickenfeathers and chickenfat. My dear Southern Gentleman. of course, I am drunk, what other way is there to be? And I'm even fond of you for Christ's sake, no *form* what? Anyway, I am sorry that home in New Orleans is swallowing all your money like a slot machine. ah, life can get HARD, can't it? especially in Berkeley.— DON'T TELL ME THOSE ACID-CATS CAN'T UNDERSTAND FIN-NEGANS WAKE? tell them that's it's just like music or singing or talking, you say and feel what you want, but don't INVENT majestics that are not THERE like you people do, also with POUND's Cantos which are nothing but dry and hard work with little joy, and Art is the Joy of Telling the Truth, bastard, just like I am telling you the truth now.

Since I last met you (New Orleans) the gods have for some reason put upon me to meet many college profs and some few men of fame. they all fell short in naturalness—they are shits and goofs. and so, at last, I see the game. the pretty facade. everybody hiding. what TERRIBLE WORD-SLINGERS they ALL are! what little inventiveness or easiness they have! shits, a worldful of shits in some disguise or other.

You said you would send me your last novel. You never did. Did you steal it from my letters? You have failed to answer a request upon last letter mailed to you. Southern Gentleman. My dear Southern Gentleman, I'd sure as hell *hate* to meet a Southern boor. I won't bother you any more, professor, you are the pro.

•

• 1 9 6 9 •

[To Jon and Louise Webb]
February 5, 1969

got the Patchen *Outsider* 4/5, and the old magic is still there;
I could recognize the angelic beatificness of a LOUJON book even
while being slugged while drunk. . . . enclosed a sixer for hardcover
edition.

every man's life has its particular misery, but I would like to
see you both write a book, yes a BOOK about THE ADVENTURES OF
LOUJON IN A LOW-DOWN CLIME, or something like that. all the times
the press went in and out the window, sometimes the same window,
out, in, out again. the time of the attempted robbery. the time
Bukowski tried to gas you. the bed up in the air. the bathtub filled
with pages. that ugly and cold Santa Fe scene. the crazy and dull
visitors. the madmen. the gangsters who push their bad work almost
with threat. the pests. the sickness again and again. flood, fire. old
papa with his beer. Bukowski vomiting in the University trash can.
the old hand press. the madness and agony of everything. all the things
I do not know. Lou on the corner trying to sell paintings. the deaf
and dumb guy in the bar. city after city. all the odd benefactors with
strings attached. the whole crazy wild story. I'm sure that there has
never been a press and a time like yours, and I think that it would
be a shame and an error if it were not recorded, because someday
somebody is going to do it and they'll get it all WRONG. well, it's
a thought anyhow. [* * *]

also *Penguin Poetry* 13 out. but won't be printed in U.S. until

June 26, this year. Bukowski–Norse–Lamantia. but we are already in trouble. the slick-poetry academy boys and critics are already after our asses. Sinclair Beiles wrote a good review of *Penguin* 13, said it was the best of the series, but *London Magazine* refused to print the review and Beiles sent it to a South African paper which also refused to print the bit. Beiles wrote Norse that he thought Hal and I were the best living writers using the English language. which is neither here nor there, but the battle's on, and Hal suggested that we fight back instead of taking it as we have all these years. so, again, I come to you two . . . Nikos Stangos, the editor, has review copies which he can mail out. and I wonder if you might know anybody who could possibly give us a favorable review, or if not favorable at least unbiased and unprejudiced before the reviewer sits down? all my work is taken from *It Catches* and from *Crucifix*. and Hal's is all good. Lamantia weak here and there. but I've agreed with Hal to enter battle. so if you know of any reviewer who might not be stricken with Creeley-itis, please let me have their addresses . . . and many many thanks. I know I've laid a lot down on you here. now must rush out. [* * *]

[To Jim Roman]
February 25, 1969

REMEMBER THE STARVING WRITER!
how's that for an opening line? anyhow, sent you a good month or so ago, upon request, a signed copy of *The Curtains Are Waving*. you mentioned a bit of remuneration. it was my next-to-last copy. did you receive it?

I hope that you haven't caught "Corringtonitis"*!

(* a refusal to acknowledge receipt of mail and refusal to answer inquiry. a disease which befalls one usually after a trip to England, say the University of Sussex at Brighton for one's Ph.D.**)

(** an over-exaggerated accomplishment which is attained more through drudgery than skill. i.e., a "lickboot," a "chilblain," a gatherer of calloused candlewick; i.e., a terrible bit of wading through shit.)

Notes of a Dirty Old Man is out,—paperback. a gathering of filthy stories and inane ravings. $1.95. you can probably located one in good you liked the dirty stories—they were easy to write—mostly after the races, tired, hitting on can after can of beer and smoking cheap cigars, sitting here under this lamp—there was this sense of ACTION—I knew that *whatever* I wrote it would be on the streets in a couple of days—no waste, no time-lag—hit the bull's eyes, BANG! and on to the next. once a week, week after week . . . it was a good piece of ass thing. now compare it—I have written two long stories, one—"The Life, Birth, and Death of an Underground Newspaper"— send it to *Evergreen*—it has been two months—no answer. another story, "The Night Nobody Believed I Was Allen Ginsberg," has been resting with *Playboy* for 6 weeks. there's just no *movement*. even if the stories go, it is not the same fast-paced type of vibration. yes, *Open City* folded, and there was lot of shit involved for it all, and I wrote it in the *Evergreen* submission. Bryan phoned the other night, high, from Frisco, saying he wants to start another newspaper, this time sex, no politics, and so I might be back on the weekly column kick if he wasn't dreaming high. so, we'll see.

but, actually, the fact you want to translate the stories into the German is a high honor to me, no shit, it gives me the creeping chills think of crawling back to the Fatherland like that—my own tongue, out—but you've got a good tongue, Carl, you speak for me, and cious thanks for the miracle. The ESSEX HOUSE boys say, however want to work it, Buk. so all's all right, only should it come off, want a contract to sign, whatever it says. so I don't think that's much bother. [* * *]

ust heard from Martin on the phone—Blazek got 3 grand for ag from the Coordinating Council of Little Mags. . . . about them got grants. he says. says Martin. how much did you get, Martin says none of the good mags got anything. which means t nothing. what is it, Carl? just one big ass-suck. all this poet- ence. all these grants. I suppose if I got one, though, I'd say ll right. then there's Levertov who gets a yearly grant from ional Foundation of the Arts, has used up a year's grant, her next year's grant in advance. it wouldn't be so sicken- hese people just aren't that *good*, Carl. I mean with the word, down, and maybe in a lot of other ways. me, they're still ire me from the post office, trying to knock me all the way kid row. I may just quit. [* * *]

Fort L., Jim, at your local book or liquor store, but look in the por- ny section. *I* don't think the stories are dirty. when they lean to sex, and many of them do, I believe that sex is a very tragic and a very laughable matter.—see Boccaccio, *The Decameron*. we are all so ludicrous and lousy with our miserable sex organs. I hope that if you read these stories, you will understand, not misunderstand the intent. I am down to one copy, but if you can't find any out there, let me know if you wish an inscribed copy, "To Jim Roman," etc. etc. whatever.

I am disappointed in your not responding to my mailing of *The Curtains Are Waving*, but hell, I *do* realize that Life does get in our way, sometimes. I have been just about out of my jughead mind for about a year and couldn't answer a damn letter to anybody. you must have thought I'd a gone to BRIGHTON, Eng. but I didn't write anybody. it was as if my head were chopped off. but now, strangely, things seem to be oozing back into place. I don't understand these mental blackouts and I'd rather not have them. I'm not a prima d. I don't play Arty. and basically I am a kind person, although it sounds unrealistic to say so. I think that finally and actually, there were too many people writing me at once and I simply gave up. I couldn't keep up. now I am corresponding again, but only with 3 or 4 and I am keeping it that way. and I feel better. I answer everybody but not at the length that I used to. [* * *]

all right then, fire engines going by. I am on FIRE! here they come! they are circling back. they are going to put me out just like a landlady who never read Rimbaud, or Bukowski. . . .

[To Jim Roman]
April 2, 1969

I think your Bukowski collection better than mine. somebody stole my only copy of my first book [* * *] and my only copy of "The Genius of the Crowd." but I'm told that this happens to all writers. those who come and beat on our doors and drink our beer and take our time—also steal our books.

[* * *] since you have shown such an interest I will be mailing you, in the next couple of days, one of the two hardcover Penguin Library editions that were airmailed to me. Dark gray binding, gold

lettering on the spine; pages thread-sewn. they've really done a beautiful job, but I do want to take care in packaging and mailing. but it *will* arrive, autographed to you, as per usual. these books will not be on sale in American until July 1969. [* * *]

[To Jim Roman]
April 14, 1969

[* * *] I *do* want to get back to doing some painting with something or other—some kind of color on paper—there has been a long gap there. I jump from painting to poetry to prose, back and forth and in between with all three—my wives, my whores. speaking of which, the mother of my child is taking said child (aged 4) to New York City to live and it's going to make a hell of a cut into my feelings—the little girl and I vibe perfectly, but with the mother, it's something else, and I can't raise the child, don't know how, so there it is—stuck again with a sad and heavy smash of pain, but the game works that way—everybody gets it, you, me, everybody; we've just got to piece together and carry on with our bit of the play until the rotten stinking curtain is rung down. [* * *]

This letter announces the short-lived magazine, Laugh Literary and Man the Humping Guns, *that Bukowski co-edited with Neeli Cherry. "We didn't get very good submissions," Bukowski recalls, "so we wrote most of the stuff ourselves, inventing the names of writers."*

[To Carl Weissner]
April 23, 1969

you SENT the letters, baby, god bless your majestic koool spirit behind those shades!!!! I already hit the univ. for sum on manus. paintings books, other shit, but this is more money in the bank and since they are REALLY FUCKING with me on the rotten JOB—poor

attendance, same old thing—this will help keep me alive, and also Marina, and if the breaks keep coming I'll simply sit here over th typer and pour out the bullshit. I can write ENDLESSLY if I wish and forgive me—but it all comes out pretty good. so, you'se a go Hun, babe. all my thanks. future letters yours—if they are wor' damn or not—I will not HIT you for letters again! so, you are ; after all! I love your guts!

ho, and I am being a bit shitty in my way—I mean thos did not return letters upon my deathbed request—I *was* dar at the time—I no longer correspond with. so, I am a shit, '

I only have one copy of *Notes,* but would LOVE to German—it would wobble my BRAINS!!! I will airmail y soon as I can get another one. hard to find them. and s to correct. just read 4 of the stories for Columbia on r did 12 reels of poetry for APPLE, signed contract, got ; coming over tomorrow with Columbia contract and happening so fast I don't know where I am. also som« film co. wants to do *Notes of a Dirty Old Man* on fi] with contract next week. must be careful not sign , rights. jesus christ, for a lousy post office clerk, thi pening. PENGUIN. and also two books coming up ROW, plus a bibliography some poor shit's doin which I will get automatic dollars. I might just the post office before they fire me. there is simp check for "Fünfzehn Dollar"—Germany—fo "At the End of Feet" and "Lilies in my Br¿ on, Carl? am I going crazy? I even win money be the fairest DREAM OF DREAMS to be able the typer and continue to write anything a' which is the ONLY way I will do it . . . '

also editing a literary magazine—L« *Humping Guns*—which should be out ir with this when a rich backer turned ou' creditors . . . but liked the poems so n . put mag out. hope to run it a while, tl until the material is excellent enough ; TIME. and how. [* * *]

[To Carl Weissner]
[July 1969]

[* * *] don't make work much more. just stay up all night and drink and listen to the radio—switching around trying to get the little Schubert songs like I have now—only the other German who went mad and wrote nothing but *songs*—better, can't think of his name. drunk now yes. but I know with you that is all right. anyhow, sick early this morning. first the female mailman. postage due. a rotten magazine. I stand in the doorway in robe, my balls hanging out. but the word is out. he is nuts. you know. I go back to bed. telegram. Hoffman. *Evergreen.* can hardly read with eyes. wants to know if names, newspaper used in story true or not. reply collect. I try Western Union. there is only a fucking machine on the phone. how can I tell the machine that I want to send the fucking thing collect? no instructions about that given by machine. I drink two beers. keep dialing for live human. one hour later get one. I tell Hoffman, don't worry. no libel. I mean I tell the telegram woman. now Bach. thank Christ. o.k., I try to sleep again. big Hemingway. sleeping alone. 50 pound beergut. bad heart. and really a coward. a fine coward. and proud of it. I think too much. doorbell again. special delivery. the PROOFS. jesus christ. what's the rush? I drink another beer. PLEASE CORRECT THE PROOFS AND PHONE IN CORRECTIONS COLLECT. boy, am I Hemingway? uh. BEST, she signs. jesus, somebody knows that I am alive. I read the proofs. the 25 typewritten pages come to 9 or 10 long galley proofs. it is hot. 90 degrees. I am naked and sick in the center of the room. my knees hurt. I lean on a red pillow. uh uh uh, I read, uh uh uh uh I read, and I think, what the fuck? this stuff is not so good. what are they so excited about? well, I find some errors. dial collect. GROVE PRESS. no, *Evergreen.* everybody is mixed up. my balls are sweating on top of the red pillow. now I know that it is not so good being Hemingway. the telephone operator garbles my name: "A Mr. Bublinskar calling collect." I'm told that nobody is there. I wait 5 minutes, spell my name to the operator: B like in Bastard, U like in unguentine, K like in Kafka, O like on Ow, W like in Whore, S like in Siff, K like in Kafka's brother if he had one, and I like in the second letter of the city Winston-Salem. I got through. Susan Bloch. I got her. what a young and knowledgeable and sexy voice. she made me feel like an old pig. I'm not an old pig, am I? no, she made me laugh. kneeling on that red pillow fighting galley proofs. there are some wonderful women

in the world, Carl, but I never meet them. anyway, I finally went to bed and slept like, if not a dead Hem, at least better than a dead O. Henry. [* * *]

[To Carl Weissner]
[August 1, 1969]

los angeles, calif. it's Friday, I don't have a clown's calendar, but I think it's August First, 1969, HOT HOT, and good old cheap Sears Roebuck fan turned on my ass; well, not exactly, I sit in my shorts, aging, drinking beer, the windows open, and the look at me, 6 p.m., coming in from their little jobs . . . they have been drowned and shitted upon. well, they belong to my club . . .

hello carl:
    good to hear; I'd though maybe the literary thumpers and back-scratchers had gotten to you and told you I was a pile of dog turds. but you are the quiet type; it didn't fit in my mind. I remember you behind those dark shades, just smiling evenly, that slight smile there all along. I read pretty good and I don't believe in poking into souls, but I thought, "if Carl has turned, it is very strange. because usually is the *constant* talkers, the OPEN-HEARTS, that will leap from boat to boat when the waters seem to change: so good to hear—it keeps my score at 100 percent. [* * *] I am afraid that my time with the female is done, and there isn't any sadness. I've had enough sex experiences to write 400 more stories about sex experiences. like *The New York Review of Sex* sent me a 25 buck check about the time I stuck my head down there and saw the STRANGEST panties I ever did see . . . plus other things. they want to see more. well, I am full of bullshit, and years. and as the little money comes in from the writing, here and there, I simply give myself more leisure time, drink more, lay around, stare at the ceiling, walk over to the typer when it calls. my boss says, "Bukowski, where have you been?" me, sitting there with a hangover and a new idea for a story. "fuck it," I tell him. "I don't have any excuses. fire me!" he just shakes his head and walks away. he thinks that I am crazy. am I crazy, Carl?
    just uncapped another bottle of beer with my short top. my landlord gives me TWO garbage cans while the others get one. the

beerbottles. I am the true Hun, Carl. but even if I were mostly Polack, it wouldn't matter. I don't know how it works.

on "Absence of the Hero," good it went, it started as a very long matter but each time I read it I saw another line or another paragraph that didn't belong. I don't have a copy of the thing around so no longer know what I wrote. but, as I was writing the thing I had this idea that I was processing something down to where it BELONGED. it gets very slippery sometimes, and there you go over the EDGE, but I finally chopped it down to where I wanted it, and I knew I had what I wanted but I had to worry about *you*—there was a chance you might think that I was just throwing cold gravy out the window. it was not so. I fought the fucking thing all the way through like an octopus with an embracing pussy. so, I'm happy you picked up on the vibe strings. it's paranoia-reality; first one is one, the other the other; then they mix; everything become the same. when *Evergreen* #70 comes out—at least the proofs read #70 —my job is over at the post office. I exposed all their little interrogations in dark rooms under their human-skin lamps (America, the beautiful!) about how they didn't care for the type of thing that I wrote while drawing their bloody and sweaty paychecks. of course, other things in there too. it runs quite long and is mostly comedy, like dying. I'll ship you a copy. you say so.

[* * *] I haven't eaten in 3 or 4 days, but that's nothing new with me. I still weigh around 220. was once down to 133. it's really much better to be light—for fucking, bumming, swimming, almost anything else. I guess the only edge a heavy man has is shitting— man, there's nothing like a heavy pooping fat stinking beershit your cheeks spread all over the silly bowl; looking down at your toes, cutting it loose! glory! then to get up and ADMIRE YOUR OWN TURDS! AH, SO MANY OF THEM! WHAT A GREAT MAN I MUST REALLY BE TO BE SO FULL OF SHIT!?!

strange thing—3 critical studies of me arrived in the mail in about two days. one a long book, another an article in a sex mag, another some burblings about me in a thing called *A Bukowski Sampler.* really, the worst one was the one by the prof, the long book—he just went on winding-out the spool of literary criticism as he had been taught to do. and to make it more cajoling complete—he called the worst poems the best ones, the best ones the worst, and very bothered with the term "surrealism," I guess something they really jammed into his anus in college. the one in the sex mag was really the best; I got drunk with the guy all night one night so he had something to talk about that I told him instead of something he *imagined* through reading my crap. after getting a ph.d. you know? well, the *Sampler* thing was all mixed-up. they meant well, but, basically, they were too young and not enough had happened to them. I don't mean that you have to be OLD to write, but I do mean that if you *are* OLD and can still write and have sailed some bloody ships, you're got a little edge. [* * *]

[To Carl Weissner]
[September 16, 1969]

September 16, 2 a.m. plus listening to some symphonic piss, but even that is better than this day which preceded it, harassed by frightened little red-faced men about attendance, or lack of, thereupon, or arguing because I had not filled out the proper forms . . . what proper form? What proper form? I'd like to believe that the proper form is some type of existence that precludes being gunned down by idiots with brain cells the size of wasps and eyes that have the stink of the shit of their souls risen to the top iris, or whatever it is called . . . Sometimes I wish I knew the language better; then other times I know that this is dangerous, not dangerous, but trappish, wasteful, like dipping the fingers into cunt butter, then standing around for a couple of years licking out the droplets. what the hell am I talking about? I don't know. and that's good.

hello Carl:
    not to insult, but your letter is the best gash of writing, straight on through that I have seen in some time. would like to use, will use in *Laugh Literary* #2 if you don't mind. #2 will be larger, easier to read with the eye, but emphasis still on CONTENT. # uno issue almost sold out, went very fast. I think that it is simply a matter of certain people knowing that your blood and guts are in the thing, instead of some kind of con. Most all of everything is con. But it seems that there *are* 500 people in the world who can tell the difference between con and the other. In the next issue, we are going to clown a bit, but the kind of laughter that comes up through the mouth after being hit with a sledgehammer. I believe that some names are going to be named and some assholes torn. But I am very very

tired of the standardized type of little mag stuff. and after standing 8 or 10 hours a night talking with the dolts about who won the old ball game, or whether Namath has a right to own a bar full of thugs while quarterbacking for the Jets—well, shit. I am not just going to turn out a little old ladies' magazine, I hope. the death-toll they count over me in their fucking pigs' pen is a pain that I have never been able to adjust to—and I am going to spit some shit back into somebody's eye—not out of vengeance—because some of what has happened to me is my own FAULT (or so I am told), but the life-juice spit of a dying man will not, I hope, be without a vernacular of its own.

and as I work less and less in their pig pens, now, at least, for the time being—some luck comes my way—the fucking *Penguin* 13—you pushing little buttons in the land of my birth—translating my slimy greasy cunt stories—and please take liberties —I trust your soul all the way through—you know what I mean [* * *]

I gave your letter to the two or 3 trusted that I know, and even those I do not entirely trust, and they laughed, each of them, reading certain phrases out loud. This is always the test: THE ULTIMATE TRUTH, NO MATTER HOW TRAGIC, THE ULTIMATE TRUTH ALWAYS MAKES A MAN LAUGH HIS BALLS OFF SIMPLY BECAUSE IT IS SO GOOD, SO ON THE MARK.

Having much luck with Dirty Old Man stories—some mag in Chicago bought reprint rights to 4 stories via Essex House for $250. [* * *] Just for kicks, one night, I didn't go to work, sat at typer, wrote thing, 7 typewritten pages, 45 minutes, called "The Copulating Mermaid of Venice, Calif." Some sex mag says it's worth $150 to me upon publication. But the beautiful thing is that I have not had to *compromise* my style. The post office may yet be told to go kiss its own ass. If it weren't for the child-support thing, I'd tell them now.

Meanwhile, certain poets drop around, mostly bad ones, complaining that they are misunderstood, blocked-off, black-listed, and some of it is true, but some of the fellows have simply forgotten how to write, or don't write, or pretend to, or play the Poet-game as a spiritual right to continual handouts from everywhere—$$$$, sex, adulation. and sometimes I get a little cruel, maybe jealous because they are living off the fat while I am hitting a timeclock, I tell them to try the steel mills and get their backbones back, but they pale at this—Christ, their little souls couldn't stand it. So, I relent, let off, get them some beers and listen to them, and next out come their poems—which most of them read to me out LOUD. They think that this improves the work.

And I say, no, I don't like it.

then they get pissed. after eating up the only 2 or 3 hours I have to do what I wish to do.

Then I tell them, look, man, I have to shit, shave, eat, make the fucking job.

And they leave off for someplace else, saying, "Hey, Marty, let me have a twenty. You know, that Bukowski, he's a rotten son of a bitch . . ."

I can stand one poet a week but when they begin to arrive 7 days a week I begin to go a little crazy. listening to them, I can't even do the simple things—like—go to the laundry—get that one extra hour sleep I need—dump the garbage—get the stink out of the sink, the ring out of the bathtub, all the shit off the floor. and then come the others—the admirers—worse than the poets—with their drinks—and their softness and their ladies—you can't insult them—everything you say—no matter how vile—is funny. You could whip the whole roomful of them but they sicken you so you drink and drink and drink and drink, while all the time there's this idea in the center of your brain— the typewriter sits there. you can't make their women; they are fascinating and fascinated but frightened. What shit.

so I miss two or three days work, they don't fire me, I make no excuses and old black cunts press their flanks against me hardhard hard, say, "Where ya been, Hank?"

"Drunk," I say.

all of their faces are dumped and burned in pain, wasted, like mine. I think, go punch out. slam it home. no good.

No good. I always dream of my perfect one. Well, I don't mean that. just an ordinary little woman with nice knees and nice ankles who likes to put on high heels and nylons and drink and look at me from across the couch. and then, hours later, make love. Not a love to *prove,* just a love that has flowed into an easy evening. but most bitches are hunters, all the time gleaming gleaming, their cunts reaching forward like cages. ah, shit. can't I get off this sex thing?

Your letter—the camels, the arabs—the everything—easy to see why the Israelites won the last war. I have always thought that man's greatest inventions went like this:

1. The Bed.

2. The Shit and Piss disposal system (which, I understand, is beginning to back up, and fail).

352

3. The Atom Bomb.
4. The Hydrogen Bomb. and
5. the rubber. [* * *]

---

*At the end of November 1969 Bukowski resigned his position
in the U.S. Postal Service and, encouraged by a promise of
regular advance royalties from John Martin, took the risk of
living solely by his writing.*

[To Carl Weissner]
[Mid-]November 1969

[* * *] anyhow, so yes, I can't approach L.A. Freep, they hate
my guts simply because of this and that and this and that, and various
rumors, true and untrue, like I threatened to beat the shit out of a
guy in a wheelchair one night . . . that's true, but I was joking and
when guys 30 years younger began to run out of the house because
I said they were next, I wondered, why please these chickenshits?
so, with various other tales I could lay upon you, Carl, I am on the
blacklist in this ass-sucking town, coteries town, big bloody cunt of
nothing town. . . .

also I am going crazy and can't stand the post office job any
longer. I have one of two choices—stay in the post office and go crazy
(I have been there eleven years) or stay out here and play at writer
and starve. I've decided to starve. so at the end of Nov. I am going
to resign my job at the p.o. so I need YOUR HELP! [* * *]

my child-support bag is only $45 a month plus this and that,
and I hope to find a cheaper place to live. [* * *]

have sold some good stories coming down from *Evergreen* to the
sex mags, so there will be various sources of income made mostly
off this old machine [* * *]

so, after Dec. one, I will be on my own, and this typewriter will
be a machine gun . . . as it was meant to be. this does not mean that
I will be writing for money but for luck. a hell of a decision to make
at age 50. . . . I toss a job away that most men would oh love. but
I am not most men. [* * *]

my little daughter is so beautiful, Karl, Carl, you never met her did you? she's singing *London Bridge Is Falling Down* from the bedroom. the woman thinks London B. is corrupt. she's a radical. o.k. when the sun hops we will be the first to record it.

[To Jim Roman]
January 11, 1970

[* * *] I am a member of the unemployed now with nothing but a typer and a couple of paint brushes to hold off the world. So keep your fingers crossed for me and hope the gods are on my side. There's my 5 year old daughter involved and if I lost her, that would do me in. But things sometimes have a way of working. There's no need to lay it down yet. There's a novel in mind and *The Days Run Away* . . . moving very nicely. but but but . . .

This letter is so gloomy, Jim, that I can't ever write it, finish it. I'll write when things are looking better.

•

AFTERWORD

It's easy, reading these letters, to see why Bukowski's correspondents saved them. Apart from the sometimes striking idiosyncrasies of format which gave them an unusual impact (and which we mostly can't see in book form), their often searing vividness—a stream of feeling and suffering more than stream of consciousness—gives them an impact which must have been easy to recognize. Besides, during these years all of those addressed in the letters printed here were aware of Bukowski's poetry and already valued it for similar vividness of impact.

Bukowski's letters have an unusual immediacy, compared to those of other noteworthy modern literary correspondents. (Think of Lawrence, Pound, Fante, or Creeley and Olson; all are variously fascinating as letter writers but give infinitely less by way of self-portrayal.) Bukowski seems, with trusted correspondents, to pour himself forth with little forethought or purpose other than to render his immediate experience. Only a small minority of surviving letters have a mainly conventional kind of purpose—answering or posing questions, conducting literary business. More often, even when the letter accompanies submissions of poems or other writing, there is a full outpouring of the self in its present situation, generally incorporating notations of the immediate mundane circumstances: people passing or working outside, activities in the apartment, toothache, hangover, radio sounds, etc.

It is a cliché to lament the decline of the personal letter in our telephone age, but Bukowski never doubted its value. "I think the letter is an important form," he writes early on.

> You can touch about everything as you run around. It lets you out of the straightjacket of pure Art, and you've got to get out once in a while. Of course, I don't restrict myself as much in the poem as most do, but I have made this my business, this freedom with the word and idea [* * *]. (22)

355

He escapes from the straightjacket of pure Art, we note, not by self-indulgence but by a *discipline* ("my business") of writing designed to earn the freedom with word and idea. Yet even so, the personal letter offers a welcome further relief: no worries about unity, shaping a whole, or revision, for instance. Still, it's a form it would be dangerous to grow self-conscious about. When Tom MacNamara proposed quoting from both past and future Bukowski letters, Bukowski sensed a danger.

> Letters? god damn, man, let's be careful. all right at outset, esp. for tightheads who have been working in sonnet form, writing critical articles, so forth; it gives them (letters) the facility and excuse for wallowing in the easiness of their farts and yawns without pressure. [* * *] then the next thing you know instead of being an o.k. thing, a natural form, it simply becomes another form for the expulsion of the creative, artistic, fucked-up Ego [* * *] and soon a lot of the boys end up working as hard or harder on the letters than they do on their poems. wherever the payoff lies, what? (103)

Self-consciousness and posing are the enemy, in all their guises and whether in writing or personal behavior. It is his suspicion of such posing that makes much traditionally admired literature unpersuasive to Bukowski:

> "I have just read the immortal poems of the ages and come away dull. I don't know who's at fault; maybe it's the weather, but I sense a lot of pretense and poesy footwork: I am writing a poem, they seem to say, *look* at me!" (14)

(His recurrent jeering at the coteries and mutual admiration societies of the "creative writing" crowd provides many amusing passages of invective throughout the decade.) Against such falseness there is unself-conscious "natural form," whether of the letter or of the kind of poem Bukowski writes. Bad poetry, false poetry, is the self-important ego on display: "I am not primarily a poet, I hate god gooey damned people poets messing the smears of their lives against the sniveling world [* * *]." (47)

The letter form is liberating when unselfconsciously undertaken—and undertaken at the typewriter, essentially. Technology helps, not inhibits, his epistolary self-expression. To Kaye Johnson he explained: "you know, u really kant get the ingress into a WORD without the typer, the typer is the carver, the ax, the cleaver, the thing with the mouth that hollers about the bloody dice. it machineguns the mind out of penury. fuck the pen." (75) When his machine broke down, he said he felt "like a man without a cock having a spiritual hard-on and nothing to ram it home with. I can't spin anything without the keys, the keys have a way of cutting out the fat and retaining the easiness." (101) Bukowski's handwritten letters are done in large printing and seem laborious; the machine allowed him speed and copiousness with less effort.[1] Spontaneity meant occasional whimsical spellings (and infrequent misspellings), it meant free play with capitalization (almost always the first person pronoun retains its capital, however) and sometimes with layout. But Bukowski is surprisingly fastidious about punctuation, consistently using the semi-colon in the traditional way, for example. Spontaneity also allowed improvisation in vocabulary: we find quite a few nonce words and coinages enlivening these letters, with only rarely a loss of intelligibility. The improvisation co-exists with a certain purity of diction: taboos on obscenity, of course, are not respected, but there is a remarkable absence of clichés, catch phrases, or ephemeral slang.[2] Perhaps most strikingly, spontaneity meant a rich inventiveness of imagery, as in the phrases just quoted.

The Bukowski letter, then, has something in common with the "spontaneous prose" described by Kerouac in 1957.[3] Or it may be seen as a kind of performance art, an improvisation analogous to that of a jazz soloist. The mood of the moment, whether exhilarated or suicidal, comradely or belligerent, is the essential subject matter. Bukowski kept no carbons of his letters, and writing with self-abandonment meant that he often professed not to remember what he had said in prior letters (as in interviews, phone calls, etc.). Responding to earlier prospects of seeing some of his letter in print, Bukowski agreed enthusiastically: "I'd like to see what I have written too" (September 30, 1965; to Blazek). But even without knowing what he might have said, he always gave permission to present the authentically embodied self warts and all, with no censorship: "I've got nothing to hide," he told the Webbs. "That I drink or play the ponies or have been in jail is of no shame to me." (31)

If the letters render and project a self with striking vividness and uninhibited fullness, we can yet remark on how narrow the focus is, how painfully constricted the life. The constriction is the price of the intensity. For Bukowski in the sixties, after periods of omnivorous reading in earlier years and after decades of wandering (see *Factotum*), the *Racing Form* would seem to be the main reading material, the hated job alternating with drinking-and-writing and playing the horses the main activities. For the now settled Bukowski, it was a period of intense physical and mental suffering and intense productivity. Writing poems and letters—he tells us as much—was what kept him from suicide or insanity: that and drink. A man too self-conscious and inarticulate to enjoy most forms of face to face meeting, especially with literary people, he found in his intense exchanges with a few kindred spirits (Jon Webb, Doug Blazek and Carl Weissner most notably) the sense of community that we all need, and the impetus to keep writing. Russell Harrison puts this well:

> the very fact that Bukowski is engaged in an extensive and ongoing correspondence is significant. It bespeaks a social need that we would not at first suspect in a writer who, in his fiction and poetry, has placed an unusual emphasis on his protagonist as an isolated individual, a loner. That the correspondence was important is evidence by his promptness in responding.[4]

Bukowski told Wantling in 1965, "Sometimes I am corresponding with 15 or more people at once, but finally after I work them over a few rounds they have their way and edge off."[5] By 1967 he was slacking off a bit: "it's all right to be a good guy and to send 12 page drunken letters to 40 different people but after a while there just isn't enough Bukowski to go around any more."[6]

Writing letters fed the impulse to write poems and indeed sometimes (especially to Blazek) the letters themselves modulate into verse as they go. And while Bukowski was never too much interested in literary chitchat, criticism, theory, or analysis, the letter form allows him to throw off a number of passing evaluative remarks about other writers, from Hamsun and Kafka to Ginsburg and Creeley, and about his sense of what literature is for, what makes it good. He never quotes Pound's phrase to name the function of literature: "nutriment of impulse" (indeed he rarely quotes at all), but he seems to agree with it. Clearly he hates any sense of literature as an accomplishment or of literary education as what gives polish to a man or woman. The literature that matters is what keeps you from dying. If he seems (to someone like me, of more conventional tastes) narrow in the range of his appreciation, he makes up for it in the passionate existential seriousness of his approach: "Poetry must be forgotten; we must get down to raw paint, splatter. I think a man should be forced to write in a roomful of skulls [* * *]" (14) Such an impatience with literature as "belles lettres" ("this fiddle," in Marianne Moore's phrase) has a long pedigree. Wordsworth, for one, the revolutionary who wanted to write like "a man speaking to men," would have agreed.

A final word should be said on the consistency and integrity of the self so vividly and dramatically presented in this book. The man who cheerfully quotes Popeye's "I am what I am" reminds me of Lawrence's jaunty citing of "The Miller of Dee":

> There was a jolly miller once,
> Lived on the River Dee.
> He laughed and sang from morn till night,
> No man more blithe than he.
> And this the burden of his song
> Forever used to be:
> > I care for nobody, no not I,
> > Since nobody cares for me.

It hardly needs saying that the insoucient attitude in both cases is only one element of a more complex stance in the world, balanced by (perhaps protective of) other instances of great sensibility. Bukowski was never without sensitivity to the uniqueness of the person he was addressing. The letters to Ann Menebroker, among those here present, are particularly revealing in this respect: their delicacy of tone contrasts markedly with the more macho strutting sometimes heard (e.g. in the letter to Marvin Malone of August 1962, a letter which refers crudely to the same Menebroker he could write so self-revealingly to). More painfully amusing, as revealing different "voices" of Bukowski's letter writing, is the early series sent to the publisher of his first chapbook, E. V. Griffith, progressing from the impersonal to the totally exasperated to the abjectly apologetic. Towards the end of the decade we find an extremely long letter to Carl Weissner provoked by his comic embarrassment at having identified Weissner in a snapshot as a girl. The tenderness of feeling for his baby daughter is another recurrent note that fills in the self-portrayal. So does a remark he made in response to the joy given him by the Webbs' publication of his second large scale book collection. "[A] book like this lifts my life up into light whether I deserve it or not," he writes, adding:

> I used to have a theory that if I could just make one person's life happy or real that would have been otherwise, then

my own life would not have failed. It was a good theory but a few whores ran me through the wringer for it, but I do think that for a while a few of them enjoyed not being spit on for a while, and so this made it o.k. for me. (77)

We come back to the literary vocation which in the long run is what makes these letters valuable to a wider public than their addressees. "[* * *] it's up to a man to create art if he's able, and not to talk about it, which, it seems, he's always more than able." (174) Deprecating, as usual, his own public persona, Bukowski writes:

I say or do nothing brilliant. The most brilliant thing I do is to get drunk—which any fool can do. If there is any dramatics in me, it must wait on the Art Form. If there is any ham in me it must wait on the Art Form. If there is any D. H. Lawrence in me it must wait on the A. F. (25)

It was D. H. Lawrence who said, "Art speech is the only speech," and these declarations by Bukowski put the emphasis finally in the same place—on the achieved writing. The ability to be buoyantly stoic, to declare, "I have nothing to hide and anything I say in a letter goes anywhere anytime, and if they don't like the taste of it, let them suck empty beer bottles" (86), is a liberating and enabling self-sufficiency. The letter writer and the poet are a single, coherent entity. One result is that, while we may find a difference of emphasis and tone in references to the same person over time, we don't find here the kind of bad faith recently noticed in the letters of Philip Larkin:

a warm and appreciative letter to X is followed, often on the same day, by a warm and appreciative letter to Y in jeering dispraise of X, and so on. Bad faith was a form of good faith; it meant that Larkin was still keeping his options open.[7]

Bukowski's letters give us a whole self in many moods. His courage and endurance and sheer hard work at his writing are exemplary. He told a correspondent that "it is good to have your own courage but it is also good to take hope and courage from the ways of others. this I haven't been able to do until lately." (185) The encouragement he found in his correspondence can be shared by us. "I wrote

360

letters to many in those days," he has said, "it was rather my way of screaming from my cage." It is gratifying for the reader of these sometimes agonized "screams" to know that the decade ends with his escape from the Post Office into a successful career of living by his writing alone.

—Seamus Cooney
Western Michigan University
Kalamazoo, Michigan

NOTES TO AFTERWORD

[1] He had to suffer the complaints of his neighbors, though, and was forced to agree not to type after 10 p.m. in his first apartment (see Jan. 28, 1964, p. 102).

[2] Neeli Cherkovski made a similar point about Bukowski's diction: "In the heart of the sixties he remained untouched by hippie terminology, employing it only sarcastically to prove a point" (*Hank*, p. 189). Curiously, one of the few literary allusions to familiar quotations that I have spotted in these letters is to Spenser's remark that Chaucer is "a well of English undefiled" (Bukowski calls the Cantos "a well of Pounding unrecognized" [5]). (Another allusion is to the last lines of Eliot's *Prufrock*.)

[3] See Jack Kerouac, "Belief and Technique for Modern Prose" and "Essentials of Spontaneous Prose" (1957), reprinted in *New American Story*, ed. Donald M. Allen and Robert Creeley (New York: Grove Press, 1965), pp. 269-271.

[4] Unpublished paper by Russell Harrison, whose *The Outsider As Insider: Essays on Charles Bukowski* is forthcoming from Black Sparrow Press.

[5] Letter of June 23, 1965, not otherwise excerpted in the present volume.

[6] To Louis Delpino, August 2, 1967.

[7] Jonathan Raban, *The New Republic* (7/19–26/93), p. 35.

INDEX TO THE LETTERS

The Index lists the recipients of the letters and other persons mentioned in them, as well as titles of literary works and magazines.

364

369

370

371

Printed November 1993 in Santa Barbara
& Ann Arbor for the Black Sparrow Press
by Mackintosh Typography & Edwards Brothers
Inc. Text set in Plantin by Words Worth.
Design by Barbara Martin. This edition is
published in paper wrappers & in a hardcover
trade edition; 600 special hardcover copies
are numbered & signed by the author; &
there are 326 numbered & lettered copies
handbound in boards by Earle Gray, each
with an original silkscreen print by
Charles Bukowski.

Photo: Michael Montfort

An internationally famous figure in contemporary poetry and prose, Charles Bukowski was born in Andernach, Germany, in 1920, and brought to the United States at the age of three. He was raised in Los Angeles and currently lives in San Pedro, California. He published his first story when he was twenty-four and began writing poetry at the age of thirty-five. He has now published more than forty-five books of poetry and prose, the most recent of which are *Septuagenarian Stew: Stories & Poems* (Black Sparrow, 1990), *The Last Night of the Earth Poems* (Black Sparrow, 1992) and *Screams from the Balcony: Selected Letters 1960–1970* (Black Sparrow, 1993). Most of his books have now been published in translation in over a dozen languages, and his poems and stories continue to appear in magazines and newspapers throughout the world.

Seamus Cooney was born in Ireland and educated there and in the United States. He now teaches English literature at Western Michigan University in Kalamazoo.